Justice Delayed

David Cesarani

JUSTICE DELAYED

HEINEMANN: LONDON

William Heinemann Ltd
Michelin House, 81 Fulham Road, London SW3 6RB
LONDON   MELBOURNE   AUCKLAND

First published 1992
Copyright © David Cesarani 1992

The author has asserted his moral rights

A CIP catalogue record for this book
is held by the British Library
ISBN 0 434 11304 2

Phototypeset by Intype, London

Printed in Great Britain
by Clays Ltd, St Ives plc

Contents

Acknowledgments

Parts of this book are based on material unearthed for the *Report on the Entry of Nazi War Criminals and Collaborators into the UK, 1945–1950*, initiated by the All-Party Parliamentary War Crimes Group, for which I was Principal Researcher. Louise London and Henry Mizrahi were Assistant Researchers on the project which was co-ordinated by Philip Rubenstein, Secretary of the All-Party Group. Beryl Hughes kindly gave permission for me to use material obtained in an interview in 1988. John Hope gave me the benefit of his extensive knowledge for the matters dealt with in chapter seven. Tony Kushner, a colleague and a friend, read sections of the manuscript, saved me from several howlers and offered many constructive observations. I would like to thank the current and past staff at the Institute of Contemporary History and Wiener Library for their help, particularly Tony Welles whose knowledge of sources on the Nazi period was of constant value. Philip Rubenstein and Warren Taylor provided me with coffee, information and assistance while I worked on the records of the APPWCG. Peter Robinson read the entire manuscript and gave valuable advice on how to improve it. Tom Weldon of Heinemann patiently guided the transition from word processor to finished product. I owe thanks to all of the above; responsibility for any errors and blemishes in the final version is mine alone. To Dawn I am indebted most heavily of all: she put up with my long absences, bouts of exhaustion and the delay which this project caused to our wedding plans. She helped with research, read each chapter (often more than once), made endless useful suggestions and just kept me going with her inexhaustible cheerfulness. Her love sustained me through what was often a grim task.

In memory of my mother,
neé Sylvia Packman, born London 1921, died London 1977,
her uncle Jankiel Pakman, born Biale Podlaska, Poland, 1903,
died Auschwitz, 1944
and his wife Lisa, born Leczika, Poland, 1904, died Auschwitz,
1942. Jankiel and Lisa were rounded up along with other
Polish-born Jews in Paris in July 1942. They were deported
from the camp at Beaune-le-Rolande on 5 August 1942. The
fate of their teenage daughter is not recorded.

Abbreviations used in the text and notes

ABN	Anti-Bolshevik Bloc of Nations
ACA-EB	Allied Commission for Austria – British Element
APPWCG	All-Party Parliamentary War Crimes Group
BAOR	British Army of the Rhine
CCG	Control Commission for Germany
CIA	Central Intelligence Agency
CIC	Central Intelligence Corps
COGA	Control Office for Germany and Austria
COI	Central Office of Information
CONCOMB	Control Commission for Germany, Berlin
CONFOLK	Control Office, Norfolk House, London
CROWCASS	Central Registry of War Criminals and Security Suspects
DP	Displaced Person
DPAC	Displaced Person Assembly Centre
EVW	European Voluntary Worker
FLC	Foreign Labour Committee
FO	Foreign Office
HO	Home Office
IGCR	Intergovernmental Committee for Refugees
IRO	International Refugee Organisation
JAG	Judge Advocates General
JIC	Joint Intelligence Committee
MG	Military Government
MI	Military Intelligence
NCB	National Coal Board
OMGUS	Office of the Military Government United States
OPC	Office for Policy Co-ordination
OSI	Office of Special Investigations
OUN	Ukrainian National Organisation
PCIRO	Preparatory Commission International Refugee Organisation

PEP	Political and Economic Planning
POW	Prisoner of War
PRO	Public Record Office, Kew, London
PW&DP	Prisoner of War and Displaced Person
RDC	Refugee Defence Committee
ROA	Russian Army of Liberation
SD	Sicherheitsdienst
SEP	Surrendered Enemy Personnel
SHAEF	Supreme Headquarters Allied Expeditionary Force
SIPO	Sicherheitspolizei
SIS	Secret Intelligence Service
SOE	Special Operations Executive
STV	Scottish Television
UNRRA	United Nations Relief and Rehabilitation Administration
VLIK	Supreme Commission for the Liberation of Lithuania
WJC	World Jewish Congress
WO	War Office

Introduction

In April 1991, Britain seemed on the edge of a constitutional crisis. A bill that had been passed once by the House of Commons, thrown out by the Lords, and passed again with a large majority stood in danger of defeat in the Upper House for the second time. This political wrangle, unprecedented in recent decades, was caused by a short and apparently quite straightforward piece of legislation. The War Crimes Bill was intended to extend the jurisdiction of British courts so that they could try persons alleged to have committed or abetted mass murder during the Second World War, in other countries, while they were not British citizens. The Bill was needed because an official Government inquiry had upheld the astonishing claims made by war crimes investigators that, after 1945, Britain had served as a refuge for Nazi collaborators and henchmen in the extermination of millions of innocents in Eastern Europe.

The saga of the war crimes campaign opened in October 1986 when the British people were stunned to learn that, for forty years, their country had been a haven for men who had worked willingly with the Nazis and committed atrocities against Jews and other civilians during the war. This was the implication of evidence brought to London by a delegation from the Los Angeles-based Simon Wiesenthal Centre. British parliamentarians and pressure groups took up the challenge posed by this astounding information and the hunt for former Nazi collaborators and war criminals – which had already taken root in the USA, Canada and Australia – was extended to the United Kingdom. Further research instigated by the All-Party

Parliamentary War Crimes Group established that after 1945 it had, indeed, been possible for mass murderers and Nazi allies to get into Britain undetected, in large numbers, and to remain here in safety. The Government responded to the weight of evidence by setting up an official Home Office inquiry under Sir Thomas Hetherington and William Chalmers, two former senior law officers.

In July 1989, the Hetherington–Chalmers Report confirmed many of the allegations made by the Wiesenthal Centre and the All-Party Parliamentary War Crimes Group. It concluded that there were at least three men who should face trial and seventy-five deemed worthy of further investigation. Driven by this knowledge, its prestigious authors recommended that the law be changed to make prosecutions possible in England and Scotland. The fact that seventy-eight alleged war criminals were still alive in Britain fifty years after the war chillingly suggested that twenty or thirty years ago there were far more at liberty. Who were these men and how did they get here? Who was responsible for the blunder exposed forty years later to the embarrassment of the whole nation? And why did it take four decades to bring to justice men who should never have been allowed into the United Kingdom in the first place?

This book sets out to answer these questions. It is based on hitherto unpublished primary sources held in the British Public Records Office (PRO) and disclosures from American archives made possible by the Freedom of Information Act. Much of the relevant British documentation is still suppressed, but with the help of other sources it has been possible to piece together a scandalous story of bureaucratic negligence and political expediency. What is more, the focus on the evolution of policy towards East European refugees and former collaborators with the Nazis has thrown new light on the post-war Labour Government, its attitude towards immigration and its controversial role in the Cold War.

Yet events in Eastern Europe before and during the Second World War are the essential backcloth for understanding how the problem of collaborators and refugees originated, and it is here that this investigation begins. Focusing on the Baltic

States, White Russia and the Ukraine, it describes the patterns of collaboration between the local populations and the Germans, the raising of police and military units, and their complicity in the mass murder of the Jews. It shows how Lithuanian, Latvian, Estonian and Ukrainian militia and police units that had voluntarily assisted in the work of the Einsatzgruppen (mobile killing squads) were turned into front-line Waffen-SS units.

At the end of the war, these men found themselves amidst the ruins of Germany in a devastated landscape awash with millions of uprooted people – refugees, slave and forced labourers, concentration camp survivors, liberated prisoners of war (PoWs) and ethnic Germans who had fled the Red Army. Men who had served the Germans in militia or police units, as concentration camp guards or in East European Waffen-SS divisions, tried to conceal their true identities and wartime careers. Some of them became Displaced Persons (DPs) and were taken under the wing of international refugee agencies; many more were repatriated to the USSR and the countries of Eastern Europe under the terms of the Yalta Agreement. But the British and Americans were particularly reluctant to return Latvians, Lithuanians, Estonians and Ukrainians who originated from areas that had only come under Russian rule in 1940. This left the Western Allies with a massive problem on their hands: what was to be done with the hundreds of thousands of so-called 'non-repatriables'?

There was enormous confusion in British circles concerning East Europeans who had fought for the Nazis. Lobbyists such as the former Latvian Ambassador in London insisted to the Foreign Office (FO) that they were all pro-Western and had been conscripted into the German ranks. Influential MPs, who saw them as allies in a future struggle against Soviet Communism, intervened with the FO to prevent them being repatriated. As a result, East European Waffen-SS men were treated more favourably than their German counterparts. Thousands of Latvian, Lithuanian and Estonian ex-combatants were discreetly held in PoW cages pending a settlement of their fate. When the Russians demanded that war crimes suspects should be handed over to them, the British authorities stonewalled and even connived in the escape of certain individuals against whom there was damning evidence of wartime collaboration.

Despite the fact that the United Nations relief organisations refused succour to former combatants, the British occupation authorities displayed no such qualms. East Europeans who had worn German uniform were cared for in separate camps and subsequently designated as DPs, even though they had not been 'screened' by any of the international refugee bodies and, if they had, would not have been eligible for refugee aid. Britain's willingness to shelter thousands of men who had fought for the Nazis and categorise them as hapless refugees was to have dramatic consequences when the DPs became a vast pool for the recruitment of volunteer labour for British mines, farms and factories.

Faced by a desperate shortage of manpower at home, in 1947 the British Government inaugurated a policy of recruiting foreign labour from among the DPs. This policy was developed at Cabinet level by Clement Attlee, the Prime Minister, Hugh Dalton, the Chancellor of the Exchequer, and Ernest Bevin, the Foreign Secretary. The European Voluntary Worker (EVW) schemes were rushed into operation despite the reservations of many civil servants and officials in London and Germany who warned that there were not the facilities, personnel or the time adequately to screen the recruits to ensure that they had clean war records. Responsibility for the process of scrutiny and security checks was fragmented and ineffectual. Screeners had only the patchiest knowledge of the non-German Waffen-SS and collaborationist units active in the east and no lists of East Europeans who had committed atrocities. Screening was so weak that, in reality, it was useful only for public relations purposes, to allow the Government to rebut claims by the USSR that Britain was accepting war criminals as workers. In private communications diplomats and officials freely admitted that 'screenings' were little more than a cosmetic process.

At the very same time, however, the Labour Government was carefully screening-out other potential immigrants and enforcing a calculated policy of discrimination against Jewish immigrants. Jews were routinely excluded from the EVW schemes and considerable efforts were made to deny them a precedent for entering the country. Nor were non-white immigrants considered desirable. The arrival of the steamship *Empire Windrush* bringing West Indians seeking work to Britain in 1948 provoked alarm in the Government. A Cabinet inquiry concluded that, because non-whites were unpopular and difficult to assimilate, it would be unwise to encourage their settlement on a large scale. The EVW schemes were an attractive solution to the labour shortage because they excluded Jews and Blacks; the price was allowing Nazi collaborators into the country.

The volunteer worker projects were also seized upon by the Foreign Office as a convenient device to solve diplomatic crises abroad. Under the guise of labour recruitment an entire Ukrainian Waffen-SS division was shipped to Britain from Rimini, in Italy, in 1947 to avoid a clash between Italy and Eastern Bloc countries which demanded its repatriation. It is certain that some of these men had served voluntarily in the Waffen-SS, while others had been drafted in from police units directly involved in massacres and deportations or were former concentration camp guards. Only a fraction were subjected to cursory screening by a team under Brigadier Fitzroy Maclean. He told the Foreign Office that some of the Ukrainians had murky war records while others admitted to volunteering for the Waffen-SS, but no further action was taken to check their wartime activities. Despite protests by MPs like Tom Driberg and Dick Crossman, the Ukrainians were shipped to England as a top priority and a year later turned into civilians. Some emigrated to Canada or South America, but most remained in England where they joined a veterans' association that openly boasted of its war service in a Waffen-SS division.

The indifference of civil servants towards the warnings that former Nazis and mass murderers might be amongst the thousands of volunteer workers was not without a precedent. It was similar to the terrible insouciance towards the fate of the Jews that had marred Britain's wartime refugee policy and restricted rescue measures to little more than token gestures. There were still other reasons for the ease with which former Nazi collaborators were able to get into Britain. Between 1945 and 1947 the political atmosphere in Europe changed rapidly and with it perceptions of one-time allies and enemies. Anticipating conflict with the USSR, the Western Allies began to utilise the remnants of the anti-Soviet forces previously marshalled by the Germans. The disclosures by Kim Philby, Anthony Cavendish and CIA operatives have revealed that MI5 and MI6 recruited anti-Soviet agents from amongst the pool of DPs, including Axis collaborators and known war criminals. In spite of the weeding of records in the public domain, there is enough evidence to suggest that the Foreign Office was fully aware of this cynical practice.

After the war, the Government received demands from the USSR for the extradition of alleged war criminals but took little serious action. Several factors contributed to the lax British treatment of Nazi agents and the men who persecuted the Jews. Britain refused to contemplate extradition to the Eastern bloc where judicial procedures were rightly held to be dubious. It dismissed as Cold War propaganda the evidence against anti-Soviet émigrés that emanated from Eastern bloc sources. In any case, war crimes were not on anyone's agenda. Britain had not been occupied, so collaboration was never a domestic issue. The bloody struggle of Palestinian Jews against British rule between 1945 and 1948 stimulated a wave of anti-semitism that stalled the flow of feeling towards the Nazis' chief victims. The facts of what happened to the Jews of Europe during the war did not significantly impinge on popular consciousness in Britain until the 1970s.

From the time of the Eichmann trial in 1960–1, a swelling number of academic books, novels and films tackled the 'Final Solution'. Although this new-found interest was centred on the USA and Israel, it had a gradual, but accumulating, impact on British society, too. Public concern in the USA gave rise to fresh war crimes investigations in the late 1970s and early 1980s, a trend which spread to Canada and Australia where there were also large émigré populations from Eastern Europe. These inquiries proved that after 1945 war criminals had, indeed, entered these countries: the unthinkable was becoming a reality.

Yet, even after the revelations by the Wiesenthal Centre that there were numbers of suspects in the United Kingdom, public opinion in Britain was sceptical and politicians frequently mocking. It required considerable pressure from MPs led by the All-Party Parliamentary War Crimes Group to elicit a pledge from the Government to investigate the initial claims. When in February 1987 the Government admitted that several of those on the list submitted by the Wiesenthal Centre were alive in Britain, disbelief gave way to indignation: the momentum for a full, official inquiry became relentless. MPs, investigative television reporters, representatives of the Wiesenthal Centre and legal officials from the USSR piled up the evidence until, in February 1988, the Government announced the establishment of the Hetherington–Chalmers Inquiry.

The Report on War Crimes was published in July 1989, but it took nearly two years to implement its recommendations for changes in the law to enable the trial of suspects in the United Kingdom. Each step of the way had to be closely fought, and the debate was highly charged. There were accusations on one side that the proponents of legislation were puppets of a vindictive, world-wide Jewish lobby. The other claimed that opponents of war crimes trials used anti-semitic caricatures in the defence of mass murderers. The controversy revealed a deep resistance to reckoning with the past and an ingrained hostility in some quarters to the agenda of ethnic minorities. While Eastern Europe threw off forty years of Communist rule and sought to come to terms with a suppressed past, parliamentarians, peers and commentators in Britain blithely deemed history, notably the history most relevant to one ethnic group, best forgotten. Behind the parliamentary fracas of May 1991 stood a mass of preconceptions and prejudices that turned what was to many people a clear-cut moral issue – should Britain be a haven for mass murderers? – into a morass of constitutional niceties and juridical hairsplitting.

The War Crimes Act became law despite the last-ditch opposition of the House of Lords. Eventually, the Government acted in accordance with the clearly stated view of MPs who, in a series of free votes, had voted by massive majorities in favour of legislation to facilitate war crimes trials, and invoked the Parliament Acts of 1911 and 1949. This was only the third occasion that they had been used since they were passed and the first time a Conservative Government had ever resorted to them. It was an astounding climax to a campaign that had been sustained for nearly five years and which would clear the path for an equally extraordinary legal process. On 10 May 1991, the Queen gave her assent to the War Crimes Act and so opened the way to the first trials of alleged war criminals to take place in Britain since the Second World War.

Shortly afterwards, a specially constituted police unit was assigned to the investigation of alleged war criminals. Led by Detective Chief Superintendent Eddie Bathgate, a senior police officer who was formerly head of the CID in South-East England, the team comprises three inspectors, one sergeant, three constables and has access to personnel from the Crown Prosecution Service as well as translators and historians. Its budget of several million pounds indicates the seriousness with which the Government regards its work. The claim that there were war criminals in the United Kingdom, which seemed so fantastic in 1986, is about to be subjected to the full forensic process of the English and Scottish legal systems. The quiet sojourn of Nazi collaborators and mass murderers in Britain has ended. For the first time it is possible to reveal how they arrived in this country, why they were allowed to remain here undisturbed for four decades and what their crimes really were.

Collaborators
and War Criminals

The settlement of East Europeans in Britain after 1945 is one, often forgotten, legacy of the Second World War. It had been Hitler's intention to occupy the countries to the east of Germany as *Lebensraum* – living space – for the 'Aryan master race'. The Slav peoples who inhabited these lands were to be reduced to the status of helots, serving the new German settlers; whole populations were to be exterminated, thinned out or redistributed around the continent according to Hitler's ethnic hierarchy. This grandiose plan collapsed ignominiously, but the genocidal policy against the Jews and the massive population transfers were put into operation, if with only partial 'success'. Although Hitler's goal of *Lebensraum* was never realised, the callous policy of evictions and exploitation resulted in millions ending the war thousands of miles from their homes – to which they would never return. The Nazi war aim of resettling the Germans in the east resulted, paradoxically, in East Europeans settling in the west – including Britain.[1]

Amongst the East European immigrants beginning a new life in this country were thousands who had collaborated with the Nazis to various degrees and for a mixture of reasons. Many had donned German uniforms to fight against the Russians, their traditional enemy, and free their countries from Soviet domination. Along with simple nationalism there were also currents of anti-Communism and, sometimes, a sense of affinity with Nazi ideology. Some had volunteered to fight with the Germans; others were offered a cruel choice between work in Germany or joining the army. Many entered the ranks of the

German forces after a career in the local police or militia, and amongst these were men who had joined the lethal onslaught against the Jews.

One of the startling paradoxes of the Third Reich is that despite the ideology of the master race, the German military and even the vaunted SS units, dedicated to the extermination of the Jews, embraced the co-operation and collaboration of so-called *Untermenschen*, or subhumans. Indeed, the use of non-Germans in military, paramilitary and rear-area support units probably enabled the Reich to shore up its eastern front after the disastrous defeat at Stalingrad in the winter of 1942 and stave off total defeat for another two years. Nor could the extermination of millions of Jews have been accomplished so completely and so rapidly without local assistance. Directly and indirectly, with the two forms of collaboration frequently overlapping, native aid was fundamental to the prosecution of the Final Solution.

The involvement of East Europeans in the extermination of European Jewry began with the local response to the murder squads that tore through the Jewish population of Eastern Europe in the summer and autumn of 1941. This murderous co-operation emerged partly out of the long history of contacts between German military intelligence and dissident nationalists in Poland and the USSR before the war. Military collaboration culminated in the establishment of the 'Eastern Waffen-SS' – several entire divisions comprised of Baltic, Ukrainian and White Russian volunteers, formerly the people most despised by the self-designated Aryan 'supermen' in the Waffen-SS. As these divisions were mangled in battle, they were replenished from units that had early on assisted the murder squads or guarded the death camps and the ghettos.

The war launched by Hitler against the Soviet Union on 22 June 1941 was an ideological war, the climax of Hitler's anti-Bolshevik crusade and the means by which he intended to put his racial theory into practice. It was to be a war of extermination against Communism – a political system and creed which he considered to be synonymous with the Jewish people. Hitler entrusted its implementation to Reichsführer Himmler, head of the SS, in a directive of 13 March 1941. This was the starting point for the work of the Einsatzgruppen, the task forces which were to carry out the destruction of Communist power. The Nazis automatically equated the Jews with Communism, but the 'Jewish–Bolshevik intelligentsia' was not explicitly mentioned as a target until late June 1941. Within a couple of months, this category was widened to include all Jews – Jewish commissars, soldiers, civilians; Jewish men, women and children.[2]

The Einsatzgruppen faced a daunting task. There were 260,000 Jews in the Baltic territories, 1,350,000 in Soviet-occupied Poland and 30,000 in Soviet-occupied areas of Romania. Within the pre-1939 boundaries of the USSR there were 1,533,000 Jews in the Ukraine, 375,000 in White Russia, 50,000 in the Crimea and 200,000 in other regions.[3] To accomplish their assignment (which included the elimination of the Communist state and party apparatus, intelligence and general security duties), they comprised barely more than 3,000 personnel. This total included clerks, radio operators, drivers and translators, some of them women. Nor were the members of these units selected for their special skills or because they were believed to display some special aptitude for the work which lay ahead. A large number were ordinary policemen released from routine police work in Germany. Many were older men who had been passed over for conscription into the regular army and had served instead in police battalions. Only a proportion came from the highly politicised, Nazi Sicherheitspolizei (Security Police) known as Sipo, the Sicherheitsdienst (Security Service) or SD – and the Waffen-SS.[4]

Given the small numbers in the Einsatzgruppen and the enormity of their objectives in a vast and strange country, the assistance of local people would be crucial. The reports filed by the Einsatzgruppen to the SS headquarters and Nazi leadership give a graphic and reliable account of local responses. However, these reports must be seen against a background of longstanding local enmities and more recent horrors which had created tensions that the Nazis readily exploited to their own ends.

Under the secret terms of the Nazi–Soviet pact signed in September 1939, Finland, Estonia, Latvia, Lithuania and eastern Poland fell into the Russians' zone of influence. The Red Army moved into Poland soon after the German invasion commenced, and the country was partitioned. At the same time, the Russians demanded military bases in the small and relatively defenceless Baltic states, which had no choice but to comply. This was not enough for Stalin. On 16–17 June 1941, the Red Army occupied Lithuania, Latvia and Estonia, claiming that it was responding to calls from Communist, pro-Russian insurgents. Rigged elections held soon afterwards resulted in the establishment of new governments which requested inclusion in the USSR. All three republics asked to 'join' the Soviet Union on 21 July, and were formally 'accepted' by the Supreme Soviet a few days later. Over the following year the process of Sovietisation led to the arrest and deportation of around 60,000 Lithuanians, 45,000 Latvians and 50,000 Estonians. The most brutal phase of this 'Red Terror' occurred on the eve of the German assault and goes a long way to account for the welcome which the inhabitants gave to the invaders.[5]

The period of Soviet occupation deepened the gulf between Jews and non-Jews in these regions. Although Jewish merchants and businessmen were ruined after the arrival of the Red Army, many young Jews welcomed Communist rule. In Lithuania, in January 1941, 355 out of the 1,968 members of the Lithuanian Communist Party were Jews. While Hebrew schools were suppressed and Jewish nationalist groups broken up, other Jewish political and cultural enterprises flourished. Jews were prominent in the new Lithuanian military establishment. During the Soviet terror in June 1941, 7,000 Jews were arrested or deported to Siberia, yet this suffering was overshadowed by the activity of local Jews who had collaborated with the Soviets or of Russian Jews who had been in evidence amongst the occupation forces. So, when the Germans arrived, they were welcomed as liberators and their anti-Jewish and anti-Communist propaganda was broadly welcomed.[6]

In Kovno, in Lithuania, local anti-Soviet partisans were already in action against the Russians when German troops arrived. They killed around 3,500 Jews between 25 and 28 June. Avraham Tory [Golub], a young lawyer and Zionist activist, recorded in his diary on 7 July:

> Soviet rule has disappeared. The Jews are left behind as fair game; hunting them is not unprofitable, because the houses and courtyards of many of them brim with riches. Slaughter the Jews and take their property – this was the first slogan of the restored Lithuanian rule. In that respect the Lithuanians are in complete accord with the Germans. . . . One of the first acts of what seemed to be the government of the independent Lithuania was a bloody massacre of Jewish men, women, and children. Like a pack of bloodthirsty dogs the Lithuanian partisans prowled the streets and courtyards, seizing panic-stricken Jews who had managed to find various hiding places. These Jews were dragged away to an unknown destination.

Tory had narrowly avoided arrest by the Russians, who regarded his Zionist work as bourgeois nationalism; he now found himself trying to survive an immeasurably more brutal regime.[7]

The Einsatzgruppen rapidly organised the 'partisans' into local militias and directed them at the Jews – with bloody effect. Within a few days, the Lithuanian partisans had been grouped into an 'auxiliary police force' of five companies under the command of an Einsatzkommando. Local police guarded Fort Seven outside Kovno in which 1,500 Jews were slaughtered; Lithuanian Ordnungspolizei (order police – the regular police force) were soon killing 500 Jews daily.[8] In Vilna, thousands of Lithuanian deserters from the Red Army formed partisan groups to attack the retreating Russians and any Jews they came across. Sporadic and random killings led to 500 deaths in a matter of days, although there was no mass pogrom.[9]

In the Ukraine the same pattern was repeated. Here, too, the descent of the Nazis took place against a long history of inter-ethnic rivalry and religious prejudices stretching back for centuries. While some Jews in the Western (Polish) and Eastern (Soviet) Ukraine had suffered from Soviet rule, others had benefited from it and identified wholeheartedly with the regime.

Lazar Kaganovich, for example, rose to the level of the Polit-buro and imposed Stalin's terror on his native Ukraine – spar-ing no one. The arrival of the Germans unleashed a wave of Ukrainian nationalism, anti-Communism and anti-semitism that led to spontaneous pogroms all over the region. However, there were examples of Ukrainians speaking out on behalf of Jews – such as Metropolitan Sheptytsk'yi – and cases of indi-vidual heroism in which Jews were saved by Christian neigh-bours.[10]

Spontaneous pogroms against the Jews occurred in Lvov, Tarnopol and Rovno. Ukrainians in Tarnopol massacred sev-enty Jews in one convulsion soon after the entry of the German forces: twenty were beaten to death on the streets in 'revenge' for action by the NKVD, the secret police, against anti-Soviet Ukrainian nationalists. Pogroms against the Jews also occurred in Dombril and Sambor. Local militia helped the Einsatzkom-mandos to round up Jews in Sokol, Lutsk and Zlokov.[11] In Lvov on 2–3 July, local forces assisted by German-trained units butchered several thousand Jews as revenge for the execution of imprisoned Ukrainians by the Soviets on the eve of their retreat from the city. Later on, 1,000 Jews were collected together and handed over to the Einsatzgruppe.[12]

For the young Simon Wiesenthal, this was when the Holo-caust began. Wiesenthal had trained as an architect and worked in Lvov until the Soviet occupation. When the Red Army moved in he lost his livelihood, like so many Polish Jewish professionals, and found work in a factory making bedsprings; his stepfather was imprisoned, and later died in gaol, while his stepbrother was shot for being a 'bourgeois'. After the departure of the Soviet forces, local Ukrainians descended on the Jews and Wiesenthal went into hiding. On 6 July he was routed out of concealment by a Ukrainian policeman and arrested. Most of the Jews who were captured at the same time were shot; he was spared and was later saved by a friendly Ukrainian guard who helped him to evade the Germans temporarily.[13]

Malvina Graf, who had fled with her family to Lvov from Cracow in September 1939, witnessed the horrors which occurred.

For three days, Ukrainian men and women ran amok like savage beasts, carrying large, thick sticks in their hands with which they would beat every Jewish man, woman and child that they encountered. So great was their frenzy that the streets were littered with shapeless masses from which occasionally emanated moans, murmured prayers, cries of pain. Beaten to bloody pulps, Jews could do nothing but watch in sheer amazement and anger – and wonder at the brutality of these animals who could be so barbaric as to beat the life out of innocent, small children.[14]

Not all the pogroms were entirely spontaneous. The Germans encouraged mob violence since it saved them time and effort if local people engaged in 'self-cleansing' operations. They played on the atrocities committed by the Soviets and exploited the popular association of Jews with Bolshevism, casting anti-Jewish actions as justifiable 'defensive' operations against 'Jewish terror'.[15] Yet German efforts to encourage actions against the Jews were not always successful and rarely occurred after the Einsatzgruppen had departed. Time and again, the authors of the Einsatzgruppen reports complained of the 'passivity' of the local populations. This was particularly so in the regions of White Russia and the Ukraine which had always been part of the USSR, where the inhabitants were more wary of defying Soviet power. In districts closer to the front line, and everywhere else as the campaign wore on without an outright German victory, Russian citizens acted with greater circumspection with an eye to the possible return of Soviet rule.[16]

However, the speed and scale of the slaughter would not have been possible without local aid. Einsatzgruppe A reported in mid-October 1941 that it was responsible for the elimination of 125,000 Jews; Einsatzgruppe B boasted 45,000 victims by mid-November; Einsatzgruppe C had accounted for 75,000 Jews by the start of that month; while by mid-December, Einsatzgruppe D had murdered 55,000 people.[17] In Lithuania, Latvia, Estonia and the Ukraine, local militia and police units were brought under German command and offered valuable support to the Einsatzgruppen in their operations. Himmler was so impressed by the role of native helpers that on 25 July 1941 he decreed the rapid formation of Baltic, White Russian and Ukrainian units. The Wehrmacht co-operated by ordering the early release of prisoners of war from these nationalities.[18]

The Lithuanians provided five companies of police for use against the Jews in Kovno and Vilna; half of all the Jews in these centres were killed by people who had formerly been their neighbours, now serving in the militia. The report of Einsatzgruppe A for 11 July 1941 noted that 'Their cooperation consists chiefly in looking for and turning over Lithuanian Communists, dispersed Red Army soldiers, and Jews. After the retreat of the Red Army, the population of Kaunus [Kovno] killed about 2,500 Jews during a spontaneous uprising. In addition, a rather large number of Jews was shot by the auxiliary Police service.'[19]

On 4 July Einsatzkommando 9 in Vilna organised the local Lithuanian police for a concerted onslaught on the Jewish population, using an execution site in the forest of Ponar which partisans had previously employed for this purpose. The Einsatzgruppe report for 13 July stressed the importance of their assistance:

> The Lithuanian *Ordnungsdienst* which was placed under the command of the Einsatzkommando after Lithuanian political police had been dissolved was instructed to take part in the liquidation of the Jews. 150 Lithuanian officials were assigned to this task. They arrested the Jews and put them into concentration camps, where they were subjected the same day to 'Special Treatment'.

This contingent of Lithuanians succeeded in murdering 500 male Jews a day until the Einsatzkommando moved on to Minsk.[20]

In Latvia, the Perkonkrusts, the indigenous Latvian fascist movement, seized Jews in Riga and participated in the subsequent massacres. The commander of Einsatzgruppe A, General Stahlecker, ordered the formation of three police battalions to serve alongside the spontaneously formed auxiliary police unit under the command of Victor Arajs. The 'Arajs Kommando' comprised five companies, numbering 500 men in all. On 6 July, it killed 1,500 Riga Jews and burned down three synagogues; 400 Jews were massacred in the Gogol Synagogue when the building was set alight. The next day, 10,000 Jews and Communists were arrested and detained; over the following weeks, thousands were taken from the holding centres in Riga to the Bikernicki forest and executed.

By August 1941, Latvian Kommandos had massacred 15,000 Jewish men in the Bikernicki and Hochwald woods. However, the Nazi commanders feared that the local Selbstschutz (self-defence militia) was not sufficiently reliable and replaced it with German police. The Arajs Kommando continued to work, now in co-operation with the German police. Meanwhile, in Riga, the Latvian Schutzpolizei guarded the ghetto set up in the autumn where the surviving Latvian Jews were held along with Jews deported from Germany. Between September and December, 29,000 Jews were marched from the ghetto to the Rumbula wood for execution. Their route was guarded by Latvian Schutzmannschaften (police regiments) under the command of Lieutenant-Colonel Osis; the killing site was ringed by Latvian auxiliary security police under Arajs and Latvian Ordnungspolizei.[21]

In Estonia the Selbstschutz annihilated the small Estonian Jewish population for the Germans. Reflecting on several weeks of work, the Einsatzgruppe A report for 12 October 1941 commented that 'The Estonian self-defence units, which were formed when the army marched in, immediately started to arrest Jews. Spontaneous demonstrations against the Jews did not take place because there was no known reason for the population to do so.' These units were ordered to arrest all male Jews over sixteen years; 'all Jewesses fit for work between the ages of 16 and 60, to be utilised to work in the peat bogs'; and to concentrate the rest of the Jews at specified sites. 'All male Jews over 16, with the exception of physicians and the appointed Jewish Elders, were executed by the Estonian self-defence units under supervision of the Sonderkommando' (special detachments or squads).[22]

Local militiamen in the Ukraine searched for Jews, rounded them up and, from August 1941, increasingly did the killing themselves. They were paid by their town or city councils, often out of funds expropriated from the Jewish communities.[23] There was never any shortage of native helpers for the SS, which was considered to be just as well. The Einsatzgruppe C report for 11 September 1941 noted: 'Primarily in the large towns, the ever increasing security tasks cannot be solved by the Einsatz-kommandos alone, since they are too small for this purpose. Mounting importance is being attached to the creation and organisation of a regular police service. Well-screened and par-ticularly reliable Ukrainians are employed for this purpose.'[24] During 1942, the number of collaborators grew enormously. For all the rhetoric about Slav *Untermenschen*, the killing oper-ations came to rest more and more on East European collabor-ators.

Following Himmler's instructions, the native Ordnungspoli-zei was boosted from three to nine regiments. The Schutz-mannschaften, known by their shortened name as Schumas, were also rapidly expanded until they numbered seventy-eight battalions in July 1942, formed from disbanded militia bodies, released prisoners of war and volunteers. By the end of the year, 47,974 men were serving in these units; for each German security battalion there were five native Schumas. Lithuanian, Latvian, Estonian, Ukrainian and White Russian Schumas guarded civil and military locations against partisan attack and took part in anti-partisan actions; they also watched over the ghettos in the Baltic, White Russia and the Ukraine, herded Jews to places of slaughter and joined the Einsatzgruppen in their renewed assault on the Jewish population during 1942.[25]

Diaries and fragments of memoirs that survive from the ghet-tos record the actions of the Baltic and Ukrainian guard units. Between the formation of the Kovno ghetto in August 1941 and its effective liquidation in October 1943, Lithuanian police battalions patrolled the perimeter. During actions to deport Jews to the death camps, Lithuanian, Latvian and German police formations worked closely together, storming into the ghetto to snatch groups of Jews. On more than one occasion, Avraham Tory's diary notes that Lithuanian police guards casually shot Jews passing by the ghetto fence. They treated the ghetto Jews as 'fair game' to be plundered at will.[26] Latvian police shared with their German counterparts the tasks of shepherding Jewish labourers in and out of the Riga ghetto. Local police were at the forefront when the ghetto was liquidated.[27] Tadeusz Pankiewicz, in the Cracow ghetto, observed that the 'Armed spies, collaborators from Lithuania and Latvia who served in the German units and distinguished themselves with displays of unusual cruelty and sadism . . . were used in the *Aktions* for the liquidation of the Ghetto.'[28]

Ukrainian guard units served in Polish ghettos, far from home, and were notoriously associated with deportation actions. The Warsaw ghetto diaries of Emmanuel Ringelblum and Abraham Lewin repeatedly describe them as 'scoundrels' and 'bandits' who seemed intent only on looting the Jews under their guard. They could also be lethal. Ukrainians scoured the tenement blocks of the ghetto looking for Jews during the great deportations between July and September 1942 and employed the utmost brutality to channel them towards the *Umschlagplatz* from where Jews were deported to Treblinka. When the hunters found a 'bunker' in which Jews were hiding they were merciless.

Abraham Lewin was a gentle man, an educationalist descended from a line of scholars and rabbis. He was a member of the Oneg Shabbas group, formed around the historian Emmanuel Ringelblum, which was devoted both to maintaining morale in the ghetto through cultural activities and to chronicling the fate of the Jews. On 9 August, at the height of the 'action', Lewin wrote:

> Yesterday was horrific in the full sense of the word. The slaughter went on from early morning until nine and half-past nine at night. This was a pogrom with all the traits familiar from the Tsarist pogroms of the years 1905–6. A mixed crowd of soldiers of various nationalities, Ukrainians, Lithuanians and over them the Germans, stormed into flats and shops, looting and killing without mercy. I have heard that people are being slaughtered with bayonets. Yesterday there were vast numbers of deaths.[29]

Writing in his diary on 14 December 1942, Ringelblum recorded:

I know of a case on Nowolipie Street where several dozen people were hiding in two walled-up rooms. The Ukrainians blockading the house threw a party in the next room. They were about to leave when they heard a child crying. They chopped down the wall and found one of the rooms, with twenty-six people in it. They shot six of them on the spot; the rest bought the Ukrainians off and went to the Umschlagplatz.[30]

Eight hundred Latvians and Lithuanians in several Schuma units were deployed in the first attempt to liquidate the Warsaw Ghetto in January 1943. This incursion was suspended in the face of Jewish resistance, but 375 Ukrainians from the *Werkschutz* – labour-gang guards – and guards from the Trawniki training camp joined the final assault on the ghetto in April.[31]

The training centre at Trawniki in Poland was set up as one element in what was dubbed 'Operation Reinhard' – the extermination of the Jews in the districts of Warsaw, Cracow, Lublin, Radom and Lvov. 'Operation Reinhard' was instigated in the autumn of 1941 after it became evident that the Einsatzgruppen alone, with their established methods, could not hope quickly to eliminate the 2,284,000 Jews in Poland, Lithuania, White Russia and the Ukraine. In September, the Einsatzgruppen commanders had started to experiment with a variety of killing techniques, including dynamite and gas, which they hoped would be faster and less wearing on their men. In using gas they were able to draw on the experience of the Nazi euthanasia programme, and this approach was soon adopted.

By the end of 1941 the Einsatzgruppen had begun to make extensive use of mobile gas chambers. These were vans with large, sealed containers into which the engine's poisonous exhaust fumes could be piped. Jews in the Chelmno district were gassed in this way from early December 1941. A month earlier, work commenced on fixed killing sites with stationary gas chambers. Eventually three camps were erected to carry out 'Operation Reinhard': Belzec, Sobibor and Treblinka.[32]

Each camp was run by just twenty to thirty-five SS men. The bulk of the personnel assigned to guard duty were drawn from Schuma units, Ukrainian prisoners of war and recruits.

They were trained at the specially established camp at Trawniki commanded by SS Sturmbannführer Karl Streibel, under the supervision of Otto Globocnik, the SS police chief of the Lublin area. Over the duration of its history, 2,000–3,000 men were processed through Trawniki for tasks that included guarding ghettos and carrying out deportations as well as duty at the extermination centres. Treblinka, Sobibor and Belzec were each allotted a company of Ukrainians numbering around 100 men.[33]

At Belzec, the black-uniformed Ukrainians manned the watchtowers and guarded the camp perimeter. They assisted the German SS men in the initial unloading and processing of trainloads of Jews, herded them up the 'Tube' to the gas chambers and helped to carry out the gassing operations. Ukrainians watched over the Jewish work details which built Sobibor – and shot them once their task was fulfilled. As the trains came into Treblinka, Ukrainian guards took up their positions on the buildings overlooking the 'ramp', removed Jews from the trains and chased them to the gas chamber operated by the ill-famed Ivan the Terrible.

Survivors present varying portraits of these Ukrainian guards. Many were open to petty bribery; some excelled in cruelty; but others seemed unwilling to be at their posts. The Germans looked on them with ill-concealed contempt. Abraham Krzepicki observed that the Germans treated the Ukrainians at Treblinka like 'second-class citizens' and frequently punished them for minor offences. Samuel Willenberg, another survivor of Treblinka, recalled that the Germans restricted contact between the Ukrainians and the deportees, since many of the new arrivals had money or valuables with which they tried to bribe the guards. For the same reason they forbade exchanges with Jewish prisoners who collected the discarded possessions of the deportees or extracted gold from the mouths of corpses.[34]

Nevertheless, the camp guards engaged in such relentless venality that the district around Treblinka acquired the reputation of a boom town. Farmers, currency dealers and prostitutes from as far away as Warsaw gravitated to the area; the guards were frequently drunk on the vast quantities of alcohol which they purchased. A Pole, Jerzy Krolikowski, who worked close to the Treblinka death camp observed: 'The Ukrainian fascists, who were totally corrupted by the wealth they had acquired with no effort, were contemptuous of its worth.' Jankiel Wiernik, a survivor of Treblinka, recollected that 'When the Ukrainians noticed that the Jews were handling the gold under practically no control, they began coercing them to steal. The Jews were compelled to deliver diamonds and gold to the Ukrainian guards or else be killed. Day after day, a gang of Ukrainians took valuables from the room where the valuables of the deportees were kept. One of the Germans noticed this and of course it was the Jews who had to pay the penalty.'[35]

The cruelty of Ukrainian guards was notorious. Moshe Bakir remembered that in Sobibor the Ukrainians formed a column from the area in which deportees were disembarked and undressed up to the gas chamber, beating the naked Jews as they passed, forcing them to run barefoot through the dirt and mud. Franciszek Zabecki, a Pole who lived in a village near Treblinka, testified that 'The cruelty of the security guards, Germans, Latvians, and Ukrainians, is difficult to describe. Sadism and torture seemed to know no bounds. I saw how guards, who were always very drunk, would open the freight doors at night and demand money and valuables. Then they would fire into the cars . . . ' Ivan the Terrible inspired horror and fear in the inmates. A prisoner told Willenberg soon after his arrival: 'Ivan, the Ukrainian guard, takes out his horseman's sword and hacks to bits anyone who tries to resist at the entrance [to the gas chamber]. He amputates hands and slices up the bodies of naked people; he tears infants out of their mothers' arms and rips them in half. Sometimes he grabs them by the legs and smashes their heads against the wall.'[36]

Yet some Ukrainians not only traded with prisoners but showed sympathy with their plight, even to the point of assisting the resistance in the camps. Several Ukrainians at Treblinka told Abraham Krzepicki that they had volunteered for the Trawniki unit only to escape starvation in a prisoner-of-war camp. He knew of one guard who 'escaped' while another was shot by the SS for some act that displeased them. In the autumn of 1943, the underground in Sobibor made contact with Ukrainian guards who had stopped believing in a German victory and were wavering in their loyalties. The guards promised to establish links between the prisoners and the partisans, but the plan for a link-up failed. Julien Hirshaut, a prisoner in the Pawiak prison in Warsaw where 40,000 Poles, Jews and others were executed, also noted a change in the attitude of the twelve Ukrainian guards in late 1943. When the prisoners mounted a revolt in July 1944, one of the guards threw in his lot with the uprising.[37]

The role of native helpers in the annihilation of the Jews cannot be separated easily from the military collaboration with the Germans. Militia and police units that helped to drive Russian troops out of towns and cities as the Germans entered frequently attacked Jews, too, and were later organised into paramilitary formations that took part in pogroms. Every element of the bewildering array of collaborationist units – Selbstschutz, Schutzmannschaft, Sicherheitsabteilung, Ordnungspolizei, Werkschutz and so on – contributed towards informing on Jews, registering them, seeking them out for deportation or execution, guarding Jews in ghettos or en route to killing sites and, often, murdering them. The police or militia battalions which the Germans sent to the front had often been engaged in murderous activities before they became soldiers. These formations were also the basic elements of combat units formed by the Germans later on in the war; many men were transferred individually or en bloc from guard duties into army brigades and divisions.

The history of military collaboration between the German Army and East Europeans long predated 'Operation Barbarossa', the German invasion of the Soviet Union. Covert links between the German Army, the Abwehr (German military intelligence), the Nazi Party and East European nationalists had begun in the 1920s. It was woven into the complicated and obscure pattern of national movements, *Realpolitik* and subversion which characterised the area well before the rise of Hitler. From 1933, German military intelligence operated routinely in the Baltic states and for several years after the Nazis came to power, Alfred Rosenberg, the party's expert on the east, flirted

with Ukrainian dissidents. These connections acquired special
significance in view of the plans to invade the USSR.[38]

After the Communist occupation of the Baltic states in 1940
and the reign of terror which followed, German military intelligence was easily able to establish a fifth column in time for the
invasion of the USSR. The Germans helped a former colonel
in the Lithuanian Army, Colonel Kazys Skirpa, to form a
Lithuanian Activist Front in Berlin in 1940. The Front was
intended as the kernel of a pro-German regime and liaised with
anti-Soviet partisans. When the Germans entered Lithuania in
June 1941, 200 armed volunteers trained by the Abwehr operated in conjunction with the Wehrmacht. Simultaneously the
partisans launched an uprising in Kovno which succeeded in
inflicting substantial damage on the Red Army.[39]

In May 1941, Latvian officers in exile in Germany formed
a National Association of Latvian Fighters. German military
intelligence trained 200 Latvian volunteers for special tasks
during the onslaught on Russia and, as in Lithuania, partisans
and self-defence groups harassed the retreating Russian forces.
Latvian partisans rose up to drive the Russians from Riga as
soon as the German military had crossed the border. The
Abwehr had also established connections with anti-Soviet
Estonians who had fled to Finland and gave special training to
eighty volunteers. When 'Operation Barbarossa' got under way,
these men were inserted into Estonia, forty by parachute and
forty by sea, to engage in sabotage actions to assist the German
advance and to organise anti-Soviet partisans.[40]

The German occupation forces quickly organised the Baltic
partisan groups into local militias: the Alytus Siauli in Lithuania, the Aiszargi in Latvia and the Eesti Kaitseliit in Estonia.
Army Group North soon established thirteen native security
battalions – Sicherheitsabteilungen – to protect its rear areas.
It was not long before Balts were making an even more direct
contribution to the German war effort: several thousand Estonians and Latvian auxiliary police were sent to the front to serve
alongside German Army units during the critical months in the
winter of 1941–2. Two companies of the Arajs Kommando,
numbering 200 men, saw active service as ski-troops from

February to April 1942. Although the Arajs Kommando
returned to its lethal work in the summer, the other assorted
police units formed the basis of the Latvian and Estonian
Legions that were created in 1942–3.[41]

Military co-operation between the Wehrmacht and the
Ukrainians went back to November 1938 and the aftermath
of the Munich agreement. At Munich, Czechoslovakia was
dismembered and Slovakia acquired 'independence'; but the
Ukrainian population in the district of the Carpathian Ukraine
pressed for autonomy, too. With the encouragement of German
military intelligence, the Ukrainians formed a National Defence
Organisation and created a militia of 2,000 regular soldiers and
13,000 reservists. The militia, or Sich, had a brief existence:
Hitler had previously agreed to hand over the Carpathian
Ukraine to Hungary, whose army occupied it in March 1939.
The Ukrainian volunteers were swept aside, although 600
escaped from the rout into Slovakia. German military intelligence maintained its contact with them in this refuge and
armed and trained them with an eye to the coming invasion of
Poland.[42]

In September 1939 these newly titled Nationalist Military
Detachments moved into Poland with a Slovakian division and
headed for Galicia, where the Ukrainians hoped to establish an
independent Ukrainian government. However, the Germans
had agreed with the Russians prior to the invasion that Poland
would be partitioned between the two powers and that most of
Galicia would fall into the Russian zone of occupation. The
Ukrainian units were recalled and stationed in Western Galicia,
where the Germans established twelve Ukrainian police regiments – Schutzmannschaften – to keep order. The Military
Detachments were disbanded and their members placed in
Schuma and Werkschutz units, often guarding Jews in forced-
labour gangs.[43]

Ukrainian nationalists continued to liaise with the German
Army, a relationship which bore fruit as the Wehrmacht prepared for the assault on Russia. In April 1941, German military
intelligence organised two units for reconnaissance and sabotage duties in the Ukraine. Code-named 'Nachtigall' and

'Roland', the first was formed from Ukrainian émigrés in Austria, the second from Ukrainians in German-occupied Poland. On 22 June 1941, 'Nachtigall' advanced with the German Army in the direction of Lvov while 'Roland' headed south-east in the direction of Kishinev, in the company of Romanian and Croatian troops. When 'Nachtigall' reached Lvov on 30 June, it joined with local nationalist forces in proclaiming an independent Ukrainian state.

In the chaotic week that followed, 'Nachtigall' and local Ukrainian militiamen murdered large numbers of Jews and handed more over to the Einsatzkommandos. But the Germans were taken aback by the proclamation of independence and the Einsatzgruppe troops began to round up the Ukrainian nationalists. To show their determination that the Ukraine would never be a sovereign entity, Galicia was split off from the rest of the Ukraine and incorporated into the Generalgouvernment, the Nazi administrative area covering central Poland. Manifestations of Ukrainian nationalism in other parts of the region were suppressed while 'Roland' and 'Nachtigall' were recalled and submerged into the 201st Ukrainian Schuma battalion. Bitterly aggrieved by the treatment of their cause, the Ukrainian fighters became mutinous. Fearing more trouble, the Germans disbanded the entire unit in December 1941 and imprisoned those of its officers who did not escape in time and join the Ukrainian underground army.[44]

As the campaign in Russia ground on, the German Army found itself engaged in more spontaneous forms of collaboration. In the huge space of the Russian interior, worn down by unexpectedly ferocious Russian resistance, German forces were soon desperately overstretched; they welcomed the services of Russian prisoners of war who volunteered to serve as drivers, cooks and orderlies. Gradually, many of these Hilfswilliger (volunteers), or Hiwis, were armed and ended up being incorporated into German combat units.[45]

The Army also formed a range of native security and anti-partisan units – called variously Selbstschutz, Schutzmannschaften, Sicherungabteilungen – to protect its rear areas. These were comprised of full-time militiamen who were based in barracks and worked in conjunction with the German security divisions. By the end of 1941, Army Group North had established fourteen battalions of Russian, Finnish, Latvian, Estonian and Lithuanian Sicherungabteilungen or security units. Other elements of the Wehrmacht started to organise collaborationist units, too. The Abwehr began recruiting Russian prisoners of war in November 1941 while the Chief of Staff of Army Group Centre set up six pioneer battalions composed of Ukrainian volunteers.[46]

During the first part of 1942 while the Wehrmacht licked its wounds and prepared for another draining offensive, the enrolment of non-Germans accelerated. The number of Hiwis grew to around 100,000 while the army surreptitiously began to form battalion-size combat units entirely of one nationality. Hitler had ordered on 16 July 1941 that only Germans and their allies would be allowed to bear arms, but in April 1942 he bowed to pressure from his Army commanders and gave permission for the formation of larger Hiwi units and so-called Osttruppen or eastern troops.[47]

There was a similar expansion of native paramilitary security units, Schutzmannschaften, to cope with the burgeoning partisan movement. The Schumas were pressed into service in a variety of functions, often distant from their home bases. During 1942, 55,000 White Russians and 180,000 Ukrainians were enrolled in the self-defence corps. There were twenty-six Estonian Schuma battalions, thirty in Latvia and fifty-one Lithuanian battalions; the White Russians numbered eleven battalions while the Ukrainians deployed no less than seventy-one.[48] This form of military collaboration reached its peak in 1943 when the Germans commanded around 150,000 Osttruppen, 400,000 self-defence militiamen and 150,000 personnel in Schumas. The number and array of non-German forces was so great that an Inspector General of Eastern Troops was appointed in December 1942 to bring some order to the topsy-turvy development.[49]

In the spring of 1943 the Army went so far as to experiment with the establishment of a Russian Liberation Army, built around a captured dissident Red Army general, Andrei

Vlasov.[50] The Russian Liberation Army theoretically embraced all the Hiwis, but Hitler prevented its actual coalescence so that it remained merely a propaganda weapon in the hands of the Army intelligence. In January 1944, the idea was revived by Himmler, and led to the coming into existence of several assorted units at a very late stage in the war.[51]

Himmler's belated interest in Vlasov was an extension of his concern to exploit the population reserves of Eastern Europe to provide manpower for the German military machine and, in particular, the Waffen-SS, which was under his control. The Waffen-SS had suffered heavy casualties during the battles of 1941 and 1942. Himmler hoped to make good these losses and to expand the Waffen-SS by drawing on foreign volunteers throughout Europe. When the reserves of enthusiasm dried up in the west, he turned to the *Volksdeutsche* or ethnic Germans, in Hungary, Romania, Yugoslavia, the Baltic and Russia. By 1943, it was necessary to seek recruits even from those who were not ethnic Germans. Reversing his earlier aversion to the idea of employing racially inferior peoples, early in 1943 Himmler permitted the Waffen-SS to recruit locally.[52]

Himmler had thrown Latvian police units into the battle lines as early as October 1941. By April 1942, three Schuma battalions – the 16th, 19th and 21st – were in front-line service operating under the 2nd Waffen-SS Motorised Infantry Brigade, one of the first multi-national Waffen-SS units. In February 1943, Himmler ordered the Latvian police battalions to form a Latvian regiment and following the addition of a further three Latvian police battalions – the 18th, 24th and 26th – the 2nd Waffen-SS Brigade was redesignated the 2nd Waffen-SS Latvian Volunteer Brigade. In addition to this move, Himmler obtained Hitler's agreement to bringing all Latvians in the ranks of the police and Waffen-SS under the umbrella of the Latvian Legion.[53]

Success whetted Himmler's appetite and with Hitler's permission he ordained the formation of non-German division-sized units. The formation of the 15th Waffen-SS Latvian Volunteer Division was announced on 26 February 1943 and in March 1943 Latvians who had registered for labour duty were

offered the alternative of military service. The response was
good: 17,900 opted for the Latvian Legion and 13,400 for other
military duties. Conscription of the cadres 1919–24 was introduced in November; recruits drafted at this time were allocated
to the 15th Waffen-SS Latvian Division and the 19th Waffen-
SS Latvian Volunteer Division, which was constructed around
the Waffen-SS Latvian Volunteer Brigade.[54]

The 15th Waffen-SS Latvian Division took up its station at
the front in the area of Velikye Luki in White Russia early in
1944, but was forced back to the Velikye river by the Soviet
offensive in January. It was joined at the front in the spring by
the 19th Waffen-SS Latvian Division, but the two units were
separated under the hammer blows of the Soviet summer offensive and the needs of the German high command. The 19th
Waffen-SS Latvian Division retreated north-westwards into
Kurland, finally becoming trapped in a huge pocket covering
the tip of the Kurland peninsula where it eventually capitulated
to the Russians. The 15th Waffen-SS Latvian Division was
removed from the front to recover from the drubbing it had
received and ended up in northern Germany, scattered in
several units. One battalion of Latvians, trapped in Berlin, took
part in the final defence of Hitler's bunker. Other elements fell
back towards the Americans, surrendering to US troops in the
region of Schwerin in May 1945.[55]

The 20th Waffen-SS Estonian Division was likewise formed
around a kernel of police units and volunteers whom Himmler
had succeeded in organising into an Estonian SS Legion, with
Hitler's consent, in August 1942. The Legion fought as part of
the Waffen-SS 'Wiking' Division and was expanded by a steady
influx of volunteers until it was brigade-size. Then in February
1943, under the mantle of registration for labour service, Estonians of military age were offered the choice of labour or military
service. Work conditions in the munitions industry were known
to be bad and 5,300 chose duty in the Waffen-SS while 6,000
opted to join the ranks of the Wehrmacht. In September 1943,
the collaborationist authorities issued a call to arms against
Bolshevism which met with great success: 38,000 Estonians put
themselves forward for military service. The 20th Waffen-SS

Estonian Division was created at the start of 1944 and only the shortage of barracks and equipment slowed up its formation.[56]

The Estonians fought on the Leningrad front during 1943 until they were driven back to the frontier of Estonia by the Red Army offensive in January 1944. They held their new position on the Narva river with legendary tenacity until the front collapsed far to the south in July–August 1944 and the Russians poured into Lithuania. This advance threatened to cut off the most northerly German army group, to which the Estonians were attached. During the autumn the Germans withdrew from the Baltic states, abandoning them to their fate. The Estonian Division was evacuated from the region and sent to Neuhammer in Silesia to rest and refit. Later it participated in the bloody suppression of the Slovak revolt in October 1944 and saw more front-line duty in Silesia before it divided into three groups, the bulk of which surrendered to the Russians near Prague in May 1945.[57]

In March 1943, Himmler took up the suggestion of Otto Wachter, the governor of Galicia, for the creation of a Ukrainian SS unit. This formation was to be designated the 14th Waffen-SS Volunteer Division Galizien since Himmler baulked at the use of the term Ukrainian. Recruitment of volunteers throughout the Ukraine was opened on 28 April 1943, with the co-operation of the collaborationist Ukrainian National Committee. The appeal for volunteers was greeted with enormous enthusiasm. By June, 82,000 men had registered for service, although only half that number were called up and just 27,000 were considered fit and suitable for service. The Waffen-SS were able to pick the cream of the recruits, while the surplus were assigned to police regiments that were deployed separately.[58]

The 14th Waffen-SS Volunteer Division Galizien was trained in south-eastern Poland from July 1943 to February 1944 and from February to March 1944 at Neuhammer, where it was reviewed by Himmler personally. Its ranks were strengthened by the addition of eighty-nine officers who had commanded the 'Nachtigall' and 'Roland' units and languished in German prison camps since the dissolution of the 201st Schuma battalion in December 1941. Five Ukrainian Schuma battalions were also disbanded and their members transferred to the Galizien Division. Before it was battle-ready, elements of the division were used in anti-partisan actions near Lvov. In June 1944 the division – now redesignated the 14th Waffen-Grenadier SS Division (Galizien No. 1) was sent to the front and was engaged in battle in July around Brody, where it was used by the Germans in an attempt to slow up the relentless Russian advance. The unit was massively assaulted and surrounded by Soviet forces. Only 3,000 of the original complement of 11,000 men broke out to the west and reached the retreating Germans; Lvov fell not long afterwards.

The remnants were regrouped at Neuhammer, where the division was brought up to strength by the infusion of recruits and elements of redundant police battalions. The reconstituted division was engaged against partisans in Slovakia during autumn 1944, a particularly vicious operation, and in Croatia in early 1945. At around this time it changed its name to the 1st Ukrainian Division and a second division was in the process of formation from surplus troops and Ukrainians stationed in Denmark and Holland. The self-declared Ukrainian Liberation Army was withdrawn to south-east Austria in March 1945, where it surrendered to the British at Radstadt on 8 May. General Pavlo Shandruk, the unit's last commander, made contact with General Anders, who led the Free Polish Forces, and through his intercession the Ukrainian Division was transferred to PoW cages in Italy.[59]

So it was that Himmler's dreams of a pan-European SS army, fighting a crusade against Bolshevism, finally crumbled away. Despite Hitler's antipathy to Slavs, Ukrainians and Balts, the Third Reich ended up as a massive employer of non-Aryan labour and was defended by over a million soldiers who were 'racially inferior' according to Nazi doctrine. A war that was intended to lead to the annihilation of the Jews, the displacement of the Slavs and the relocation of Germans to a new *Lebensraum* did, indeed, end in a massive redistribution of population. Millions of foreign workers, conscripted labourers, Wehrmacht Hiwis, East European Waffen-SS men and refugees ended up in Germany. When the Third Reich was finally over-come, the victorious Allies were astonished to find it awash with a displaced population as cosmopolitan as it was wretched.

2

Germany, Year Zero

When Stephen Spender drove into Germany in July 1945, on a mission to report on the state of German intellectual life after the Third Reich, he saw 'broken streets, filled with broken people'. Later on he recorded, 'My first impression on passing through was of there being not a single house left. There are plenty of walls, but these walls are a thin mask in front of the damp hollow, stinking emptiness of gutted interiors. Whole streets with nothing left but the walls standing are worse than streets flattened. They are more sinister and oppressive.'[1]

In this devastated landscape innumerable personal dramas and tragedies were played out. Wives looked for husbands, parents sought their children, brothers and sisters searched for one another: there was the joy of reunion and the grief of loss. Overlaying this panorama of euphoria and suffering was the constant battle to get food, find work, obtain transport and just survive. At another level, communities of people – members of national and ethnic groups displaced from their homes – tried to orientate themselves. Some yearned to go home; some did not, or could not return; and others no longer had anywhere to go. The armies of the Western Allies – the USA, Britain and France – along with the international relief agencies wrestled to impose order on this chaos and to help the millions of people whose lives had been shattered.

Simultaneously, politicians vied with each other over the fate of nations and national groups. The Russians demanded the immediate return of Soviet citizens; but what was the position of those who came from states that had been annexed by the

USSR in 1940: did they count as Soviet citizens? And what of those Russians who did not want to go back or feared retribution for their collaboration with the Nazis? For the wretched mass of humanity, the uncertainty and turmoil was a nightmare; but there were some groups and individuals who took advantage of the shambles to hide, disappear temporarily or change identity. And amidst the tumult, the intelligence agencies of half a dozen countries pursued a covert agenda that was dictated more by the war they anticipated would soon come than by the one that had just passed. All of this was played out amidst the devastated ruins of the Third Reich.[2]

The cities and towns in western Germany had been pulverised by two and a half years of air raids and months of ground fighting. In Cologne, 66 per cent of houses were destroyed; in Düsseldorf, 93 per cent were uninhabitable; in Frankfurt, 80,000 out of 180,000 homes were wrecked. Throughout the British Zone of Occupation, of the 5.5 million residential housing units existing before the war, 3.5 million were either obliterated or seriously damaged. Germany was paralysed: of 13,000 km of rail track in the British Zone, only 1,000 km were operating; half of the locomotive stock was out of commission; of 12,000 coaches, 5,000 were disabled and the rest damaged. Every bridge over the Rhine was wrecked; elsewhere the British found that 740 river and 540 canal bridges were down. Half of the telephone switchboards operating before the war were inoperative. Although German industry was less badly damaged than military intelligence had thought, the country was temporarily prostrated and the standard of living had sunk to subsistence level.[3]

The scale of physical destruction was matched by the magnitude of human dislocation. Seven million German soldiers had surrendered in the west; the roads were clogged with Wehrmacht columns marching into captivity. One and a half million German civilians had fled from the Red Army towards the US, British and French areas of operation. Ten million city and town dwellers had escaped the bombing and moved into the countryside: the intact towns and cities were brimming with refugees.[4]

In addition to the displaced German population there were over eight million foreign workers who, by the end of the war, formed almost 30 per cent of all industrial workers and 20 per cent of the total labour force in Germany. Of these, around 15,000 were Estonians, 60,000 were Latvians and 90,000 were Lithuanians. These figures were dwarfed by the 1,456,000 Poles and three million Soviet citizens, amongst whom there were many who would also designate themselves Ukrainians or Lithuanians. Finally, there were the non-Germans who had donned the uniform of the Wehrmacht as Hiwis and Osttruppen; who served as Flakhilfer, the crews of anti-aircraft batteries; members of the paramilitary Schumas or Ordnungspolizei; the men who had fought in the eastern divisions of the Waffen-SS; concentration camp and ghetto guards; and those who had slaughtered Jews during the sweeps by the Einsatzgruppen or in the death camps; all of whom had retreated into the Reich with the German forces. In May 1945, up to 20 per cent of the 7.8 million troops wearing German uniforms were non-German.[5]

An estimated seven million human beings were on the move, heading in every direction. Yet there was a mass of people who were intent on staying where they were: the Allied zones of occupation had become the resting place for tens of thousands of non-combatants from Eastern Europe: civilian collaborators, their families and the families of non-Germans in German uniforms. Along with the 350,000 *Volksdeutsche*, ethnic Germans, who had left their homes in the USSR, were 11,500 people from the North Caucasus, 72,000 Ukrainians and 44,600 White Russians (from Volhynia). When German power in the Baltic crumbled away, 15,000 Estonians and 5,000 Lithuanians and Latvians had made their way into Germany.[6]

Leonard Mosley, a leading war correspondent and an acute observer, noted that mixed in amongst the mass of displaced persons (DPs) there were thousands posing as victims of Nazi oppression. He distinguished between the forced labourers, the voluntary workers who had gone to Germany in response to the lure of higher wages and the outright supporters of Nazi Germany who had withdrawn into the Reich with the retreating

German forces. 'The genuine "slaves" just wanted to go home, and besieged the Military Government authorities to get them home as quickly as possible; the others showed no such anxiety to quit the Germany which, they claimed, had treated them so brutally. They were having a fine time. They could steal plenty of food and drink; no one interfered if they terrified the local farmer and his daughters.' Other observers confirm that the Germans were robbed at will by roving gangs of DPs.[7]

The initial responsibility for the maintenance of order and the restoration of basic amenities lay with the Supreme Headquarters Allied Expeditionary Force (SHAEF). Relief work and the arrangement for the repatriation of displaced persons devolved upon SHAEF's Displaced Persons branch, which operated according to a predetermined plan for the administration of German territory that fell under its control.[8] In July 1945, Germany was divided into three Allied zones of control and in the west SHAEF handed over to the zonal Military Governments. Authority in the British Zone of Occupation in Germany was vested in the Control Commission for Germany (CCG), with its headquarters in the picturesque Westphalian town of Lemgo. The parallel body in Austria was the Allied Commission for Austria – British Element (ACA–BE), based in Vienna. The political direction of non-military affairs from London was exercised through the Control Office for Germany and Austria (COGA) up to April 1947, and thereafter by the Foreign Office. Both CCG and ACA–BE had a division handling Prisoners of War and Displaced Persons (PW&DP).[9]

In the first phase, SHAEF and the United Nations Relief and Rehabilitation Administration (UNRRA) worked in close co-operation. Once immediate emergency care for refugees and concentration-camp survivors had been arranged by military personnel, UNRRA civilian officials started to gather DPs into centres where they could be registered and controlled. UNRRA ran the camps set up to house the DPs and organised regular supplies of food as well as basic welfare services. These camps were frequently managed by the inmates themselves, not least because of the drastic shortage of personnel.[10]

The Army had the task of screening those eligible for relief and admission to DP centres. Under the constitution of UNRRA, DP status was denied to war criminals, quislings, collaborators, traitors and ex-Wehrmacht personnel. But the British military authorities, influenced by the disputed status of the Baltic states, were less choosy and would accept into the camps under their control Balts who had fought against the Russians or been conscripted into the German Army. Since UNRRA would take on former combatants if they had a certificate of eligibility from the military authorities indicating that they had not entered the Wehrmacht by choice, it was not difficult for ex-combatants to get into one sort of camp or another. Nevertheless, many DPs showed alarm at the interrogation and registration process. After it became known that some were being 'evicted' from DP camps for practising deception or because they were suspected of war crimes, large numbers of them opted to live as best they could amongst the German population or entered refugee centres run by the civil authorities.[11]

While they may not have known it at the time, East Europeans guilty of war crimes actually had little to fear from investigations. The teams of Allied officers tracking down war criminals were almost exclusively concerned with Germans and Austrians. They were guided by the Central Registry of War Criminals and Security Suspects (CROWCASS), an enlargement of the list compiled by the United Nations War Crimes Commission (UNWCC), but this excluded East Europeans since the Russians had refused to participate in UNWCC. The prime task of East Europeans was simply to avoid repatriation and this was relatively easy. In the chaos of war it was quite acceptable to claim that identification documents had been lost. Most Allied military personnel lacked familiarity with the geography and languages of Eastern Europe and had little way of checking false claims of nationality.[12]

Donald Cameron Watt, later a professor of international history at the London School of Economics, was a young sergeant in British field security in 1945 with the job of interrogating East Europeans and detecting suspicious cases. He recalled,

The problems in finding such people was enormous . . . They were not Germans and so not officially Nazis. They were unlikely to have any documented history that could be discovered . . . I would start my interrogation by asking their name, date of birth and religion. The last question could be a give-away because Nazis tended to say just, 'I believe in God' . . . The dodgy ones we passed on to more specialised interrogation centres. The others were sent to DP camps.[13]

After setting up temporary care and welfare facilities, SHAEF and UNRRA moved on to the huge task of repatriation. Within the SHAEF areas of Germany, Austria and Czechoslovakia there had been 5,922,000 people who wanted to go home, of whom Soviet citizens formed by far the largest proportion at around two million souls. Because of further refugee movements after the war ended, the total number of DPs continued to increase and in the case of certain national groups counterbalanced the number being repatriated. Between 1 May and 30 September, over eight million people were returned to their homes, 2,034,000 to the USSR alone.[14]

At the close of the inter-Allied conference at Yalta in February 1945, an agreement had been signed that obliged the British and Americans to repatriate, by force if necessary, tens of thousands of Soviet citizens – prisoners of war and civilians. The agreement stemmed from the concern of the Western Allies to secure the speedy repatriation of their nationals who had been captured by the Germans and liberated by the Red Army. Before the war was over, thousands of former Red Army soldiers were being sent back to Russia, but in the closing months of the campaign in Europe the British and American forces found that up to 10 per cent of the 'Germans' they captured were, in fact, Russians. They also came across the millions of Russian volunteer and compulsory workers in Germany.[15]

In their anxiety not to offend Stalin, and so delay the return of British and American PoWs, the Western Allies quickly negotiated the arrangements for the transfer of millions of Russians. The agreement concluded at Halle on 23 May 1945 detailed the rate of movement of people and the points at which the handover would take place. Russian repatriation missions were enabled to visit PoW camps and circulate amongst displaced civilians to help organise the flow. Between May and September 1945, over two million Soviet citizens were successfully repatriated, but thereafter the number willing to return tailed off sharply. It became necessary to move thousands of 'recalcitrants' by force, often under traumatic circumstances. The many Russians who had served in the Wehrmacht and so become part of the Russian Army of Liberation, led by Vlasov, dreaded retribution at the hands of the Soviet Government. Cossacks and other members of the various units of Osttruppen could expect no mercy. But their pleas to the British and Americans were swept aside and their efforts to resist repatriation nullified by the use of force.[16]

American and British officers and soldiers were deeply unhappy about the task they were ordered to perform. Their protests were amplified by the newspaper publicity given to the awful scenes accompanying the movement of Vlasovites and Cossacks, the stories of suicides and beatings as men were bludgeoned into freight cars bound for the east. During the autumn, American policymakers began to question the policy and in December 1945 its terms were significantly altered. American troops would no longer be expected to repatriate by force Soviet citizens, while Russian PoWs captured in German uniform would be sent back only if the Soviet authorities could prove that they were Soviet nationals who had voluntarily served the enemy.[17]

British policy remained unchanged for several months more: Bevin and the Foreign Office were too wary of provoking the Russians by any departure from the Yalta Agreement. However, individual commanders blatantly disregarded or circumvented the instructions. Italy, under the overlordship of Field Marshal Sir Harold Alexander during 1945, was a haven for all brands of Soviet nationals who had collaborated with the Germans. Nevertheless, the British PoW and DP camps in Italy were obliged to disgorge hundreds of unwilling returnees until the Cabinet, disturbed by the mounting evidence that the practice was costing lives and Britain's reputation, officially discontinued the policy at a meeting on 6 June 1946.[18]

During the winter of 1945-6, UNRRA cared for 357,000 DPs in Germany and Austria. Amongst these were 285,000 Russian citizens who refused repatriation, including Balts and Ukrainians who denied that they had Soviet nationality. Of the 178,904 Balts, 50,572 were in the British Zone of Germany and 979 in Austria. This hard core of non-returners became an economic burden on the occupation authorities and a political embarrassment since Russian propaganda accused the authorities of harbouring groups of anti-Soviet agitators and obstructing repatriation. Partly in response to Soviet concern and partly because of the dwindling stocks of food and other supplies, UNRRA tightened up the conditions which had to be met before an individual could get relief. However, the process was hampered by the shortage of interrogators and the confusion over the criteria for eligibility.[19]

It is almost impossible to know how many East Europeans were masquerading as DPs, but the numbers were certainly substantial. Due to the capture of German records which listed Balts who had left their homes voluntarily to work or live in Germany hundreds were evicted from UNRRA camps. By December 1946, 90 per cent of the Balts in UNRRA DP centres had been investigated, of whom 2,224 had been declared ineligible for privileged DP status, while a further 23,919 were deemed doubtful cases. These figures indicate that over half of the entire number of Balts in the British Zone were suspected of having either voluntarily moved to Germany to work there or voluntarily fought in the German Army. Even then, this did not represent the total number of displaced Balts: some were in PoW camps, while others were in camps administered directly by the German authorities. No less than 49,000 people were in camps run by the British military, where the conditions of acceptance were notably lax.[20]

Meanwhile, the repatriation drive continued. Although the rate of repatriation slowed down dramatically after the end of 1945, from then until the cessation of its activity in July 1947, UNRRA still assisted the return of one million people. After that time the DP problem was taken over by the International Refugee Organisation (IRO), which had been set up by the

UN General Assembly in February 1946 to care for refugees and seek permanent homes for the remaining displaced persons.[21]

Who were the people who could not or would not go home? UNRRA passed on to the Preparatory Commission for the International Refugee Organisation 650,000 DPs who refused to be repatriated or whom the Western Allies regarded as exempt from the Yalta Agreement. Of this residue, 22,000 were Estonians, 78,000 Latvians and 48,000 Lithuanians. In addition there were also 49,000 non-repatriable Balts in British military camps. It was also estimated at the end of the war that there were two million displaced Ukrainians in the areas occupied by all the Allies. By November 1946, after the bulk of Soviet Ukrainians had willingly gone home, there remained 55,000 self-designated Ukrainians in the British Zone, including approximately 8,000 in the 14th Waffen-SS Galizien Division, which was held near Rimini in Italy. Amongst the recalcitrant Poles there were tens of thousands who claimed to be Ukrainians from the area of the Polish Ukraine that was now Soviet territory.[22]

The IRO took up the challenge of finding new homes for these 'recalcitrants'. Many of them refused to return to their homes because they abhorred Soviet rule, while others feared vengeance as a consequence of their anti-Soviet activity during the war. Some were outright Nazi collaborators or fanatical anti-Soviet fighters who had joined the Waffen-SS with enthusiasm. A few were straightforward war criminals, as yet undetected, who had participated in horrific crimes. Britain was to play a significant part in solving the DP problem by admitting the hard core to its shores. The evolution of this policy was complicated and impelled by a mixture of motives. To understand its origins, it is necessary to look in detail at how British policymakers reacted when they first confronted the unexpected problem of East European collaborators.

'Keep the Balts for As
Long As Possible, and
As Quietly As Possible'

The Baltic had been one of the most stupendous killing grounds
during the first phase of the Holocaust. Between 22 June 1941
and 1 February 1942, Einsatzgruppe A operating in north-west
Russia and the Baltic succeeded in murdering about 218,000
Jews. The small Jewish community of Estonia, numbering no
more than 2,000, was completely exterminated: it was one of
the first areas which the SS declared 'Judenrein', free of Jews.
More than two-thirds of Latvia's pre-war Jewish population of
100,000 was wiped out. In Lithuania, once a centre of Jewish
religious, cultural and artistic life, around 130,000 Jews were
slaughtered and the world of the *shtetl* destroyed for ever.

This had all taken place with little effort at concealment,
but there was negligible opposition to the Germans' genocidal
policy. On the contrary, hundreds of anti-Communist partisans,
militiamen and German-run native police assisted in the massacre. Whatever motivated their collaboration, the members of
the local administrations were complicit in the murder, while
the Baltic combat units which served at the front against the
Russians prevented the liberation of Jews still surviving in the
ghettos of Vilna and Kovno. They helped to win time for the
Germans to push the extermination to its limits.[1]

Yet the policy adopted by the British Army and the Foreign
Office hardly reflected this at all. Balts captured in German
uniform were treated with bemusement at first, but quickly
won respect from British soldiers – who knew little of the
carnage in the states which these men had left behind – for

their good behaviour, intelligence and obvious talents. The political echelon in Germany and London treated the Balts mainly as the subjects of a knotty diplomatic problem: should Britain recognise the legality of the Soviet occupation of the Baltic states in 1941? If so, then the Balts ought to be repatriated under Yalta. If not, then they were exempted. In March 1945, the Cabinet made it clear that Balts were not to be deemed Soviet citizens, which entailed protecting them from Russian demands for their repatriation.

But what of war criminals that were found amongst them? The Foreign Office was so afraid of appearing to give credence to Soviet claims to the citizenship of Balts that it was unwilling to hand over a single person on any other than the most exhaustive grounds. So, for a medley of reasons – ignorance, confusion and diplomatic principle – the British acted as the champions of the Baltic people stranded in Germany. Had more been known about the extent to which Balts were compromised by the bloodbath in their former homes, it is questionable whether such a stance would have been taken. At the time, however, the Balts were amongst the most popular of the millions of DPs swilling around Central Europe.

British attitudes were typified by the history don turned soldier, A. G. Dickens. In May 1945, Arthur Dickens found himself in Lübeck, the once beautiful, but now ravaged medieval port city. He was based there for the last five months of his Army service, charged by the Military Government with the job of setting up and editing newspapers as a medium for information and re-education directed at the German population. In the course of this work, Dickens was struck by the number of foreign DPs in the area. Like other commentators he remarked on their unruly behaviour and expressed sympathy for the cowed Germans who were preyed upon by bands of DPs roaming through the countryside. He noted wryly that German-owned bicycles were a favourite target for DPs, presumably so they could pedal back to their distant homes.

Dickens soon encountered several thousand Baltic refugees, many of whom had been evacuated to Lübeck when German rule in the Baltic states finally collapsed. They made a much better impression on him. The 6,000 Estonians and a similar number of Lithuanians wanted to set up a newspaper and begin cultural activities; the Latvians, of whom there were 10,000, had their own National Liberation Committee and appeared well organised. The Baltic peoples, he wrote in his diary, 'are almost all anti-Russian and live daily in fear of being repatriated to their countries, now absorbed into the Soviet Union.' Dickens went out of his way to assist them to adapt to their new situation and expressed concern at the possible fate that awaited them: 'However small the merits of the case for the preservation of the three Baltic states, it would seem highly undemocratic to compel these minorities to return. As individuals, many I have encountered show every sign of balanced political views and might well make good democratic citizens.'[2]

In all, there were known to be around 50,000 Balts in the British Zone of Germany in September 1945, of whom over 20,000 had served in the German armed forces. Latvians formed the largest contingent of non-German surrendered enemy personnel: 15,000 went into captivity in British camps in May 1945. Most of these men, mainly members of police and Waffen-SS units, were transferred to a camp at Zedelghen in Belgium at the end of September.[3] However, there was enormous confusion about who they were, their military history and what should be done with them.

Under the terms of the Yalta Agreement nationals whose countries had been absorbed into the USSR after 1 September 1939 were deemed to be exempt from repatriation to the USSR. Although the Foreign Office had wobbled with respect to recognition of the Soviet annexation of the Baltic states, lack of consistent pressure from the USSR and fear of upsetting relations with America had meant that the situation was left as it was in 1940. Britain still denied the legitimacy of the Soviet occupation, so the Balts were exempt from voluntary or forcible repatriation.[4]

Matters relating to the Balts were handled by the Northern Department of the FO, under Christopher Warner. Warner had helped to formulate the Foreign Office line that it was vital to retain the wartime alliance with the USSR and it was he who conceded the policy of forcible repatriation. Until he lost hope in continued co-operation with the Russians, he trod warily on any issue that threatened to offend them. Warner was ably assisted by Thomas Brimelow, who had served at the Moscow Embassy in 1942–5 before moving to the Northern Department. Brimelow was justifiably considered an expert on Soviet affairs; he knew Russian well and had devoted himself to the study of Marxism–Leninism. Although he toed the FO line in 1945–6, he was to emerge as a leading cold war advocate of tough policies towards the USSR. Brimelow had an important influence on Robert Hankey, known as Robin throughout the foreign service, who succeeded Warner as head of the Northern Department in March 1946. As a result of his readings of Marxist–Leninist texts, in which he was assisted by Brimelow, and his personal dealings with the Soviets while he was counsellor at the British Embassy in Warsaw during 1945–6, Hankey too developed a deep suspicion of Russian intentions. Together these men were a driving force behind the adoption of cold war policies; their perspective exercised a telling effect on the handling of East European collaborators and alleged war criminals.[5]

The Foreign Office first came to grips with the post-war dilemma of what to do with the Balts in July 1945 when they were alerted to rumours that the French were repatriating them. Officials at the FO told SHAEF that, even though Whitehall had not yet formulated a definitive policy on the Baltic states, efforts should be made to safeguard Baltic nationals. Arrangements were even made to transfer surrendered Balts out of French hands and into the British and US Zones of Control. During September the British Government made its views known publicly, but the French subsequently denied that any such actions had been contemplated and the crisis blew over. However, the scare had prompted Warner and Brimelow to urge Sir Alfred Duff Cooper, Ambassador to Paris, to intervene with the French and showed how sensitive they were both to demands by the Soviets and to any threat to the well-being of the Balts.[6]

As the Allies deliberated on the fate of Axis collaborators

and forcibly repatriated certain groups, such as Cossacks, the
Balts appealed to the British authorities for sympathetic treatment and tried to put as much distance as possible between
themselves and their former German comrades-in-arms. They
used the 'Latvian Red Cross', a non-recognised body, as a front
for their pleas against repatriation. For example, in June 1945,
a large group of Latvians in Flensberg, near the Danish border,
submitted a petition to the British in the name of the 'Latvian
Red Cross', claiming that the Latvians were not Nazi or anti-
Western, but simply anti-Bolshevik. Significantly, the petition
also denied that the Latvians were members of the Waffen-SS.[7]

In August, Dr Alfreds Valdmanis, describing himself as the
former Latvian Minister in Germany, wrote to Field Marshal
Alexander imploring him to separate captured Latvian Waffen-
SS men from surrendered German troops and asking for an
improvement in the conditions under which they were being
held. Valdmanis argued that the Latvians were not from the
same mould as the German Waffen-SS and pleaded that they
be dealt with as a distinct entity.

Valdmanis certainly knew something about the Latvian Waffen-SS. He had been the Minister of Justice in the collaborationist Directorate General that had functioned under the control
of Heinrich Lohse, the Reichskommissar for the Ostland. During
1942 he had negotiated with the Germans, offering 100,000
Latvian recruits for the front in return for a measure of national
autonomy. As long as the Germans appeared willing to make
political concessions, Valdmanis and other members of the
collaborationist regime encouraged Latvian youth to register
for military service. Thanks to their efforts the Germans had
no need to resort to conscription to form the two Latvian
Waffen-SS units that were established during 1943.[8]

Latvians stranded in the British Zone had a powerful advocate in the person of Charles Zarine, the Minister of the Latvian
Legation in London. Before the Soviet occupation and annexation of Latvia in 1940, Zarine had been the accredited diplomatic representative of his country. Since the Western Allies
refused to recognise the Soviet annexation, he enjoyed a curious
diplomatic half-life in which he continued to act as if an inde-

pendent Latvian state still existed. Zarine submitted memoranda and letters to the Foreign Office that set out to prove that Latvians in German uniform, including Waffen-SS, were victims of circumstances.

On 5 September 1945, Zarine explained that membership of the Latvian Legion had been voluntary and the unit had been 'forcibly' embraced by the Waffen-SS. He maintained that Latvians had protested against this and stated that they only wanted to fight Bolshevism. True to their intention, they had never directed their arms against the Western Allies. Zarine noted that the British now had many Latvians in their PoW cages and complained that, according to information he had received, they were being held along with German Waffen-SS men. He asked that since they were not enemies of Britain they should be separated from the German troops, released and treated as DPs. Two weeks later, the Latvian Legation pleaded that the ex-Waffen-SS Latvians should be allowed to get rid of their 'hated' German uniforms.[9]

The Foreign Office treated these representations with caution, as shown by Brimelow's comments on the Valdmanis letter. 'The chief point', he minuted, 'is that the Latvians who were captured in German uniform did not deserve the fate which has befallen them of being imprisoned in German SS pens. It is not a very strong point. The Latvians as a whole were not SS minded, but some of them were and it may well be that at least a proportion of the prisoners richly merited what has happened to them.'[10] Yet the Latvians were always heard respectfully and often with unconcealed sympathy. During October 1945, the Foreign Office pressed the War Office for intelligence that would throw light on the status of Baltic nationals in the German Army; in particular it sought clarification whether they were really SS men.[11]

At the end of the month, Brimelow informed Cecil King, a political adviser to Field Marshal Montgomery, the Commander in Chief, Germany, of guidelines for the treatment of Latvians and other Balts. They were to be kept immune from repatriation and were to be permitted some degree of organisation; beyond that, the Foreign Office was unwilling to make further concessions:

> We regret that we cannot recommend favourable treatment for Latvians (or other Baltic nationalities) captured in German uniform and now held as prisoners of war. It is impossible to distinguish between those who enlisted voluntarily and those who joined up under duress. The War Office says that the only concession which can be made is that of segregation from the Germans and any relaxation of security, particularly change of uniform, is most undesirable in view of the fact that they are unscreened and in many cases have fought voluntarily against the Soviet Union.[12]

This could only be a holding position: the British military could not continue to house and feed these men indefinitely. Whitehall would have to decide on their fate.

At the start of December, King cabled the Foreign Office, with reference to Brimelow's earlier communication, giving the Control Commission's view on what should be done with the 24,000 Baltic nationals captured in German uniforms. 'Present policy of military authority is to discharge into the zone only members of disarmed Wehrmacht normally resident in it. Other Germans and non-Germans in the Wehrmacht are held until their discharge has been arranged to their place of origin.' Of course, in the case of the Balts this was impossible. 'May we agree to discharge Baltic disarmed Wehrmacht into British Zone? If so we should assume from Brimelow's letter under reference that they should be treated as German civilians and not (repeat not) as DPs.'[13]

So, as far as the officials in Germany were concerned, the Balts were collaborators and could not expect relief from UNRRA sources. In fact, this point had been made as long ago as the end of September by Brigadier Kenchington, the chief of the Control Commission's Prisoner of War & Displaced Persons Division.[14] But the Whitehall view was that these men could not simply be dumped into the German population and left to sink or swim. Brimelow commented, 'I think we should try to keep the Balts for as long as possible, and as quietly as possible, in the status of Prisoners of War, until a decision has been made about their ultimate disposal, and if they have to be disbanded before such a decision is reached, they should be treated not as German civilians, but as Baltic DPs.'[15]

Even this position was rapidly undermined. The International Red Cross in Belgium wanted advice on the question of the 12,000 Latvians, 2,000 Estonians and 2,7000 Lithuanians in the Zedelghen camp. Were they PoWs? Were they to be handled as Germans? Could their families have DP privileges? The Refugee Department of the FO quickly disillusioned Brimelow as to the part they or the international relief agencies might play in caring for the Balts: since they were not Allied nationals, had not left their homes due to enemy action or persecution, Balts did not come under the aegis of UNRRA or any other body.[16]

Moreover, Christopher Warner and John Troutbeck, head of the German Department, were worried about the Russian response. The Soviet Union was suspicious about the reasons why disarmed East European units were still being held intact by the Western Allies and even allowed to engage in anti-Soviet propaganda. Troutbeck warned that the Balts were the sort of group 'against which the Russians have been making such outspoken protests'. He recommended that they should be disbanded and discharged, without giving them the privileged status of DPs; Warner concurred.[17]

Brimelow was in a dilemma. If UNRRA denied the Balts DP status, then they could not enter DP camps and would have to shift for themselves amongst the German population. But what was to stop them sticking together and embarking on anti-Soviet activities? Once they were discharged, the British would lose all control over them. What was more, the Russians might claim that if they were treated as discharged Wehrmacht soldiers, then by the same logic they ought to be returned to their homes. Then again, the British could not support them endlessly and risk accusations from the Russians that they were being held in protective custody by the British Army. It was a miserable, frustrating and tense situation.[18]

Out of the blue, the Russians broke the logjam by demanding

that either the Balts should be returned to their places of origin or disbanded and discharged. This message was conveyed to Field Marshal Montgomery by Marshal Zhukov, the most senior Russian general, and triggered an instant response. Montgomery recommended holding the Balts outside the British Zone or discharging them into DP camps. Since the former was expensive, the Foreign Office opted for the latter.[19]

The British authorities in Germany already had a highly sympathetic attitude towards the Balts. They were 'well disciplined and have been most co-operative'. Since their families were already in DP camps, it was proposed that the ex-soldiers should simply be released and left to join them. The camps in question were maintained by the Germans, so there would be no cost to the British; but the British military could keep an eye on them. 'This will not prejudice any decision eventually re. their future disposal.' Yet the communications that went between the FO, the Control Commission and British military headquarters in Germany show an awareness that the Baltic troops were not free of suspicion as to their wartime activities. The military in Germany assured London that 'Before discharge they would be carefully screened and we are prepared to accept any security risk entailed in making them DPs.'[20]

There is no evidence, however, that such screening ever occurred. On the contrary, the efforts by UNRRA to apply eligibility tests for qualification as DPs were fiercely resisted by the Balts on the one hand, while on the other the British military authorities explicitly stated that they would designate Balts as DPs even though they failed to meet UNRRA criteria. In January 1946, around 16,500 Balts acquired DP status en masse, despite the fact that they were former combatants, many of whom almost certainly volunteered to fight with the Germans.[21]

If screening did take place, the proof that Balts had fought in the Waffen-SS was not taken very seriously. In July 1946, six months after the discharge and supposed screening of the Balts, Lieutenant-Colonel E. Fogarty, a member of the military authority for the Schleswig-Holstein region, discovered that at the Grossenbrode DP Camp there were '500 SS bearing blood gp markings under the armpit'. The blood-group tattooed under the left arm was unique to the Waffen-SS and it was looked for by investigators at the most preliminary stage of screening surrendered enemy personnel. During the summer of 1945 it was common to see long lines of half-naked German soldiers with their left arm raised, filing past tables at which sat the PoW screeners: Waffen-SS men identified in this way were then separated and held for interrogation. Although these Balts had been in PoW cages prior to their discharge and ought to have been screened thereafter, a compact group of 500 had now been 'revealed'. It was hardly surprising that Fogarty commented, 'The presence of these in a DP Camp is regarded by this HQ as a serious matter in view of political repercussions.'[22]

UNRRA, prodded by its Soviet members, challenged the sleight of hand by which a whole class of men of dubious eligibility was turned into DPs. In the autumn and winter of 1945/6, the camps run by UNRRA applied tests for eligibility in order to whittle down the numbers in receipt of relief and to facilitate increased repatriation. If UNRRA officials detected someone who was suspected of volunteering to serve the Germans moving by choice to Germany to live or work there, or committing war crimes, they were evicted from the DP camp. Baltic DPs saw little difference between Soviet repatriation missions and eligibility tests, and frequently believed that UNRRA officials were Soviet agents. As soon as UNRRA eligibility tests were applied to the Balts there were howls of protests and a flurry of lobbying by their supporters in Britain. As a result, the British acted as the protectors of the Balts, partly as a consequence of the Yalta Agreement and partly due to sheer confusion about the role of Baltic collaborators.[23]

On 8 February 1946, Charles Zarine visited Sir George Rendel, Britain's former Ambassador to Yugoslavia, who was now Superintending-Under-Secretary at the Refugee Department of the Foreign Office. Zarine's mission was to protest against the way in which UNRRA was handling the Latvians. He felt that they were vulnerable to a variety of pressures and needed help. Several weeks later he submitted a memorandum in which he recommended admitting the Latvian DPs to an Anglo-Saxon country.[24]

A few days later, the *Manchester Guardian* reported that the US Army intended to submit the 90,000 Balts in the US Zone to a strict investigation in order to differentiate those who deserved preferential DP treatment from imposters and ineligible persons. According to US sources it was suspected that as many as 40 per cent of the Balts had engaged in military collaboration with the Germans. This report triggered questions in the House of Commons, where Konni Zilliacus, a left-wing Labour MP, asked how many Balts in the British Zone were being employed by the British Army and how many had formerly fought for the Germans. The Jewish Labour MP Maurice Orbach also wanted to know why the Army was employing men who had worked for the Nazis and complained that they were being allowed to indulge in anti-Soviet propaganda.

These questions were answered by John Hynd, the Chancellor of the Duchy of Lancaster, who was the Minister in charge of the Control Commission for Germany and Austria (COGA). Hynd responded to the charges made by Zilliacus by declaring that 'no information' was available, but he told Orbach that non-German Balts were being treated as DPs until the 'wider questions' regarding their treatment were resolved.[25]

In fact, American policy on the Balts created a minor nightmare for the British. The Embassy in Washington informed the Foreign Office:

> Some 90,000 of these persons will be subject to an intensive screening programme which will determine whether they are eligible to continue receiving preferential treatment given DPs in camps in Germany. Screenings already completed indicate a very high average of former collaborators among the Baltic populations. Almost 40% of the men were estimated to have served actively in the German Army. The majority of the women, it is said, worked willingly for the Germans.[26]

This American initiative exposed the embarrassing situation in the British Zone and placed the British under severe pressure to differentiate collaborators and eject them from DP camps.

Lieutenant-Colonel Hammer at the War Office sought urgent advice from the Refugee Department of the Foreign Office: what should the British do? Thomas Brimelow advised that in principle voluntary collaborators should be denied DP status:

> we realise that it will be difficult to do the screening with certain fairness; but it should be done on general grounds of justice and also to forestall criticism from other governments. We must, however, continue for the present to refuse to use compulsion in the repatriation of persons of whose guilt as War Criminals, Traitors or Quislings substantial *prima facie* evidence has not yet been supplied.[27]

The American move led to much debate within the FO and a good deal of cynicism about American intentions. John Pumphry, an assistant private secretary at the Foreign Office, which had now taken responsibility for the Control Office, minuted, 'The US policy is all right, but it would be nice to know how it works in fact. Presumably PoW and SEP [surrendered enemy personnel] are automatically deprived of privilege, and any who took German nationality. But the screening of collaborators from slave-workers must be a hitty-missy operation. Perhaps Refugee Dept. would say whether the British authorities screen Baltic DPs into good and bad categories.'[28] In practice, the British authorities just arranged to transfer UNRRA rejects and those ineligible for DP status into sixty assembly centres over which they had retained control.[29]

All through 1946, the Foreign Office was bombarded with letters from Zarine and supporters of the Latvian cause, protesting against the merest hint of screening. In January, one official, John Galsworthy, commented on the earlier Red Cross appeal on behalf of the Balts: 'Ex-Wehrmacht Balts in our hands have many advocates . . . '[30] Zarine intervened at the Foreign Office several times during the first six months of the year to protest against US policy, although Sir George Rendel explained that the British could not interfere in the American Zone. The Duchess of Atholl, who chaired the right-wing British League for European Freedom, wrote to *The Times* to rouse opinion against the alleged forcible repatriation of Balts. There were protests in the *Tablet*, too.[31]

The well-organised pro-Balt lobby was also active in Parliament. Towards the end of December 1945, Sir Basil Neven-Spence, a Conservative MP, demanded to know from the Minister of State for the Foreign Office, Hector McNeil, how many Balts were being handed over to the Russians. In March 1946, Mr Pickthorn MP questioned if the Prime Minister was aware of reports that Balts were being repatriated by force. In May 1946 Alfred Bossom MP, the President of the Anglo-Baltic Friendship Society, asked for Balts to be allowed into Britain to work as agricultural labourers and a few months later tried to prevent the deportation of seventeen Balts who had entered the UK illegally. Bossom and Zarine were naturally in close touch with one another. Tom Driberg was another MP who entered the debate about Latvian prisoners of war.[32]

In June, the harassed Foreign Office obtained from the Control Office for Germany a firm denial that the British were repatriating Balts, except in the case of proven war criminals. All Balts were entitled to DP status and were not treated as collaborators even if they were ex-combatants, unless it could be shown that they had voluntarily entered the German forces or freely migrated to Germany before September 1939.[33]

Crucially for the fate of the Baltic DPs, British patience with the Russians was wearing thin. Ernest Bevin, the Foreign Secretary, was fiercely anti-Communist, but he had subordinated his personal suspicion of the Soviets for the sake of preserving the wartime alliance. By the summer of 1946, he was well on the way to giving up hope that it would be possible to work with Moscow. It was symptomatic of his toughening stance that in June he persuaded the Cabinet to agree that the forcible repatriation of Soviet citizens should cease.[34]

The Foreign Office now decisively rejected Soviet demands and developed a sceptical attitude towards UNRRA screening methods. Sir Alexander Cadogan, Britain's representative at the UN, told Sir George Rendel in September 1946 that the Soviet line on 'collaborators' was unacceptable. Men who fought against Communism were not automatically 'collaborators' and should not be treated as such. He strongly resented the way in which the Soviet diplomats tried to make UNRRA act on the basis of their ideological assumptions. Rendel concurred entirely and roundly criticised the way UNRRA was handling the DPs, expressing to colleagues in the Foreign Office the hope that the emerging International Refugee Organisation would adopt different criteria.[35]

The IRO would not take the field until July 1947, and in the meantime Balts in Germany continued to rail against the behaviour of UNRRA officials. On 15 January 1947, the Refugee Defence Committee added its voice to those already raised in protest against the screening policy. The committee was an impeccably honourable body under the Presidency of the Rt Hon. Earl of Halifax, with Professor Gilbert Murray and Sir Norman Angell as vice-presidents. In a memorandum on the status of the Balts, the committee complained, 'Each Baltic citizen who served in a German formation has, in order to retain his DP status, to prove that he joined up under compulsion. The burden of proof is *on the accused* . . . And who in the chaotic conditions since 1941 would still carry *proofs* of his compulsory call-up?' As a consequence, 30–40 per cent of them were being stigmatised as Wehrmacht, paramilitary or Waffen-SS members.

The memorandum countered that the Balts were victims of the Germans, not collaborators or criminals. It was the Allies who should prove that membership of the Wehrmacht and paramilitary formations had been voluntary. Balts who had served in the Allgemeine-SS (the general duty, non-combat SS) or the Waffen-SS should have their cases reviewed immediately by competent boards. It concluded:

Our committee urges that these excellent Baltic refugees during their continued stay in Europe shall be subjected to no more stresses, whether by pressure of Soviet Russia or those who regard the DP problem as an intolerable burden, that the repatriation drive cease and that only those who served in SS formations be still screened by Eligibility Tests, and that the status of 'de facto' statelessness be accorded to those DPs, and that only those duly proved by a Joint Board to have voluntarily

served with the enemy should be penalised under the Eligibility
Tests.[36]

Shortly afterwards, the committee submitted another memorandum rejecting the accusation that the Balts had voluntarily
joined the Wehrmacht or the Waffen-SS and demanded to know
how many Balt DPs had been rendered ineligible as a result
of recent screening procedures. The Control Commission in
Germany provided the necessary information: 'CCG rules that
all ex-Wehrmacht Balts are to be eligible for DP status unless
CCG has definite proof they served in SS.' This policy differed
from that of UNRRA, which placed the onus of proof on the
individual: a prospective DP had to show UNRRA camp officers that he had been conscripted. As a result, the mass of
Balts were excluded from UNRRA care, but were 'eligible for
reception in British camps'. Whereas UNRRA had rejected
1,752 Balts, the British had turned away only 130 cases.[37]

At around the same time, Zarine addressed a further attack
on UNRRA to Robin Hankey, now head of the FO Northern
Department. He lamented that 'the "screening" process
remains a continual worry' to the Latvians. However, he was
careful to distinguish between the conduct of UNRRA personnel and the British: 'In general the military government
officials give great satisfaction, but the ways of UNRRA often
leave much to be desired.' In a subsequent communication, he
explained to Hankey, 'Quite frankly I must confess that the
disquietening news about the screening does not come from the
British Zone, though there has been much uneasiness on the
subject of screening and fear that what was taking place in the
American Zone might also happen in the British . . . '[38]

During the course of 1946, Balts in British custody were
steadily released without any screening having occurred.
Twenty-six who were being detained at the huge PoW centre at
Rimini were sent to Germany and released into the population.
Three hundred Latvian DPs in northern Germany were permit-
ted to begin work on ships in the Baltic in the summer. Major-
General Brownjohn at the British Control Commission head-
quarters recommended that Balts be allowed to settle in the

British Dominions since they were the 'best and most useful class to take'.[39] The policy of undiscriminating release was extended to the backyard of the Foreign Office. Twenty-six Balts who had fought against the USSR had ended up in Britain in a PoW camp at Knutsford, Cheshire. They had been kept there, concealed from the Russians, until the summer of 1946. Then they were stealthily transferred to Germany and designated as DPs.[40]

The obstructive attitude of British officials towards the screening of DPs may be understandable in view of the pressure from the Soviet Union to repatriate all Balts forcibly. All the same, a distinction existed between Soviet demands which were purely ideological and those which had some forensic basis. Foreign Office officials always proclaimed that genuine war criminals ought to be placed under Soviet jurisdiction if they were detected. Yet even here the cautious and increasingly cynical perception of Russian motives cut across the effective implementation of measures to root out men and women who were suspected of war crimes.

One device which the Soviets used to achieve their aim of mass repatriation was to claim that just by virtue of having fought against the USSR during the war former East European combatants were traitors. With rather more substance, the Russians argued that Balts in the Waffen-SS were war criminals in a generic sense. The argument that these men ought to be delivered into their charge to face trial and punishment had some basis in the procedures to which all the Allies had agreed since, in 1946, the International Military Tribunal at Nuremberg had declared the Waffen-SS to be a criminal organisation. Officers were to be detained and carefully interrogated; other ranks were to be detained in separate PoW camps, too. In a number of cases, the Russians actually identified individuals against whom specific allegations could be made. But the British response in every instance was to stonewall.

Early in 1946, the Soviet press began to cavil at the way the Balts were being handled in the British Zone and in Denmark, claiming that the British were preventing them from returning home. It was certainly true that in Denmark the British military had detained several Balts, but only because they had been in the SS or had worked for German intelligence. The rest were being discharged into DP camps as per instructions. These men were offered facilities for repatriation if they wished it, otherwise they remained in DP centres in Denmark until they were transferred elsewhere. The only exceptions were the suspected war criminals and it was here that the Soviet Union tried to exercise leverage.

Sir William Strang, chief political adviser to Montgomery, informed the Foreign Office that the Russians were insisting that the British transfer 'certain named Baltic personalities who are alleged to have been concerned with the formation of Baltic SS units to fight on the Russian Front'. Sir William was immediately wary of the Soviet demand and sought guidance from London: 'Intelligence Bureau point out that this request may be a preliminary demand for the handing over of all Baltic SS. Since the persons concerned are neither war criminals nor renegades in the accepted sense, I should be grateful if you would instruct Political Division Lubbecke [sic] as to the reply they should return.'[41]

Despite the fact that these Balts had fought for the Germans and were in many cases members of the Waffen-SS, a criminal organisation, the Foreign Office declined to accede to Soviet demands. There is no sign either that the FO initiated any inquiry of its own into the war record of these men. Instead, the reply, formulated largely by Brimelow, stated:

> We cannot regard Baltic nationals as war criminals or traitors when the only charge against them is that they fought against the Soviet armed forces, but we have no wish to withhold them from justice if they are war criminals in the accepted sense. You should therefore insist in each case on the production of satisfactory *prima facie* evidence that the person concerned has been guilty of a war crime in the ordinary sense of the word, and in doubtful cases you should refer to this Office for instructions.[42]

For fear of setting a precedent for the mass repatriation of Balts who fought against the USSR, and thereby accepting the legitimacy of the Soviet annexation of the Baltic states, the men of the Baltic Waffen-SS were harboured in British camps. This was the logical corollary of FO policy and in its own terms reasonable, but they were then treated more leniently than their German equivalents and there does not appear to have been any thought given to their investigation or to the application of any judicial proceedings against them. Indeed, even in cases where the Soviets presented *prima facie* evidence that a man was a war criminal, the British military authorities prevaricated.

On 28 November 1945, Russian Army officers entered the Zedelghen camp with the aim of arresting SS-Standartenführer Kripens, the commanding officer of the 32nd Regiment of the 15th Waffen-Grenadier SS Division (1st Latvian). The British military command knew of their intentions and consented, since the Russians were acting within their rights. Kripens resisted arrest and attempted to commit suicide, but he succeeded only in injuring himself and had to be taken to a British military hospital to recover. In the meantime, the matter was taken up in London, where Charles Zarine had been alerted to what had happened. He wrote to Christopher Warner at the Foreign Office the very next day, complaining that the incident should not have been allowed to occur and pleading Kripens' case.[43]

In the course of internal investigations, the War Office confirmed that Kripens was believed by them to be a war criminal and that they had agreed to hand him over to the Soviets. All this had been done in ignorance of the fact that he was a Latvian, which had led to the embarrassment. However, according to Foreign Office official John Galsworthy, 'no harm has been done by the promise to surrender him, since his "war criminality" should presumably override his Latvian citizenship'. In other words, the only factor which concerned the FO was the possibility that the Kripens case might serve as a precedent for the Soviets to demand the wholesale repatriation of ex-Waffen-SS Balts. It was with relief that they noted that Kripens was a real war criminal, as against the *pro forma* sort which the Russians usually demanded, since this enabled them to say that no precedent had been set after all.[44]

In January 1946, the Foreign Office agreed to give Kripens to the Russians since it would have been too costly in political terms to keep him. But his handover was to be hedged with conditions. Above all, the FO demanded proof that he had commanded an SS unit in Russia. The War Office supplied information that Kripens was not a member of the SS, but belonged to the Latvian Legion and, according to unconfirmed War Office sources, 'all Latvian units were volunteers and members of Waffen-SS'. Amidst this confusion, Brimelow asked Colonel Isham at the War Office for clarification. Given the sensitivity of the repatriation issue, he told Isham that it was vital to have the facts and it 'ought to be possible for your experts to say whether or not all Latvian formations were "SS" and where they were in action on Soviet territory'. Brimelow, who was by now toughening up his stance towards the Russians, was unhappy that any concession had been made over Kripens. He was backed up powerfully by Gerald Fitzmaurice, who handled the legal work of the FO, including alleged war crimes cases.[45]

The War Office replied promptly. Kripens had indeed been sworn in as a member of the SS; the Latvian Legion was formed in April–May 1943, comprised of police battalions that operated under SS supervision. But the WO questioned the degree to which membership was 'voluntary' and noted that all non-German units received an SS designation. What did the FO mean by SS? To Brimelow it was now clear that Kripens was a member of the SS and in charge of an SS unit, but in his opinion it was not certain whether Kripens was 'a furious Nazi'. With this in mind, he wrote:

> We think that the Russians should now be asked to supply evidence to satisfy Headquarters, British Army of the Rhine, that they have a *prima facie* case against him for committing acts contrary to the laws and usages of war. In view of the difficulty of establishing whether persons from the occupied countries joined the SS voluntarily or under compulsion, if it is finally decided to hand him over to the Soviet authorities we should prefer not to give as one of our reasons for doing so the fact that he belonged to an SS formation.[46]

This was a crucial decision. Many of the Latvians in British

PoW and DP camps were former Waffen-SS troops; by taking such a stand on Kripens, the Foreign Office had created a double standard by which non-Germans in the Waffen-SS were treated far more liberally than their German counterparts. It was normal practice for the British Army to hold all German Waffen-SS men in special cages and to subject officers to detailed interrogation. The International Military Tribunal at Nuremberg declared the entire Waffen-SS to be a 'criminal organisation'. However, for fear of creating grounds on which the Soviets could demand the handing over of all Latvians and other nationalities, just by virtue of their service in the Waffen-SS, the British rendered them virtually immune to investigation.[47]

Unless very strong evidence could be provided to show that Latvian Waffen-SS men were war criminals, they would not be handed over to the Russians. This was not an unreasonable position to take, but at the same time neither the military authorities nor the FO itself made thorough efforts to check the origin of the Latvian Waffen-SS units or the question of whether service in them was voluntary. Their decisions were based on sketchy information, often emanating from pro-Latvian sources. Above all, it was influenced by a growing resentment of Russian behaviour and the conviction that each brush with the Soviets was a skirmish in a widening and deepening conflict.

For all these reasons, between November 1945 and May 1946, while Kripens was in hospital, the British authorities continued to block Russian efforts to have him transferred into their charge. Then, in February 1947, the Foreign Office was somewhat alarmed to discover via a letter intercept that Kripens was alive and well and at large in Germany. Brimelow contacted the Judge Advocates General Department, the Army's legal branch, which handled war crimes cases, to ask what had happened. He was eventually told in clipped Army prose:

1. Following attempted suicide at Zedelghen Camp 28 November 1945 Kripens was detained in hospital till May 1946 recover-

ing from his wounds and suffering acute mental disorder. During the earlier part this period Russian Military Mission frequently approached HQ LoC [Headquarters Lines of Communication] to claim transfer but on no occasion did they proffer any specific charge or evidence of a *prima facie* case although asked to do so in accord with paragraph 4 of your quoted letter [JAG instructions]. He was therefore not, repeat not, handed over being unavailable in hospital. Eventually Russians apparently lost interest.

2.   In July 1946 Kripens was discharged as a DP and is presumed to have rejoined his wife in the Latvian UNRRA camp at Talava, nr. Oldenberg.

3.   This disposal was in full accordance with current Western disbandment policy here: (A) Members of Latvian nominal SS formations not treated as SS and not within automatic arrest categories. (B) Racial Balts ex-Wehrmacht eligible for conversion to DP status. (C) Full Colonels discharged unless war criminals, security suspects or certain professional categories.

4.   On becoming eligible for discharge he requested discharge papers in a false name as he feared possible persecution by Russian agents who he alleged frequently visited UNRRA camps. This was refused, but in view of nature of case he was given option of remaining a PW.[48]

Somehow a full colonel of the Waffen-SS, who had served in a unit which drew recruits from police formations involved in the massacre of Jews and brutal anti-partisan operations, whose handover had been demanded on several occasions by the Russians, was allowed to melt into the German population. This extraordinary tale of laxity and indifference was repeated throughout the British Zone of Occupation.[49]

At the start of 1946, the Political Division of British Army of the Rhine asked for guidance from the Foreign Office on the employment of Balts by Hamburg University. One, a Lithuanian, was known to have been involved in the recruitment of SS units. The FO replied that it had no objection to his working in the university; nor did it suggest any further inquiry into this man's interesting wartime career.[50]

In another case, several Baltic women accused of being *Aufseherinen* – guards – at the women's section of Ravensbruck concentration camp simply disappeared. This curious affair came to light in April 1947 after Robin Hankey, now head of the Northern Department, was petitioned by Charles Zarine seeking the release of five imprisoned women who claimed that they had been 'ordered' to work in a 'Labour Education Camp' at Kiel. Inquiries by the Control Commission confirmed that the women had been overseers in a Gestapo camp at Nordmark, near Kiel, and were being detained pending investigation on suspicion of war crimes.

During April–May 1945, the 17,000 female inmates of Ravensbruck were evacuated to Schleswig-Holstein, and it is possible that this was the route by which the Latvian women arrived in the Kiel district. The women's camp at Ravensbruck had been the domain of Dorothea Binz, who had terrorised female prisoners. *Aufseherinen* under her command wore field-grey uniforms and black boots and were equipped with whips. The alleged guards were being held in a civilian internment centre while inquiries were made into their stories, and the Control Commission informed London that if they were acquitted they would be regraded and released into DP camps for Baltic people.

Hankey passed this information on to Zarine, but six months later, in November 1947, Zarine pressed Hankey again. On further investigation Hankey found that three of the women had been released, but concerning two others there was no information at all. Moreover, one woman who had been named in the earlier communications between the Control Commission and London appeared to have vanished altogether. Brimelow told the Judge Advocates General Division that he was 'somewhat puzzled' by this, but the matter was allowed to peter out.[51]

Another example from 1947 illustrates the lackadaisical procedure in dealing with Balts who had served in the Waffen-SS. During the autumn, it appears that the Control Commission acted to solve the problem of the remaining Baltic troops still held in custody, possibly in view of the opportunities for their recruitment into labour schemes. One of these men was Nikolajs Karlsons, a former lieutenant-colonel in the Latvian Waffen-

SS. Karlsons' case was first brought to the attention of the Foreign Office in July, but a decision was handed down only in September. Under the edict of the Nuremberg Tribunal all high-ranking German Waffen-SS officers were classed 'Category 1' offenders and were subject to investigation and possible trial by German courts. Other ranks of offender were classified 'Category 2'; they had to face only a British Review Board which was empowered either to release them or, if they were judged 'a danger to security', to order their internment.

One of the headquarters staff at the Control Commission explained to the Foreign Office that 'As an Obersturmbannführer Waffen-SS he [Karlsons] would be Category 1 (Criminal) case were it not for the fact that the 15th (Latvian) Division was formed compulsorily. He will, therefore, be brought before a British Review Board for final categorisation as Category 2 or released by the Reviewers and interrogation staff so that he may join his family.'[52] Leaving to one side questions about the pre-history of men serving in the rank and file of 15th Waffen-SS Latvian Division and the question of whether service in it was voluntary or compulsory, it is highly implausible that a lieutenant-colonel would have arrived at his post 'compulsorily'. Once again, a double standard was applied to a member of the Waffen-SS who in other circumstances would have been deemed highly suspicious.[53]

Undoubtedly there were serious diplomatic issues at stake regarding the fate of former combatants and refugees from the Baltic states, and in dealing with individual cases the Foreign Office was cleaving to a well-defined policy. But, regardless of its own predilections, the Foreign Office was being heavily lobbied by outside bodies with an interest in protecting the Balts.

Charles Zarine assiduously undermined the Soviet ideological definition of 'war crimes', a task which found considerable sympathy in the Foreign Office. However, in the course of lambasting UNRRA for being an instrument of USSR repatriation policy he even challenged the use of 'war crimes' by British officials as a rationale for eviction from DP camps and forcible return. 'You say that nobody but war criminals will be sent, and for this we remain deeply grateful. It would be even more reassuring if we knew what is the Anglo-Saxon conception of "war crimes" which is to count.' Zarine referred to lists of alleged Latvian war criminals being published in the Soviet press. These included Colonels Kripens, Rucelis, Sigailis, Janums, Griselis, Parups, Reisters, Winters and Arajs. Zarine argued that 'They were great national patriots, men of quite modest means; anti-Bolshevik, of course, but certainly not to be described as fascists. I should feel very relieved if His Majesty's Government would allow them to come to the safety of this country.'[54]

Of the men dubbed 'great national patriots' by Zarine, Arajs was a notorious mass murderer and even the War Office had conceded that Kripens was probably a war criminal. The other officers had served voluntarily in Waffen-SS units (colonels are not conscripted) and some of them had gone willingly to the front as early as the spring of 1942. They commanded men who had entered German service by choice, often having previously been in police units that had participated in atrocities against Jews, Communists, partisans and Russians.

Robin Hankey restated the official FO position in his reply to Zarine: 'I can do no more than assure you that no Latvians will be repatriated against their wishes unless it can be shown that they are war criminals. I think you can be assured that the British authorities will not in any case hand over a Latvian unless a *prima facie* case is made out against him.' Zarine was placated by this response. The FO had eliminated nationality as a criterion for repatriation in the case of Balts – as it would do later with Ukrainians. It then rejected membership of the Waffen-SS as sufficient grounds to warrant handing a man over to the USSR, even though it was declared a 'criminal organisation' at Nuremberg. Only the more carefully prepared, *prima facie* case of criminality would suffice. But it was asking a lot of any of the Allied governments to prepare exhaustive legal documentation in the chaos of the post-war years. If the will had existed, such niceties could have been dispensed with. However, on the basis of experience in the Kripens case and others of a similar character, there was little fear that the British would prove overly co-operative in the event of Russian demands.[55]

4

'Good Human Stock':
Population Policy, Immigration
and Foreign Labour Recruitment

When the Labour Party took office in Britain following the
General Election of July 1945, the country was exhausted and
its economy depleted. To finance the war Britain had amassed
£3,000 million in debts and liquidated £1,000 million of overseas
investments. Losses of shipping amounted to £700 million while
the value of property destroyed by enemy action was estimated
at more than twice that. The country's foreign trade had been so
ruthlessly sacrificed to military needs that exports had shrunk to
a third of their 1939 level. Production of coal, the most basic
raw material for any industrial recovery, stood at well below
that of peacetime. A massive effort would be needed to achieve
economic recovery, but progress was critically hampered as
long as five million men and women remained in the armed
forces and a further four million were tied down by the
munitions industries and logistical support. With the cessation
of Lend-Lease in August 1945, Britain faced economic ruin.[1]

On 17 August, Hugh Dalton, the new Chancellor of the
Exchequer, told the Cabinet that its first priority must be the
reconversion of industry to peacetime production, the boosting
of manpower available for the export industries by rapid
demobilisation and the control of expenditure. Reconversion,
demobilisation and cost-cutting were all closely linked. It was
vital to restore the export industries and start earning foreign
currency, but this could not be managed before steps were
taken to free the labour necessary to operate the factories and
dig the coal to power them. Dalton's warnings were listened to

respectfully, but Ernest Bevin, the Foreign Secretary, backed by the service chiefs, insisted that cuts in Army manpower were impossible if Britain was to maintain its overseas commitments.[2]

Throughout 1946 Dalton called for demobilisation to be accelerated in order to return workers to production in the raw-material extraction and export industries, without success. British forces were vital to the management of regional crises in Greece, Italy, Palestine, India and the Far East: as Bevin reminded the Cabinet, large-scale reductions in the size of the Army would weaken British influence abroad at a crucial juncture and make it even more difficult to keep order in these areas. But maintaining the Army was costing £1,000 million a year directly, when the annual national income for 1946 was £7,974 million. Indirectly, the loss of manpower to productive industries was crippling the export drive. It seemed that it would be possible to support the armed services and simultaneously increase production only if conscription was extended into peacetime so that new recruits could be drafted into the Army to replace those who were demobilised. This option was full of difficulties and was not likely to be popular.[3]

During the bitter winter of 1946–7, exceptionally heavy demand for coal, combined with low output from the mines, led to a dire shortfall in the amount of coal available for industry. Electricity had to be rationed, factories were closed and unemployment temporarily soared to over two million. With the loss of production, the balance of payments deficit widened. In January 1947 Herbert Morrison, who as Lord President of the Council was charged with economic co-ordination, presented to the Cabinet an economic survey for the coming year. The survey was prepared by a powerful ministerial committee that included Dalton, Stafford Cripps, President of the Board of Trade, and George Isaacs, the Minister of Labour. It identified a 'manpower gap' which was projected to rise to over 600,000; this shortage could be remedied only by cuts in the armed services, postponing the raising of the school-leaving age or the conscription of women into national service. The Cabinet rejected all of these proposals.[4]

In one respect, however, the *Economic Survey for 1947* did have an impact. It suggested that 'foreign labour can make a useful contribution to our needs', an idea which gained ground in various quarters. In a letter to *The Times* in February 1947 Lionel Robbins, the influential economist, suggested obtaining 100,000 'native and foreign' workers to boost production in the coal mines.[5] Thomas Balogh, later Lord Balogh, wrote to *The Times* the following day to pooh-pooh the idea of finding 100,000 men from anywhere. But it was taken very seriously by Clement Attlee, the Prime Minister.[6]

In February 1946, Attlee had set up a Cabinet Foreign Labour Committee charged with investigating the possibility of recruiting foreign workers for British heavy industry and agriculture.[7] The Foreign Labour Committee (FLC) eventually threw up a number of schemes. Dalton was placed in charge of a committee to resettle in Britain Poles from the Polish armed forces and direct them into essential, undermanned industries.[8] In May 1946, the FLC decided to enact a plan to recruit 1,000 Baltic women to work in sanatoria and hospitals in Britain. A few months later, the programme was expanded to find 5,000 women for domestic service in medical facilities and for training as nurses. Finally, under the pressure of the coal crisis, the Cabinet approved a scheme to bring 100,000 European Voluntary Workers (EVW) to Britain for employment in domestic labour, agriculture and the coal and textile industries.[9]

Although the trigger for this massive importation of labour was the fuel crisis of 1946–7, the idea of a 'manpower gap' and the solutions to it were rooted more deeply than the immediate post-war crisis. During the 1930s it was commonly believed that Britain's population was both shrinking in size and declining in quality. The birth rate was certainly falling and the population was ageing; it was more of an open question whether the physical and mental abilities of the people of Britain were also degenerating. This, however, was the conviction of a vocal body of eugenicists and progressive politicians, many of them in the ranks of the Labour Party. Eleanor Rathbone MP, John Maynard Keynes and William Beveridge were only the most prominent amongst those who, on the basis of studies produced by eugenicists like Karl Pearson and Cyril Burt, argued for greater state provision in the realms of child welfare, health care, income support and family planning, with the aim of making it possible for parents to have larger families and ensuring that those children who were born were healthy and well looked after.[10]

Anxiety about the size and state of the population had many facets. There was a fear that a shrinking population would cramp economic development by reducing demand; it threatened to diminish the manpower available for the military and so impair the defence of the Empire; finally, the absence of surplus population in the 'motherland' would reduce the supply of British migrants to the Dominions, weaken ties with the old country and leave the Anglo-Saxon populations outnumbered by non-white peoples. These concerns were carried into the war years and lay behind the establishment of the Royal Commission on Population in March 1944.

The Commission presented its report in June 1949, although advisory and expert committees had published their findings as early as 1945. On the basis of this demographic research, the report concluded that population growth in the British Isles was slackening and it went on to examine the causes of this phenomenon, its ramifications as well as possible remedies. No doubt with the welfare state in mind, it considered ways to increase the birth rate by improving the economic position of the family and providing facilities for child care so that the option of parenthood would not be inhibited by the necessity of having to give up work. The Commission also reviewed the consequences that might follow if the population were allowed to decrease. 'The question it should be observed is not merely one of military strength and security; that question becomes merged in more fundamental issues of the maintenance and extension of Western values, ideas and culture.'[11]

In addition to such portentous considerations, the report reiterated that the future of the Commonwealth was at risk. 'We think it is important for the maintenance of the solidarity of the Commonwealth that the British contribution to further Dominions immigration should be substantial.'[12] How was all

this to be achieved if family reproduction fell below 'replace-
ment level', as might happen once the post-war baby-boom
waned?

One chapter of the report looked closely at migration as a
factor in any population policy. It assumed that Britain had to
continue encouraging emigration to the Commonwealth, but
noted that if the country kept exporting population at the same
time as total numbers were declining it would be necessary to
find 170,000 young adults over the next ten years to fill the gaps,
particularly 'for industries that are comparatively unattractive'.
Immigration could fill this void, but it was replete with difficulties in view of who was acceptable: 'Immigration on a large
scale into a fully established society like ours could only be
welcomed without reserve if the immigrants were of good
human stock and were not prevented by their religion or race
from intermarrying with the local population and becoming
merged with it.'[13]

This openly racist formula limited the Commission's scope
to Northern, Central and Southern Europe, and Eire. The
historical models for desirable immigrants were Flemish and
French Protestant refugees, but 'There is little or no prospect
that we should be able to apply these conditions to large-scale
immigration in the future.' As a result, it saw a continuous mass
influx as an undesirable consequence of failure to encourage
population growth at home.[14] It was notable that the report did
not mention either Jewish immigrants or war-time workers from
the British Colonies in the West Indies, Africa and Asia as
desirable additions to the British population.

However, in view of the imperative of supplying the Commonwealth with emigrants of British origin, it saw some hope
in a dual policy of continued emigration balanced by 'selective
immigration'. 'This combined policy has much to commend it,
for it would ensure that the needs of the rest of the Commonwealth for manpower were met as far as possible from people
of British stock and that of Great Britain, with its much larger
population, would take on as much as possible of the problem
of assimilating people of other than British stock.'[15]

The Royal Commission was not a lone voice. Its report was

the summation of a long and intense public debate on population which had attracted a wide range of participants. Political and Economic Planning (PEP), the influential think-tank, had contributed an impressive report of its own, published in April 1948. The PEP report differed from the Government's view that foreign labour could have a decisive impact on the manpower gap, suggesting instead that there was simply a maldistribution of existing human resources. Nevertheless, like the Royal Commission it saw immigration as a way of counterbalancing the drain on population due to necessary emigration, offsetting the decline in fertility and helping to solve the political problems created by the persistence of DPs and refugees in camps in Europe.[16]

The authors of the PEP study were heavily influenced by eugenic theory. Although they saw merit in encouraging immigration, they insisted that it had to be scientifically managed. 'Careful selection of immigrants can eliminate mental defectives, people with mental disorders or inheritable defects, and social misfits.'[17] According to PEP, 'the obvious sources of recruitment to the British population in the immediate future have been created by the war'. These included the Polish Resettlement Corps, DPs and German prisoners of war. Some poor and overpopulated European countries such as Italy, Greece and Eire might also serve as reservoirs. Again, the Colonies were not mentioned with favour: 'The absorption of large numbers of non-white immigrants would be extremely difficult, though the comparatively small group of people of Indo-British origin in India and Pakistan, some of whom may prefer to come to Britain, would present no major problem.'[18]

All the same, if immigration had little to offer in terms of long-term population planning, in the short and medium term it promised valuable economic benefits. Selection was the vital issue: 'In selecting from the diverse sources reviewed above immigrants whose stay is likely to be permanent, the British authorities should apply high standards, particularly with regard to intelligence, health and war-time record, though humanitarian considerations must never be left out of account.'[19]

The most explicit and forceful application of the eugenicist line came from the Fabian Society in *Population and the People: A National Policy*, a cogent tract issued in October 1945. This pamphlet was produced by a Fabian Society committee under Dr W. A. Robson, and represented one in a long series of efforts to promote progressive social measures by pointing to the alleged decline in the state of health and mental ability of the British people. Indeed, the authors saw the direst consequences in the running down of Britain's human resources: 'a declining standard of life; a hardening of the political arteries; a reduction of military power; a diminished influence in world affairs; a less adventurous and less vital social life'.[20]

Alongside enlightened social policies, emigration and immigration policy had a role to play in blunting this threat. 'From the population point of view we need to encourage potential parents of healthy stock to settle in the British Isles, and to discourage those whom we already have from leaving.' The immigrants had to be carefully selected to protect the British political tradition and ensure that they were assimilable in other senses: for example, they had to show adaptability to the 'British way of life'. All-important demographic considerations dictated that 'parents of young children and potential parents, provided they are mentally and physically sound, are the most desirable'. The Fabian Society concluded that 'Men and women of European stock, between the ages of 20 and 30, are the immigrants best suited to assist population policy . . . The utmost care should, of course, be taken to admit only those physically and mentally sound, and free from criminal records, who will introduce a sound stock into the country. The eugenics of immigration cannot be overstressed.'[21]

The Labour Party leadership of 1945 had imbibed progressive eugenic theories, tinged with Social Darwinism, in their youth at the turn of the century and during their political apprenticeships. Beveridge and Keynes, two of the mightiest influences on their thinking, had long been associated with these ideas.[22] The notion of a manpower gap resonated with the concern about declining population that had haunted the inter-war decades and provided ammunition for their argu-

ments for social welfare. Throughout the great debate on population in the mid-1940s, the linkage between immigration strategy and population policy would be reinforced.[23] This was the
intellectual background to the policy of recruiting foreign
labour; it was shot through with racist assumptions about 'good
human stock' and assimilability. In the end, it would benefit
Balts, Ukrainians and ethnic Germans; Jews, Blacks and Asians
would be the victims.

Prisoners of war in Britain were being used for labour all
through the hostilities. By December 1945, 92,600 Germans
and 131,800 Italians were employed in heavy, unskilled work;
they were joined by tens of thousands more brought over from
Canada. However, this was a finite resource since the Geneva
Convention obliged the Government to repatriate them within
a certain time period. The bulk of Italian PoWs were sent home
during 1946, the Germans by mid-1948.[24] It appears that during
the summer of 1945, there had been a plan to bring Balts to
Britain as 'reparation labour', but this was not put into effect.
Balts who had fought for Germany would wait a bit longer for
their chance to enter Britain as workers.[25]

Women from the Baltic countries were the first to benefit
from labour recruitment. In September 1945, the Ministries of
Health and Labour drew up a plan to bring women DPs of
Baltic origin to serve as domestics in tuberculosis sanatoria and
hospitals. The scheme, dubbed 'Balt Cygnet', received Cabinet
approval in April 1946 and the selection process swung into
action. Between October 1946 and May 1947, 2,575 women
arrived under the auspices of this operation.[26]

Pressure to expand the recruitment scheme came from a
variety of sources. The Preparatory Commission of the IRO
was faced with the task of resettling around 650,000 refugees
and DPs who would not or could not return to their places of
origin. These people were a burden on the resources of the
occupation authorities and a political embarrassment since they
were constantly the target of Soviet propaganda. Charles Zarine
lobbied the Foreign Office for the admission of Balts as agricultural workers and was echoed by Alfred Bossom in the House
of Commons. The Society of Latvians in Great Britain, a

member of the Baltic Council, acted as a domestic pressure group advocating immigration of Latvian DPs to Britain as a way of solving their part of the DP problem. Officers in the Control Commission, like Major-General Brownjohn, pushed for them to be resettled in the Dominions.[27]

The impetus for the mass recruitment of male DPs came from the winter crisis of 1946–7. On 17 January 1947, in the course of the same meeting which debated the *Economic Survey for 1947*, the Cabinet discussed proposals to relax the regulations governing the entry and employment of aliens. At its meeting the following week, the Home Secretary and Minister of Labour were asked 'to arrange that the employment of individual foreigners in this country including ex-prisoners of war would be facilitated in proper cases'. At the Prime Minister's personal insistence, George Isaacs, the Minister of Labour, was asked 'to arrange for the recruitment of suitable labour from among displaced persons in Europe'. Isaacs rapidly drew up a scheme, code-named 'Westward Ho!', aimed at obtaining no less than 100,000 foreign workers to fill the manpower gap. The new policy was accepted by the Foreign Labour Committee and made public in ministerial replies to parliamentary questions later that month.[28]

What was never stated openly was the 'racial' hierarchy operated by the recruiting schemes. Officials in Germany and London consistently expressed preferences for the Balts. Major-General Brownjohn described them as the 'best and most useful class to take'; A. W. H. Wilkinson of the Foreign Office Refugee Department dubbed them the 'elite of the refugee problem'. Crawford, one of the assistant secretaries at the Control Office for Germany and Austria, praised the Balts to John Hynd, the Chancellor of the Duchy of Lancaster, as the most talented and orderly of the DPs and good material for resettlement. It was no surprise that they were the first target group to be enumerated by Hynd.[29]

British enthusiasm for the Balts was not shared by the French. In May 1947, a Franco-British agreement was concluded which allowed each country to recruit foreign labour in the other's zone; but the French specifically ruled out recruit-

ment among national groups which were considered fascistic
or which had engaged in collaboration. This policy was due
largely to the influence of the French Communist Party and
Communist-controlled trades unions, which objected to importing anti-Communist Poles and Balts: they preferred *Volksdeutsche*, ethnic Germans, to either group. The British were only too
happy to leave the *Volksdeutsche* to the French and to ignore the
Poles completely, since they considered that the Balts were 'a
much better type than the Poles, more intelligent, honest and
reliable'.[30]

Indeed, the fact that the Balts were considered untouchable
by the French was regarded as a positive advantage by the
cynical Evelyn Boothby, who was Assistant Head of the Foreign
Office Refugee Department. After he had seen a copy of
the French proposals, he told his colleague Mary Appleby,
who worked at the Control Office in London, 'This is quite
acceptable from the Foreign Office point of view, especially
since the French would appear to favour the recruitment of
Volksdeutsche whereas we are more anxious to recruit from
among the more politically embarrassing elements. There
would appear to be little risk of our competing with each other,
while the choice of candidates would be much wider for both
parties.'

Boothby regretted that the FLC declined to prioritise
officially national groups on political grounds, although he
understood why it would be awkward to do so. Notwithstanding
this, he believed that 'in practice, the recruitment missions are
bearing in mind such factors as the undesirability of recruiting
Poles and the desirability of recruiting Balts'. Finally he added,
'You may be interested to know that for political reasons we
consider that whereas possible priority should be given to Balts,
Ukrainians, Yugoslavs and Soviet Citizens (including White
Russians), we have no objection to the recruitment of
Volksdeutsche, provided that they are not given priority over
the above categories of non-German displaced persons.' There
was no mention of Jews on his list.[31]

Poles, Ukrainians, *Volksdeutsche* and Jews were all initially
excluded from the pool of potential volunteers. Poles were

barred from EVW schemes because of the antgonism already created by the Polish Resettlement Corps. Government ministers had spent hours negotiating with British trades unionists to persuade them to accept Polish workers and had been forced to agree to quite stringent conditions governing their employment.[32] Ukrainians were probably excepted because of their uncertain status and fear of Russian reactions; *Volksdeutsche* were considered to be little better than enemy aliens and a potential provocation to public opinion in Britain.[33]

This selectivity was carefully concealed. In its outline of the 'Westward Ho!' operation, the British element of the Allied Commission for Austria informed local officials:

> there will be no discrimination on grounds of nationality, as this is primarily an industrial scheme, but for the time being the Ministry of Labour wants to concentrate on certain nationalities and this priority must be observed in interviewing and calling forward arrangements. This intention to concentrate on certain nationalities will not be given publicity and should not be disclosed to DPs or persons not directly concerned.[34]

Poles threw up especially delicate questions. The Control Commission preferred that as many as possible of the Polish DPs left in Germany should return to Poland; Whitehall concurred since it was felt that Britain had taken in enough Poles already. But they did not want to offend those Poles in the armed forces or the Polish Resettlement Corps by letting this be known. So although public statements had been made to the effect that there would be no discrimination, Foreign Office officials agreed that this did not rule out other tests of suitability: the criteria for exclusion would simply be disguised.[35]

The Control Office in London told the Berlin office, 'We do not consider Poles can be explicitly excluded from this scheme without causing political repercussions. At the same time it is important to avoid anything which might seriously impair the good repatriation prospects now open.' J. P. Wakefield, an FO civil servant, minuted that such a proposal '*is*, however, discriminatory'. Robin Hankey resolved the dilemma by commanding: 'Let discrimination against Poles be hidden as far as possible, please.' This instruction was passed on to the Control Office by Wilkinson, who explained that in order to avoid an 'outcry', 'we should like discrimination against Poles to be kept, as far as possible, hidden'.[36]

Before very long, the reserves of acceptable nationalities were all but exhausted. Since the EVW schemes were limited to persons without dependants, the Ministry of Labour had to decide whether to start accepting Balts with families or whether to broaden the range of national groups.[37] There was intense pressure to do the latter, not least because of competition from the French, who had a free run of the *Volksdeutsche*. 'Balt Cygnet' was extended to embrace Ukrainians on 24 Februry 1947 and at the same time the British officials in Vienna pleaded for the inclusion of ethnic Germans.[38]

The scruples of the Home Office, which was uneasy about ex-enemy nationals coming to Britain, were squared by the agreement of the Foreign Office that they would not be allowed to seek naturalisation in this country. By the end of March 1947, labour recruiters were empowered to select amongst *Volksdeutsche* too.[39] These ethnic Germans had functioned as a fifth column in countries throughout Eastern Europe which became victims of Nazi aggression. After the German conquest, they were promoted to administrative and police positions and were often the most brutal rulers on behalf of the Third Reich. Himmler recruited several Waffen-SS divisions from amongst the *Volksdeutsche* in Hungary, Romania, Yugoslavia and the Baltic before he turned to non-Germans. When the German tide ebbed, these agents of Nazism abandoned their homes and fled into the Reich. The Allies had no illusions about their standing: UNRRA and the IRO refused to give them DP status because they had collaborated with the enemy and left their homes voluntarily. Sir George Rendel commented that they had 'served before the war as outposts for Nazi infiltration'.[40]

Only Jews remained beyond the Pale. Despite the presence of thousands of Holocaust survivors in the British Zone, clamouring to be taken out of Germany, Jews were consistently excluded from all the labour recruitment schemes. Many of the Jewish DPs wanted to go to Palestine or the USA, but some might have opted for the United Kingdom if they had been given the chance. In fact, the British Government, which was simultaneously keeping Jews out of Palestine, did all it could to bar them from British territory or areas under British control. The Home Secretary, J. Chuter Ede, explicitly laid out the policy of excluding Jews in a memorandum presented to the Cabinet in November 1945. He cited the shortages of housing, clothing and jobs as the chief reason for not allowing any large-scale immigration, least of all elderly or sick people who would be a 'burden on the community'. In addition, the Cabinet minutes record that 'the admission of a further batch of refugees, many of whom would be Jews, might provoke strong reactions from certain sections of public opinion. There was a real risk of a wave of anti-semitic feeling in this country.'[41]

This policy was ruthlessly enforced. In October 1945, a small number of Baltic refugees reached Britian illegally – mainly as stowaways or sailors jumping ship. The Home Office wanted to deport them to the British Zone of Germany where they could be placed in DP camps, but the Foreign Office reacted violently to this idea. Brimelow told A. R. Judge, of the Aliens Department of the Home Office, that 'if we were to admit these Balts into Germany, our case for maintaining our refusal to admit the Polish Jews who are now streaming into Berlin would be seriously prejudiced'.[42] It was preferable for these 'illegal landers' to be allowed to stay in Britain rather than to create a precedent for Jews to enter the British Zone which might serve as a jumping-off point for migration to Palestine or Britain.

The instructions to the British Control Commission in Germany and Austria were quite explicit about the exclusion of Jews. After requesting permission to recruit *Volksdeutsche*, the Vienna office was told that 'Ex-enemy nationals, Jews and Volksdeutsche are to be excluded from the field of recruitment but the possibility of considering some Volksdeutsche at a later date will be further examined.' Vienna continued to press the case of the ethnic Germans and used the example of the French as support for their argument: 'We think that if the French and ourselves are to compete in recruitment that we should work on the same lines and we note from the Draft Zonal Instruction issued in Germany that there will be no distinction on grounds of nationality. We therefore ask authority to recruit displaced persons (excluding Jews of any nationality) on the understanding that we will give priority in the transfer to the most acceptable classes.'[43]

At the end of April 1947, Major-General Winterton, who was second in command in the British Zone of Austria, sent to Lord Pakenham, who replaced Hynd as Chancellor of the Duchy of Lancaster with responsbility for COGA, an account of DP recruitment and aims in Austria:

> I attach a list of the national groups of DPs in Austria (33,000 Jews) in the order of priority which we would wish to operate, if we were obliged to operate a priority system at all. It seems to us, however, much more simple and more effective to recruit from the whole body of DPs without regard to nationality, except that we should exclude Jews and Polish men because of the opposition from public opinion at home, and persons whom we acknowledge to be Soviet citizens, because of the certainty of trouble with the Soviets if we recruit such people.[44]

Why were Jews subjected to this discrimination? The Director of Social Administration in the British occupation authority in Austria, W. R. Iley, informed a colleague at the Foreign Office that he saw major obstacles to the acceptability of certain DPs to British public opinion, especially to workers and trades unionists. 'For example, the situation in Palestine and anti-semitics [sic], clearly prevent the recruitment of Jews.'[45] It was certainly true that the conflict between Jews and the British in Palestine was responsible for adding intensity to the anti-Jewish feeling in Britain which had persisted all through the war and been only partially dampened by the revelations from the death camps. This animosity was to reach a peak in the summer of 1947 when the murder of two British sergeants in Palestine provoked anti-Jewish riots and attacks on Jewish-owned property around the country.[46]

Yet there was still considerable sympathy for Jews who were the victims of Nazi persecution. The August 1947 riots provoked a considerable backlash in the British press, which deplored the outbreak of anti-Jewish violence in this country so soon after the defeat of Nazism. Yet the Government appears to have capitulated entirely to a vociferous racist element, and allowed the situation in Palestine to overshadow all other considerations. As a consequence, only a few hundred Holocaust survivors were admitted to Britain after the war. Pressure on the Government to do something to aid the DPs had some success with the establishment of a Distressed Relatives Scheme under which British citizens could bring over to the UK members of their family who had suffered at the hands of the Nazis. Between 1945 and 1950, 5,520 people entered Britain by this means, but only a portion of these were Jews – around 2,000, including 743 Jewish children who had lived through the experience of the camps and the ghettos.[47]

Had the political will existed to facilitate Jewish immigration to Britain, it might have been possible to provide a haven for the Jews in the DP camps. It was, after all, possible to settle over 114,000 Poles and 91,000 European Voluntary Workers in Britain despite some native antagonism. However, the Jews were never mentioned positively in the discussion of population or immigration policy, they were not considered to be easily 'assimilable' nor were they regarded as an asset to the country. On the contrary, Jews were a 'problem'. As a result they were barred from the EVW schemes and only a couple of thousand were permitted to settle in Britain after the war at a time when 200,000 East Europeans were being absorbed, admittedly not without difficulties, into British society.

The other losers were West Indians and Asians from the British Empire. Black and Asian soldiers had fought in the British armed forces during the war and vital workers for the munitions industry had been brought over from the Caribbean under the Overseas Voluntary Service scheme. But at the end of the conflict they were viewed as an unwanted element in the population: large numbers of wartime workers and servicemen were quickly repatriated.[48] Yet the lure of the 'mother country' and the bridgehead established by earlier immigrants drew more Afro-Caribbeans to Britain. The arrival of 492 Jamaicans in June 1948 on board the SS *Empire Windrush* became a *cause célèbre* – or *cause de scandale* – attracting questions in Parliament and articles in the press out of all proportion to the numbers involved. The Labour Government reacted to this with alarm; inter-departmental meetings were held and the issue of non-white immigration was discussed in the full Cabinet. Notwithstanding the manpower gap and the relative ease with which the population accepted 200,000 foreign workers of European origin, Black and Asian immigration – even on a comparatively small scale – was treated as a crisis.[49]

Rather than accept Jews or Blacks and Asians to solve the labour shortage, the British Government expressed a clear preference for Central and East Europeans – even if they had been collaborators with the Nazis. Of course, there were pressing arguments for allowing DPs into Britain and reasons why Jews and non-white immigrants might be considered a 'problem'. But there was a powerful case to be made for Jews, Blacks and Asians, and it was acknowledged at the time that the absorption of Poles, Ukrainians and Balts had not been trouble-free. Substantial efforts were made to win over trades unionists and public opinion to the idea of settling these people in Britain; awkward questions concerning their wartime record were carefully circumvented or swept under the carpet. In considering why East Europeans were deemed worth this exertion, but Jews, Blacks and Asians were not, it is all but impossible to avoid the conclusion that racism was at work. At the time, it would have been dressed in the rhetoric of eugenics and even regarded as a progressive position; today it just looks ugly.

The Waffen-SS Comes to Britain I: The Balts

Once the decision had been made to recruit foreign labour from amongst the DPs, the question of who these people were and where they came from should have been critical. Yet the urgency propelling the recruitment schemes and the speed with which they were implemented was allowed to prevent any but the most primitive screening. Ignorance about the war history of former Baltic Waffen-SS men might have excused such careless procedures earlier on, but there is enough evidence that the truth was now known to suggest that this was being replaced by indifference. In Germany, where the recruiting took place and in England, where the volunteer workers arrived, it was apparent that men who had served in the Waffen-SS were amongst these selected. This information might have provoked qualms of conscience, or a tightening up of screening methods; but nothing of the sort happened. On the contrary, caution seems to have been thrown aside and the consequences concealed from public view.

The fact that Britain was importing members of the Waffen-SS was not news to those like Kanty Cooper or Sue Ryder who were involved in the selection process in Germany. Kanty Cooper was a former pupil of the sculptor Henry Moore. She had given up art in 1937 to join a relief unit in Republican Spain and from then on had worked with refugees and war orphans in almost every trouble spot in Western Europe, including a long stint with UNRRA in France and the British Zone of Germany. In 1947 she was based in Lemgo, where she was involved in the recruitment of Baltic women for work in hospitals in Britain.

The Balts made a good impression on Cooper, as they did on so many other British observers. 'They were enemies of our ally Russia', she wrote in her memoirs,

> and collaborators of our enemy Germany. Some of their men had joined the German army. But because they were cultivated, clean and reliable people they were usually the first asked for on emigration schemes. They belonged chiefly to the middle or upper-middle classes and many of them spoke excellent English. Most of the women would look more at home in the drawing room than in the kitchen, yet they were all prepared to act as scullery or ward maids for the first three months of their stay in England.

When she accompanied the first batch of seventy-five women going to Britain under 'Balt Cygnet', one wore an ermine coat and fur-lined boots.[1]

After a period at Lemgo, Kanty moved on to Düsseldorf, where she helped to set up one of the EVW processing centres. Here she assisted the selection teams and watched as every day hundreds of volunteers went through the interview, medical check, blood test and X-ray. It was humdrum work, but not without exciting moments. 'Our interest', she recalled, 'was kept alive by the variety of the problems.' For instance,

> the medicals necessary for the schemes revealed Balts who had been in the SS, the tell-tale blood-group tattooed under their arms. It was the work of the eligibility officer to decide if a displaced person came under IRO mandate and to discover all his particulars, but occasionally I received last-minue con- fessions from DPs about to emigrate that they had registered under false names. Fear that reprisals would be taken against their families, left behind in their Communist homelands, led them to take this step.[2]

Such deception was repeated on a large scale, made possible by a staggering absence of concern amongst British officials at the time. Kanty Cooper herself was more concerned by the possible 'loss of identity' and psychological effect of these lies on the deceiver than on those who were being misled. She appeared untroubled by indications that thousands of former Waffen-SS soldiers were being shipped to Britain – where they would eventually be allowed to set up new homes – without any detailed knowledge of what they had done during the bitter fighting on the eastern front and before.[3]

Sue Ryder, now Baroness Ryder of Warsaw, was another relief worker in Germany at this time. In a debate on the War Crimes Bill in the House of Lords in 1990, she recalled, 'During my relief work in Europe in 1945–46, I witnessed that tattoo marks under the armpits of several non-Germans who had recently been recruited by the SS were erased prior to them being examined for emigration to Britain under the Westward Ho! Work Scheme. Hardly any screening occurred.'[4]

How is it possible to account for this astonishing nonchalance? The labour recruitment schemes were rushed into operation with little thought for the mechanics of security screening. There was confusion as to who was responsible for these checks and the available resources were always inadequate. Reliance was placed on UNRRA and IRO eligibility screenings which were flawed and on the reports of camp commandants who were often overly sympathetic towards their charges. Above all, there was simply no political will to ensure thorough screenings: the dire need for manpower and the fear that France would attract the best DPs meant that the politicians placed enormous pressure on civil servants to hasten the process. Security was blatantly sacrificed for economic and, ultimately, political requirements.

The Cabinet invested George Isaacs with the responsibility for drawing up a plan to bring over foreign workers at its meeting on 30 January 1947. Within a few days, he presented an outline to the Foreign Labour Committee and orders were issued to the relevant departments to begin work. As if to underline the urgency of the project, the Foreign Office noted anxiously that the French had already initiated a similar programme. A. W. H. Wilkinson in the Refugee Department minuted on the Cabinet decision that 'we may find that other countries will have skimmed the cream of the displaced persons, especially the Balts who are undoubtedly the elite of the refugee problem'. However, at the very same moment, Foreign Office officials raised the awkward question of who was going to screen these 100,000 people who were about to come to Britain.[5]

Soon after the Cabinet decision to investigate large-scale recruitment, the Ministry of Labour established a Displaced Persons Operation Committee to determine which areas of industry most required an injection of manpower, to organise the process of recruitment in Germany, to make the transport arrangements and to prepare the reception facilities in Britain for the DPs once they arrived. The Ministry of Labour also entered into discussions with the CCG to set up the machinery for recruitment.[6]

The Control Office for Germany supplied the details of how many Baltic, Polish, Ukrainian and Yugoslav refugees and DPs there were in the British Zones of Germany and Austria.[7] By the second week of February, the Ministry of Labour had prepared a detailed plan which was submitted to the Foreign Labour Committee for approval. A few days later in Parliament Attlee and Isaacs signalled that foreign labour recruitment was now under way.[8] The Control Office in Germany were informed that recruitment was about to begin and told that they should prepare for the arrival of the Ministry of Labour teams. The first six-man group arrived on 3 March 1947, followed by a second a week later; eventually twenty-five Ministry of Labour officials would be employed in Germany, with secretarial back-up provided by the Control Office, as well as a smaller unit operating in Austria.[9]

The Ministry of Labour set up its central office in Lemgo, with regional branches in Kiel, Hanover and Düsseldorf. In each of these cities a collecting centre was established where volunteers for the labour scheme could be processed before they were passed on to the Transit Camp at Seedorf (later moved to Münster). Successful applicants were then shipped out from Cuxhaven to Hull or Harwich and sent on to the nine Holding Hostels scattered around the British Isles.

The first officials to arrive in Germany prepared the publicity for 'Westward Ho!' Leaflets were distributed around DP camps inviting those interested to attend a meeting. The DPs were then addressed by a representative of the Ministry of Labour and provided with forms to fill out and hand to the camp director if they wanted to be considered for recruitment. After a few days, a Ministry of Labour official would return to the camp and interview each person who had submitted a form; on the basis of this encounter he would decide whether the prospective candidate was suitable and also what industry he would best fit. Candidates then received a medical examination by the camp doctor. The results of the interview and the medical were passed on to the regional centre for assessment; those who were regarded as suitable were then summoned to one of the collecting centres and dispatched to the Transit Camp. Here they received another health check; it was also at this point that Home Office officials made the only serious attempt to assess their political and military record.[10]

From the first, there were instructions from the highest level to minimise any delay in getting workers to Britain. Concern about the pre-history of the DPs was carelessly swept aside. At the meeting of the FLC on 14 February 1947, ministers decided that 'no emphasis should be placed on the political background of particular national groups who were suitable for work in this country'. John Hynd, Chancellor of the Duchy of Lancaster and the Minister responsible for the Control Office, added a corrigendum to the minutes specifically calling on the FO not to place obstacles in the way of recruitment amongst groups 'such as White Russians to whose entry into this country objections might be made on political grounds'.[11]

The urgency of getting labour to British industries was such that pressure was applied to abandon all but the most cursory security checks – partly for fear of losing potential recruits to the French. At the second meeting of the FLC in February 1947, George Isaacs pointedly asked for the Control Commission in Germany to assist 'in speeding up those arrangements, particularly those for "vetting" of recruits'. Hynd, the responsible Minister, was 'invited' to consult with the Ministry of Labour to find ways of accelerating the documentation necessary for processing candidates.[12]

This impatience was faithfully transmitted down the line: J. W. L. Ivimy, one of the assistant secretaries at the Control Office in London, telegraphed the British occupation authorities in Vienna to inquire what was the minimum of screening that could be considered viable.

> Home Office are prepared to discuss the degree of security screening required for entry into the UK. We would like specific proposals from you as to relaxation of existing checks which you consider necessary to facilitate movement on scale envisaged. Chancellor [of the Duchy of Lancaster, John Hynd] is particularly anxious to ensure that documentation does not become a bottleneck.[13]

The record of a discussion by British officers in Vienna clearly shows that they understood how unrealistic it was to expect any serious intelligence work or screening to be done. Addressing a meeting of officials in the splendour of the Schoenbrunn Palace, Major G. H. Redfern, the intelligence officer responsible for security, stated that 'Intelligence Organisations could not carry out any intelligence screening of DPs with their present resources.' Colonel Logan Grey of the PoW Division said that camp commandants could make a contribution to the screening process, but the Government would 'have to decide what political screening was necessary'. The meeting concluded that 'Social Administration Division after consulting with Intelligence Organisation should agree what intelligence screening was possible in the time available and put up concrete proposals.'[14]

When they submitted their plans to put 'Westward Ho!' into operation, officers at the sharp end of the recruitment process made sure that Whitehall could not be in any doubt as to the vulnerabilities of the system. The following message from the Vienna office is revealing – particularly when it is borne in mind that the British authorities in Austria had to cope with only a tiny fraction of the numbers awaiting processing in the British Zone of Germany:

It is considered that detailed security screening is impossible in view of the shortage of staff and would be of little value owing to the lack of records and knowledge of former background. It is in any event considered undesirable because of inevitable delays. Agree that a check should be made against Central Security Records and that views of Camp Commandants should be sought on those DPs who are living or who have lived in the camps. In addition arrangements can be made for the Austrian Police to certify that particular DPs were not known criminals or for other reasons undesirable immigrants to UK for a check against MG [Military Government] Records. These checks need not cause delay as they could be undertaken between the time of acceptance and travel without holding up the travel arrangements . . . If it were agreed by Home Office that screening on these lines would be sufficient we consider that documentation need only be on a normal DP movement basis i.e. by nominal rolls, and need cause little or no delay.[15]

The use of nominal rolls, that is the list of DPs, entailed simple cross-referencing from one list to another, with no interview or any other sort of screening. Those on the list would be given leave to land collectively and their travel documents would be validated automatically, without individual visas being needed or any detailed face-to-face examination.

Similar pressure was felt by the Control Commission in Germany, and there it generated the same mixture of confusion and helplessness. British Army personnel, Control Commission staff, representatives of the Ministry of Labour and international relief agencies met in Lübeck on 17 March 1947 to draw up a plan for the recruitment, selection and transport of EVWs from Germany to Britain under 'Westward Ho!'. The minutes of the conference, transmitted to the FO via the Control Office in Berlin, stated, 'We feel onus for any security screening required should be on Home Office and not us. Though we would give all possible help. This follows normal procedures for such schemes. If Home Office requires security screening strongly recommend they send out personnel to do it here since it would have bad psychological effect on DPs if numbers of them were returned to camps here on rejection on arrival in UK.' To add to the confusion, British officers in Germany were 'vague as to whether this is a resettlement scheme or merely a foreign workers scheme'.[16]

There was, of course, a vast distance between the concept of importing temporary labour and facilitating the immigration of permanent settlers. Recruiters and screeners may have been less than sedulous in their scrutiny of volunteers because they anticipated that the people in question would return to Germany. In fact, over 90,000 EVWs were to settle in Britain and become British citizens. Despite its superior knowledge of the labour schemes, the Foreign Office was prepared to accept laxity as the price of speed. Reviewing the plans for processing recruits, A. W. H. Wilkinson remarked of the security and medical checks: 'if these are too stringent, there may well be an awkward delay, especially in Austria'.[17]

A few days later, the authorities at Lübeck elaborated on the security controls which they felt able to provide by themselves:

Public Safety Branch will screen for criminals and 'wanted' DPs. Names and descriptions of 'wanted' persons will be sent by Central Records Office to all DPAC [DP camp] Commanders who will check prior to initial interview of DPs by Ministry of Labour. An extensive search of Mil. Gov. [Military Government] Records will also be carried out. It is considered that this is sufficient safeguard against the inclusion of criminals amongst those recruited for this scheme.[18]

These methods were subsequently confirmed and issued as instructions to officers in the British Zone; the same was true for Austria. But they were unreliable and ineffectual.

In both zones, great weight was placed on the testimony of camp commandants. But how trustworthy were they? Sir William Strang observed in his memoirs that 'The military government staff sympathised with the Germans against the displaced persons, whom they regarded as a serious danger to good government . . . Our combatant soldiers, who were in actual charge of the camps, seemed to sympathise more with the displaced persons.'[19] Another official, J. W. L. Ivimy, told the FO that camp commanders were frequently lenient towards their charges, whom they had got to know and often to like.

He noted the 'unsatisfactory results of such previous screening as had been done'.[20]

It was quite useless to check the names of East Europeans against Austrian and German police records except to weed out those who had committed criminal offences since their arrival in those countries. Nor would the Military Government Courts have provided much information about suspected war criminals: they would have data only on known cases. Military intelligence shifted the burden of screening on to Home Office officials, but all that they had at their disposal was the 'black list' which contained details of delinquents and common criminals. Even the chief list of wanted war criminals compiled by the United Nations – CROWCASS: Central Registry of War Criminals and Security Suspects – was ineffective when it came to non-Axis personnel. Few East Europeans were on the list, little was understood about their activities and the Soviet Union was erratic in making such material available.

The Home Office officials who conducted this security check were under enormous pressure: in the first two months of 'Westward Ho!', 11,500 EVWs arrived in Britain – an average of more than 200 per day. This would have meant that the interviewing officers could barely have spent more than a few minutes with each recruit. Even if they had been superbly equipped for the job, screening such large numbers would have been a virtually impossible mission to perform with any effectiveness. As it was, the security aspect of the operation was lamentably conducted. The main concern of the Home Office seems to have been to make sure it could deport back to Germany any unsatisfactory workers or troublemakers: once this was conceded by the FO, the conditions of entry were made extremely slack. Over the course of a few days in March 1947, civil servants from the Home Office and Ministry of Labour hammered out the entry requirements and conditions of landing for EVWs coming to Britain under 'Westward Ho!'.

The Home Office eventually accepted the principle of issuing identity cards on the basis of nominal rolls, even though this rested on the UNRRA screening which had originally been responsible for extending DP status to the inmates of the camps.

No visas would be required and the only checks would be made against the 'black list' of known criminals who should be denied entry; this could all be undertaken close to the point of embarkation and completed 'speedily'. Home Office officials wanted to retain the use of photographs on the ID cards, and the Ministry of Labour reluctantly granted this as long as it could be left until the volunteers reached Britain. As a result they dispensed with one of the most elementary means of ensuring that the name on a list and the person claiming to bear that name actually belonged to each other.[21]

Could greater efforts have been made and were the British authorities aware of the dangers they were running? The surviving (available) documents suggest that they knew they could have been more assiduous and that they were urged to be more careful. For example, the slapdash attitude towards screening volunteer labour was not shared by the French. In the course of negotiating the Anglo-French agreement on recruitment, the Control Office in Lübeck reported to London that 'The French lay great stress on security screening by the French Service de Sécurité before accepting any DPs.'[22] There is no sign that the equivalent British security services played any part in keeping people out – although they may have played a shadowy role in getting them in.

Soviet diplomats at the United Nations vociferously objected to the recruitment of DPs for labour in Britain and the way in which it was conducted. Through the medium of UNRRA, they accused the British of taking DPs who should have been repatriated or who were suspected as war criminals. This criticism obliged the British delegate to UNRRA, Lord Inverchapel, to ask the Foreign Office for details of 'Westward Ho!'. 'May I also have full information on measures which have presumably been taken to exclude war criminals from the recruitment scheme, because this point was also raised by the Russian representative.'

The Foreign Office replied:

No war criminals were knowingly registered as displaced persons. Persons admitted to displaced persons camps were originally screened by the CCG or UNRRA as far as this was possible and they have since been rescreened by CCG. The selection from among those who volunteered for the Westward Ho! operation is made by Ministry of Labour officers. There is a further security check by the Home Office representatives who interview and grant visas to those who are accepted for entry into the UK. It is not pretended that these screening operations are 100% thorough, but they are as complete as possible in the circumstances. We are looking for useful workers and not criminals of any category.[23]

This reply might have provided Lord Inverchapel with a useful figleaf, but it would hardly have stood up to detailed scrutiny. The criteria for eligibility to DP status differed wildly between UNRRA camps and British Military Government holding centres. In thousands of cases, former combatants were turned into DPs by the British even though they had fought for the Germans in Waffen-SS units and would never have attained such a privileged position through the normal channels. Once they were turned into DPs they formed part of the pool of labour from which EVWs were recruited. In order to avoid slowing down the flow of manpower, the Ministry of Labour did all it could to minimise security screenings; military intelligence waived responsibility for the process and left it to the Home Office, which was hardly equipped to deal with people from half a dozen nationalities who may have committed war crimes thousands of miles away. The pool from which the DPs came was heavily polluted; the filtration process was wholly inadequate; the toxin ended up in Britain.

Doctors at the EVW hostels who examined Latvian men coming off the boats from Cuxhaven were the first to note the characteristic Waffen-SS tattoos under their left arms. A commotion broke out at the hostel in Hans Crescent in London, in October, when the resident medical officer, who happened to be a Pole, discovered the tell-tale marking and started to question the men. Poles were especially sensitive to the havoc caused by the Waffen-SS, which had played a brutal part in the suppression of the Warsaw Uprising in 1944; but when the doctor displayed an interest in the tattoo, the Latvians became alarmed and protested that they had left political screenings and interrogations behind them. To make matters worse, the *Daily Graphic* had got hold of the story and printed an alarmist version of what had happened.

Charles Zarine immediately took the matter to Thomas Brimelow at the Foreign Office – whom he now addressed with familiarity as 'My Dear Mr Brimelow'. He wrote: 'As you know, a considerable proportion of the younger men now coming as EVWs served in the German armed forces under the compulsory mobilisation carried out by the Germans.' The Latvian recruits were formed into a 'Latvian Legion' which 'fought with valour on the eastern front against the Bolshevists'. 'They were not fighting for Germany and the nazi cause, but for the freedom of the Latvian people. At that time the primary danger to be averted was a repeated Russian invasion. The ultimate aim of all Latvian soldiers was to turn against the Germans at a later stage when the Russian danger had been avoided.'

This was a highly coloured and selective account of the career of the Latvian Legion and failed to point out that it had grown from Latvian police battalions that had participated in the massacre of Jews. The core of the Latvian Waffen-SS was formed without compulsory mobilisation; it would anyway have been possible for young Latvians to opt for labour service or other units such as the *Flakhilfer*: Latvians were never compelled to serve in the Waffen-SS. It is also difficult to reconcile Zarine's version of their intention to fight the Germans with the role of the Latvian Waffen-SS in the last-ditch defence of Pomerania, not to mention the fanatical stand of one battalion of the 15th Waffen-SS Latvian Division in the defence of Berlin.

Zarine went on to explain away the blood-group tattoo. 'In the latter stages of the war,' he wrote,

the German military commanders had found it a useful practice to examine the blood of the men and to tattoo the mark of the respective blood group somewhere on the body. Then in the case of casualties the blood transfusion could be administered speedily. The Germans intended to carry this out through all their armed forces, but started with their own SS units and the next on the list were the Baltic soldiers. The rest of the army they had not yet managed to treat in this way, and as apart from the Baltic soldiers only the SS had these marks, unscrupulous propagandists have often used this to prove that the Latvian men have been members of the SS and therefore politically undesirable and unreliable, whereas in fact it was a purely medical expedient.[24]

This was utter nonsense. The blood-group tattoo had been used by the Waffen-SS since early in the war and was never extended to the Wehrmacht. The notion that the Latvians had almost accidentally arrived in a situation that marked them out as Waffen-SS was pure deception.

The response of Foreign Office officials revealed either extreme gullibility or willing complicity. A. W. H. Wilkinson wrote:

While it seems quite in order for the examining doctor to ask questions about these tattooings, such questions should, I feel, be of a medical and not a political nature, and we might draw the attention of the Ministry of Labour to this point. As all EVWs are screened before coming here, I think that we can deal effectively with the allegations which may impute that these Balts were SS men – an accusation which lacks much of its former importance now that German PoWs can be civilianised.[25]

Far from showing any alarm at the arrival of the Waffen-SS in Britain, Evelyn Boothby, of the FO Refugee Department, chastised the Polish doctor, whom he considered 'may well have acted irresponsibly'. Thomas Brimelow was equally scathing. He had already contacted the Ministry of Labour:

and been given an assurance that in future the MO [Medical Officer] will be asked to confine his attentions to the sick and NOT to meddle with blood groups. At the same time I told the Min. of Labour that there were obvious political objections to the admission of genuine SS men and expressed the hope that the political screening on the far side was being well done. All we need say to M. Zarine is that the Ministry of Labour are taking steps to see that there is no repetition of this unfortunate incident.

Boothby conveyed the substance of these remarks to Zarine in a letter a few days later.[26] Zarine acknowledged the letter, adding, 'I should like to say how much I appreciate the prompt action that the Foreign Office took in this matter, and their humane approach to the questions concerning the Latvians coming to work in this country.'[27] There was, indeed, cause to be grateful for what amounted to a cover-up of a potentially explosive story.

Not long after this, Zarine took up the protests of Latvians passing through the EVW transit camp at Münster in Germany, where, he was informed, similar questions were being asked about the blood-group markings. At the Münster camp, doctors were specifically searching for the Waffen-SS tattoo and noting the names of those bearing them. One of the British officials there had said that 'instructions had been received to watch out for tattoo marks and to stop the sending to Britain of men who bore these marks'.[28] Evidence was soon at hand that even if this was the case at Münster, the earlier Seedorf transit camp had offered no such obstacle to former Waffen-SS men being accepted for foreign labour schemes in Britain.

In the middle of November, Dr Franz Burger, a lecturer working for the Central Office of Information (COI), visited the EVW camp at Bedhampton. Burger was a naturalised German Jew who had arrived in Britain as a refugee during the 1930s after a long spell in a concentration camp. Like many other refugees he had obtained work with government agencies that required German-speakers. It was the duty of the COI to supply lectures on life in Britain to EVWs and help their assimilation into British society; German was frequently used as a *lingua franca* amongst Central and East Europeans. After he had finished delivering his lecture on 'The British Way of Life and Government', he struck up a conversation in German with one of the Latvian EVWs and was astounded to learn from him that 'he had not only served in the "Wehrmacht" but was a member of the S.S.'.

In a memorandum to his superiors, Burger reported: 'He told me he joined up as a volunteer at the outbreak of war and was made a P.o.W. when Germany surrendered.' The man said he had been held first by the Americans and then by the British, who treated him as an SS soldier, which presumably meant detention, interrogation and an appearance before a Review Board. In this case, the suspect was 'acquitted' and discharged whereupon he had found his way into a DP centre. The Latvian informed Burger that there were 'many other men in the same position [that is, former SS men] among the residents of the camp'.[29]

There was no advantage for this man to gain by inventing such an incriminating story, so there was every reason for believing it to be true. Burger was appalled at the prospect that this volunteer worker and others like him had been registered as an alien and, after serving as an EVW, would soon be at liberty to settle anywhere in the country. He might also have expressed indignation that the man's entry into Britain had been in defiance of all the criteria which supposedly screened out undesirable elements. In particular, the Latvian boasted that he had volunteered to serve in the German armed forces and had been in the SS – a clear breach of the conditions of eligibility for DP status according to UNRRA, IRO and, supposedly, candidacy for EVW recruitment.

The COI passed on the letter to the Ministry of Labour, where it was handled by A. F. Rouse, an assistant secretary. He passed it on to the Foreign Office with a covering note that explained a great deal about how such a situation could have been allowed to come about. 'I seem to remember from my days in Germany', he wrote, 'that some Balt DPs were compulsorily enrolled in German paramilitary units, a number of which turned overnight into SS units, and that this accounted for a number of men on screening being placed in the "white" category. Perhaps you could confirm this and let us have the complete story for use on appropriate future occasions.'

Rouse's hazy recollections seem to confuse several different elements in the history of the Latvian Waffen-SS. Latvian paramilitary units were indeed sent to the front and later designated Waffen-SS, but they were police units and included formations like the Arajs Kommando. These had not been formed compulsorily; in many cases their members had spontaneously

assembled into anti-Soviet militia units and later hunted down
Jews. The Latvian Waffen-SS had been turned into DPs with-
out going through the same process of screening as the German
Waffen-SS. The assistant secretary continued:

> The line adopted by this Department on the screening is, of
> course, that if individuals have been accepted by the Control
> Commission, UNRRA, or PCIRO [Preparatory Commission of
> the IRO] as clean, we have not concerned ourselves with the
> question at all. The Home Office have hitherto been satisfied
> with the acceptance of people on this basis from the screening
> angle and we ourselves have simply been at pains to take as our
> recruiting field those who have been appropriately screened.[30]

If Rouse was correct, and he ought to have known how EVWs
were screened, then the Home Office had abrogated all responsibility for security and was relying on the test for eligibility for
DP status to eliminate undesirables. But the walls of the DP
camps were notoriously porous; Latvian ex-Waffen-SS men had
no trouble getting initial DP status; if they were subjected to
screening subsequently, there was persuasion from London to
have their past put to one side.

In their discussion of the query, FO officials referred directly
and unquestioningly to Zarine's coloured history of the Latvian
Legion and his dismissive explanation for the tattoos. Wilkinson
added, 'It is obviously undesirable that bona-fide SS men
should be brought here under "Westward Ho!" but I think
that the extensive and repeated screenings which these people
have undergone in Germany, coupled with the notorious reluctance of UNRRA to render assistance to anyone with even a
minor collaborationist record, makes it unlikely that double-
dyed Nazis would be able to come here.' According to Arnold
Walmsley, of the FO, 'We have been told by MI4c that an
enquiry has shown that up to the last few weeks of the war all
Balts fighting for Germany had to be in the Waffen-SS'.[31]

The Foreign Office also wrote to the Prisoner of War and
Displaced Person Division at Lemgo to get clarification from
them. In a clear hint of the preferred answer, the letter concluded, 'It would seem undesirable that persons should be

barred from "Westward Ho!" simply on the strength of bearing these marks . . . '[32] This probably elicited the formula elaborated in the winter of 1945–6 when the Balts were granted DP status: following that fateful decision, the argument about screening went around in circles.

Wilkinson subsequently drafted the reply which Evelyn Boothby sent to the Ministry of Labour. It embodied the information provided by Zarine and MI4c that 'up to a few weeks before the German collapse, *all* Balts who were enrolled in the Wehrmacht were classified as members of the *Waffen*-SS, a military formation distinct from the political *German* SS'. The tattoos mentioned by Burger were dismissed as 'perfectly innocuous'. Finally, 'As all persons selected for "Westward Ho!" have been screened and re-screened by our security authorities as well as UNRRA and the Preparatory Commission of the International Refugee Organisation. I think there is little, if any, possibility of any persons with an undesirable wartime record being brought to this country.'[33] This breezy and confident tone was somewhat at variance with the earlier message to Lord Inverchapel that 'It is not pretended that these screening operations are 100% thorough, but they are as complete as possible in the circumstances. We are looking for useful workers and not criminals of any category.'

The impression builds up inexorably that Foreign Office officials knew that the Waffen-SS was coming to Britain, but did all that it could to conceal this fact. It would have been politically embarrassing if the Soviet Union discovered that large numbers of anti-Soviet former Waffen-SS men were in this country; it would have been disastrous to labour relations in an already touchy area if the trades unions had found out. The appearance of a cover-up is conveyed most strongly by the handling of a bizarre incident early in 1948.

Foreign labour was required most urgently in the coalmines: it was the crisis here, after all, which triggered the EVW programme. British miners had taken a good deal of convincing before they would accept foreigners working in their pits, but by late 1947 the mines were receiving a steady supply of men recruited in Europe. All those selected for underground work

were subjected to medical checks by National Coal Board
(NCB) doctors in Germany prior to assignment to mines in
Britain and it was during these checks that the Waffen-SS
blood-group tattoos came to light. Afraid that the tattoos would
be easily spotted by other miners either when they were underground or in the works' showers, NCB doctors rejected these
men for labour in Britain. Suddenly the whole raison d'être of
the EVW scheme was in jeopardy.

On 12 March 1948, Sir Harold Wiles and Messrs Armstrong
and Swanee of the NCB convened an urgent meeting with
civil servants from the Foreign Office and the Home Office.
Armstrong explained that 'since there had been the utmost
difficulty in breaking down resistance to the employment of
foreign workers, which resistance still persisted in coalmining
areas, it would be fatal to the general scheme of recruitment of
foreign workers to admit any workers who could be remotely
suspected, however wrongly, of being associated with the
German SS, at any rate at the present stage'. A. W. H. Wilkinson attempted to soothe his anxieties by presenting a completely
fictional and wholly misleading account of both the Latvians
in the Waffen-SS and the meaning of the tattoos. He said that
'it was the Waffen-SS who were responsible for the recruitment
and oversight of foreign workers recruited to the Wehrmacht
and this largely explained the association'.

Wilkinson asserted that the 'IRO, whose mandate did not
permit them to admit to their care persons wilfully assisting
the enemy, did not regard the markings as indicative of collaboration and there was no doubt that the incidence of desertion
was one of the reasons for the markings'. His claim concerning
the IRO was made on very uncertain grounds, while the explanation that blood-group markings derived from the 'incidence of
desertion' was pure fabrication. Nevertheless, the other officials
were willing to accept this line.

Beryl Hughes, one of the few high-ranking women civil servants in the Home Office, said that the Home Office 'had
originally felt some misgivings' but were now satisfied 'particularly as the individuals concerned would be especially interrogated by Home Office Immigration Officers before leaving the

Continent'. When the meeting broke up it was decided that since the numbers involved were probably small the NCB doctors should be permitted to continue their policy of barring all those with tattoos from entering mining work. Later on, when foreign workers were deemed more acceptable, the policy might be amended. In the meantime, they would be happily accepted for other occupations in Britain for which they were not obliged to remove their outer clothing: literally, a 'cover-up'.

Curiously, although Wilkinson was sensitive to the suspicions of the mineworkers he felt none himself. His prime concern was to avoid disruption to the EVW recruitment programme and he had no objection to former Waffen-SS soldiers being employed elsewhere in Britain. He was also at pains not to alienate the Baltic representatives in London. Indeed, Wilkinson undertook to 'placate Mr Zarine and his confrères' if they found out that Balts were not being accepted for labour in the mines. Finally, the Foreign Office took measures to ensure that no information regarding the importation of the Waffen-SS leaked out. Individuals who were rejected for mine work would not be told the real reasons; it was also 'agreed that the question of tattoo-marks should not be mentioned to any but the Board's medical advisers'.[34]

To those who wanted to find out, there was no lack of evidence that something in the recruiting process was seriously awry. In April 1948, there were disturbances at the Münster transit camp when Poles attacked Latvians serving in the camp police. The officer in charge of the camp reported to the Ministry of Labour that the Poles resented the Latvians, who they complained 'are very "SS-minded" because the majority of Latvians in Germany have served during the war with German SS units'.[35] This riot in a major clearing centre for EVWs moving to Britain might have been expected to raise eyebrows at the Ministry of Labour and at the Foreign Office. Instead, a discreet silence was maintained over the extraordinary traffic in besmirched souls. Managers of nationalised industries, civil servants and politicians covered up the arrival of thousands of men who, had they been Germans, would have been subjected to arrest and interrogation.

The history of the Baltic Waffen-SS was complicated and there may have been grounds for giving them the benefit of the doubt, but it is hard to reconcile the sensitivity shown towards public opinion in general, and the feelings of miners in particular, with the proclaimed innocence of these men. If the Waffen-SS tattoos were so 'innocuous', what was to be feared? Or did the British public and members of the NUM know enough about the Waffen-SS and its history to force civil servants to conceal their arrival lest it provoke an uproar?

The Waffen-SS Comes
to Britain II: The Ukrainians

Riccione, a small town south of Rimini, is best known today as a popular holiday resort on Italy's Adriatic coast. In the summer of 1945, it was the location for several vast PoW camps where thousands of Germans, Yugoslavs, Russians and Ukrainians idled away the time in stuffy Nissen huts or sprawled around the dusty parade grounds while politicians decided their fate. The rows of barracks stretched away in all directions, surrounded by a less than daunting barbed-wire fence that was patrolled intermittently by lethargic British soldiers. Prisoners frequently worked outside the camps; many formed relationships with Italian women and marriages between Ukrainians and Italians were frequent. It was not uncommon to find newly constituted families lodging in the huts.

Until June 1946 the Foreign Office had stuck doggedly by the terms of the Yalta Agreement, permitting Soviet repatriation missions to scour PoW and DP camps in order to identify their citizens. These missions succeeded in persuading the majority to return home voluntarily; but those who would not go by choice or were known as collaborators, quislings or war criminals were repatriated by force. As late as May 1947 the PoW camps around Rimini witnessed terrible scenes as Soviet citizens under British armed guard were placed on trains to take them northwards into Russian hands. This operation led to a grim rollcall of suicides and fatalities when the Russians discovered that they were being transported back to the Soviet Union. The accompanying publicity was so embarrassing that it finally persuaded the British Government to abandon forced repatriation. Amongst the beneficiaries of this policy change were the 9,000 Ukrainians of the 14th Waffen-SS Galizien Division.[1]

The Ukrainians had been in the Riccione–Rimini camp since the end of May 1945, although how they got there is something of a mystery. According to the most authoritative account, British field commanders in southern Austria deemed them Polish or of indeterminate nationality and simply allowed the division to walk from Klagenfurt to the Adriatic coast, where they reported to a PoW cage. Having surrendered as an intact unit they remained in their regimental formations, with their officers and NCOs, and were well organised and tightly disciplined. Ukrainian Orthodox priests led services in the camp quad every Sunday; there was even a primitively built church – a battered hut adorned by a cross. Around the camp, and inside its ill-guarded perimeter, hundreds of Ukrainian women and children had joined their menfolk. There were also numerous Italian women who had married Ukrainians and moved into the barracks with their husbands. Together they anxiously awaited the determination of their fate.[2]

However, the Ukrainians were not alone. Supplies and support reached the members of the division from Ukrainians around the world. As long as the threat of repatriation hung over it, British Government ministers and civil servants were bombarded with letters and petitions from Ukrainian lobbyists in several countries pleading that the men in the division should be protected. Archbishop Ivan Buchko, a high-ranking Vatican official who watched over the affairs of the Ukrainian Church, directed his supplications to Sir D'Arcy Osborne, the British representative at the Vatican; the Ukrainian Socialist Party addressed Clement Attlee; Ukrainians in Brazil and Canada added their voice.[3] Support was not confined to the Ukrainian communities: Richard Stokes, the right-wing, Catholic Labour MP for Ipswich and doughty champion of anti-Communists everywhere, and the Quakers were counted amongst their friends.[4]

But what was to be done with a fully intact former Waffen-SS division? Gordon R. Bohdan Panchuk, head of the Central

Ukrainian Relief Bureau in London, had a number of ideas. Bohdan Panchuk, as he was usually known, was a Canadian citizen of Ukrainian extraction who had served in the Royal Canadian Air Force. While still on active service in Britain he had taken an interest in the fate of Ukrainians captured by the British. After the war, he emerged as the leading Ukrainian lobbyist in the UK and eventually became President of the Association of Ukrainians in Great Britain (which he established in 1948). Eager to get his fellows out of the PoW camps where they were vulnerable to Soviet pressure, Panchuk first suggested in a letter to the Foreign Secretary that they should be formed into a British Foreign Legion. As secondary options, he put forward enlistment directly into the British Army or transportation of the division to England.[5]

His primary idea was not as preposterous as it may sound. Italy was a headache for British foreign policy-makers who feared an imminent Communist takeover, either by the ballot box or by a coup d'état. On top of that worry, they feared that Yugoslavia might launch an attack on either Trieste or southeastern Austria in pursuit of longstanding territorial claims. In order to fend off either possibility Bevin insisted in keeping British troops, at great expense, in the Venezia Giulia region. It was just conceivable that he might buy the idea of holding the Ukrainians – who were die-hard anti-Communists – in readiness for dealing with either civil unrest or a border incursion. After all, during 1945 the British had armed surrendered Japanese troops in south-east Asia to help suppress nationalist and Communist insurrections. Panchuk provided Bevin with a heavily sanitised version of the Ukrainian Division's history which made its members out to be no more than anti-Soviet patriots who had been betrayed by all sides; there could be no reason for the British to wish them ill and there might well be a basis for friendly co-operation.

On 29 March 1946, Bevin met with Lieutenant-General Sir Frederick Morgan, the former Deputy Chief of Staff of SHAEF who was now head of UNRRA operations in Germany, to discuss the Ukrainians. Morgan had a penchant for detecting Communist (and Jewish) plots everywhere and sympathised with those who feared repatriation to Soviet territory. He and Bevin agreed that Britain would extend its protective mantle over the Ukrainians on the premiss that, since they could have come from the area of the Ukraine under Polish rule before 1939, their citizenship was in doubt. This decision was ratified by the Cabinet in May, although the exact fate of the division was left unresolved.[6]

Its future in Italy was limited. The elections for a constituent assembly held in June 1946 showed that a coalition of Christian Democrats and right-wing Liberals would be able to deny power to the left. While the threat of a Yugoslav swoop on Trieste remained potent, Italy's internal crisis eased. In fact, the presence of the Ukrainians began to loom as an obstacle to restoring full stability to the region. Italy had negotiated a peace treaty with the Allied powers, including Russia, which gave them the right to extradite from Italian soil any of their nationals, or citizens of other Allied nations, accused of collaboration or war crimes; if the Ukrainians remained in the country and the Russians demanded their handover, they could become the cause of diplomatic friction. As the conclusion of the peace treaty drew nearer, minds in the Foreign Office were concentrated on what to do with the now redundant Ukrainian Division.

Once again, the ever-helpful Bohdan Panchuk came up with a possible solution. Wearing the hat of the Ukrainian Relief Association he approached civil servants in September 1946 with a proposal to employ the Ukrainians in Britain as agricultural workers. A. B. Bartlett at the Ministry of Agriculture asked the FO for its opinion and Robin Hankey replied that he could see no problem, as long as it was clear that the men concerned did not fall under the categories for repatriation as determined by the Yalta Agreement.[7]

At the same time, the FO was being prodded by the influential world-wide Ukrainian lobby. Anthony Hlynka, a right-wing member of the Canadian Parliament, demanded a visa to go to the British Zones of Germany and Austria to visit fellow Ukrainians. The Control Office did not miss the potential of this intervention and immediately suggested that the FO ask

Hlynka about settling Ukrainian DPs in Canada.[8] Not long afterwards, a long memorandum on the virtues of the Ukrainian Division arrived at the Foreign Office from the Supreme Ukrainian Liberation Council, the offspring of the wartime collaborationist Ukrainian Liberation Committee headed by General Pavlo Shandruk, the unit's last commander. The Council now networked Ukrainians throughout the world and had links with the Canadian communities and with Bishop Buchko in the Vatican.[9]

Almost simultaneously, Christopher Mayhew, Parliamentary Under-Secretary of State at the Foreign Office, was handed a petition from the Ukrainians at Riccione–Rimini via Alderman H. Hynd, the MP for Central Hackney, who had recently visited the camp. The petition asked for the right to settle in the British Commonwealth, particularly in Canada, or at least permission for the men to go to the British Zone of Germany to join their relatives there. (They also wanted welfare and educational support so that they could run classes for the younger members of the division, which gives some idea of their ages.) Finally, the Ukrainians wanted information about their ultimate fate.

Comments by FO officials at this time reveal that the outlook for the Ukrainians was bleak. Thomas Brimelow noted that since they 'are surrendered enemy personnel, they presumably do not qualify for any government assistance'. There was no room for them in the British Zone of Germany, nor was there much hope that they would be allowed to enter Canada. A. W. H. Wilkinson, of the Refugee Department, concurred with this pessimistic forecast: 'As they admit to having aided the enemy voluntarily, they are excluded from any form of UNRRA or IRO assistance in resettlement.'[10] In his reply to Alderman Hynd, Mayhew was apologetic that he had to be so 'negative and inconclusive'. However, he held out the hope that 'the decision which will shortly be taken as to the disposal of these Ukrainians will provide an answer to the requests which they have submitted in the petition'. Indeed, Mayhew told Hynd that 'the question of the disposal of these Ukrainians is now very much to the fore'.[11]

The status of the Ukrainians was about to undergo a near-miraculous transformation from that of international pariahs to potential citizens of Great Britain, able to settle anywhere in the world. Towards the end of 1946, with the conclusion of the peace treaty between Italy and the Allies threatening like a black cloud on the horizon, the War Office and the Foreign Office made frantic efforts to find a place to deposit the division. The Control Office firmly excluded Germany as an option; after inquiries the use of PoW camps in North Africa were also ruled out, although why is not clear.[12] Then, as if in answer to the prayers of the Foreign Office, four days after Italy signed the peace treaty in Paris the Foreign Labour Committee quite independently agreed to expand the DP recruitment schemes and set up 'Westward Ho!'. Foreign Office officials pounced on this development as a way out of their predicament.

A. W. H. Wilkinson was apparently the first to make the connection. Not long after the FLC meeting he drew up a cogent memorandum setting out the case for dispatching recruiting missions to Italy, 'where a most serious position exists'.

> The project of removing innocent political dissidents to North Africa is meeting with considerable difficulties, and if these unfortunate people are to be protected from forcible repatriation it will be necessary to find them a home elsewhere. As every other alternative refuge has been turned down, it would appear desirable on both political and humanitarian grounds to allow them to come to this country. If a mission were to be sent to Italy to recruit labour for this country, it would not only help to solve a serious political problem but would also show the Italians that we are doing our best to relieve them of a serious burden on their economy, a potential danger to law and order and a source of friction with their Slav neighbours.[13]

Nor was the British Ambassador in Italy slow to see the opportunity offered by the EVW programme. He wrote to Sir George Rendel, Superintending Under-Secretary of the Refugee Department of the FO, calling for recruitment to be opened in Italy at the earliest moment.[14]

At this point, 'political and humanitarian' reasons dramati-

cally overrode the original functions of foreign labour recruitment. The EVW programmes, which were intended to relieve
the critical shortage of manpower in Britain, were turned into
a chute down which to eject 'politically embarrassing elements';
British mines, farms and factories were to be the immediate
dumping ground. Politicians and officials at the Ministry of
Labour and the Home Office protested against this perversion
of the schemes, but the political impetus built up relentlessly,
crushing all opposition.

Christopher Mayhew urged Bevin to put the case for recruitment in Italy to the Overseas Reconstruction Committee, which
was determining the deployment of foreign labour selection
teams. Mayhew was concerned chiefly with anti-Communist
Yugoslavs who were likely to become the object of attention of
Tito's Government, but the same logic applied to the Ukrainians: 'I think therefore that we should try to bring some of them
here as soon as possible, subject to the conditions that those
who come here are (1) innocent and in danger of reprisal if
they return to their own countries, and (2) useful material from
a Ministry of Labour point of view.'[15]

The Ministry of Labour, whose work was cut out trying to
cope with the flood of EVWs from Germany and Austria, did
not see it in quite that way. For a couple of days in March,
Minister and officials vainly tried to halt the evacuation of the
Ukrainian Division and the plan to drop it in their laps as
'volunteer' labour. George Isaacs told Frederick Bellenger, the
Minister of War, that the Overseas Reconstruction Committee
and Ministry of Labour did not see how it was possible to
accept more EVWs until the present wave was absorbed.[16]
Evelyn Boothby, who had earlier told the Ministry of Labour
that 'urgent steps' should be taken to send a recruiting mission
to Italy, would have none of this shilly-shallying and brushed
aside the Minister's reservations, while Sir George Rendel
impatiently demanded that the Foreign Office should get the
Prime Minister to write to George Isaacs, forcing him into
line.[17]

On the same day, Bevin wrote to Arthur Greenwood, Lord
Privy Seal, and Bellenger telling them of the 'parts I think the

War Office and the Ministry of Labour should play in solving the very dangerous problem with which HMG is at present faced in Italy, where large numbers of innocent people for whom we are in varying degrees responsible will shortly be in danger of forced repatriation to their countries of origin where it is only too probable that an unjust fate would befall them'. To ensure the maximum effect, Bevin sent to Attlee copies of these letters with a strong covering note explaining why it was essential to evacuate the Ukrainians and Yugoslavs to Britain.[18]

Panic gripped the Foreign Office as the ratification and implementation of the peace treaty drew near: soon the Russians would be entitled to demand the return of the Ukrainians as either alleged war criminals or Soviet citizens and it would be impossible to resist them. Impatient about the progress of recruitment in Italy, Rendel asked Mayhew to lean on John Hynd to admit DPs into Germany, too. Mayhew passed on this message in uncompromising terms:

> we are faced with an acute crisis over the question of the refugees and DPs in Italy, where, owing to the impending entry into force of the Peace Treaty, it is probable that unless some immediate action is taken to remove a number of these people from Italy to some place of comparative safety in the near future, large numbers of them may have to be handed over by the Italian Government to the Governments of their countries of origin under article 45 of the Peace Treaty with Italy, which obliges the Italians to hand over on demand any Allied subjects accused by their Governments of being 'war criminals', irrespective of whether a prima facie case can or can not be made against them. As you know the East European Governments are apt to regard any of their nationals who refuse to return as being 'war criminals', and these Governments have their own methods of dealing with political dissidents.

If the Italians did not comply with Yugoslav demands, it was even possible that Tito's army would invade Italy.[19]

In this haste to get the Ukrainians, along with the 'innocent' Yugoslavs, out of Italy, security screening was subordinated to speed of movement. The Foreign Office and the War Office

delegated the task of examining the Ukrainians held at Riccioni
to Brigadier Fitzroy Maclean and the Special Refugee Screening
Commission which had been set up in December 1946 to screen
Yugoslavs held in Germany and Austria. Maclean had been
attached to Tito's partisans during the latter part of the war
and knew Yugoslav wartime policies inside out. As a former
diplomat in Moscow, he was also highly knowledgeable about
Russian affairs, and in a short time managed to turn in a
shrewd report on the Ukrainian Division.[20]

On 21 February 1947, Maclean arrived in Rome hot-foot
from Rimini, where he had spent two weeks with the Refugee
Screening Commission. From Rome he reported to Whitehall
that, even though the members of his team were working at
full stretch, it had been possible to screen only 200 men – a
fraction of the total. He told the Foreign Office, 'Really careful
screening of the whole camp would take many months.' There
were no proper camp records: a list of camp inmates had to be
drawn up with the help of the Ukrainians themselves 'who were
thus in a position to withhold any information they wished.
None have identity documents of any kind.' He reported that
the 'Camp is organised on politico-military lines under a fanatical Ukrainian nationalist leader [probably Pavlo Shandruk]
who formerly served with Skoropadski [the leader of the short-
lived German-puppet republic of the Ukraine in 1918] . . .
Ukrainian nationalist badges and flags are freely displayed.'

According to Maclean all the Ukrainians had been captured
in German uniform and 'most of those interrogated have admitted freely that they volunteered to fight for the Germans'. He
personally had only a hazy idea of the history of the Ukrainian
Division thinking, quite wrongly, that it had been formed in
late 1944. Although 'it is hard to obtain any information regarding their earlier activities', he noted that 'there are indications
that some may have served in SS units'. Maclean was frankly
dubious about the unanimous assertion by the men that they
hailed from the Western Ukraine, that is, those portions which
fell under Soviet rule only after 1939. Regardless of whether
this was true he thought that very few would volunteer to return
to Russia, which made the prospect of enforcing the peace

treaty quite horrific. The camp was ill-guarded and Maclean regarded it as an achievement that, despite the ease with which it was possible for the inmates to escape, 'hitherto only 10% of the total have done so'. 'Any attempt to repatriate these 8,000 Ukrainians would involve a major military operation as apart from those who escaped or committed suicide, everyone of them would actively resist repatriation.'

In conclusion Maclean noted that 'it must of course be borne in mind that we only have their own word for it that they come from the Polish as opposed to the Soviet Ukraine and they have not committed atrocities or war crimes; on the other hand we have no means of disproving their statements and those interrogated give an impression of telling the truth'. Characterising repatriation as unviable, Maclean advised that a refuge be found for the Ukrainians but that, wherever they were sent, 'their existing politico-military organisation should not be allowed to remain in existence'.[21]

Forty-two years later, during a television interview about his work at Rimini, Sir Fitzroy Maclean recalled that 'it was a hopeless proposition'. He told Tom Bower, 'First of all, we were not qualified to screen the Ukrainians. We didn't have the necessary language experts or anything like that.' Asked if he had suspected that some of them were murderers, Maclean admitted, 'I think it was fairly clear that quite a number of them must have been in the SS as part of the Ukrainian SS Division. There was every probability that there were war criminals amongst them.'[22]

In a subsequent message to London, Maclean noted:

> The ultimate disposal of these Ukrainians seems to present as many problems as their immediate disposal . . . they would not appear to be repatriable. On the other hand, it is hard to see how, with the best will in the world, men who by their own admission volunteered to fight for the Germans against the Allies can be regarded as eligible for international relief under the terms for the proposed IRO.

The British Government was faced with the choice of leaving them to their fate in Italy 'with all its political, economic and even military complications' or assuming responsibility for them itself.[23]

The detailed report of the screening commission reached London some days later. It made no bones about the patchiness of its operation: 'Individual screening by us being impossible, it was decided to question a small cross-section chosen in accordance with Wehrmacht formations.' The screeners relied on Major Jaskewycz, the Ukrainian camp leader, for a history of the division whose formation he dated from 'the late summer of 1944'. Yet the investigators noted several cases when serious discrepancies opened up between the story which Jaskewycz told and that given by interviewees, several of whom 'stated that they had volunteered for armed service with the Germans as early as July 1943'. Further interrogations revealed the existence of the '14th Galician Waffen Grenadier Division' – although only one of the officers let on that it was a Waffen-SS unit. The screeners thought that it 'had some SS training' and observed the use of distinctive Waffen-SS ranks for the officers and NCOs.

The Screening Commission settled for the version which dated the unit's existence from 'September 1944' and suggested that it had been formed around the 'remnants' of the division destroyed at the Battle of Brody. After that it had fought for 'only about one month', at the end of the campaign in Austria. Even so, the report concluded that 'The great majority of them voluntarily enlisted in the German Armed Forces and fought against our Allies, Soviet, Russian and Yugoslavian.' There were, therefore, 'prima facie grounds for classifying them as traitors, i.e. as ineligible for IRO schemes'. It was, consequently, somewhat surprising that the report recommended turning the men into DPs, protecting them from the Soviets and transferring the division out of Italy as a matter of urgency.[24]

The decision to save the division was underpinned by the verdict on its nationality, but here the Refugee Screening Commission relied on a previous screening by Soviet officers in August 1945. The Soviet mission, under General Vasiliev and Colonel Jakovliev, had visited the camp twice on 17 and 20 August, with scant results: the bulk of the men insisted that they were from the pre-war Polish Ukraine. This account was readily accepted by Major Denis Hills, the British officer who had been conducting parallel inquiries on behalf of the Western Allies. Hills, later a confidant of Idi Amin before he fell foul of the Ugandan regime, was adamantly opposed to the policy of co-operation with Russian demands. He subsequently boasted, 'I found myself shielding the Ukrainian Division of 8,000 men from forcible repatriation.' After a rudimentary survey of the camp's inhabitants, he concluded that it was impossible to separate the genuine Polish Ukrainians from the Soviet Russian ones. Before the arrival of the Soviet repatriation mission, Hills recalled, 'I warned the Ukrainian camp leaders and their commandant, Major Jaskewycz, to be absolutely firm with the Moscow officers; they were not to fear them and they would not be under duress. I would be present to see fair play.'[25]

Hills stuck by his decision despite all the later revelations about the alleged war criminality of some Ukrainians in the unit. He told Tom Bower in 1989, 'Of course I knew about the SS and I was wary, but I had to make up my own mind about these people.' Challenged with the question of whether he had checked the men for war crimes, Hills replied, 'I don't know. It was not my brief and the Army were not interested. We wanted to find out where they came from because on that decision depended their own future.' When asked if he had consciously disobeyed the orders to detect Soviet citizens and war criminals so that they could be repatriated, Hills boldly answered, 'Entirely, yes.' He said that he did not accept the validity of the Soviet accusations, but 'legally they should have been returned'.[26]

The screening for nationality was thus extremely suspect and few British officials subsequently believed that all the men were really former Polish citizens. According to the authoritative study of the repatriation process by the American historian Mark R. Elliot, 20–50 per cent of the men were really former Soviet citizens who ought to have been repatriated, but 'in this instance at least, the British, as well as the Americans, screened the interned soldiers in such a casual fashion that every last soldier could opt for resettlement in Britain'.[27]

Regardless of any doubts about the men's nationality, the decision to preserve the Ukrainians and transport them to Britain under cover of the EVW scheme was astounding in view of the unambiguous evidence that the majority of them had volunteered to fight for the Nazis. Their arrival and subsequent treatment was in total defiance of every single immigration regulation – but this is less than surprising in view of the consistent political interest that was attached to their well-being. In the worsening climate of the cold war, the Ukrainians were not simply possible victims of Soviet malice; they were potential allies against the new enemy. Ideological affinity now merged with humanitarian sympathy to strengthen the determination to get them out of Italy and into Britain.

The degree of importance accorded to the Ukrainians was illustrated yet again by the outcome of a fresh crisis which blew up at the end of March 1947, when it was found that no shipping was available to transport the division to Britain. The War Office informed the FO that the seven ships needed for the task could not be made available – except at the cost of slowing down the repatriation of Poles and German PoWs from the Middle East. Foreign Office official Cecil Edmonds impatiently commented, 'I think there is no doubt that the Ukrainians should have priority. With them it is now or never and "never" would involve the most serious political complications.' The inter-departmental competition for resources had to be resolved by an appeal from Hector McNeil directly to the Prime Minister. The day after the Cabinet met on 1 April, Edmonds told G. N. Tuck at the War Office that the Prime Minister had decided: the shipping would be assigned to the movement of the Ukrainians.[28]

Shifting a full division of soldiers, even without heavy equipment or arms, is not an easy business. The process of transportation was scheduled to begin on 25 April and it was not expected to be completed until mid-May. In the interim, questions were raised about the final destination of the Ukrainians – which led quickly to the matter of their security status and screening. Now it was the turn of the Home Office to come up

against the powerful forces which were speeding the division to
British soil.

The War Office had prepared the movement of the Ukrainians with customary thoroughness. Two large transit camps
were readied for the division's arrival, whence the men would
be distributed around twenty-five 'labour camps' a fortnight
later. But the War Office had no patience for screenings and
made its views abundantly clear: Lieutenant-Colonel Chancellor relayed to the Foreign Office the military's hopes that there
would be no delays in the operation due to such checks and
asked the FO for specific assurances on this score. Edmonds
replied instantly: 'The Minister of State's [McNeil] telegram
to the Secretary of State [Bevin], 13 March, makes our position
quite clear. They are to be scattered and used for labour and
adequately screened at leisure afterwards.'[29] This was a significant admission that the unit had not been screened properly in
Italy and that the whole issue was deferred indefinitely. In fact,
the processing of the division had been so sloppy that in
October 1947 a meeting was held at the Foreign Office to
discuss the embarrassing discovery of over seventy DPs who
had slipped into Britain along with it.[30]

None of this was known to the Home Office, which was
formally responsible for the entry of non-British nationals. The
first inkling which the key officials in the Immigration and
Aliens Departments had of a large-scale influx was a summons
to meet the Permanent Under Secretary at the Home Office,
Sir Frank Newsame. Beryl Hughes, who worked in the Aliens
Department, recalled that she and another colleague bundled
themselves into a taxi to rush over to Newsame's Whitehall
office, where they were 'issued with a fait accompli'. Newsame
had made 'every possible representation' on behalf of the Home
Office, but he was told that 'the Prime Minister decreed' the
arrival of the Ukrainians.[31]

Getting the Ukrainians into the United Kingdom was all
very well, but they could not remain in PoW camps for ever.
What was to become of them? Carew Robinson, an assistant
secretary in the Aliens Department of the Home Office, testily
asked Evelyn Boothby whether any consideration had been

given to their 'ultimate disposal'. He stressed that from the Home Office point of view it was most undesirable for the Ukrainians to be discharged from PoW status and turned into civilians. Irritated by the lack of consideration shown to the Home Office, he asked whether the Foreign Office had considered emigrating the Ukrainians to Canada – so throwing the ball deep into their court. Robinson reminded the FO that the country was already absorbing 4,000 Poles daily: it would be very difficult to accept more aliens into the British population.[32]

Boothby tried to soothe his Home Office colleague, assuring him that Canada House was being consulted while other options were being explored, too. It was anticipated, for example, that 1,500 of the men would go to Argentina.[33] This fell far short of what the Home Office wanted to hear: just how many thousands of unscreened, ex-enemy soldiers were to be allowed to settle in Britain? To ram home this point Carew Robinson reiterated that 'At present the Home Office supports the view . . . that conversion of these Ukrainians to civilian status ought to be avoided if possible.'[34]

The deadlock between the two ministries remained, so the Foreign Office next offered terms for a compromise. A. W. H. Wilkinson suggested to Carew Robinson, 'While we consider that the ultimate status of Ukrainians coming to this country as PoWs is not a matter of immediate concern . . . it would be helpful to know whether there would be objection to individual Ukrainians being given civilian status in order to obtain visas for foreign countries that would be denied them if they were PoWs.' The FO was anxious to ensure that no Ukrainian would lose the right to emigrate 'because of such a technicality'. Wilkinson probably had Canada in mind when he continued, 'We understand that certain governments willingly grant visas to civilians who are not in custody and we are, therefore, anxious, as I expect you will also be, to ensure that no Ukrainian loses the chance to emigrate.'[35]

This was a disingenuous request. Canada would not permit the entry of PoWs or men in custody; but the Foreign Office proposed to circumvent this perfectly sensible restriction in order to get the Ukrainians out of Britain. In other words,

Wilkinson was asking the Home Office to assist in deceiving the immigration service of another country. The request appears all the more unscrupulous if it is recalled that the dilemma of what to do with the Ukrainians would never have arisen if the correct immigration procedures had been applied to them by the British authorities in the first place: they would never have been allowed into the country.

As it happened, the Home Office saw no objection to Ukrainians who were ineligible for residence in Britain being discharged from PoW status 'merely to facilitate emigration'. Carew Robinson assumed, however, that care would be taken to see that they did, indeed, leave the country.[36] The Home Office was holding firm: the Ukrainians were simply not eligible for entry and settlement in Britain in any officially accepted manner. If they were to be civilianised, it would only be to enable their departure. This line emanated from the highest political level: the War Office was told, 'As regards the men themselves, the Home Secretary has taken the view that every possible expedient should be adopted for their eventual disposal other than by conversion into civilian status in the United Kingdom.'[37]

By July there had still been no solution to the question of 'ultimate disposal'. Foreign Office officials thrashed around looking for a panacea, but found themselves trapped in a vicious circle. They had virtually promised the Home Office as a condition for getting the division into Britain that its members would not be given civilian status; but unless the men were civilians they could not get visas to emigrate to any other country – least of all Canada, which was the destination most favoured by the FO and the Ukrainians themselves. On top of that, the men were still effectively unscreened and it was hard to conceive of their civilianisation until that task was accomplished. But, as Boothby noted, 'if a general decision about their status is taken, it will not be so easy to screen them'.[38]

Efforts to persuade the Canadians to take the Ukrainians proved to be unavailing: nothing would change unless the men were discharged from PoW status, which begged the question

of security checks. The FO explored the possibility of recon-
vening the Refugee Screening Commission 'for a *total* screening'
– itself a damning acknowledgment of the failure to screen the
division adequately before it arrived. However, having
ensconced the division in England, where its members were
doing some useful work, the FO resigned itself to a more relaxed
view of its prospects. According to Boothby, 'there is no very
great hurry about screening as long as the Soviet Government
does not press us to explain our action in bringing the Ukrainians from Italy'.[39]

In fact, the British Government had been playing an elaborate game of cat and mouse with the Soviets over the Ukrainian
Division since the decision to move it to England, if not earlier.
On 3 June, George Nikolaevitch Zaroubin, the Russian
Ambassador, protested to the Foreign Office that Soviet citizens
were being transported to Britain in defiance of the Yalta Agreement. Alarmed by this intervention at such a sensitive juncture,
the War Office sought advice from the Foreign Office. Brimelow
instructed them to tell Colonel Kleshankov, who ran the Soviet
repatriation mission in Britain:

> that we propose to screen the whole Division and that if we find
> any men whom we regard as liable to compulsory repatriation
> under the Cabinet ruling on the subject, with the terms of which
> he should be familiar, we will segregate them and discuss with
> him the arrangements for their repatriation. Similarly, if
> amongst the remainder there are any who volunteer to return
> to the USSR, we should not stand in their way, and we shall
> also segregate them and discuss arrangements for their repatri-
> ation with Col Kleshankov. We shall deal with war criminals
> as we should deal with war criminals of any other nationality.
> As for the rest, we are prepared neither to repatriate them
> against their wishes, nor to give Col Kleshankov access to them
> and if he objects to this, he should be told to make this complaint
> through the diplomatic channels.[40]

In the formal governmental reply, Sir Orme Sargent, Permanent Under Secretary at the Foreign Office, told Zaroubin that
the Soviets had been given free access to the camps where

alleged Soviet citizens were held, but that by mid-June they had identified only a few hundred who fell into the repatriable categories. These Soviet citizens had shown that they did not want to return to the USSR 'and HMG for their part do not propose to send them there by force'.[41] The reply made no mention of the Ukrainian Division and did nothing to appease the Soviets.

The USSR next launched an attack via the Soviet press, accusing the British of plucking from captivity men who should have been returned to Russia. Hector McNeil dealt firmly with this challenge, engineering a parliamentary question which enabled him to assert that the Soviet repatriation mission had checked over the division. In reply to another protest from Zaroubin, Sargent repeated the line that the unit had been cleared according to nationality: the men were not Soviet citizens.[42] But the results obtained by the Soviet screening mission in 1945 were dubious – not least because of Denis Hills' efforts to protect the Ukrainians. Nor had it been properly screened for war criminals.

The arrival of a complete Waffen-SS division did not escape notice in Britain. Felix Wirth, a well-known journalist working for the Foreign Press Association, contacted Tom Driberg MP to express his astonishment at the news. Wirth conceded that the men were probably non-repatriable on the basis of nationality, but thought that it would be 'much more interesting to determine by careful investigation, if any of these people could be classed as war criminals under one of the numerous Allied decisions'. He continued: 'Little is known, on the whole, of the Ukrainians' terrible role as Germany's faithful and active henchmen in the slaughter of the Jews in Lwow and other towns in that part of the world as well as in the murder factories throughout Eastern Europe. The notorious Ukrainian SS Division "Galizien" and other Ukrainian formations bear the full responsibility for a good deal of the monstrous outrages perpetrated there.' Driberg passed this letter on to the Foreign Office, seeking 'an assurance that the former record of these Ukrainians had been carefully investigated'.[43]

At around the same time, Richard Crossman, the Labour

MP for Coventry East, received a letter from an anguished Jewish correspondent, M. L. Hyman, protesting that while genuine DPs – including Jews – were being denied entry to Britain the Government was bringing over 8,000 Ukrainians from an enemy unit. Crossman asked McNeil for his response to this accusation.[44] Such objections were not confined to Jews. The Foreign Secretary himself was the target for an angry missive from L. W. Carruthers, a resident of Guildford, who identified the unit as the SS Galizien Division and asked if it was credible that an SS division could be brought to England.[45]

McNeil was also taxed about the division in the House of Commons. The first question was probably a plant, asking him 'how many Ukrainian personnel of the former SS Division, Galizien' were being brought to Britain, if they were screened and whether any demands had been made for their extradition: it enabled him to deny all these charges. He described the Ukrainians misleadingly as 'ex-Wehrmacht personnel' and members of the 1st Ukrainian Division who were coming to Britain as PoWs. McNeil said, 'A cross-section of this Division was screened by a Soviet mission in August, 1945, and a further cross-section was screened by the Refugee Screening Commission in February of this year.' He acknowledged that the Russian Government had requested that members of the division be sent to the USSR, 'but since the overwhelming majority of the men concerned' came from Polish territory occupied in September 1939 the Government did not intend to comply with these demands. This answer hardly did justice to the doubts expressed by Maclean and his team.

McNeil was then challenged by two Jewish MPs, Daniel Lipson, a Tory, and Barnett Janner, from the Labour Party. Lipson wanted to know if the men were going to be employed in England, possibly hoping to stir up trouble with the trades unions who had made strenuous objections to the employment of Poles and EVWs. But McNeil declined to take the bait and simply retorted, 'I am confident that they will.' Janner, a leading member of the Anglo-Jewish community, was more direct: 'Is my Right Hon. Friend aware that members of this Division were exceptionally brutal, that they murdered hundreds of people in cold blood? Will he take all steps necessary to see that none of those who come into this country took part in any of these sadistic and vicious incidents?' Before the Minister could reply, Richard Stokes was on his feet insisting that the Ukrainians loathed the 'Muscovites' and the Germans equally, and only desired independence from both. Eventually McNeil was able to deal with Janner's supplementary, only to assure him that 'we have taken the most extensive precautions to see that anyone guilty of crime is so treated, and I have no doubt that there will be further screening processes associated with these men'.[46] He clearly did not share the doubts of his officials that it would 'not be easy to screen them'.

The brush with these MPs provoked some introspection in the Foreign Office. Evelyn Boothby consulted with David Haldane Porter, who had been the head of the Screening Commission at Rimini; Haldane Porter also met with Thomas Brimelow and General Blomfield at the War Office; but the result was only more obfuscation and disinformation. When Hector McNeil, briefed by his civil servants, delivered his answers to Driberg and Crossman, he was economical with the truth. He again described the Ukrainians as 'ex-Wehrmacht personnel' who were coming to Britain as PoWs, not as EVWs. McNeil also asserted that 'cross-sections of these men' had been screened in August 1945 by the Soviets and in February 1946 when 'a further group were subjected to a very exhaustive screening process at the hands of our own Screening Mission', neither of which had revealed any guilty men.[47]

In formulating these answers, the Foreign Office displayed the utmost complacency concerning accusations against the Ukrainian unit, even though they must have been aware of the inadequacies of the 'screening' to which it had been subjected. When confronted by the charge that the former Waffen-SS division might be notorious for its wartime activities, A. W. H. Wilkinson minuted dubiously that 'in the absence of any evidence against individuals, it is unlikely that any war criminals will be found'. Evelyn Boothby commented, 'It seems unlikely that any Jew-baiters wil be found amongst the men . . . ' Paul Gore-Booth, the head of the Refugee Department, told Mr

Carruthers that the division was not an SS unit and was 'free' from atrocities. Only some of its members might have served in the Galizien SS Division 'which it is alleged did not have such a clean record'. In any case, it had been screened, so there was nothing to worry about.[48] This was a mixture of fact and wishful thinking; it was certainly not founded on a thorough-going check of all individuals in the unit.

Bohdan Panchuk let McNeil know that he was gratified by the way the Minister had fielded the questions in the House of Commons. But Panchuk's agenda had moved on: with the division now safely in Britain, he wanted to know what could be done to help some of the Ukrainians move on to Canada and what would eventually happen to the rest.[49] At this stage, the Foreign Office was still in a quandary concerning the emigration of the Ukrainians and was content to let the matter rest for the moment while some solution was found to the screening problem. Gradually, it moved towards a tripartite solution: some Ukrainians would be assisted to emigrate to Canada; some would be sent to the British Zone of Germany; others would be civilianised and allowed to settle in Britain – despite the oft-stated and well-founded misgivings expressed by the Home Office.

Towards the end of 1947, the Foreign Office and the War Office made preparations to civilianise the bulk of the Ukrainians, which would enable them to stay in Britain if they chose to do so. When Panchuk returned to Whitehall in November and promised Boothby that he could arrange for the emigration of Ukrainians with relatives in Canada, this offer was treated as an option only for the Ukrainian PoWs who were not acceptable for civilianisation and settlement in the United Kingdom. Those whose presence could not be tolerated in either Britain or Canada would be 'repatriated' to Germany, regardless of the feelings of the Control Commission.[50] However, efforts to normalise the status of the Ukrainians by turning them into civilians and allowing them to settle in Britain were temporarily upset by another Soviet intervention and a dramatic claim that the men were, indeed, war criminals.

George Zaroubin had returned to the offensive, with a list of thirteen White Russians and Ukrainians in Britain who, he alleged, were guilty of collaboration, treason and war crimes. All the men on the list were Soviet citizens and it gave rudimentary details about their wartime activities. Nikolai Volosyuk, a native of White Russia, had served as a policeman in the town of Kobrin during 1942–4, when he had murdered and robbed local people. He was traced to London: Zaroubin even submitted a Post Office box number for the man. Vitold Golovach, another White Russian, was accused of working as mayor under the Germans in Budslav, where he participated in the deportation of Russian citizens to Germany. He was said to be in a PoW/EVW camp at Bramley. Ivan Dvoretski, from Molodechno in White Russia, had taken part in mass shootings alongside the Nazis and had fled with the German Army. According to Zaroubin he ended up in PoW/EVW Camp 104 at Gosfield, in Essex.

Josef Ilyuschits, a deputy police chief and killer from the Kopecha district in White Russia, was also alleged to be in a PoW/EVW camp, No 106 at Vitcan Street, Revental, in Essex. Anatoli Korzun, who had volunteered for the German-run security services in Starobinsk district of White Russia, where he had assisted in bloody anti-partisan operations, was located in Camp 137. Pavel Manets, a commander of a police detachment, was in Camp 286, Purfleet, Essex; Ivan Medved, once a policeman in Kobrin, was now in Petworth Camp, Sussex. Alexander Ogloblin, a Ukrainian intellectual from Kiev – he was a history professor – had served as president of the town council before fleeing with the Germans. Based in Prague for the latter part of the war, he took part in efforts to set up Nazi spy rings behind Russian lines. Apparently in London, he now worked for the Ukrainian Scientific Institute.

Another Russian citizen accused of intelligence work for the Nazis, Boris Rogulya, was at an unknown address in England with his wife. Rogulya, a teacher from Minsk in White Russia, had attained the rank of major under the Germans and had been honoured for his work as organiser of an anti-Soviet White Russian nationalist party and deputy president of the puppet assembly of White Russia set up in 1944. Alexei Romanovski came from the same province as Rogulya, and had served in the German police until July 1944, killing several partisans; he was alleged to reside in camp 613/2 at Flockborough (sic). Philip Fistunov, another White Russian, had served the Germans as district chief in Minsk; after fleeing in the summer of 1944, he worked for the Sicherheitsdienst. He was captured by the British in May 1945, near Bremen, and was 'sent to work' in England. Also somewhere in the country was Alexander Chernukha, who had previously served as a platoon commander in the police and conducted anti-partisan operations which led to many deaths. Finally, there was Ivan Sheremei from the province of Brest on the Russo-Polish border, who had gone over to the Germans and entered the police in Kossov, whereupon he terrorised the local inhabitants; he was in Whitley Camp, near Godalming in Surrey.[51]

Zaroubin was told that inquiries would be made and, from the available documentation, it seems that there were desultory efforts to trace the men. The Aliens Department of the Home Office undertook a search through the list of registered aliens, but could not find any of the thirteen. Of course, if they had been amongst the 8,000 Ukrainians this would have been no surprise since the division had evaded the normal immigration registration procedures. Beryl Hughes suggested trying the War Office, but the Director of PoWs had already replied to inquiries that after an 'exhaustive search' only one name could be identified. A few days later, the Foreign Office requested the American Embassy for any information it might have about this individual; there the story, as far as it can be reconstructed from public records, ends.[52]

Undeterred, Zaroubin stormed back with an even longer list – 124 names of officers of the 14th Waffen-SS Galizien Division, from junior lieutenant to full colonel, who were being held in PoW Camp 17. The Ambassador demanded that these men should be handed over as both war criminals and Soviet citizens in accordance with the decisions taken at Yalta and Potsdam. The Foreign Office was unimpressed and unhelpful: Wilkinson commented, 'This list has obviously been lifted wholesale from a nominal roll of Ukrainian PoW officers and is not accompanied by any evidence. Unless the Soviet embassy can provide evidence that these men are (a) Soviet nationals, (b) guilty of war crimes or of wilful collaboration with the enemy, I do not think that we should take on the responsibility of providing such evidence ourselves by screening these men.'[53] The last part of his riposte was particularly revealing: the officers had not been screened – but the FO declined to oblige the Soviets by undertaking the task themselves.

Nevertheless, Hankey ordered some steps to be taken. The Home Office and the War Office were, again, asked if they had any information about the men on the latest list and, as before, replied that they did not. However, Ian Roy at the Aliens Department added two uncomfortable pieces of information. First, he noted that 'arrangements to confer civilian status in the United Kingdom upon selected Ukrainian prisoners of war are in progress,' and that once they were civilianised it would be a difficult business to arrange for their extradition as alleged war criminals. Should such a case occur, it would prove 'embarrassing and unwelcome'. But the sting was in the tail: 'individuals against whom undischarged allegations of war criminality exist would not be acceptable for civilian employment in the United Kingdom.' That being the case, the Home Secretary expected that the named officers would be sent to Germany and only then discharged.[54]

The Foreign Office would have none of this and even expressed irritation at the delay to the civilianisation process. Wilkinson cited the Refugee Screening Commission report as proof that no more than a 'handful' of the Ukrainians might hail from the pre-1939 USSR. To his mind it also showed that 'the "SS" part of the description of the Galizien Division was largely a misnomer and that it could certainly not be held to apply to the bulk of the Ukrainian PoWs in this country.' He understood the desire of the Home Office to 'avoid the grant of civilian status to persons likely to be considered as war criminals, but I do not think that it would be fair to send persons to Germany just because they have had the misfortune to feature on a nominal roll of camp inmates which has fallen into Soviet hands.' Other officials backed him up on this point, although some suggested that a more intensive screening should be made of the division in England.

Wilkinson disagreed strongly with the suggestion of detailed checks: the Ukrainians were already being interviewed 'with a view to their civilianisation in the UK' and those not selected would have to be sent to Germany within a fixed period of a few weeks. In his view, 'a fairly simple screening should suffice to show which of these 124 are Soviet nationals by our definition, and we might put this to the WO, who may otherwise be perturbed at the prospect of a thorough screening which may prove beyond their powers.' Wilkinson wanted to move fast and to his mind that meant resolving only the question of nationality on which the Soviet claim was based; he was simply not interested in anything else. In his words, 'I do not think that a full-blooded screening is called for at this stage.' There never had been one: there never would be.

Robin Hankey, who was by now rigidly opposed to any concessions to the Soviets, added his thoughts: 'I do not see why we should allow ourselves to be frightened by the Soviet Embassy in this way into sending into Germany (where they would be a pure embarrassment) a number of men who are now performing useful work for us here.' They had received a 'preliminary' screening by Maclean which had shown them to be exempt from repatriation under the Yalta Agreement; moreover, the Russians had produced 'no evidence whatsoever' to show that the men were traitors or war criminals. Hankey even had doubts about the wisdom of asking the Soviets to provide *prima facie* evidence of war criminality because he feared that if the Soviets provided it the men would have to be repatriated and 'I am not sure what our answer would be in such a case.'[55]

It might be thought that the obvious answer should have been: 'Here they are.' But Hankey appears to have equivocated at the prospect of facilitating the Soviet demand, even if it was supported by evidence. There were certainly good reasons for doubting the validity of Russian claims, but on the other hand Fitzroy Maclean had himself expressed serious reservations about the nationality and war record of the Ukrainians. Even though German Waffen-SS officers from the rank of lieutenant to colonel would have been vigorously interrogated, the FO took no action itself in this case and applied the familiar double-standard for the non-German Waffen-SS. So, when Hankey replied to Zaroubin, he told him that before the matter could be taken any further the Soviet Union would have to show that the 124 officers were Soviet citizens and provide *prima facie* evidence that, if they were, they were traitors, or, if not, war criminals.[56]

Zaroubin was in no mood to compromise either. He riposted that the men were officers of a Waffen-SS division, an organisation proscribed under the Nuremberg Tribunal, who had participated voluntarily in combat against Russia. But still the Foreign Office refused to budge. Relying on the material supplied by Panchuk, FO officials accused Zaroubin of confusing treachery with war criminality. Even if the men were Soviet citizens, the British objected to returning them: in disregard of the Yalta Agreement the FO no longer recognised their collaboration as a crime. Exhaustive evidence of particular acts would be needed before any of these men were treated as war criminals. Wilkinson muddied the waters further by suggesting that some of the officers may have been in the Waffen-SS, but had joined the unit before it was a Waffen-SS formation and that later the designation had been dropped. The incredible confusion about the war history of the Ukrainian Division could have been cleared up with a minimum of effort, but uncertainty suited the Foreign Office. When he eventually responded to the Ambassador, Hankey called for proper evidence of war criminality and disputed whether the officers had, in fact, knowingly joined the Waffen-SS.[57]

The Soviets had been held at bay, yet again, but their intervention enabled the Home Office to mount a final attempt to prevent the settlement of the Ukrainians in Britain. To the Home Office Aliens Department, the Ukrainian officers belonged indubitably to the 'SS Galician Division'. On 2 July, Beryl Hughes told C. R. A. Rae of the Foreign Office, 'You know that we are very reluctant to agree to the inclusion of these men in the field of selection as European Voluntary

Workers while there is an undischarged accusation of war crimes against them.' She had been provided with information by an immigration officer at the Münster DP transit camp which indicated that 'these Officers may be war criminals'. They were in communication with another Ukrainian, Harass-owski, who was currently being held by the Americans as a war criminal. Hughes concluded, 'I cannot think that the Offi-cers with whom he was corresponding in the United Kingdom can have had careers which differed very greatly from his and it would be patently unfair to allow them to escape arrest merely because they happen to be in the United Kingdom.'[58]

It took a long time for the FO to reply. Almost at the end of August 1948, Hughes heard from Anthony Lambert: he was dismissive. 'While we sympathise with your desire not to discharge as civilians any persons against whom there is an undischarged accusation of war criminality, our feeling here is that it is most improbable that the Soviet authorities will be able to substantiate their claim that these men are both Soviet citizens . . . and war criminals.' Hughes learned that the Foreign Office would feel regret if the civilianisation of the Ukrainians, which was 'desirable on other grounds', should be held up by reason of the Soviet claims. Lambert also warned that if the Home Office insisted on waiting for *prima facie* evi-dence, it might be more than a year before it arrived. Finally, he brushed aside the matter of Waffen-SS status and added, significantly, that 'in the past "SS" markings of the kind described in these papers has not proved a bar to the employ-ment in this country of European Voluntary Workers, especially those coming from the former Baltic states.'[59] Now that a pre-cedent had been established for employing former Waffen-SS troops in Britain on an individual basis, the way was clear for the quiet rehabilitation of an entire Waffen-SS division.

Robin Hankey likewise played down the doubts communi-cated by the Home Office. 'I see that HO [Home Office] considers that some of these men really might be war criminals. We don't want to protect *real* war criminals, I take it.' He regarded the members of the division as non-repatriable Polish citizens and maintained that even if it had been a Waffen-SS formation, this was still not sufficient cause for delivering them to the Russians. Despite the wary screening reports from Italy, the Russian interventions and the doubts of the Home Office, no major independent investigation was launched by the FO at this time. Rather, the FO again ignored the warnings of Maclean's screening unit, bulldozed its way past the Home Office and, at the same time, prepared the way for transporting some of the men to Canada.[60]

Panchuk, by now a familiar figure at the Foreign Office, was pressing impatiently for the full civilianisation of the unit as early as April 1948. In July, he was sufficiently confident to write an angry note to the Director of Prisoners of War at the War Office, complaining about the delay. C. R. A. Rae commented sympathetically, 'We know that HO are delaying the civilianization of 124 officers claimed by USSR, pending a decision by us . . . but I know of no case for delaying the rest.'[61] That month, it was agreed that the 8,300 Ukrainians who remained in Britain after the failure to secure large-scale settlement in Canada or Argentina would be converted from PoWs into EVWs.[62]

From August 1948, the Aliens Department supervised the transfer of the Ukrainians into camps, where they lived as EVWs for the next year. They were subject to interviews by immigration officers, but the interviewers had no language skills or knowledge of events in the Ukraine during the war; their object was mainly to register the Ukrainians as aliens. Home Office officials like Beryl Hughes suspected that 'there must have been some bad eggs', but no one wanted to make any further trouble. As long as the men worked and behaved themselves, the Home Office was happy to overlook its doubts about their antecedents: 'Once the Home Office had swallowed the bitter pill it wanted to make use of them.'[63]

By the end of the year, 8,225 Ukrainians were en route to British citizenship or a new life in Canada – now opened to them since they were no longer PoWs. Only thirty-two were denied the right to settle in the UK due to 'bad records', probably referring to criminal offences committed while in Britain, and another forty-five chose to return to Germany. The

Home Office was even obliged to stomach the settlement of several hundred infirm men and reluctant workers due to another round of spirited lobbying by Panchuk. While genuine DPs and distressed relatives struggled with red tape and bureaucratic delays to get into Britain, the Ukrainians enjoyed a high road to all the privileges of British nationality. J. A. Tannahill, a civil servant from the Ministry of Labour who later wrote the story of the EVWs, commented, 'The Ukrainian prisoners of war had succeeded in getting better terms for themselves than the refugees . . . '[64]

Despite the FO's initial misgivings about Panchuk and his Association of Ukrainians in Great Britain, by the spring of 1948 he enjoyed a cosy relationship with Foreign Office personnel. At first, the FO declined to recognise the Association and complained that Panchuk was trying to 'sneak' Ukrainians into Britain by the back door. Within a few months, antagonism was replaced by a co-operative spirit which did not stop at turning a blind eye to the passage of alleged war criminals through the British Isles.[65]

In March 1948, the British Embassy in Denmark told the FO that eight 'so-called Ukrainians in prison' were being demanded by the USSR. They were alleged to be war criminals and the Soviets had provided 'detailed charges' although without much hard evidence to back them up. What should be done? The Foreign Office advised the Ambassador to hold out if the Ukrainians were not Soviet citizens. Not long afterwards, London was informed that two of the men were out of prison and en route to Canada and Argentina, via England. C. R. A. Rae passed on this news to Panchuk, who had expressed his concern for the men's fate. But Panchuk already knew: he told C. R. A. Rae that the men were in 'our house' and he had personally seen them off to Canada. It is not clear how they got into and out of Britain, or whether the usual immigration channels had been circumvented – but that must remain one explanation of this strange episode.[66]

In April 1948, Frank Savery alerted a colleague in the FO to the information that at a recent meeting of the Association of Ukrainians in Great Britain representatives were heard boasting of the Association's expansion due to the membership of men discharged from the 'SS Galician Division'. Wilkinson rushed into action to diffuse Savery's anxiety, serving up the familiar mixture of half-truths to the effect that not all the men were Waffen-SS and suggesting that not every member of the unit would necessarily be civilianised. But he noted that the Ukrainians ought to be more discreet. Wilkinson then conveyed this message in a letter to Panchuk – whom he now addressed as Gordon. Panchuk wrote back contritely to 'My Dear Wilki': 'I agree with you entirely and will continue to deal with every possible discretion, as I have done to date, with all matters concerning the Ukrainian prisoners of war in this country, particularly so as not to leave an undesirable impression on public opinion.'[67]

The complicity between certain Foreign Office officials and the Ukrainian lobby extended to concealing possible war criminals. In the light of the Maclean report, officials should have known that amongst the men of the Ukrainian Division there were probably Nazi collaborators and mass murderers. Yet when Bohdan Panchuk submitted to the Foreign Office a long memorandum setting out the case for the recognition of Ukrainian nationality, A. W. H. Wilkinson commented: 'I am afraid that in his zeal to commend the national claims of his near compatriots, Mr Panchuk . . . forgets that the national anonymity of many Ukrainians is often a matter of distinct advantage to them, especially where alleged "war criminals" and "quislings" are concerned.'[68]

Yet, from the moment that they were discharged as PoWs, veterans of the Galizien Division gathered together and celebrated their wartime exploits in Waffen-SS uniform. During the 1950s, 1960s and 1970s, the émigré communities in Yorkshire were a hotbed of anti-Soviet politics and a power-base for the virulently right-wing Anti-Bolshevik Bloc of Nations (ABN). Despite the fact that the ABN was led by members of the pro-Nazi regime that held power briefly in Lvov in June 1941, who still held pro-fascist views thirty years later, local Ukrainians even persuaded the Provost of Bradford to unveil a plaque in Bradford Cathedral in honour of its work. Fiercely

protective of their language and cultural heritage, the Ukrainians in Britain combined perfectly respectable lives with unyield-
ing allegiance to the ideals which had led many of them into
the ranks of the Waffen-SS in 1943–4. They behaved as if they
had nothing to fear.[69]

Indeed, a large-scale screening of 200,000 refugees, DPs and
immigrant workers who had entered the country between 1945
and 1950, mounted by the Home Office in 1951–2, seems to
have been more concerned to weed out Communists and pro-
Soviet fifth columnists. There is evidence that when interviewees admitted to wartime membership of pro-Nazi collaborationist units, their potentially incriminating statements were
glossed over. The questionnaires used in 'Operation Post
Report', which might have provided essential evidence for
tracking down war criminals in Britain, were filed away and
forgotten for forty years.[70]

The transportation of the 14th Waffen-SS Galizien Division
to Britain in May 1947 was not a covert operation, but the
division's history was sanitised and efforts were made to minimise its public profile. Parliamentary questions were deflected
and the protests from other departments of state were neutral-
ised by the use of misleading and selective information. Even
if the Soviet claims that the unit contained war criminals were
flimsy, no great efforts were made to check them. The caveats
in the various screening reports were overlooked, while the
reservations of the Home Office were brushed aside. The frequently expressed suspicions concerning the division and the
men in it were not followed up. Responsibility for this negligence lay primarily with the Foreign Office. At times it appears
as though the FO was actually operating a cover-up, as in 1948
when the cocky behaviour of the Ukrainians threatened to
reveal their presence. They may have felt comfortable and
confident in their new home, but the FO appears to have been
rather more edgy. If the reasons for the importation of the
14th Waffen-SS Galizien Division were purely 'political and
humanitarian', why had it been necessary to go to such lengths
to mislead MPs and the public and do so much to play down
the fact that they were in the United Kingdom? The newly

emerging history of the cold war, based on declassified US documents and fragmentary material that has survived the weeders in the British Public Records Office, suggests the disturbing possibility that the needs of British intelligence played at least some part in saving the Ukrainians.

EVWs, the Cold War
and the Intelligence Connection

By the time the European Voluntary Worker (EVW) programme was wound up in 1949, it had served as a channel
through which at least 10,000 former Waffen-SS soldiers had
been brought to Britain. This was not the result of an oversight
or an accident: the relevant government departments and their
political masters knew exactly what had been going on. There
were, of course, reasons why the importation of these men could
have been regarded as unexceptionable or, at least, justifiable:
civil servants and ministers were well versed in reciting them.
However, the evidence of what was at best obfuscation and at
worst a cover-up indicates unease in Whitehall. This may be
explained simply by reference to the fear of upsetting public
opinion, but there is another dimension to the reticence
accompanying the arrival of Nazi-collaborators in post-war
Britain: the use to which some of these men were put in the
service of military intelligence during the first rounds of the
cold war.

Following the German invasion of Russia, Great Britain and
the USSR become unlikely allies. Winston Churchill, the Prime
Minister in 1941, had in earlier years been a fervent anti-
Bolshevik; as Secretary of State for War during 1919–20 he had
launched British troops on a half-baked war of intervention to
topple Lenin's government. However, as soon as the Soviet
Union was locked in the struggle to defeat Nazism, he put aside
all notions of continuing hostile activity against the Russians
and insisted on full co-operation between all arms of the British
and Soviet military, including military intelligence.[1]

Until 1944 there was a consensus between politicians, Foreign Office officials and the generals that such co-operation was necessary and desirable. But, once the Chiefs of Staff and the Foreign Office began to prepare for the post-war world their views diverged starkly. The diplomats placed great faith in the twenty-year friendship treaty which had recently been concluded with the USSR and displayed extreme nervousness at any gesture which the Russians might interpret as hostile, so jeopardising the alliance against Hitler. By contrast, the Chiefs of Staff were moving towards an appreciation that, once Germany was beaten, the USSR would emerge as Britain's foremost enemy in Europe. For the duration of the war the FO was able to stifle the misgivings expressed by the military and insisted on regarding Russia in a beneficent light. Any moves which might upset Stalin were suppressed, especially efforts directed towards gathering intelligence on the Red Army.[2]

With the arrival of the Labour Party in government, the balance of power in Whitehall paradoxically shifted in favour of the anti-Communism espoused by the military. Attlee, Bevin and Dalton did not need instruction in the malevolence of Soviet intentions: they had fought Communist entryism in the Labour Party and the trades unions during the inter-war years, and had become familiar with the instruments and goals of Soviet foreign policy via the international bodies to which the party was affiliated. By contrast, the insouciance which the Americans displayed towards Russia at the 1945 Potsdam Conference irritated Attlee. He remarked in his memoirs, 'We were also acutely aware of the combination of Russian old-time and Communist modern Imperialism which threatened the freedom of Europe. I thought that the Americans had an insufficient appreciation of this danger and indeed of the whole European situation.'[3]

By July 1945, the Post-Hostilities Planning Sub-Committee, which combined War Office and Foreign Office officials and the Chiefs of Staffs, had unambiguously identified Russia as the object of British defence planning. It took longer before the Foreign Office broke decisively with its wartime policy of appeasing Stalin, but in April 1946 Christopher Warner circulated a memorandum entitled 'The Soviet Campaign Against This Country and Our Response to It' which set a new tone. After reviewing recent developments in Russian foreign policy, Warner concluded, 'The interests of this country and the true democratic principles for which we stand are directly threatened. The Soviet Government makes coordinated use of military, economic, propaganda and political weapons and also of the Communist "religion". It is submitted, therefore, that we must at once organise and coordinate our defences against all these and that we should not stop short of a defensive–offensive policy.'[4] This toughly worded statement from the formerly pro-Soviet and taciturn Warner electrified the Foreign Office: it became British policy to build up Germany as a potential ally against Russia and to try to maintain the strategic border with Russia as far to the east as possible.

Military and diplomatic thinking now coalesced. Under the direction of the newly created Ministry of Defence a strategy for withstanding Russian aggression began to emerge. The Foreign Office paper 'Strategic Aspect of British Foreign Policy', issued in October 1946, advocated a state of armed preparedness and alertness against Russian pressure. The FO experts reviewed techniques of Soviet expansionism and specifically drew attention to the threat of Communist fifth columns in countries such as Italy. While it held that little could be done to free states that had fallen under the sway of the Red Army, it argued that it was vital to prevent others succumbing to Communist domination. To this end it was considered essential 'to support and encourage as far as we can our friends in those countries, and so to keep alive in them the connexion with the Western democratic ideas which our policy towards them represents. The best hope of this is in Poland, since the Poles are born conspirators.'[5]

There was only a short step from blunting Soviet influence in Western democratic countries to encouraging covert action in the Soviet sphere of control itself. The use of the intelligence services as the tool of this policy was amplified in a memorandum on 'Future Defence Policy' prepared by the War Office on the orders of Field Marshal Montgomery, Chief of Imperial

General Staff, in March 1947. As well as calling for 'active opposition to Soviet ideological expansion, especially in areas of strategic value', it defined amongst its aims the 'retention of British intelligence organisation at a high standard of efficiency'.[6] 'Future Defence Policy' was the basis for a governmentally approved anti-Soviet defence strategy: the scene was set for the cold war.

British military planners were not slow to take their cue from the establishment of the CIA in July 1947 as the instrument by which America intended to answer what it, too, saw as Soviet expansionism.[7] Sir William Slim, Commandant of the Imperial Defence College, put it to the Chiefs of Staff that Russia was waging a war against the West which had to be countered by 'all possible means'. Slim, the hero of Burma, went far beyond political or propaganda weapons and proposed that techniques 'should be employed to foster social unrest' in the Communist bloc. The Chiefs of Staff concurred with his prognosis and recommended to the Cabinet Defence Committee that it was time to face the reality of a cold war, although they recommended fighting it with political means only. That was before events in Central Europe radicalised opinion in the West. In March 1948, following the Communist coup in Czechoslovakia, the Chiefs of Staff were clamouring for 'special operations' against Communist regimes.[8]

Bevin was also shocked by the belligerency of the Soviet Union. While he continued to stress resistance to Communism in the political and ideological realm, he agreed to the establishment of a section in the Foreign Office dedicated to 'political warfare'.[9] The military continued to demand more: in September 1948, the Chiefs of Staff advised 'taking all possible means short of war not only to resist the further spread of communism but also to weaken the Russian hold over countries she now dominates'. Britain, like America, was moving from a passive to an active strategy of containment in which covert action played a substantial part, ranging from interventions in the electoral politics of democratic countries with powerful Communist Parties to encouraging internal unrest within the Soviet bloc. A few months later, Britain and the United States launched the first, major covert operation against a Communist country – the ill-fated expedition into Albania that was betrayed by Kim Philby.[10]

The Joint Planning Staff identified the Soviet satellites as the Achilles heel of the Eastern bloc. In the event of war, they might pose 'a serious police and internal security problem to the Russians with great possibilities for exploitation by the Western Powers'.[11] But how was this to be achieved? How were the agents to be found and the networks established that would provide essential intelligence or engage in subversive activity in peacetime and form the basis for covert operations should the cold war turn hot?

To begin with, British military intelligence was able to draw on pre-war anti-Soviet contacts that had been maintained despite the wartime alliance with Russia. The Secret Intelligence Service (SIS), otherwise known as MI6, had targeted Russia since the Bolshevik Revolution. During the early 1920s it had established bases in the Baltic states and Scandinavian countries from which SIS personnel, disguised as Passport Control Officers, ran agents inside the USSR. Tallinn in Estonia and Riga in Latvia were hotbeds of espionage, while British operatives in Helsinki, the Finnish capital, were even involved in cross-border operations by the anti-Bolshevik underground. SIS officers like Harry Carr, chief of operations in Helsinki from 1925 to 1941, formed strong links with White Russian émigrés and members of the dissident nationalities within the Soviet Union.[12]

Throughout the 1920s and 1930s, Carr and his colleagues, Alexander McKibben, based in Tallinn, and Leslie Nicholson, who was in Riga, built up an extensive range of contacts across the Baltic republics. The Director of Military Intelligence in Estonia, Colonel Villen Saarsen, was a particularly rich source of information for Carr – as he was for the Germans, for whom he was also providing services. Ants Oras, a genuine Anglophile, who was Professor of English at Estonia's Tartu University, was also a frequent visitor to the British Legation in Tallinn, where his brother worked as Secretary. McKibben had meanwhile cultivated Walter Zilinskas, a Lithuanian diplomat, and Nicholson had suborned Robert Osis, a Latvian Army officer.[13]

Carr also made links with Ukrainian exiles, notably the assiduous intriguer Stefan Bandera. The Ukrainians, along with the White Russians, formed the core of the Prometheus Organisation – a loose alliance of anti-Bolshevik émigrés and nationalists dedicated to subverting the Communist regime in Moscow. Originally it was funded and directed by the French and Polish secret services, but in the 1930s Stewart Menzies, the head of SIS, established a strong financial and political association between the Prometheus plotters and British intelligence interests.[14]

During the war, SIS struggled to stay in touch with its friends in Eastern Europe. Despite the Russian occupation of Estonia in 1940–1, Ants Oras maintained contact with the British via the Anglo-Estonian Friendship Society, which he had helped to found along with an English resident, H. C. C. Harris. Before long, Harris feared that he would be accused of espionage and tried to get out of Estonia; finding his exit blocked by the Soviets, who refused to give him a visa, he committed suicide. Whether or not he was a 'spy', Oras was implicated in espionage activity on behalf of the British and faced interrogation by the NKVD, from whose clutches he had a lucky escape. The indefatigable Professor later played a role in the anti-Nazi resistance which regularly sent boats between Stockholm and Tallinn carrying couriers and material for the underground. The Germans were aware of this traffic: in 1944, the Sicherheitsdienst intercepted one of the boats plying across the Baltic Sea, as a result of which hundreds of Estonians in the 'Anglophil movement' of the underground were caught by the Gestapo. Many of them later escaped and resumed their underground activity.[15]

Confined to Stockholm as the Germans overran more and more territory, SIS operatives kept open channels to Latvia and Lithuania via Dr Valdemars Ginters, the representative of the Latvian Central Council in Sweden, and Walter Zilinskas, who was in touch with the Lithuanian maquis. Through these lines of communication Carr and McKibben had some knowledge of the anti-Nazi and anti-Soviet resistance in the Baltic, and it was on this foundation that they set out to reconstruct their networks after the change of direction signalled by the military echelons in mid-1944.[16]

Even before the war was over, SIS was making use of captured Soviet soldiers liberated by the advancing Allied armies in the West. When Nazi collaborators and former members of the Baltic Waffen-SS sought refuge in Sweden after the German collapse, they were pounced upon by both the Swedish and the British military intelligence – neither of which asked many questions about the Balts' wartime activities. This was the first linkage between SIS and former SS men.[17]

One of the earliest post-war recruits for SIS was the Lithuanian intellectual Stasys Zakevicius. He had served as an adviser to the Germans during the occupation and decamped from Lithuania to Denmark in their train. In the chaos of northern Europe in 1945 Alexander McKibben's agents ran into him and won him over. Zakevicius, who altered his name to Zymantas when he changed his role, brought into the service of SIS Stasys Lozoritis and Jonas Deksyns. They established links with the anti-Soviet partisans in Lithuania, many of whom had gone into the forests after serving the Germans in various capacities. Their ranks included former members of the Schutzpolizei – who had escorted Jews to the killing grounds, ringed the areas and participated in the shootings – and the short-lived Lithuanian Waffen-SS.[18]

The lynchpin of the Lithuanian underground was General Povilas Plechavicius, a national hero and pre-1939 military veteran. During the German occupation Plechavicius had bargained with the Germans, offering to raise men to fight for them if the volunteers would be incorporated into a Lithuanian national army. His well-publicised appeals to Lithuanian youth to join the crusade against Bolshevism and to ensure that the Russians never returned to Lithuania were highly successful. The Germans were astonished with the results when, in a short time, 16,000 Lithuanians presented themselves for military service. However, the Germans alienated the General by refusing to meet his terms for a Lithuanian national army and contemptuously dispatching the bulk of Lithuanian recruits to Germany. Relations between the Lithuanians and the Germans soured so badly that armed clashes involving units on both sides occurred in Kovno and Marianpole. Finally, Plechavicius broke off his negotiations and ordered the thousands of Lithuanians already in German uniform to desert and go into the forests. He was then imprisoned in a concentration camp.[19]

When the war ended, Plechavicius found himself in the British Zone of Germany. In February 1946 the Soviets demanded that he should be handed over to them as a traitor and a war criminal, but they were rebuffed by the British even though the demand was accompanied by detailed information. According to the Intelligence Bureau of the Control Office, 'Plechavicius is in our Zone, and we have good reason to believe that the Russians are aware of this. There are, however, vital intelligence reasons which preclude the possibility of our handing him over to the Russians.'[20] In fact, Plechavicius was supplying SIS with valuable details of the anti-Soviet underground in Lithuania which was being co-ordinated from Germany by VLIK, the Supreme Committee for the Liberation of Lithuania. But VLIK and the underground were almost wholly comprised of former Nazi-collaborators, men like Plechavicius who at the very least had worked with the Germans as long as collaboration served their purposes.

In response to the Intelligence Bureau's request for advice on how to meet the Russian demand for Plechavicius, Cecil King replied, 'The answer depends on the nature of the evidence on which the Soviet authorities base their claim for the surrender of this man. Unless he is a war criminal in the accepted sense, we are under no obligation to hand him over. If the case is doubtful it should be referred to the Foreign Office with full particulars.'[21] Plechavicius then disappears from the public record, although it is known that the CIA made use of his knowledge and contacts during 1948, while he was still in the British Zone.[22]

The British authorities protected Plechavicius from the Soviets for two crucial years, despite the fact that he was implicated in the brutal German occupation of Lithuania and had presided

over the recruitment and deployment of military and paramilitary units which were involved in numerous actions against Jews
and pro-Soviet partisans. Even if the British refusal to accord
legitimacy to the Soviet occupation of Lithuania meant that the
Foreign Office could deny that Plechavicius was a traitor, he
was still a collaborator with a vile regime. Yet he never had to
face investigation or stand trial. In this case it is difficult to
treat the diplomatic rationalisations of the Foreign Office as
anything more than a convenient cover for holding on to an
intelligence asset.

After the Germans had been driven out of Latvia, former
collaborators and soldiers in sundry German units took to the
forests or went underground to continue the fight against the
Red Army. British military intelligence was alerted to this anti-
Soviet resistance movement by partisans who escaped across
the Baltic Sea to Sweden. SIS then used the exiled Latvian
Central Council to establish ties with anti-Soviet elements still
inside Latvia. As early as October 1945, SIS recruited Latvian
agents from amongst the refugees and smuggled them into
Latvia to firm up its links with the groups still holding out in
the forests. The British evinced few signs of concern about the
backgrounds of these new operatives.[23]

Later groups inserted into Latvia would be composed almost
entirely of former Waffen-SS men. The connection was forged
via Robert Osis, who had been used by SIS before the war.
Osis had thrown himself into collaboration with the Nazis and
risen to the rank of Lieutenant-Colonel in their service. During
the liquidation of Jews in the Riga ghetto between November
and December 1941, he had commanded the units of Latvian
police, the Schutzpolizei and Schutzmannschaften, that had
herded Jews to the killing site in the Rumbula forest and
guarded the perimeter while the massacres were carried out.
Interned in Germany at the end of the war along with other 'ex-
Wehrmacht Balts', he met Feliks Rumnieks, who had enlisted in
the Latvian Legion, the precursor of the Latvian Waffen-SS
formations. Osis wanted to tell SIS that he was alive and willing
to work for them again, so Rumnieks made his way to Sweden
and tried unsuccessfully to reach British intelligence through

the Latvian Central Council. Osis had more luck and managed to resume his ties with SIS, who got him out of Germany and into Britain, where he undertook various duties for British military intelligence. Rumnieks was later rescued from incarceration in a Swedish DP camp and sent back to Latvia by the SIS; his career as a British agent was terminated when the KGB arrested him not long afterwards.[24]

Charles Zarine, the head of the Latvian Legation, who had been such a persistent lobbyist in favour of the Balts in the Waffen-SS, also proved to be a useful assistant to the SIS in the search for agents. He put the British intelligence services on to Rudolph Silarajs, a former officer in the collaborationist Latvian Air Force, who was languishing in one of the DP camps in Belgium which were home to so many Latvians in 1945–6. Through Silarajs, SIS was introduced to several other Latvian collaborators who were duly transferred to Britain. Of these, Vitold Berkins had worked for the Nazi Sicherheitsdienst in Riga, while Andrei Gladins had been a member of the Arajs Kommando. Berkins and Gladins were trained at a specially established centre in Chelsea, London, before being sent on their missions. Zarine, who gave his blessing to their secret enterprise, was fully aware of the role of Latvian former DPs in these covert operations.[25]

By now, 'Westward Ho!' was bringing thousands of former Baltic Waffen-SS men into the country. No less than 9,706 Latvians had arrived in England by 1949, and although not all of them were ex-combatants, these formed a large proportion of the total number. So it was even easier for SIS to recruit physically fit young men with military training and even combat experience. Bolislov Pitans, an ex-Latvian Waffen-SS soldier, had arrived in England in 1947 as an EVW and ended up working as a baker. He was approached by SIS for a special mission in 1950 and sent into Latvia with two Estonians, also former members of the Waffen-SS.[26] Lodis Upans was yet another member of the Arajs Kommando to enter the employ of the British secret service at this time. No questions were asked about his homicidal background and former MI6 officer Anthony Cavendish has confirmed that suspicion of being a war criminal was no obstacle to the recruitment of a Balt willing to take part in clandestine operations. Cavendish ran the operation in the Baltic which was intended to infiltrate dissident Latvians recruited in the West, from amongst DPs and former Waffen-SS men, back into Latvia where they would link up with the alleged anti-Soviet partisans. He told Tom Bower in an interview in 1989 that 'If somebody was needed to do a job and if he had committed war crimes, I would use him to do the job, ones I felt essential.'[27]

The same pattern emerged with respect to special operations in Estonia. British intelligence officers plundered the human cargo brought to Great Britain by the EVW programme and unflinchingly selected men who not only had fought for the Germans, but had worn the uniform of the Waffen-SS. Alphons Rebane was plucked from a textile mill in West Yorkshire, but in his previous career he had been a battalion commander in the 20th Waffen-SS Estonian Division and had actually won the highly-prized Knights Cross in February 1944. After the division was evacuated from the Baltic front to regroup in Silesia, Rebane continued to lead his unit in the last-ditch defence of the Third Reich. In March 1945, he fought his way through to the West with several hundred of his men.[28]

Rebane went into captivity with the remnants of his command and a few hundred other Estonians who were in the reserve battalion which was stationed in Denmark when the Germans capitulated. But, thanks to Britain's generous treatment of Balts in the Waffen-SS, these Estonians were transformed into DPs and accepted as candidates for the EVW schemes. Large numbers were among the 2,891 Estonians who came to Britain under 'Westward Ho!'. Of course, it was still not easy to find the right men, but the SIS could rely on its friends in the Baltic Legations. August Torma, the head of the Estonian Legation, like Zarine, had cultivated the Foreign Office and had regularly intervened on behalf of Estonian DPs and former combatants. Later he was to be closely associated with covert missions to 'free' his homeland. It is possible that once Rebane reached England he was located through the intercession of Torma, who, along with his other Baltic colleagues, made strenuous efforts to establish links with their nationals coming to Britain under the work programmes.[29]

From the moment Rebane was in the pay of SIS it was simple for them to identify dozens of suitable Estonians. The former Waffen-SS officer asked SIS to find and bring to England the former General Inspector of the Estonian Waffen-SS Division, his wartime comrade Vaino Partel. With their combined knowledge of the unit it was easy for them to draw up lists of its wartime complement. Then, with the assistance of the British, they tracked the men down in DP camps and EVW hostels and offered them employment on special missions connected with the 'liberation' of their old country. In this way numerous ex-Waffen-SS men like Leo Audova and Mark Padek were recruited into SIS. By late 1950, no fewer than forty volunteers had been assembled and several groups prepared for covert operations in Estonia.[30]

It seemed to make little difference to British military intelligence, or the Foreign Office for that matter, if Balts who offered their services for covert purposes were alleged war criminals. In March 1949, Zarine wrote to J. Y. Mackenzie at the Foreign Office to let him know that one Colonel Janums was in London on the business of Dauvagis Vanagi – the association of Latvian ex-servicemen. Janums had been a key figure in the internal security apparatus of the collaborationist regime which had worked under the Nazis in Latvia. As Chief of the Personnel Department of the regime's Home Affairs Committee he had authority over all of the Latvian police units operating under German command. In 1943, he helped to recruit volunteers for the Latvian Legion and subsequently took command of the 33rd Regiment of the 15th Waffen-SS Latvian Division.[31]

Pro-fascist as well as anti-Soviet, Janums had found a congenial home in Berlin while Latvia was under Soviet occupation during 1940–1. He had played absolutely no part in resisting or even questioning the aims and methods of German rule and had served in the ranks of the Waffen-SS to the bitter end. Dauvagis Vanagi, the organisation for which he now worked, originated when ex-Waffen-SS Latvians in PoW camps in the US and British Zones of control banded together for welfare purposes and to defend themselves from Soviet repatriation missions. Gradually, it established a firm grip over these holding centres and routed out Latvian social democrats and Communists, whom it regarded as Soviet stooges. Another former collaborationist who was crucial to organising imprisoned Latvians was Dr Alfreds Valdmanis, whom the British permitted to travel freely through their zone, doing 'welfare work' amongst 'ex-Wehrmacht Balts'. Within a short time most Latvian veterans were enrolled in highly organised networks dominated by once leading members of the civil and military arms of the quisling regime in Latvia.[32]

By 1950, the CIA was funnelling money into Dauvagis Vanagi, which came to serve a variety of cold-war functions. It was a fount of anti-Soviet propaganda and, more importantly, a source of trained manpower for use in operations in Soviet-held territory.[33] The reason for Janums' visit to London appears to have been to develop a similar project with the British. According to Zarine,

> Mr Janums is a man of understanding and realises the factors that go to make up the present situation. He does not, therefore, wish to be an embarrassment. He feels, however, that in view of the rather intimate knowledge he has of the ways and psychology of the Russian Army – both from his having served with the Tsarist Army and fought against the Red Army – it might be of interest and value for him to have a talk with someone from military circles here if this could be arranged.[34]

Mackenzie took the hint and passed the information to Lieutenant-Colonel Stoney of MI3, explaining that 'the Colonel [Janums] is anxious to discuss the future of his organisation with the appropriate officer in the War Office, and I should be grateful if you would let me know as soon as possible who would be prepared to receive him'. Stoney saw Janums shortly afterwards. He later reported to Mackenzie that 'Like most dispossessed Balts, I think he is hoping for a war!' The Latvian wanted the British Army to give training to the 150 Latvian officers in the United Kingdom and the 300 in the area of the British Army of the Rhine 'before they get too rusty'. Janums specifically mentioned the 100 Latvians in the CMWS – a paramilitary service set up by the British to guard military installations in the British Zone of Germany. But Stoney informed him that 'As the policy is not to train CMWS – whether Yugoslavs, Poles or any other refugees – in other than armed guard duties, I could not make him any promises.' Janums may have left a disappointed man, but as Stoney told Mackenzie, 'I did get one piece of information' which made the encounter worthwhile from his point of view.[35]

Because so many files pertaining to Colonel Janums are restricted, it is not easy to connect his visit or his proposal with other aspects of British military policy or the activity of the secret services. However, there is powerful collateral evidence to suggest that Janums' mission was neither an isolated, individual gesture nor a hopelessly eccentric one. The British Army was, indeed, employing former Waffen-SS men in various capacities. Konni Zilliacus, the left-wing Labour MP, and Maurice Orbach, a Jewish parliamentary colleague, had complained about the use of Balts in auxiliary Army units after a front-page story in the *New York Times* on 4 February 1946 drew attention to the practice. Despite their protests the use of former enemy soldiers was not curbed: in fact, it burgeoned until hundreds of Baltic ex-combatants and collaborators were receiving British Army pay. They were employed as drivers in all-Baltic transport companies, engineer units, and as armed guards protecting British military installations – including such sensitive and strategically important locations as headquarters buildings, ammunition dumps and airfields.[36]

These transport, engineer and guard companies on the surface performed mundane tasks that could have been carried out by German civilians or by British troops. So why did the Army insist on what was a controversial policy – about which little is known even to this day? What might have been the real purpose of Baltic paramilitary formations may be inferred from the origin and career of parallel units established by the US Army. So-called Labor Service Units composed entirely of Latvians, Estonians and Byelorussians were created by the American forces early in 1946 and continued to exist well into the

1950s. From US Army documents declassified in the 1980s, it is now clear that they were intended as holding and training units for men destined to play a crucial role in a third world war.

According to US military doctrine in the late 1940s and early 1950s, there was an imminent risk of a war with the USSR which would result in an exchange of atomic weapons. The final victor would be the power that survived this exchange and was able to establish control over its enemy's territory. One means by which the USA intended to accomplish this would be the insertion of special operations groups behind the lines to establish links with the anti-Soviet forces, which, it was fervently believed, would emerge to take power from the battered Communist authorities. Exiles from the Soviet satellite countries would be perfect for this task: the Labor Service Units were a means to recruit and train them, and hold them in a state of readiness.[37]

Representatives of the émigré communities seem to have explored the same idea with British Government officials on more than one occasion. In April 1948, Bohdan Panchuk and another Ukrainian, M. Andrievsky, met with C. R. A. Rae at the Foreign Office to discuss 'the formation of Ukrainian military units' to serve against the USSR. Andrievsky also gave to the FO a list of Ukrainians in Germany who were 'in danger', and proposed that Britain and America should help to save them by moving them to a haven somewhere else. Due to the weeding of the PRO files it is hard to work out why these men may have been 'in danger'. It is possible that they were Soviet citizens whose repatriation was being sought by the Russians, but they may have been guilty of something far nastier than being born in the wrong place.[38]

The existence and, presumably, the purpose of these units was also known to Charles Zarine, who discussed them with Alexander McKibben of SIS. After the outbreak of the Korean War, Zarine, like many other exiles, believed that a showdown with Soviet Russia was imminent and that the West would wish to make use of the émigrés for intelligence purposes and covert action. Since the British Army was employing Latvians and

Estonians in armed formations until the late 1950s, this may not have been a fanciful notion.[39]

Covert activity sponsored by the USA which has come to light under the Freedom of Information Act offers a useful analogue for reconstructing the work of the British secret services, which, by contrast, have succeeded in retaining a vice-like grip on documents, critical and trivial, that offer any insight into their history. Yet the US experience offers more than just an instructive but necessarily somewhat speculative parallel. There are several well-documented cases of collaboration between the intelligence agencies of the two countries which throw light on the role of the SIS, in particular. This material reveals that British intelligence protected alleged East European war criminals and 'shared' their services with the Americans.[40]

It is now well known that as the Allied Armies drove into the Third Reich, the US Army Counter-Intelligence Corps (CIC) and British military intelligence were working together on several separate missions to locate German scientists, industrialists and members of the German Army and Nazi intelligence communities who could provide useful information for the Western Allies. The grotesquely misnamed 'Operation Applepie' was devoted to securing the members of the SS head office department, RHSA-Amt VI, who were responsible for intelligence work relating to the USSR.[41]

The British element of 'Operation Applepie' was quite successful and found several individuals who had worked in RHSA-Amt VI. Amongst them was Nikolai Poppe, a Russian scholar of oriental languages and peoples. Poppe had been at Leningrad University until 1941 when, with the city under threat of capture by the Germans, he fled to the Caucasus and found work at a teaching institute. A year later, the Wehrmacht summer offensive left him in territory under German control. Poppe now put his expertise at the disposal of the Nazis and collaborated with them in the formation of a puppet regime amongst local tribesmen. He also provided significant topographical data to assist the German military effort as it penetrated the Russian defences in the Caucasus mountains.

However, in the winter of 1942 the débâcle at Stalingrad forced the Germans to retreat. As their armies evacuated the Caucasus, Poppe went with them and took up an offer of work at the SS-sponsored Wannsee Institute in Berlin.[42]

The Wannsee Institute, where Poppe arrived in 1943, was run by the Foreign Intelligence Section of the SD, whose head was Walter Schellenberg. In his memoirs, Schellenberg ranked the establishment of the Institute as one of his most valuable achievements. It was 'a library which contained the largest collection of Russian material in Germany' on political, scientific, economic and military aspects of the USSR. During 1943–4, it sifted data on the Soviet war effort and furnished intelligence for the German forces; it also contributed to the efforts to mobilise East Europeans in the defence of the Reich. Here Poppe laboured until the Third Reich collapsed around him.[43]

Poppe ended up in the British Zone of Germany immediately after the war and seems to have lived there unobtrusively and undetected for over a year. However, in the summer of 1946 the Russians obtained information of his whereabouts and demanded that he be handed over to them. In July 1946 General Sir Bryan Robertson of the Military Government was asked by Colonel-General Kurochkin to deliver Poppe, whom he described as 'an active agent of the Gestapo', into Soviet custody.[44] At around the same time, British intelligence learned that Poppe was somewhere in the British Zone and insisted that they be given access to him. The urgency of getting hold of Poppe before the Russians did was increased by news reports in the American press that he had been captured.[45]

In fact, to everyone's embarrassment, Poppe was becoming an international *cause célèbre*. During September, he had managed to get a letter to a leading academic contact in Britain, Dr Haloun of the Chinese Department at Cambridge University. He gave Haloun an anodyne version of his wartime career, seeking the don's intervention to get him out of Germany. Soon, leading British orientalists were pleading with the Foreign Office for Poppe to be allowed into Britain. Haloun wrote to Sir John Pratt, former head of the Far Eastern Section at the

Ministry of Information, making the case for Poppe's salvation and serving up essentially the same story that the former collaborator had given to him. Pratt accepted it and suggested to colleagues in the FO that 'Pope [sic] should somehow be spirited into this country from Berlin' and given work at a British university.[46]

However, when the Intelligence Division and the Foreign Office made inquiries about Poppe, the Control Office for Germany told them that 'the whereabouts of Poppe are still unknown'. For nearly a month there was no trace of him, until he was located by the Control Commission and detained. They reached him just in time: a Russian mission to catch him was also on his trail and not far behind. It is notable that even after Poppe was safely under lock and key, the Foreign Office persisted in denying that it had knowledge of his presence. The reasons were made clear after the Control Office, fully aware of Soviet efforts to find him, finally admitted it knew where he was: 'It has never been our intention to hand over Poppe.' On the same day that Thomas Brimelow was discussing Poppe's case with F. Pickering of the Intelligence Division of the Control Office, Anthony Lambert, another Foreign Office official, was claiming in response to inquiries that 'we are genuinely unable to trace him'.[47]

At the start of November 1946, Nikolai Poppe was securely in British hands and was being interrogated as part of 'Operation Applepie'. Preparations were made to deflect the Russians should they seek him again. The Control Office in London told its Berlin branch that if the Russians did learn that he was incarcerated by the British, 'Follow normal procedure of asking Russians to submit *prima facie* case against Poppe and refer to us again when case submitted for advice whether he should be surrendered.'[48] In other words, the London Office was telling British officials in Berlin to play for time by using legal niceties to delay what should have been the automatic, obligatory return of a man who was known to be a Soviet citizen and a traitor.

The Foreign Office engaged in a prolonged internal debate on Poppe's future, exploring ways to justify denying him to the Russians. Lambert tried to explain away the time Poppe had spent at the Wannsee Institute by arguing that 'Poppe was a scholar and specialist, no other trade was open to him.' Yet even he had to agree that it was a poor case. Brimelow went straight to the heart of the problem when he minuted: 'Are we not compelled to hand him over under the terms of the policy laid down by the Cabinet for the repatriation of the Soviet citizen?' This was also the view of the Foreign Office's legal adviser. Notwithstanding the lobbying by British academics, Lambert, too, conceded: 'If we refuse to hand Poppe over to the Russians, the latter may be expected to make considerable publicity out of the case on the grounds that we are sheltering a traitor to the Soviet Union and a war criminal. It is difficult to judge how embarrassing such propaganda would be, but there is no doubt that action on our part in this sense would not improve our relations with the Russians.'[49]

The decision-making process concerning Poppe reached to the topmost levels of the Foreign Office. Hankey saw that Poppe's version of his wartime activities was utterly threadbare. Given the indefensible nature of the case, 'Should we not be under very serious criticism, knowing what we know, if we set him up as a Professor at Cambridge or something.' But Christopher Warner wondered, 'Is there any way by which if he "disappeared" he could usefully carry on his specialized career?'[50] Why did these senior Foreign Office figures want to fight so hard for Poppe? What was it about his 'specialized career' that made him such a valuable asset that it was worth defying the USSR on what was an open-and-shut case under the Yalta Agreement on the repatriation of Soviet citizens, quislings, traitors and war criminals?

Poppe was vital not because he was an expert on Mongolia nor even for what he could tell the British about the USSR that he had already told the Germans. What made it impossible to give Poppe up to the Russians was what he could tell them about the extent of Western intelligence-gathering based on exploiting many other traitors and war criminals who ought to have been surrendered to the USSR. Major-General Shoosmith made this utterly clear when he told the Control Office in mid-December, 'It is feared that if he were returned to the Russians he would reveal under interrogation the names and possible locations of his former colleagues, which would result in further demands for extradition of people who are the subjects of an important investigation.'[51] Foreign Office officials and, no doubt, their political masters were fully aware of the real reasons for protecting Poppe, even at the cost of a diplomatic incident. Thomas Brimelow recorded a meeting with an intelligence officer, D. E. Evans, who told him that 'Poppe would be in a position to give the Russians valuable information about "Operation Applepie" which, as far as I can gather, is an attempt to collect all the information which the Germans had about the Soviet Union.'[52]

The problem remained of how eventually to dispose of Poppe once he was sucked dry by the intelligence services. Declassified US Army Counter-Intelligence Corps documents supply the answer. In the spring of 1947, the British approached the Intelligence Division of the US Army with a request. As Colonel Peter Rhodes explained to the Deputy Director of Intelligence at the headquarters of the European Command of the US Army at Frankfurt, Poppe was now living in the British Zone, under an assumed name:

> His presence in the British Zone is a source of embarrassment to British Military Government, as the Soviet authorities are continually asking for his return as a war criminal. The British feel that Mr Poppe is valuable as an intelligence source and have asked me if it is possible for US intelligence authorities to take him off their hands and see that he is sent to the US where he can be 'lost'.[53]

Once in the hands of US intelligence, Poppe acquired a new identity and was taken to America. His entry to that country in blatant disregard of stringent rules to exclude Nazi collaborators was secured by the active intervention of top US State Department officials, including George Kennan. For a while Poppe assisted the Office for Policy Coordination (OPC), the precursor of the CIA, before resuming an open, academic career. But his poisonous activities were not over yet. He played a small but nasty part in the anti-Communist witch-hunts con-

ducted by Senator Joe McCarthy in the 1950s. His testimony
to the Senate Internal Security Subcommittee played no small
part in driving the distinguished Sinologist Professor Owen
Lattimore out of the USA. Poppe eventually settled in Seattle,
where he still lives.[54]

The case of Nikolai Poppe is the case of an individual, but
under the authority of directives authorising covert action that
were issued by the National Security Council in 1948–50 whole
groups of East Europeans were saved from investigation and
justice for similar reasons. John Loftus, a former federal prosecutor in the unit devoted to tracking down suspected war
criminals in the US – the Office of Special Investigations of the
Criminal Division of the United States Justice Department –
has provided powerful evidence that in 1948 the OPC, under
the direction of Frank Wisner, established a network of former
collaborationists and transported to the USA the bulk of the
30th Waffen-SS Byelorussian Brigade. Christopher Simpson
has assembled evidence that Wisner, acting as the first chief of
CIA clandestine operations, and his colleagues in the State
Department were responsible for an even more widely ramified
system of recruiting CIA agents from amongst displaced East
Europeans, with no regard at all for the possibility – or knowledge – that they were war criminals.[55]

Wisner was a former member of the Office of Strategic Services (OSS), the American wartime intelligence agency created
from scratch by General William Donovan. At the end of the
war, he was involved in the covert enlistment of General Reinhard Gehlen in American counter-intelligence work. Gehlen
had headed the Wehrmacht's intelligence department responsible for Foreign Armies East and had assembled a mass of
information on the Red Army and the Soviet Union. As the
Third Reich disintegrated and the US Army streamed all over
southern Germany, Gehlen sent out emissaries to make contact
with US military intelligence. He then traded his treasure-
house of information for his own security and the integrity of
his entire wartime apparatus. After the OSS had been convinced that Gehlen could offer them a ready-made source of
intelligence about the USSR – and even networks of agents

behind Russian lines – Gehlen's outfit was simply transferred under the wing of the US Army.[56]

From 1947 onwards, Wisner was at the hub of a circle of American intelligence officers and diplomats who dealt with the Soviet Union. They included Allen Dulles, George Kennan, Charles Thayer and Charles Bohlen, who would emerge as the architects of America's cold-war policy. Kennan, Thayer and Bohlen had all served as young diplomats in Moscow before the war, where they had become close friends with a number of their German counterparts. Several of these men, notably Hans 'Johnny' von Herwarth, would later be responsible for the recruitment of East Europeans into the German armed forces or play a part in intelligence operations directed against the USSR. Aware of this, the Americans made every effort to track down their former colleagues and friends. Charles Thayer launched an initiative that led to the US Army locating Herwarth, who had played a leading part in organising the Osttruppen and Vlasov's 'Russian Army of Liberation'.[57]

In his memoirs, Thayer frankly confessed why he held such an interest in Herwarth: 'none of us had as yet any inkling of what had really happened on the Russian Front since June 22, 1941 . . . If we could find Johnny, there were a lot of questions he could answer, and from my experience before the war I was sure those answers would not only be reliable but expert.' Herwarth was as useful as Thayer hoped he would be and soon gave him a record of all his wartime work, including a memorandum on the Ukrainian Question in which he set out the story of the recruitment of dissident Ukrainians to fight against the USSR. Herwarth thus inducted the Americans into the realm of collaboration between the Nazis and East Europeans and planted the idea, which would prove so attractive to cold warriors, that the Soviet Union was a house of cards that could be toppled if the subject nationalities were aroused and turned against their Communist masters.[58]

Herwarth also introduced the OSS to other Germans, such as Gustav Hilger, a German Foreign Office official who had specialised in Russian affairs. Hilger was an expert on Russian collaboration; he had been one of the first German officials to explore the potential of the turncoat General Vlasov and was heavily involved in the political aspects of raising collaborationist units for the German cause. Hilger, and those like him who were taken into the service of the CIA, was to have a major influence on shaping America's cold-war foreign policy and covert operations against the USSR.[59]

Subversion was one of the tasks allotted to Wisner's section of the CIA and East European émigrés were to become an important tool in his armoury. Inspired by Herwarth's and Hilger's version of events inside Russia during the war, the CIA prepared to send East Europeans behind the Iron Curtain to link up with the alleged anti-Soviet partisan movements in the Ukraine and Byelorussia. Others were readied for the possibility of a third world war when they would function as a fifth column behind Russian lines and assist in displacing the Soviet administration. In pursuit of this policy, between 1947 and 1951, several groups of émigrés were parachuted into Albania, the Ukraine and Byelorussia.[60]

British military intelligence participated in these operations and utilised networks of émigré Ukrainians and Byelorussians on lines similar to those used in the case of the Baltic region. Stephan Bandera and Yaroslav Stetsko were the chief links between SIS and the Ukrainian émigré movement. Bandera had been a leading Ukrainian nationalist before the Second World War and had long been associated with British intelligence: Philby described Bandera's OUN/B faction as 'the darlings of the British'. Indeed, SIS continued to use OUN/B personnel after 1945, despite its intimate collaboration with the Nazis and its complicity in the massacres of Jews in the Ukraine in 1941.[61]

The British authorities did little to curb the activities of the formerly pro-Nazi OUN/B when it was using strong-arm tactics to establish its hegemony over the Ukrainian refugees, DPs and ex-servicemen in the British Zone of Germany.[62] By 1950, the influence of OUN/B extended to the Ukrainians in Great Britain. Although much of the material on the political activity of the Ukrainian émigrés is still withheld from public view, a sufficient amount has been released to indicate that even the

Foreign Office was alarmed at the rightward, neo-fascist trends that became evident in British Ukrainian circles. In 1949, Ukrainian EVWs felt bold enough to hold public meetings and pass resolutions in support of the aims of the anti-Soviet – and rabidly right-wing – émigré movement. Its leaders, such as Yaroslav Stetsko, who had accompanied the Nazis to Lvov in 1941 and had been at the head of the short-lived Ukrainian government, appeared to be able to travel to and from Britain with ease. Stetsko was well known to Foreign Office officials and in June 1949 felt confident enough to ask for a private meeting with Ernest Bevin.[63]

The Ukrainians in Great Britain would, therefore, have been fertile recruiting ground for the SIS. During 1951 at least three teams of British-trained Ukrainians were parachuted into the Western Ukraine; although it is not certain if these groups were furnished from the Ukrainians in Britain, it is not difficult to surmise that some of them, if not all, may indeed have come from this abundant, local source. These operations were mounted in full co-operation with the CIA and align exactly with independent American activity at the same time. Operating by analogy, it is hard not to see the Waffen-SS Ukrainian Division fulfilling the same function as the Waffen-SS Byelorussian Brigade, which Wisner imported into the USA. This may not have been the original motive for its preservation or transportation to the United Kingdom, but once it was *in situ* its presence must have been fortuitous for the men responsible for organising the contribution of SIS to the secret war against Russia. With the now fully authenticated American example in mind it may be thought that serendipity alone is an inadequate explanation.[64]

Despite the patchiness of the information that is available concerning the British secret services and the émigrés, it is almost certain that co-operation with Nazi collaborators was not confined to the operations in the Baltic or the Ukraine. John Loftus, formerly of the US Office of Special Investigations, has alleged that the SIS, inspired by Philby, also recruited Mikolai Abramtchik, a member of the collaborationist Byelorussian Central Council which was convened by the Nazis in

1943 as a device to legitimise the raising of more Byelorussian volunteer units. Abramtchik was discovered by the British in a DP camp, one island in the archipelago of collaborationists where most of his followers also lived; but Philby happily passed him on to Wisner, who was not to know that Abramtchik was, in fact, a double agent.[65]

Members of Vlasov's army also found their way into British service, even though they were traitors and prime cases for repatriation. In 1944, Major Len Manderstam, an officer in SOE, personally intervened to save forty men belonging to the Russian Army of Liberation (ROA) on the premiss of training them for operations behind the German lines. Manderstam was born in Riga in 1903 and was caught up in the Bolshevik Revolution as a youth. Having fought in the Red Army he changed sides, became violently anti-Communist and barely avoided the executioners' squad for plotting against the Bolsheviks while studying at Moscow University. He managed to escape from Russia with his family and settled in Latvia, before going to South Africa where he worked during the inter-war years. In 1939, he volunteered for military service with the British, travelled to England and found his way into SOE.

Early in 1944, Manderstam was made head of the Russian section of SOE, charged amongst other things with the task of persuading Russian troops in the German ranks to desert. Through this work he came across Russian officers and men from the ROA and it occurred to him that they would be perfect material for SOE. Manderstam organised a centre where they could be trained, but the Russians objected to this use of Soviet citizens captured in German uniform. There was a good deal of argument within SOE as to the propriety of going on with the scheme and several brusque exchanges with the Foreign Office, too. But Manderstam was appalled by the policy of forced repatriation and did all that he could to subvert its implementation. He found a good deal of support for his way of thinking amongst his SOE colleagues, not least from Major-General Colin Gubbins, who was at its head. SOE successfully deceived the Russians and, as Manderstam recollected many years later, 'Nothing gave me greater pleasure during the war than the disappearance of my forty Russian parachutists from the Kempton Park POW Camp.'[66] It is not clear what became of these men and others like them, but Gubbins was connected with all of the senior figures in SIS who were later involved in covert activities against the USSR such as the parachute drops into the Ukraine.

The Joint Intelligence Committee, the body responsible for co-ordinating intelligence activities, was certainly aware of Vlasovites who had reached Britain. Beryl Hughes recalls that in 1947 or 1948 the JIC approached the Home Office departments handling aliens and immigration affairs seeking 200 native Russian speakers as teachers for SIS operatives. It did not prove difficult to find candidates: the immigration officers simply went through the interviews with EVWs and called in those whose place and date of birth suggested that they would prove useful. In this way more than 100 Russians were located for the War Office, which ran the courses. No questions appear to have been asked about how these men got into the country or about their wartime activities.[67]

Beryl Hughes' information about the use of Vlasovites has been echoed in the case of Ukrainians by Rupert Allason MP, who told the House of Commons, during a debate on the War Crimes Bill in March 1990, that 'Quite a number of them [Ukrainians] came at the invitation of the British Government and of British intelligence.' According to Allason, who writes on the intelligence services under the *nom de plume* of Nigel West,

> They went up to RAF Crail, then the language centre operated by most of the services. RAF Crail has now been closed and its operations have been transferred to Bodmin. The Ukrainians went to Crail, and I have obtained evidence from people who served there and were taught Russian by people who openly boasted about the atrocities that they had committed against Jews in the Baltic countries during the war. Those boasts were known to British national service men going into the Intelligence Corps and they must have been known to the British Government in subsequent years.[68]

It is tempting to use a conspiracy theory to explain the

evidence that the DPs in British camps in Europe and those brought here under the EVW programmes provided a handy pool of anti-Soviet East European émigrés, just at the time when SIS was setting out on clandestine operations against the USSR. In the world of secrets where such covert activities take place, anything is possible and suspicion is fuelled by the bizarre restrictions on access to British material pertaining to 'national security'. Many of the files on 'sensitive' matters which are withheld at the PRO may actually contain trivial information; some might even prove that there was no collusion between the Government bodies responsible for the policy towards DPs, PoWs and EVWs and the intelligence agencies which exploited them.

However, the authenticated history of the OSS and the CIA offers a parallel for the British secret services and helps in the interpretation of the fragmentary evidence that is available. On this basis, it seems highly likely that intelligence considerations played some part in the decisions to shield East Europeans from repatriation. Although the cold war played no part in the instigation of the EVW schemes, there is little doubt that they provided a conduit through which valuable intelligence assets could be transported to Britain and resulted in the creation of émigré communities that were ripe for exploitation. In this sense it is very possible that SIS 'piggy-backed' on the handling of the East Europeans without ever interfering directly in the matter.

Given the number of exchanges beween senior civil servants in the Foreign Office and officers in the intelligence divisions of the Control Office in Germany and London, the War Office and the intelligence services, it is hard to believe that they did not know what was happening. If the permanent under secretaries in the Foreign Office were aware of the use to which PoWs, DPs and EVWs were being put, it is equally incredible that their political masters were unaware. Since Attlee, Bevin, Dalton and other Cabinet ministers were party to the evolution of British policy towards Russia, this information would not have seemed unacceptable or outlandish to them. British attitudes towards East Europeans were formed within the context of the cold war: the pursuit and prosecution of war criminals, the disdain for collaboration and the revulsion felt for the Waffen-SS were all tempered by a pragmatic sense that war criminals, collaborators and ex-SS men could prove useful in the new struggle to ensure British security. In any case, as the horrors of the war years receded and new concerns pressed in on popular consciousness, complacency made conspiracy redundant.

Justice Delayed

When Rebecca West arrived in Nuremberg in 1946 to cover the trial of the major war criminals, she described it as 'the citadel of boredom'. The urge for retribution was muted by the sheer tedium of the proceedings and the questionable legitimacy of the trials, not to mention an uneasy sense in some quarters that perhaps the wrong people were in the dock. In England the shortage of newsprint meant that it was not even possible for those who were interested to follow the trials properly. Once they were over, although lesser trials continued for years, a great silence fell over the darkest chapters of the war. Few books were published in English that could inform people of what had happened to the Jews, least of all the fate of the great Jewish centres in Eastern Europe. Only a handful, mainly journalistic, ventured to tell the story and these were based largely on the testimonies and documents produced for the Nuremberg Tribunal: the voice of the survivors was not heard.[1]

It was against this background of war-weariness and ignorance that the British authorities handled accusations concerning alleged war criminals in the United Kingdom. Later on, natural scepticism that war criminals might be found in Britain was buttressed by a complacency that stemmed from incomplete knowledge of what had happened during the war. It may be a paradox which defies easy understanding, but in the 1990s awareness of the Holocaust is deeper and more pervasive than was the case immediately after it ended. The notion that the free world reeled before the revelations of what had occurred under the Nazis is a myth. 'The Holocaust' was not an issue: in fact, it did not even exist as a historical or cultural concept.[2]

Misconceptions about the fate of the Jews stemmed from the manner in which the Final Solution was camouflaged by the Nazis and the way it ended. The main killing centres, Belzec, Treblinka and Sobibor, were in the east, tucked away amidst the forest and marsh land of Poland. They had actually ceased operating in the autumn of 1943 and the SS had gone to great lengths to cover up the traces, planting trees over the sites of the camps and setting up farms where the barracks had once stood – as if they had never existed. Auschwitz–Birkenau remained a subject of confusion to the Allies until 1944 since it was an agglomeration of concentration camps, barrack-cities housing forced labourers and industrial zones with an extermination centre in its midst. When the Red Army overran Auschwitz–Birkenau, as had happened when Majdanek was liberated, the Soviets did not allow Western journalists more than perfunctory access to the site. Because the Russians occupied all the main extermination centres, they remained virtually unknown to the West, unvisited and unrecorded.[3]

The camps which the Allies liberated in the west – Bergen–Belsen, Dachau, Buchenwald and Mauthausen – were primarily concentration and labour camps. The horrific conditions in them were due to catastrophic overcrowding and the collapse of all amenities in the last six months of the war. Hunger and illness decimated the camp populations, which had been bloated by the influx of survivors of the forced marches from camps further to the east that were evacuated as Russian forces approached. The thousands of corpses which staggered the GIs and British soldiers who arrived at these places were as much due to the ravages of disease and sheer neglect as to deliberate brutality or the murderous intentions of the camp overlords. Not only did the camps thus give a false impression of the *modus operandi* of Nazi genocide: they gave a distorted impression of who constituted its victims. Jews formed only a proportion of the inmates in these camps: in Buchenwald, there were just 8,000 Jews out of a total of 81,450 prisoners. Consequently, press reports of the liberation of Buchenwald hardly mentioned

Jews at all, while in the case of Belsen the preponderance of Jews was played down for other reasons.[4]

For the West, the liberation of the camps became an emblem for the end of the war – a symbol that was charged with ideological significance. As it was portrayed in the newspapers and the newsreels, the Allied victory had ended the genocidal policy against the Jews and those designated as 'sub-human' by the Nazis. Right had triumphed over an evil that was now fully exposed: 'liberation' provided a perfect *ex post facto* validation of the oft-proclaimed reasons for fighting the war.[5] In fact, Himmler had ordered the end of the Final Solution in October 1944 and by the closing stages of the war he was bargaining with the Red Cross, for his own advantage, to save Jewish lives. The Allied armies had rescued thousands of Jews from death by intentional neglect, as well as widespread random violence, but not from the mass destruction typical of the years 1942 and 1943. Indeed, details about the systematic slaughter visited on the Jews in the east remained vague; the role of Germany's Eastern allies, satellites and puppets was shrouded in mystery; the activity of collaborators in the Baltic, eastern Poland and Soviet Russia was almost completely unknown. Since the Russians had no desire to publicise the extent of collaboration between Soviet citizens and the Nazis, it would remain so for decades. People in the West could feel justifiably proud of what they had accomplished, but they had only half the story.[6]

Even then, the liberation of the camps had less impact than is commonly thought to be the case by generations born since 1945. After Majdanek had been overrun, the Russians released horrific photographs of the gas chambers and crematoria which fell into their hands almost intact. The British press treated the reports and the photographs with diffidence: the *Illustrated London News* actually apologised to its readers for bringing the ghastly business to their attention at all. *The Times* complained that the Majdanek newsreel was too shocking for public consumption and should not be screened. After Bergen–Belsen was opened to the press, the *Illustrated London News* printed the photographic record in a detachable supplement, 'for our adult readers only'. Rather than mustering the courage to face the truth, large sections of Fleet Street capitulated to squeamishness and avoided it altogether or treated the massacre of the Jews in the same way as a titillating court-room scandal, like pornography.[7]

The plight of the Jewish survivors did elicit a visceral outpouring of concern, but only for a brief period. By the autumn of 1945 Jewish DPs were being perceived as a 'problem' and a source of irritation by British commanders in Germany. Jews who had no homes to go to and no country to which they wished to be repatriated cluttered up the DP centres and presented intractable difficulties, the most serious being their almost unanimous desire to go to Palestine. It had been British policy since 1939 to restrict Jewish immigration into Palestine pending a settlement of the Palestine question. As tension between Jews and Arabs in Palestine mounted and pressure for a resolution of the claims of both sides increased, the clamour of the Jewish DPs added to the Government's dilemmas. In the interim, the authorities in Germany denied separate status to the Jews lest they appeared to endorse the notion that the Jews were a distinct national group and so add weight to Zionist demands.[8]

Initially the Americans had taken the same line, but it ran against the grain of sympathy for the survivors of Nazi bestiality and set off a wave of indignation at home: the US Army was ordered to change its policy to take account of the special situation of the Jews. But British military officials still refused to treat them as a separate category: German Jews were housed with German refugees, Jews from the Baltic states with Lithuanian and Latvian DPs. Not content with placing Jewish survivors in centres where they were cheek by jowl with people who a few weeks before had been trying to murder them (and who did not bother to conceal their unceasing hatred of Jews), the British military authorities insisted on using former concentration camps as DP facilities. As a result, Jews streamed out of the British Zone and into the American Zone where, by 1946, 90 per cent of the Jewish survivors were to be found.[9]

Intolerance towards Jewish DPs spread to the British public, whose attitude towards the Jews was framed by the intensifying conflict in Palestine. The Zionist movement believed that the electoral victory of the Labour Party – which had declared its support for the creation of a Jewish state at its 1944 annual conference – would result in a decisive shift in its favour. However, it was soon apparent that Jewish demands for immediate mass immigration into Palestine would not be met. In Palestine, frustration at the plight of Jewish survivors in DP camps prompted a surge of anti-British violence. In October the various Jewish underground fighting groups, the Haganah, the Irgun and Lehi, combined to mount a series of punishing attacks on British targets. Although the Army poured in reinforcements the situation continued to deteriorate: Jews were killed and injured in the course of rioting in Tel Aviv in November, while in December there were fierce gun battles between the Jewish underground army and British forces.[10]

British discomfort was made worse by the attitude of the United States. For his own domestic reasons President Truman publicly exuded sympathy with Zionist aims. In July 1945, he sent a mission to Europe to report on the problem of the Jewish DPs and as a result of its findings the administration increased its pressure on the British authorities to permit the immediate immigration of 100,000 Jewish DPs into Palestine. These demands gained weight from the poignant reports of conditions in the DP camps and the impatience of the Jews which manifested itself in anti-British riots. The report of the Anglo-American Commission of Inquiry which investigated the problem in the first months of 1946 finally called for the entry of the 100,000 DPs into Palestine.[11]

In America the British were the objects of vilification: during 1946 right-wing Zionists took full-page advertisements comparing the British in Palestine with the Nazis, sentiments which were echoed in less extreme form throughout the American press. In Palestine the cycle of terror and counter-terrorism worsened. On one day in April, Lehi killed six British paratroopers in cold blood, provoking anti-Jewish rioting by their comrades in several Jewish towns. In June, Irgun gunmen kidnapped five British officers from the officers' club in Tel Aviv; two weeks later, a bomb planted by the Irgun shattered

Kovno, Lithuania, soon after the German occupation.
Jews are killed in the streets by local police,
militia and civilians while Wehrmacht troops stand by.
(Wiener Library)

Lvov, Ukraine, in July 1942. Ukrainians beat Jews
to death following the arrival of the German Army and Ukrainian
military units which proclaimed an 'independent' Ukraine.
(YIVO, New York)

Lithuanian 'Selbstschutz', or self-defence force,
marching away a column of Jewish women in 1941.

Ponary, near Vilna in Lithuania, the killing site where 100,000
Jews were murdered by the Einsatzkommando and local militia,
police and 'Selbstschutz'. These corpses were unearthed in 1944
after the liberation of Vilna. (*Documents Accuse*, Ginteras, Vilna)

Volunteers in the Latvian
'Selbstschutz' on their
way for training to form
a police battalion
in August 1941. (Dauvagis Vanagi)

Two youthful guards
at Belzec death camp
in 1942. Identified in
their native Ukraine
years later, they were
tried in Lvov in 1965 and
executed. (Courtesy of M. Tregenza)

'Askaris' – the Nazi slang for native troops –
during the destruction of the Warsaw Ghetto, April 1943.
Several hundred men from Ukrainian and Baltic police
and guard units were employed in the operation.
(The Stroop Report)

Young Latvian volunteers in a Waffen-SS grenadier regiment
resting behind the Front Line, 1943 or 1944. (Dauvagis Vanagi)

Latvians at the NCO training school for SS men,
Arnheim, Germany, 1943. (Stober, *Die lettischen Divisionen*)

Latvian Waffen-SS volunteers captured by
British troops in June, 1945. (Imperial War Museum)

Colonel Arvids Kripens who evaded Soviet officials seeking his arrest for war crimes in 1946 by attempting suicide while held in a British POW camp in Belgium.

Screening a DP at a refugee centre in Belgium.
(UNRRA photograph)

Archbishop Ivan Buchko meeting soldiers of the 14th Waffen-SS
Galician Division at the British POW camp near Rimini, 1946 or
1947. He successfully lobbied the British Government to prevent
the unit being repatriated to the USSR. (Shandruk, *Arms of Valor*)

The Ukrainian Church in the POW camp, Rimini, 1946–7.
(Shandruk, *Arms of Valor*)

Front page of the
Leicester Mercury,
11 November 1960,
following the exposure
of the Estonian
collaborator
Ain Erwin Mere.

As Minister of Labour in the collaborationist Latvian régime,
Paulis Reinhards helped recruit volunteers for the Latvian Waffen-
SS. He later settled in Britain and died in Gravesend in 1990.
(Searchlight)

the King David Hotel which housed the British Army headquarters in Jerusalem, with a terrible loss of life. British
reprisals were harsh: much of the Jewish population endured
collective punishments such as curfews, while over 1,000
'illegal' immigrants were deported from Haifa to Cyprus.[12]

The violence in Palestine spilled over on to the streets of
British cities. Following the reprisal flogging of a British officer
and three sergeants in Palestine, two synagogues in London
were vandalised. Matters were not helped by the *Daily Herald*
and *Sunday Pictorial*, which carried scare stories about Jewish
terrorists infiltrating Britain and planting bombs in Whitehall.
In January 1947 a *Sunday Times* editorial went so far as to
challenge British Jews to denounce terrorism in Palestine.[13]
Although the Government announced in March 1947 that Britain was pulling out of Palestine, the friction between Jews
and the occupation forces continued without let-up. British
repression, which included the hanging of Jewish terrorists, and
the policy of turning away illegal immigrants inflamed Jewish
feeling there and abroad.

This vicious dyad reached its climax in July–August 1947.
In July the *President Warfield* – soon to become world-famous as
the *Exodus-1947* – was chartered by the Haganah to take 'illegal'
immigrants into Palestine. The boat was intercepted by the
British Navy, boarded and taken into Haifa harbour where, in
full view of the press and film cameras, the 4,500 passengers
were forcibly removed and placed on a ship which eventually
took them to Hamburg. There, before an amazed world public,
the Jews were disembarked into the country that they loathed
most of all. It was a public relations disaster for the British
Government.[14]

Meanwhile, another violent and terrible drama unfolded.
On 30 July, two British sergeants were hung by the Irgun in
retaliation for the hanging of three of their men. A huge photograph of the atrocity was printed on the front page of the *Daily
Express* on 1 August and every British newspaper gave the story
massive coverage, infused with rage at the behaviour of the
Palestinian Jews. In Palestine, British soldiers went on the
rampage and killed five Jews; in Britain, the following days

saw the most widespread anti-Jewish rioting in modern British history. On the August Bank Holiday weekend, mobs of youths shouting anti-semitic slogans raged through the Jewish districts of Liverpool, Manchester, Salford, Glasgow, East London and other towns. Jewish-owned shops and properties were destroyed, synagogues were vandalised and cemeteries desecrated: relations between Jews and Gentiles in Britain reached their nadir.[15]

In this way the Palestine imbroglio cut directly across sympathy for the Jewish victims of Nazism. Anti-semitism, which had persisted throughout the war, surged to a new level of intensity. In May 1945, a group of Conservative MPs started badgering the Home Secretary to say when the Jewish refugees who had fled to Britain on the eve of the war would be repatriated. These calls to rid the country of German Jews were echoed in the press; in the London borough of Hampstead, anti-alien feeling culminated in a petition blaming refugees for the housing shortage.[16] When Polish Jews fled westward after pogroms in Cracow and Kielce in 1946, the military authorities in the British Zone of Germany did their best to exclude them. Ignoring the terror that the pogroms had naturally created amongst the remnant of Polish Jewry, the senior British officer in charge of UNRRA, Lieutenant-General Sir Frederick Morgan, declared that the exodus was 'nothing short of a skilful campaign of anti-British aggression on the part of Zion aided and abetted by Russia' to embarrass the British over their Palestine policy.[17]

Several speakers at the annual Conservative Party Conference in 1947, aroused by the events in Palestine, hardly bothered to conceal their hostility towards the Jews. During the following year measures were introduced into both Houses of Parliament to ban the slaughter of animals according to Jewish religious law. The insidious rumours that associated Jews with the black market were given fresh impetus by the 1948 Lynskey Tribunal, before which two Jews were accused of corrupt dealings with a Minister of State.[18]

This upsurge of anti-Jewish feeling so soon after the war, and the exposure of where racism had led, shocked British Jewry.

But the war had not been fought for the Jews: it had been an anti-fascist war and once fascism was defeated, as the newsreels made clear, the job was done. No explicit connection was made with racism or anti-semitism at home. Indeed, popular anti-semitism was still rife in Britain and local fascism was making a come-back. In November 1946, the veterans of the British Union of Fascists, many of them former wartime internees, gathered in East London to revive the movement; by February 1948 Oswald Mosley was back and there was violence on the streets of East London again. The reports of Jewish terrorism in Palestine created a mood which the fascists were easily able to manipulate.[19]

The International Military Tribunal at Nuremberg, which sat from November 1945 to September 1946, and the subsequent trials of other war criminals had only a limited impact on this atavistic tendency: in fact, they were something of a non-event at the time. Contemporary commentators as diverse as Rebecca West and Peter Calvocoressi repeatedly remarked just how long drawn out the process was. West called it 'boredom on a huge historic scale . . . Every person within its walk was in the grip of extreme tedium.' All those involved were fed up with war and its effects and just wanted to get on with the new exciting business of enjoying the world at peace. In December 1945, when *Reynolds News* polled 150 of its readers on their reactions to the trial, 72 replied that they were 'not interested'. Even Norman Birkett, the distinguished High Court judge who was appointed as the alternate British member of the Tribunal, was not immune to the stale atmosphere. By May 1946 he was complaining in his letters home that 'life is slipping away': it was a 'shocking waste of time'.[20]

The emotional and intellectual impact of the evidence was subject to the law of diminishing returns. Calvocoressi noticed that the numbers of people killed by the Einsatzgruppen were so high that they were meaningless. When SS General Ohlendorff admitted to responsibility for the deaths of 90,000 people, 'there were many who found it impossible to grasp or believe this statement'. One of the American prosecutors, Colonel Telford Taylor, was so aware of the obstacle to credulity that he addressed it in his closing speech against the military echelon: 'Crime has been piled upon crime in this case until we are in danger of losing our sense of proportion. We have heard so much of mass extermination that we are likely to forget that simple murder is a capital offence.'[21]

Public reaction in Britain was lessened still further by circumstantial events. During 1946 the Government imposed newsprint rationing on the newspaper publishing industry in an attempt to curb imports of raw materials. Calvocoressi considered that:

> It was a calamity that reports of the Nuremberg proceedings were restricted in England (as elsewhere) by the lack of newsprint. At the conclusion of the trial a spate of letters to the press showed that those who had taken an interest in the trial had been deprived of the opportunity of forming sensible views about it. Almost the whole of the evidence remained unrevealed to a very great proportion of the readers of newspapers.

Rebecca West likewise attributed popular dissatisfaction with the trials to the inadequate coverage: 'the public, which had read the war correspondents' stories but not the transcripts of the trials (because the newspapers had no space to print them) shrieked that the sentences were too lenient and the judges pro-Nazi'.[22]

The more common response was negative: that the trials were unjust and the penalties too harsh. 'As soon as the sentences and verdicts of the Tribunal had been announced,' wrote Calvocoressi in 1947, 'voices were heard in England urging a reprieve for the condemned, among them being some of note and authority.' He attributed this to the blunting of consciousness by the sheer scale of the crimes and the intervening physical and chronological distance: the British public was more excited by a salacious murder case at home than by the evidence against Ernst Kaltenbrunner, chief of the SS head office from 1942, or Fritz Sauckel, the Labour Minister who presided over the deportation and exploitation of millions of foreign workers. There was also a feeling of unease amongst the population and opinion leaders after accounts of the horrors wrought at Hiroshima and Nagasaki reached the West: 'Developing a guilty conscience, they began to feel that in the face of this wrong it had been unjust to punish the German leaders for their misdeeds.'[23]

The backlash against the trial of Nazi war criminals began the moment the Tribunal ended its work at Nuremberg, even though there were still dozens of major figures from the German military, diplomatic corps, industry and the SS awaiting the due process of law in other courts. Sir John Wheeler-Bennett, the distinguished historian, was one of those called in to assist in the prosecution of the German generals in 1948–9. He recalled that by this time, 'The British people were bored to death with war crimes trials and there was ironically enough a general sympathy for von Manstein . . . '[24] This recoil had many sources in addition to the 'itching abscesses of ignorance and hatred' which Rebecca West ascribed to deficient reporting.

One of the most comprehensive and Olympian presentations of the misgivings aroused by war crimes trials was delivered by Lord Hankey in his 1950 book, *Politics, Trials and Errors*. Maurice Hankey was an eminent former civil servant who was part of the furniture of the British Establishment: he had been Secretary to the Committee of Imperial Defence from 1912 to 1938 and had served for a time in Churchill's War Cabinet as Minister without Portfolio. In between sundry post-war activities, Hankey took the time to fire off several broadsides against the Nuremberg Tribunal, the parallel trials in Tokyo and the subsequent prosecution of German generals and diplomats.

Hankey argued that the very notion of war crimes was tainted, since it was conceived in the embittered atmosphere of wartime. The trials were unfair since they represented 'victors' justice': their legal basis was dubious since the defendants were being tried for categories of crimes that were new and which had been created *ad hoc* and *ex post facto*. Particular charges such as waging a war of 'aggression' were vague and were equally applicable to the Allies – especially the Russians. He protested that the defendants were denied the right to a proper defence because they were forbidden to raise such awkward questions as the role of Britain and France in 'permitting' the war, their descent on Norway in 1940 or Russia's unprovoked aggression against Poland in 1939, Finland and the Baltic states in 1940.

Above all, Lord Hankey saw no advantages to be gained by war crimes trials and set out to undermine the claims made for the Tribunal by its advocates. Trials would not hinder future wars and would do little to strengthen the writ of the United Nations since the manner in which they were being conducted actually compromised its authority. Nothing would be achieved in terms of rehabilitating Germany: Germans would still worship Hitler if they wanted to and would blame his lieutenants both for the wrongs of the Third Reich and for its ultimate collapse. Rather than returning the country to the fold of Western European nations, the trials threatened to alienate the German population. In his eyes an important potential ally against the Soviet Union was being slapped in the face unnecessarily.

In the midst of his argument, Hankey used a curious and revealing analogy to attack the idea that war crimes trials against Nazis would help to uproot the evil they espoused. 'That again is doubtful. To take this point: how many autocrats before Hitler, and how many religious fanatics, and how many countries have tried to uproot the Jews? Even in England in the year AD 1290 King Edward I decided to drive them out of the island; they did not return until the Stuart and Hanoverian era. Yet they flourish more than ever.' This was the only mention of Jews in the course of his 145-page case against trying war criminals. Rather than dwell on the atrocities which they had committed against the Jewish people, he used the course of Jewish history as a parallel for the resilience of fascist and Nazi ideas.[25]

This deeply ambivalent attitude towards Jews, which pervaded sections of the British civil service and much of the political nation at large, was a nebulous yet all-powerful barrier to detecting or screening-out Nazi war criminals, their agents and allies. It combined readily with anti-Communism and the accusation that the trials were invalidated because the Russians were allowed to get off totally free. The writer Montgomery Belgion in his *Epitaph on Nuremberg* (a work warmly commended to readers by Lord Hankey) saw a conspiracy at work behind the Nuremberg Tribunal. He complained that the press had chosen to stir up public feeling about Belsen and Buchenwald only when the camps were liberated and when trials would be likely to start. But they wrote nothing about the massacre at Katyn or the camps run by Stalin's NKVD. In this early example of revisionism, Belgion also argued that the killing of resistance fighters and commandos was justified by their 'stab in the back' activities, while the RAF's carpet bombing of German cities was a crime in its own right. According to Belgion, 'The Nuremberg Trial was a gigantic "put up show" . . . a gigantic piece of propaganda . . . '.[26]

These were not isolated or eccentric views. Both Houses of Parliament saw major debates in which opponents of war crimes trials put the case against their continuation. Finally, in 1948, the Government agreed to suspend further legal action. Richard Stokes, the right-wing Labour MP, took a leading part in the opposition in the House of Commons against war crimes trials. Stokes was a curious figure. In the late 1930s he had been a member of the pro-German Right Club which was run by Captain Archibald H. Maule Ramsay, who declared its aims to be 'to oppose and expose the activities of Organised Jewry'. Stokes was also active in the equally anti-semitic Militant Christian Patriots. In 1940 he had called for a negotiated peace with Germany and campaigned for the release of Sir Oswald Mosley and other fascist detainees (including Captain Ramsay!) during the war. In 1945–7 he made several interventions in Parliament and with the Foreign Office on behalf of the Baltic Waffen-SS and Yugoslav collaborators.[27]

Stokes led the attack in an adjournment debate on 4 December 1947 which originated out of concern for the fate of anti-Tito Yugoslavs who were threatened with repatriation. In the course of the debate, Stokes threw cold water on the business of finding and trying any war criminals. He was upbraided about this by Eric Fletcher, the MP for Islington East, who 'gathered from what he [Stokes] said that he did not regard the Nuremberg trials as being fair trials of war criminals. He was objecting to any war criminals being sent back to some countries, but I am not sure what he would do with them.' To this Stokes replied, 'I find the greatest difficulty in deciding who is a war criminal. For example, is the man who lets off an atomic bomb a war criminal, or not? That may be a great crime against humanity.'[28]

The pressure to abandon trials grew steadily. During a debate in the House of Lords in May 1948, the Lord Chancellor, Lord Jowitt, hinted that the Government was considering their abandonment. He told the peers: 'I think that the indefinite prolongation of the trials . . . is no longer performing a useful or a desirable purpose.'[29] Although Ernest Bevin assured the House of Commons in June 1948 that the Government intended to press on with war crimes trials, by July Christopher Mayhew was sounding a different note. He announced that the Government now felt that it had met its obligation to examine and hand over Yugoslav suspects: 'It is now more than three years since the end of the war, and it is clearly not possible for us to continue this process of search and surrender for an indefinite period of time.'[30] The amnesty for the Yugoslavs was to set a precedent.

Stokes meanwhile returned to the offensive in July and October 1948, moving from anxiety about Yugoslavs to outrage at the treatment of some of the most senior German military figures, Field Marshals von Manstein, von Rundstedt, von Brauchitsch and Colonel-General Strauss, who were still awaiting trial. In this last matter, Stokes was not alone; the young Labour MP Michael Foot was amongst other parliamentarians who protested about the handling of the generals' case. In his response, the Under Secretary of State for War, Michael Stewart, confessed to the House, 'I am well aware of the disquiet which is felt by many people in the country and which has been voiced by many hon. Members tonight.' However, he defended the decision to persist with judicial proceedings.[31]

The generals' case became a *cause célèbre* for opponents of war crimes trials and occasioned many of the arguments against such trials which were to be repeated decades later. The accused were held to be old men in poor health – in 1948, Rundstedt was seventy-three, Manstein sixty-one and Strauss sixty-nine years old. Moreover, their alleged crimes, which had occurred over three years before, were deemed to be too distant in time to permit a fair trial. They had only been obeying orders and had, if anything, disliked the regime they served. General Sir George Jeffreys MP described them as 'elderly and distinguished officers who fought against us according to their lights as honourable opponents, and who we now know as an absolute fact were politically opposed to the regime in many ways and some suffered as a result'.[32]

In fact, these generals had loyally served Hitler to the end; Rundstedt had actually masterminded the Ardennes Offensive in December 1944. Manstein had distributed the 'criminal orders' on the eve of 'Operation Barbarossa' which exempted his troops from any disciplinary measures if they shot captured commissars or 'Jewish–Bolsheviks' and later justified 'the necessity of severe retribution against Judaism' with the excuse that Jews were supporting the partisans. They all accepted the other 'criminal order' which sanctioned the execution of captured British commandos.[33]

Nevertheless, opinion at the time was running strongly against trials and it gained force when Winston Churchill added his voice to the defence of the 'aged German generals' and even contributed to the Manstein defence fund. Speaking during the debate on the King's Speech in October 1948, Churchill accepted that there could be no end to the search for those guilty in certain exceptional cases, such as the Waffen-SS massacre of captured British troops in 1940 near Dunkirk, but he asserted, 'The time has come to stop these denazification trials.' He was not deflected from his speech when the Jewish Labour MP Sydney Silverman interjected, rather rudely, that the Manstein case was no different from the other one. On the contrary, in his closing peroration Churchill declared, 'Revenge is, of all satisfactions, the most costly and long drawn out; retributive persecution is, of all policies, the most pernicious.' This passionate appeal to end war crimes trials was the climax of a successful campaign. That day, Herbert Morrison, the Lord President of the Council, announced that as from 1 September 1948, Britain would not hold any further trials.[34]

Seven months later, the Foreign Office Minister in the Lords, Lord Henderson, made a definitive statement of the new Government's new war crimes policy: there would be no new trials; the Germans would be handed the responsibility for any further cases that came to light; extradition demands would be treated with great reluctance and only assented to in exceptional cases; otherwise, requests for the extradition of 'traitors and collaborators' from areas under British control would no longer be entertained.[35] From this point onwards, it was established policy to treat accusations against alleged war criminals in the United Kingdom with extreme reserve and to take a negative attitude towards the question of extradition.

Henderson's statement was occasioned by a debate in the Lords on 5 May 1949 which was part of the public campaign to free Manstein, the sole general in custody awaiting trial after Rundstedt and Strauss had been released on grounds of ill-health. His case was raised again by the Bishop of Chichester, supported by Viscount Simon and Lord Hankey and echoed in the Lower House ten days later. Members of Parliament stressed that too much time had been allowed to pass, and the conditions were now quite different to those which had obtained when Manstein had been arrested. One MP, Mr Skeffington-Lodge, asked Emanuel Shinwell, the Secretary of State for War, whether he did not realise that 'large sections of public opinion condemn the cat-and-mouse policy which has been followed in this and other cases, and owing to the long delay in bringing this man to trial, will not my hon. Friend look at it again and decide to call it off? It would be a good gesture, which would help our future relations with the Germans.' This was a point made by other MPs: at a time when it was important to help Germany recover and normalise, such a trial would do no good.[36]

The cold war was now fully under way and perceptions of Germany had changed radically. In 1949, the West German Republic was founded and the first elections were held for the new West German parliament, the Bundestag; West Germany was characterised as an emerging democracy and a potential bulwark against Soviet aggression. At the end of 1950, America,

Britain and France agreed that West Germany should be allowed to rearm – although it was five years before this aim was realised. Bitter argument over rearmament raged inside Germany and abroad, where Jewish opinion, especially, was scandalised by the decision. Eventually, the re-establishment of a German army was facilitated by West Germany's membership of the European Coal and Steel Community in 1951 and its entry into the European Defence Community in 1952, which showed that the revived German military force would be penned within the associations of West European nations. The appointment of former Wehrmacht officers to the Bundeswehr, the West German Army, demonstrated graphically that the era of the Nuremberg Trials was long past.

Jews in Great Britain were muted as they beheld this metamorphosis. The *Jewish Chronicle* was resigned to the change in the public mood and recognised that the USSR had supplanted the Germans as public enemy number one. Nevertheless it criticised the efforts to forestall the trial of Manstein and the campaign for the release of convicted German war criminals which was steadily gaining momentum. After 1949 it routinely covered war crimes trials in Germany and never failed to scorn the light sentences passed against diplomats and generals who, in its eyes, were directly or indirectly responsible for the deaths of many thousands of Jews. But this concern was not emulated anywhere else in the British press.[37]

A silence descended over the history of the genocidal campaign against the Jews of Europe. During the late 1940s and throughout the 1950s barely more than a dozen books were published in English which tackled the fate of the Jews. Most of these did so on the basis of the Nuremberg Trial evidence which was dominated by German documents and reflected the perpetrators' point of view. They also duplicated the absence from the trials of specific attention to crimes against the Jews: the virtual destruction of European Jewry had, in fact, been subsumed under the 'crimes against humanity' alongside such outrages as Lidice and Oradour sur Glane and the brutal conduct of the German occupation regimes in general.

Peter Calvocoressi's 1947 account of the Nuremberg Tribunal

was one of the first in this genre and is a powerful echo of the case against the Nazi leadership. Yet only one of its chapters dealt with war crimes and crimes against humanity and, even then, a relatively slim portion was devoted to the fate of the Jews, albeit written and illustrated with great skill. The tone of the book was defensive: Calvocoressi was already writing against the tide. The first comprehensive history of the Holocaust was Gerald Reitlinger's *The Final Solution*, which appeared in 1953. By profession Reitlinger was an art critic, but his fine sensibility was so revolted by the vulgarity, corruption and wickedness of the Nazi hierarchs that he devoted several years to producing three important works on the Nazi period that remain in use today.

Although it was a pioneering work, Reitlinger's history attracted little attention. It was reviewed for the *Jewish Chronicle* by Max Beloff, who took the opportunity to ruminate on the lack of awareness about, or interest in, the examination of the Jews. Beloff remarked that although there was now irrefutable proof that millions of Jews had been systematically murdered, 'public opinion outside Jewry nowhere really accepts this fact; and nowhere takes account of its implications in framing policy, either in the West or behind the "Iron Curtain" '. He ascribed this absence of concern to the difficulty of grasping what had happened and the error made at Nuremberg of burying mass murder amongst 'political' crimes.[38]

One book published in the mid-1950s did make a tremendous impact. Lord Russell's *Scourge of the Swastika* became a bestseller and went through four English editions in the space of one year. Russell had been Deputy Judge Advocate General to the British Army in Germany from June 1946 to July 1947 and again from October 1948 to May 1951. In this capacity he had advised the Commander in Chief with respect to the war crimes trials in the British Zone of Occupation. In May 1951 he returned to London and rose to the office of Assistant Judge Advocate General. During this time he wrote his 'short history of Nazi war crimes', but when it was completed in 1954 the Lord Chancellor attempted to block publication on the grounds that authorship of such a book was 'incompatible with the holding of judicial office'. Russell defiantly resigned his post so that when the book appeared it was already a *cause de scandale*; it received mixed reviews, but had massive sales.

For generations of schoolchildren and adults in the late 1950s and early 1960s, the Holocaust meant two books: *The Diary of Anne Frank* (published in English in 1952) and *The Scourge of the Swastika*. Russell's account was hugely popular, but not necessarily for the right reasons. It won notoriety for the photographs of shrunken human heads found at Buchenwald and naked women being humiliated by camp guards; the text was interspersed with stories of sadism, perversity and even cannibalism. Reviewing the book for the *Observer*, Edward Crankshaw complained that 'the most serious problem of our age is exploited with a tastelessness and sensationalism normally associated with the worst kind of journalism. It is no answer to say that Lord Russell has limited himself to extracts from the published records: the same defence could be made by any hack serving up selected extracts from divorce or murder cases.'[39]

This was not what Russell had intended. In his Preface he wrote: 'This book is intended to provide the ordinary reader with a truthful and accurate account of many of these German war crimes.' He earnestly wanted to show that whereas there had been war crimes in past conflicts, between 1939 and 1945 they were not only committed on an unprecedented scale, but were integral to the Nazis' conception of war and conquest. However, the book was selective in its approach and was ultimately self-defeating. It concentrated heavily on atrocities against prisoners of war and Western European populations. The extermination centres at Chelmno and Treblinka were covered in less than two pages, while Belzec, Sobibor and Majdanek were not mentioned at all. Although his chronicle ended with a twenty-five-page description of the Final Solution, his fatigue and that which he expected of readers can be inferred from his own concluding comment, which began: 'This dreary catalogue of murders could be continued but it would always be the same old story.' Outrage, because it was so unremitting, gave way to exhaustion and numbness.[40]

This failing was all the more regrettable because *The Scourge of the Swastika* filled a vacuum. As the jacket notes asked rhetorically, 'How many in Britain realise that, of the 3,000,000 Jews living in Poland in September, 1939, not more than 50,000 could be traced in 1946 as a result of the German policy of mass extermination. How many know that 3,000,000 prisoners were killed at the Auschwitz Camp alone; that at one time, 10,000 people *a day* were put into its gas chambers. Since the war there have been many books by German officers defending the Nazi war machine. It is as well to read the other side of the story.' Incredible as it may seem, the Holocaust was, in a sense, further from public consciousness ten years after the war ended than it was forty years afterwards.

The extermination of the Jews certainly had little profile in the arts. The first novel of the Holocaust to make an impact in English was John Hersey's *The Wall*, which came out in 1950. It was virtually unique for many years until the translation of the stories about Auschwitz by the pseudonymous Ka-Tzetnik (Yehiel Dinur). There was little memoir literature available, either. Dr Filip Friedman, who was to emerge as a pioneering historian of the Holocaust, published *This Was Oswiecem* in 1946; but five years later Joseph Leftwich, a *Jewish Chronicle* reviewer, remarked that most personal testimonies were still in Yiddish. The appearance of *I Came Back* by the Christian Polish woman writer, Krystja Zywalika, was a comparatively rare phenomenon.[41] Eyewitness accounts by members of the British armed forces who had been involved in the liberation of the camps or the interrogation of leading Nazis, some of whom became major historians of the period, touched on the Final Solution, but only incidentally.[42]

In this unpropitious atmosphere it was relatively easy for the Government to downplay allegations against suspected war criminals in Britain and to block extradition demands. Nor was it an excessively arduous policy to follow: between 1945 and 1985, there were only seven requests for the extradition of alleged war criminals resident in the United Kingdom, two of which were made by the USSR, with which Britain had no extradition arrangements in any case.[43]

One of the earliest and most notorious cases was that of Wladyslaw Dering, a Pole who arrived in England with the Polish Army in 1946. Dering had qualified as a doctor in pre-war Poland and had been in practice as a gynaecologist when the Germans conquered Warsaw. By his own account he joined the Polish resistance, was arrested by the Gestapo in July 1940 and sent to Auschwitz. Inside the camp he hid the fact that he was a doctor, but he got a job as a male nurse and in 1941 was assigned work in the new prison hospital where he was soon performing surgery in the operating theatre. Before very long, he was assisting a German doctor named Clauberg to perform hideous experimental operations on Jewish inmates, part of Nazi biological investigations to determine whether it would be possible to keep Jews for work purposes but, by forced sterilisation, prevent them from having children. In January 1944 he was allowed to leave the camp and was sent to work in Clauberg's hospital in Silesia. When the Russians overran the hospital he was briefly detained, but after his release travelled to Warsaw where he obtained false papers from the underground with which he was able to flee the country. He reached Italy, enlisted in General Anders' Polish 2nd Corps and in August 1946 arrived in England as an Army doctor.[44]

Six months into his new life, Dering was taken into custody by the police as a result of war crimes allegations made against him by the Polish Government. It had not taken long for the post-war Polish authorities to place Dering on their list of wanted persons. His name had consequently been entered on the CROWCASS list which was shared by all the Allies. Even though he was suspected of 'torture' on a list in British hands, and was wanted by the Poles, the Czechs and the French, he was able to enter the country without any difficulty. Since many other Polish turncoats and Ukrainians and White Russian collaborators also joined the 'Anders Army' in 1944–5, his method of ingress may stand as a model for unknown numbers of other war criminals from Eastern Europe. However, Dering was identified, interrogated by the War Office as well as other departments and held in Brixton Prison pending the outcome of extradition proceedings.[45]

The interrogations and the submission of material from Poland took a long time, but this suited the Foreign Office. It was totally opposed to meeting the Polish demand, even though officials understood that there could be a propaganda backlash against Britain if they refused to hand over Dering. Their reasoning was that 'he would not get a fair trial' in his native country and it appears that they did everything they could to play for time. One Foreign Office official wrote to Ian Roy in the Aliens Department of the Home Office, 'We are being pressed very hard by the Polish Embassy and it is not easy for us to hold them off much longer.' The Home Office seems to have agreed that a trial or an extradition process was undesirable, but Dering was an embarrassment and it wanted to get rid of him: as far as Ian Roy was concerned, 'my own feeling is that to arrange his emigration perhaps to some South American country, may well prove to be the best solution'. The Northern Department of the Foreign Office concurred: 'The best solution would be to arrange for emigration abroad at the earliest possible moment . . . we should rather not have him here at all.'[46]

In the course of these discussions, no one at the Foreign Office seemed unduly concerned with the appalling character of the allegations against Dering: he was just the passive object of a diplomatic wrangle. Only Ernest Bevin appears to have considered the moral issues and commented on the internal debates, 'I must say that I am not very impressed with this – I feel that all our concern seems to me to be to protect these monsters.'[47] Nor was Lord Jowitt, the Lord Chancellor, much swayed by the Foreign Office apprehension of recognising the Polish legal system: in April 1948 he ruled that there was a *prima facie* case against Dering. At the end of the month, the Foreign Office finally announced that he would be extradited to face trial in Poland. However, Dering's counsel asked the Home Secretary, Chuter Ede, for more time to prepare a defence, while several MPs protested that Polish justice could not be trusted.[48]

As a result of these interventions, the deportation process was halted and the evidence was re-examined. The Home Office then detected a flaw in the case made by the Poles: the one eyewitness whom they had been able to bring to England (from France) to identify Dering had failed to pick him out in an identity parade. Chuter Ede cancelled the deportation order. The *Jewish Chronicle* was atonished by this reversal and at least one MP, Eric Fletcher, expressed consternation, but after more long-drawn-out legal wrangling, Dering was freed.[49] For a year and a half, he practised in a London hospital before going abroad to work for the British colonial administration in Somaliland. He stayed there for ten years and after returning to Britain received the OBE in recognition of his medical work in the colonial civil service. Dering settled down in Ealing and went back to the humdrum of general practice, in a surgery on Seven Sisters Road, Finsbury Park.

Dering did not escape judgment in the end. In his novel *Exodus*, published in 1959, Leon Uris referred to Dering, to the effect that he had willingly and callously performed thousands of brutal operations without anaesthetics on Jewish prisoners. In June 1962 Dering launched a libel case against Uris and the publishers of *Exodus* claiming that he had been grievously maligned. The case came to court in April 1964 and a succession of eyewitnesses recalled their awful experiences in the Auschwitz hospital. Dering 'won' since it could be shown that he had carried out under 200 operations, but the jury showed what it thought of his conduct by awarding him a halfpenny damages. It was a sensational result and received blanket coverage in the press.[50]

The Polish authorities were rebuffed a second time, in September 1948, following a request for the extradition of Helena Mateja, who was accused of betraying over '100 members of the Polish underground' to the Gestapo. According to the Polish Government, 'As a result of her activities the above mentioned were sent to concentration camps and executed.' There is no sign that these charges were investigated by the British Government; like the Dering case, raison d'état was allowed to override other considerations. The Foreign Office replied to the Poles that the extradition of Mateja 'cannot be permitted because of the political nature of the charges against her'. Citing a 1932 treaty covering extradition between Poland and Britain, FO officials claimed that the offence was not 'criminal' but was defined according to ideological criteria. When the Poles protested that 'conspiracy to murder' *was* covered by the treaty, the Home Office department responsible for extradition matters dismissed the case on the grounds of 'insufficient evidence'. There is no indication of any inquiries being made in this country, or any investigation of whether Mateja had entered Britain on false premisses.[51]

The next case concerned an Estonian by the name of Ain Erwin Mere, who had come to England in 1947, probably as an EVW. In 1960 he was living in Leicester, where he worked as a hosiery knitter. A member of the city's small Estonian community, he led a quiet life there until November 1960 when the people of Leicester were stunned to find Mere the subject of a war crimes investigation by the Soviet Union. Mere had been a major in the Estonian Army at the time of the Russian occupation in 1940 and had remained in the armed forces under Russian command until 1941 when he deserted to the Germans. After a brief period as a prisoner of war he was sent to Tallinn as an officer in the Estonian Selbstschutz, the anti-partisan self-defence corps. Then, because of his language skills, the Germans gave him the task of reorganising the Estonian police force.

While he was Chief of Police in the collaborationist Estonian regime, Mere had been in charge of all the locally recruited Hilfspolizei and Schutzmannschaften. He was responsible directly to the German Sicherheitsdienst and worked hand in glove with the SS, SD and Gestapo. According to his Russian accusers, he supervised the running of the Jagala prison camp, in which thousands of Jews and Communists were executed. It was also alleged that he had personally taken part in the mass murder of Jews at Kalevi-Liiva. This was one of the notorious killing sites at which the work was done that enabled Einsatzgruppe A to boast that at the end of 1941 Estonia was truly 'Judenrein' – free of Jews. In April 1943, like so many collaborators in police and militia units, Mere was assigned to the Estonian Legion. At the end of the war he was captured by the

British, but came to Britain in 1947 and married a fellow Estonian in Portsmouth before moving to Leicester in 1955.[52]

Interviewed by the *Leicester Mercury*, Mere did not dispute the allegation that he had been a police chief under the Nazis. He simply said that his job had been confined to 'pay, clothing, food and cigarettes' for the policemen and security forces under his auspices. It might be thought that his remarkable admission might have stirred feathers at the Home and Foreign Offices, but not a bit of it. Despite the fact that a freely confessed collaborationist police chief was in the country, no steps were taken to investigate the charges against Mere or to question how a man who had voluntarily aided the enemy had managed to take up residence in a sedate suburb of Leicester. Instead, in December 1950, the Government told the UN War Crimes Commission that, since the change of policy announced by Mayhew and Henderson in 1948, it no longer felt under any obligation to deport alleged war criminals. What was more, the Government pointed out that it did not recognise the legality of the incorporation of Estonia into the USSR, so there was no legal basis for proceeding.[53]

The Russians had tracked down Mere many years after the British had announced that they would not accept further extradition cases. But was it right to apply this rule to individuals who were undetected at the time of the ruling? Strict application of the 1948 decision would mean that East European murderers in England would be protected from facing justice just because they had been cunning and kept their heads down for long enough. Mere was eventually tried *in absentia* in Tallinn. Dozens of eyewitnesses testified to his activities in wartime Estonia and detailed evidence was provided exposing his role in the Jagala camp. In March 1961 he was sentenced to death, but this had little effect on his life in Leicester, which returned to normal. He died there in April 1969.

Not long afterwards, two other cases of alleged Baltic war criminals in Britain came to light as a result of investigations by the World Jewish Congress (WJC). Jewish organisations like the Association of Baltic Jews in Great Britain had long been helping in war crimes trials such as the Riga Ghetto case in Hamburg in 1951. They had sought evidence against mass killers like Victor Arajs amongst survivors in Germany and England; but they had never before looked for the murderers on their own doorsteps. Yet the WJC alleged that Veide Vittenbergs and Karlis Vittenbergs, two district chiefs in occupied Latvia, were now living in Britain. The story was reported in the *Jewish Chronicle* and the WJC attempted to create interest in the case, but it seems to have got no further.[54]

All the same, the tide was slowly turning. In 1957, 1958 and 1959 there were major trials in West Germany which showed that significant war criminals were still alive and free. Hermann Krumey, arrested in April 1957, had been a member of the Einsatzkommando responsible for the deportation of Hungarian Jewry in 1944; Erich Koch, arrested in October 1958, had been the Gauleiter of the Ukraine whose reign of terror was virtually unparalleled in the East. There were also well-publicised trials of East European collaborators, such as the Kovno trial in September 1962, which almost for the first time brought to light the role of native East Europeans in the Holocaust.[55]

All of these, however, paled by comparison with the capture and trial of Adolf Eichmann. This was the catalyst for an upheaval in perceptions of the Second World War and marked the beginning of a fundamental transformation of consciousness, the birth of 'The Holocaust'. The dramatic story of Eichmann's identification, apprehension and trial were reported extensively between May 1960 and June 1962. First of all, the British press was transfixed by admiration for the skill with which the Israeli secret service had conducted Eichmann's abduction and clandestine shipment to Israel. Then it was riveted for months on end by the trial and all that it revealed about the sheer scale of the Final Solution and the elaborate manner of its implementation. Finally, the death sentence triggered a controversy that was sustained from the pronouncement of the sentence in December 1961 to Eichmann's execution the following June.[56]

The Eichmann trial had profound cultural ramifications. Hannah Arendt, a brilliant German–Jewish intellectual who had emigrated to the USA before the war, covered the trial for the *New Yorker* and published her articles in book form as *Eichmann in Jerusalem: A Report on the Banality of Evil*. Her reflections on the trial and the story it appeared to tell caused an uproar within the Jewish world. To Arendt, the extermination of six million Jews would not have been possible without a mixture of stupidity, passivity and co-operation on the part of the victims themselves. She indicted the Jewish leadership in occupied Europe for playing into the hands of the Nazis by complying with their orders and forming intermediary councils to act as functionaries of the Final Solution, instead of calling on Jews to resist or flee. Many Holocaust survivors were appalled at these comments and set about putting the record straight, as they saw it.[57]

From the mid-1960s, a torrent of memoirs by survivors and studies by Jewish historians chronicled the Jewish resistance in the forests, the ghettos and the camps. The Yad Vashem Institute founded in Israel in 1954 to support the study of the Holocaust provided an institutional base and an impetus for this research. In 1968, an important conference on 'Jewish resistance' was held by Yad Vashem in Jerusalem and the volumes of studies by the Institute swelled in dimensions and numbers. The Eichmann controversy had actually been pre-empted by a more scholarly, but no less significant or more polite exchange of views, when Raul Hilberg had published his enormous three-volume history, *The Destruction of the European Jews* in 1961. This classic study had exerted a deep influence on the way in which Arendt had reported the trial, since it was based almost entirely on German records and ended with Hilberg's severe judgment on Jewish behaviour. If Hilberg galvanised the academic community, Arendt electrified the public: 'The Holocaust' was an issue at last.[58]

Throughout the 1960s, novels, poetry, plays and memoirs dealing with the Holocaust proliferated. André Schwartz-Bart's *The Last of the Just*, Elie Wiesel's autobiographical *Night* and Yevgeny Yevtushenko's poem *Babi Yar* all appeared in English translations in 1961; Leon Uris published *Exodus* in 1959 and followed it with *Mila 18* on the Warsaw Ghetto uprising. In 1963 Rolf Hochhuth, a German playwright, created a storm with *The Deputy*, a drama based on the researches of historians which indicated that the Vatican had ignored pleas to save the Jews. Finally, the survivors began to recount their stories, unmediated by lawyers, historians or professional writers: Kitty Hart's *I Am Alive* in 1961, Rudolf Vrba's *I Cannot Forgive* and Alexander Donat's *Holocaust Kingdom* in 1963. It was not by chance that in 1965 Elie Wiesel issued his famous call for silence on the subject of the Holocaust; but the momentum to which he had contributed carried on into the 1970s, with the definition of Holocaust Studies as an academic discipline and the founding of publishing houses devoted solely to bringing out material on the Final Solution.

Popular culture was soon touched by this explosion. As well as best-selling novels like those of Leon Uris which reached millions of people, the film industry in America and Europe began to explore – and exploit – the Holocaust as a subject. *The Diary of Anne Frank* was filmed in 1959, *Exodus* in 1960; the American director Stanley Kramer brought to the screen *Judgment at Nuremberg* (1961) and *The Ship of Fools* (1965), based on another Holocaust-related novel. Sidney Lumet's powerful 1964 film *The Pawnbroker* was one of the first to attempt a depiction of the Final Solution from the deportations to the death camps. By the 1970s, 'Holocaust films' were well on the way to becoming a genre. In Britain, television also tackled the subject, with a full and uninterrupted episode of the immensely popular 1975 series *World at War* starkly entitled 'Genocide'.

Television was to prove decisive in shaping the 'post-Holocaust' consciousness of a whole generation. The American mini-series *Holocaust*, directed by Gerald Green in 1978, might have been a soap opera, but just for that reason millions of people watched it who had never confronted the tragedy of the Jews even on a superficial level. Although the most far-reaching developments in academic studies and popular culture occurred in the USA, Israel and Germany, when the war crimes issue was raised again in Britain in the mid-1980s, the atmosphere was quite different. There was curiosity about the Final Solution, not to say fascination, where once there had been torpor and the desire to move on to something bright and cheerful;

people simply knew more about what had happened to the
Jews during the war, even if it was a bowdlerised and shallow
understanding; Auschwitz, for good or ill, had become a universal symbol of evil, a metaphor applied to nuclear catas-
trophe, famines and even ecological disasters. It would no
longer be possible to brush aside the suggestion that there were
alleged Nazi war criminals in Great Britain: public interest was
too intense, the story was too 'hot'.

The War Crimes Campaign in Britain, 1986–1989

As consciousness of the Holocaust burgeoned in the United States and Canada, public attention turned to the persistent allegations that there were large numbers of East European war criminals living in these countries. Powerful movements grew up demanding that government agencies should investigate such claims and, if they were proven, act against the suspects. By the mid-1980s, this concern had spread to Australia, too. Britain remained the only Anglo-Saxon country to absorb large numbers of East Europeans after the war that had not engaged in an exhaustive process of self-examination.

By this time, the Simon Wiesenthal Centre in Los Angeles had emerged as one of the most powerful engines driving the pursuit of alleged war criminals. Its team of researchers embarked on a deliberate policy of handing over to individual governments lists of suspects in their country and leaving it to local campaigners to force the authorities to do something. It was from the Centre in Los Angeles that the British Government received the most forceful stimulus to act; but the initial impulse did not come solely from outside Britain. Members of Parliament were expressing doubts about Britain's record on the prosecution of alleged war criminals before the dramatic missive from Los Angeles reached Mrs Thatcher, the then Prime Minister, in October 1986, claiming that seventeen alleged war criminals were living in Britain.[1]

The initiative of the Simon Wiesenthal Centre was the catalyst. British public opinion and the campaigning skills of several dedicated MPs were to be decisive in forcing the pace on the issue once it broke in the opening months of 1987. Yet the war crimes debate never lost an international flavour and time after time it burst the usually parochial boundaries of British political life. The campaign for the War Crimes Act constantly overlapped with foreign news stories and commingled with other major controversies: the Barbie case and the Waldheim affair in 1987–8; the storm over Prince Philip's presence at the funeral of Hirohito, the Japanese Emperor, in 1989; the revolutions in Central and Eastern Europe in November–December 1989, followed quickly by waves of nationalism and intolerance resonating with enmities that had been frozen under Communism for forty years; the anniversaries of Second World War events, such as Dunkirk, in 1990; the Iraqi invasion of Kuwait and the Gulf War during 1990–1. It spanned the careers of three Home Secretaries, as many Foreign Secretaries and two Prime Ministers, and survived despite Cabinet splits, personal feuds and a constitutional crisis which put the House of Commons on a collision course with the House of Lords. In short, the struggle for the War Crimes Act has been one of the most extraordinary chapters in recent British political history.

Rooted in the events of the 1940s, the war crimes issue nevertheless threw a discomfiting beam of light on British society in the 1990s. Campaigners ran up against the indifference of politicians and bureaucrats for whom crimes committed in Eastern Europe forty years ago were simply not on their narrowly focused agendas. They had to contend with the British culture of secrecy, prising files out of Government departments and the Public Records Office only after months of tiresome badgering. Reinforcing the glacis of apathy and official reticence was sheer prejudice: time and again the promoters of the War Crimes Bill were accused of motives that belonged to antisemitic myths about the Jews and had no bearing at all on the true well-springs of the campaign. The debate in Parliament and the press revealed deeply running and frightening currents of racism in British society; even when interpreted charitably these attitudes still reeked of the most abysmal provincialism and religious bigotry.

The first large-scale hunt for East European war criminals

in the post-war era began in the United States. It was spurred by a rash of sensational newspaper articles and books in the mid-1970s, culminating in Howard Blum's *Wanted! The Search for American Nazis* (published in 1977), which identified several notorious Nazi collaborators and revealed graphically how they had entered the USA. During 1977, two members of Congress, Elizabeth Holtzman and Joshua Eilberg, pressed for official hearings on the questions raised by these publications. Their efforts led to a series of Congressional hearings in 1977 and 1978 which provided enough evidence to persuade the Administration that action was necessary. Congress agreed to amend US immigration law to enable persons to be stripped of their US citizenship and deported if it was proven that before their arrival in America they had been collaborators or had participated in atrocities. A Special Litigation Unit of the Immigration and Naturalisation Service was established to investigate and act against suspects, although its early sallies were not encouraging. In 1980 it was renamed the Office of Special Investigations (OSI) and transferred to the Justice Department.[2]

Between 1980 and 1988, the OSI sent agents to Eastern Europe to collect evidence on alleged war criminals in the USA and built up files on suspects. Legal action was initiated against eighty persons; of these cases thirty-five resulted in denaturalisation, and thirty individuals were deported or extradited – the most famous being Karl Linnas, who was returned to face trial in Estonia in 1987. In 1988, the OSI had 600 open cases, with 25 before the courts. The controversial Ivan Demjanjuk case also came to light as a result of its work. Demjanjuk's extradition to Israel and subsequent trial prompted criticism of the OSI and its *modus operandi*, but its pioneering operation upheld the claims that hundreds of war criminals had entered the USA after 1945. And it demonstrated that there were legitimate, legally sound means to rectify this blunder. In a succession of countries, the OSI served as a model for dealing with alleged war crimes.[3]

The knock-on effect was felt firstly in Canada. During the 1960s and 1970s the USSR had demanded the extradition of several alleged war criminals, but the Liberal Government headed by Pierre Trudeau blocked any inquiry into whether these cases were symptomatic of a larger problem. Trudeau was probably motivated by fear that an official investigation would unleash a wave of ethnic antagonism between the large Ukrainian– and Jewish–Canadian populations which would damage his party. In 1977, encouraged by developments south of the border, the Canadian Jewish Congress adopted a more belligerent approach. It secured the support of an MP who inaugurated the first attempt to change the law to enable prosecution of alleged war criminals in Canada. However, Trudeau persevered with the strategy of temporisation. An internal Government report poured cold water on the viability of proceedings in Canada and in spite of the successful extradition of Helmut Rauca, a seventy-three-year-old German accused of mass murder, further progress was impeded.

With the arrival in office of Brian Mulroney, at the head of a Conservative Government in 1984, circumstances changed dramatically. Mulroney in some ways resembled Mrs Thatcher in Great Britain: a self-made man, he believed that he had battled his way to the top against vested interests and entrenched elites. He, too, had many Jewish contacts and considered that they had proved more loyal supporters than the Wasps who disdained his lower-class, Irish background. For these personal reasons, as well as electoral opportunism, Mulroney took a sympathetic view of the latest intervention by the Simon Wiesenthal Centre. When Sol Littman, an American representative of the Centre, produced a list of 1,000 alleged war criminals and claimed that Dr Joseph Mengele, the so-called 'Angel of Death' from Auschwitz–Birkenau, was in Canada, the media went wild, but Mulroney was most likely predisposed towards acting in any case. At the start of February 1985, Justice Jules Deschenes was appointed to lead an official inquiry into the allegations and to recommend what steps should be taken.

The Deschenes Commission heard evidence from April 1985 until June 1986 and commissioned historians to deliver authoritative accounts of post-war immigration into Canada as well as of the wartime activity of the immigrants. Its sittings were accompanied by controversy as Jews and Ukrainians fought out the issues in the press. Tangential events – such as the extradition of Ivan Demjanjuk and the trial of two Canadians who denied that the Holocaust had taken place – added to the ethnic discord. The Commission's report was finally published in March 1987, although sections of it were kept under wraps by order of the Justice Minister, Ray Hnatyshyn. Jews and Ukrainians argued over its merits, but Hnatyshyn immediately recommended legislative action and in June 1987 Bill C-71 was introduced to amend the Criminal Code, the Immigration Act and the Citizenship Act. By September 1987, the law had been changed to enable proceedings against alleged war criminals in Canada; a few months later, Imre Finta, a former Hungarian policeman, was arrested under the Government's new powers.[4]

Developments in Australia overlapped with those in Canada. Australian activists drew succour from the achievements of both the OSI and, more importantly, the revelations of the Deschenes Commission. It was not, however, a new issue. Throughout the late 1960s and 1970s, the Australian Government had been troubled by the activity of Croatian terrorists who were carrying on wartime feuds in their new home. Measures taken against these men uncovered former members of the Ustashi, the Croatian military force which had collaborated enthusiastically with the Nazis in their genocidal policy against the Jews, as well as murdering thousands of Serbians. In 1979, Mark Aarons, a journalist with the Australian Broadcasting Corporation, exposed a leading Croatian collaborationist living in Australia and soon afterwards the Wiesenthal Centre made allegations against other men.

The inception of the OSI in America encouraged the campaign for action in Australia. However, progress was stymied by conflict within the governing Australian Liberal Party, and it was several years before any effective moves were made. The impetus for real action came from various sources. There were the successes of the OSI, including the revelation that a Latvian war criminal, Konrad Kalejs, had reached the USA via Australia, where he had lived for several years after leaving Europe. The concurrent investigations in Canada showed that Britain had been derelict in its handling of DPs after the war and had actually used Commonwealth countries as a dustbin for awkward East Europeans. Finally, Mark Aarons' radio series *Nazis in Australia* created a sensation which Labour Prime Minister Bob Hawke could not easily ignore. Once again, a change of premier was vital for following up the breach in the walls of indifference made by the media and campaigners. In June 1986 Hawke responded to the lobbying efforts of Australian Jews by establishing an inquiry under Andrew Menzies, formerly a senior official in the Federal Government's Attorney General's Office.

The Menzies Report was handed to the Government in November 1986. It confirmed that there was a 'significant number' of suspected war criminals in Australia and recommended that appropriate action be taken by the authorities. A few months later the Attorney General was charged with the establishment of a Special Investigations Unit and asked to look into the options for dealing with proven war criminals. Just under a year after the Menzies Report, a bill was introduced into the federal Parliament to amend the War Crimes Act to enable the prosecution of suspects in Australia. By 21 December 1987, the bill had passed through all its stages.[5]

Britain, which had served as a transit camp for East Europeans en route to Canada and Australia, remained untouched by these developments until August 1986 when Greville Janner, a Labour MP and a prominent figure in British Jewry, wrote to the Home Secretary concerning an all-but-forgotten extradition case. Janner asked Douglas Hurd, the Home Secretary, what results had followed from the Soviet Government's 1971 request for the extradition of Kyrylo Zvarich, a Ukrainian born in the USSR. This superficially innocuous inquiry brought to light a familiar record of inertia.

During the war Zvarich had been a member of the Ukrainian police battalion based at Zabalotya, his home village. Eyewitnesses in the USSR who had been his neighbours told the local press that they could testify to several occasions on which he had mercilessly gunned down innocent people – Jews and non-Jews – in Zabalotya. Ukrainians in Britain, who were aware of inquiries into his case, informed the Soviet authorities that Zvarich was living in Bolton under the name of Stanislaw Piotrowski. In 1971, the Russian government instigated proceedings for his extradition: testimonies were collected from over seventy eyewitnesses and submitted to the Foreign Office in support of the extradition demand. However, the FO did not even bother to reply; no inquiries into the allegations were made by officials in this country.

In 1979, the man who commanded the unit in which Zvarich had served and two of his colleagues were tried in the USSR and found guilty of mass murder. The investigations revealed that on 9 January 1943 a Ukrainian police unit had massacred over 100 Jews at a village called Tur. According to Kondrat Scheuchuk, who drove the carts laden with Jews to the execution site:

> They were taken off the road and then they were ordered to lay face down in the snow. If someone raised their head they were struck with rifles and ordered not to raise their heads. And then they were told some of them to get up, get up and force [sic] them to undress and some were completely naked and they were taken to a pit and some of them, because it was cold were running to the pit. They were pushed into the pit and shot there. There was about 100 people there and the shooting lasted about 2 hours. I knew Zvarich. I knew Dufinitz [the unit commander]. I knew Zvarich because we were shepherds together when we were boys.

Despite this additional evidence, in 1983 the British authorities rejected a further Russian bid to bring Zvarich to trial. He died in Bolton in 1986.[6]

Janner was subsequently told by Tim Renton, then Minister of State at the Foreign Office, that the Government had explained to the USSR how the absence of an extradition treaty between the two countries prevented any action by the British Government. As well as this, he pointed to the lapse of time since the alleged crimes were committed. The crucial point, however, was the reluctance to hand over anybody to the Soviet legal system.[7] The war crimes issue was finally being drawn to the attention of Parliament but, before Greville Janner could get to grips with these explanations or excuses for inactivity, moves were being made in America that would accelerate the process beyond anyone's expectations.

Two days after Greville Janner received Tim Renton's letter, members of the Simon Wiesenthal Centre delivered to Donald Ballantyne, the British Consul General in Los Angeles, a document with the names of seventeen alleged war criminals living in Britain. They asked for the list of men, mainly Balts accused of committing crimes against Jews in Lithuania, Latvia and Estonia, to be forwarded to Mrs Thatcher, the Prime Minister. According to *The Times*, 'It is believed to be the first time that alleged Nazis have been traced to Britain.' This was not actually correct, but the effect was much as if lightning had struck from a clear sky.[8]

Within a very short time, one of the names was leaked to the press. On 26 October 1986, the *Sunday Times* reported that Antanas Gecas, a seventy-one-year-old retired mining engineer living in the Edinburgh suburb of Newington, was 'seeking legal advice'. Gecas had been interviewed four years earlier by the OSI and had admitted to serving as a platoon commander in a Lithuanian police battalion that had been involved in anti-partisan operations and civilian killings. He testified, 'My unit had to surround an area to protect the Germans from attack while the executions were taking place. I took no part in the shootings; that's abhorrent and I'm a Catholic.' A few days later, in the Scottish *Daily Record*, Gecas explained how he had surrendered to the British in Italy in 1943 and then fought in the Polish Corps, by which route he arrived in Scotland after the war. Since then he had been a model citizen, had worked for the Coal Board and put himself through evening classes where he studied mining engineering. Twelve years after arriving in Scotland, he had become a British citizen.[9]

With this new material in the background, Janner wrote to the Prime Minister to ask if she had received the list from Los Angeles. This was clearly an opening gambit: the real question was what the Government would do about the list. Ten days later Mrs Thatcher replied, 'We are considering this matter urgently, and I shall let you know our conclusions as soon as I can.' To keep up the momentum, Janner asked for a debate in the House of Commons and sought out like-minded MPs to join his quest. On 24 November 1986, the All-Party Parliamentary War Crimes Group was formed with the Rt Hon. Merlyn Rees MP, a former Home Secretary, elected as its chairman. At two later meetings, the Rt Hon. Peter Archer, a Labour MP and a former Attorney General, and Alex Carlile, a Liberal MP, were elected as vice-chairmen. Both Archer and Carlile, like Janner, were Queen's Counsel, an important asset in a campaign that was to involve complex legal issues. Janner acted as honorary secretary of the group along with Stefan Terlezki, a Conservative MP from Cardiff whose Ukrainian background was seen as vital so as to avoid any appearance that the Group was launching a witchhunt against the émigré communities. The honorary treasurers were the Rt Hon. Roy Mason (subsequently Lord Mason), a one-time Labour Minister of Defence, and John Wheeler (now Sir John Wheeler), a backbench Conservative MP of considerable standing who was chairman of the influential Commons Home Affairs Select Committee. John Gorst, the Conservative MP for Hendon North, a constituency with a large Jewish electorate, joined as an officer of the Group in February 1987.[10]

Initially the All-Party Parliamentary War Crimes Group confined itself to clarifying the questions relating to the extradition, deportation and denaturalisation of war criminals. Despite the increasing media interest in identifying specific cases and their own natural frustration at the lack of official activity, the MPs restrained themselves from making such disclosures. But following the Group's third meeting in January 1987, three months after the Wiesenthal Centre list was handed over, Merlyn Rees wrote to the Prime Minister asking what action was being taken. Mrs Thatcher told Rees that the matter of the list raised 'important issues and difficult questions of law'. But she assured the Group, 'We are looking at the matter urgently and carefully and I hope to be able to give you a response in the near future.'[11]

Outside Parliament pressure was growing. The authoritative anti-fascist magazine *Searchlight* in an editorial 'Time to Come Clean' attacked the Government for 'stonewalling' in the face of mounting evidence that Britain had connived in the escape of war criminals in the 1940s. In fact, it was to be a Scottish Television programme, *Britain – The Nazi Safe House*, that provided the breakthrough. Broadcast in Scotland on 28 January and screened nationally by Channel 4 in February, Bob Tomlinson's report cited the case of Kyrylo Zvarich. Gecas was shown speaking about his unit's role in a massacre of 150 people near the Russian town of Slutsk. The report exposed in addition the 'ratlines' by which war criminals had escaped justice after the war, but showed through an interview with Neal Sher and Eli Rosenbaum of the OSI that it was not too late to catch up with them.[12]

The following day the press was full of the programme and the accusation that Britain had been remiss in its pursuit of Nazi war criminals. Capitalising on the outcry, Janner asked John Biffen, Leader of the House of Commons, why there had been no action by the Government since the letter from Mrs Thatcher. With the Zircon affair (an attempt by the Ministry of Defence to suppress a BBC television programme about a satellite project) rumbling around the Government, the war crimes issue seemed one more instance of official secrecy blocking information about clandestine operations. This impression was reinforced by the publication of Tom Bower's book *The Paperclip Conspiracy*, which proved conclusively that the British had deliberately recruited scientists, engineers and industrialists from Germany after the war and had ignored evidence that some of the men had been fervent Nazis or had acquiesced in the use of slave labour.[13]

Possibly because of the influence wielded by proprietor Robert Maxwell, the press magnate whose Czech–Jewish family was murdered by the Nazis, the Mirror Group newspapers were particularly agitated by the torrent of disclosures. The *Daily Mirror* was scathing towards Mrs Thatcher who, it noted, 'brushed away a tear after visiting' Yad Vashem in Jerusalem, but was now 'brushing aside requests for help in prosecuting Nazi war criminals hiding here'.[14]

Douglas Hurd bowed to the weight of opinion and met with Merlyn Rees on 24 February, but could offer him little of substance. The Home Secretary told the chairman of the All-Party Parliamentary War Crimes Group that the Government had taken legal advice and had been informed that there was no way that British courts could prosecute a man who, when he was not a British citizen, had committed crimes in another country – even if he had subsequently settled in Britain and acquired British nationality. Deportation of such a person would be 'difficult, if not impossible'. So, although the Government could confirm that at least six of the seventeen on the list were definitely alive and living in Britain, plus two more probables, there was nothing that could be done about them.[15]

Hurd's confirmation that several suspected Nazi war criminals were alive and in Britain was a stunning disclosure and it dominated the headlines the next day, causing more discussion than any previous revelation. MPs were now seriously irritated that months after the list of seventeen names had been given to the Government, the Home Secretary seemed unable to come up with a plan of action. Ted Leadbitter, a down-to-earth veteran Labour MP, wrote to the Home Office asking incredulously whether or not any checks had been made on the alleged war criminals when they were first allowed into Britain. Other members of the War Crimes Group were threatening to 'name names' and so embarrass the Government into acting. The *Independent* was leaked the list of seventeen suspects and published it, but with the names blanked out.[16]

Neil Kinnock, the Leader of the Opposition, may have sensed that to much of the population, particularly the readers of the popular press, this was a black and white issue and one that gripped the imagination. He asked Biffen on 26 February whether he would accept that there was 'a great and growing concern both in this House and outside about people alleged to be Nazi war criminals who are apparently still living in our country'. Biffen replied that it was a matter which was in the mind of the Home Secretary, Douglas Hurd, and mentioned that Hurd would soon be meeting with members of the Simon Wiesenthal Centre.

Biffen's reply was followed by an intervention from Ivor Stanbrook, a Tory backbencher, whose first parliamentary utterance on the subject was to typify all his later statements concerning war crimes. Stanbrook asked Biffen: 'Does my rt hon. Friend agree that there is something distasteful and abhorrent about the activities of so-called "Nazi-hunters"?' He wanted an assurance from the Leader of the House that there was no intention 'to bend or change our law to accommodate their clamour'. Biffen acknowledged that such concern would be borne in mind by all those who 'wish to live by the rule of law', but the exchange did not end there and escalated into the first of many acrimonious jousts between proponents and opponents of war crimes legislation.

Pointedly mimicking Stanbrook's own words, Greville Janner angrily asked Biffen if he did not agree that it was 'distasteful and abhorrent that people guilty of war crimes should be living in freedom in Britain and not be brought to justice'. Before he could finish what he was saying, Stanbrook snapped at Janner across the chamber, '*Alleged* to be guilty.' But Janner ploughed on and called for an undertaking that the Home Secretary would make a statement on how alleged war criminals had entered the country and what would be done about their presence here. Hardly bothering to conceal his views on the matter, Biffen answered that 'assertions of guilt' were not the same as proof of guilt; the rest would be up to Douglas Hurd.[17]

Having been stymied in the House of Commons, the campaign now moved to the media. Paulis Reinhards, the Minister of Labour in the Latvian collaborationist regime, was named in the *London Daily News* and the *Daily Mirror*. According to the Simon Wiesenthal Centre, during the war the eighty-four-year-old Latvian, who now lived in Gravesend, had been involved in the recruitment of the Latvian Waffen-SS as well as of volunteers for the collaborationist police. Scottish Television added to the uproar when it passed on to the Director of Public Prosecutions in England and to the Scottish Crown Office a fresh list of thirty-four names provided by the Soviet authorities.

The announcement that members of the Simon Wiesenthal Centre would soon be arriving in Britain to meet with the Home Secretary raised press expectations to fever pitch.[18]

Rabbi Marvin Hier, Dean of the Los Angeles Centre, and his delegation arrived amidst a brush fire of press coverage. Names of alleged war criminals were now being printed with abandon. The *Sunday Express* disclosed the names of Mikhail Suliman and Maryan Bula, who lived in Bradford, and Leo Marnwyckyi, a resident of Peterborough. Suliman was said by the Russians to have worked under the Germans as a policeman in Lvov during 1941–4. Marnwyckyi, sixty-five years old, was accused of volunteering for service in the SS in 1942 and training at the Trawniki camp before joining an SS unit at Ponyatove in Poland. In this capacity such a unit would have participated in sending thousands of Jews to the gas chambers. Marnwyckyi denied these claims and was reported as saying only that he had fought in the Galizien Division, been a PoW in Italy from 1945 to 1947 when 'they [the British] brought me here'.[19]

But the leader writers and columnists in the heavyweight papers were reacting in a different spirit. Neal Ascherson, writing in the *Observer*, commented wearily that 'The Nazi-hunting season is upon us again.' He confessed that even though he was aware of the substance to the allegations he was made uneasy by the 'competitive zeal' to hunt down 'guilty old men'. In his weekly column Ascherson concentrated on the story of the Galizien Division about which he commanded an impressive amount of information. It was his 'guess' that 'evil deeds were done' by some members of the division, but he applauded the original decision to transport the unit to England and saw little virtue in the current war crimes mania. Taking a different tack, but reaching a similar conclusion, Simon Jenkins, also in the *Observer*, commended Simon Wiesenthal and his supporters for 'sustaining a running confrontation between Europe and its past'. Jenkins was more concerned with sensitivity to history than with the principles of justice, so his scorn for Hurd's apparent efforts to duck the issue did not lead him to endorse the war crimes campaign as such:

There have been allegations of deliberate deception by the Foreign Office and the War Office, of appeasement-minded officials turning a blind eye to Nazis, of one policy being declared and another enacted. There is no case for changing Britain's laws to meet the Wiesenthal demands. But the Home Office's coyness looks suspiciously like a yearning to forget. In this matter forgetting is not an option.[20]

The Wiesenthal Centre delegation saw Douglas Hurd and senior officials of the Home Office on 2 March. Marvin Hier underlined the importance of the new evidence which had been uncovered and the reliability of the sources, stressing that even West Germany now accepted material from the USSR. Efraim Zuroff then showed how the Canadian and Australian governments had been persuaded to act on the strength of similar submissions and urged the British to follow suit. But Hurd told them that the Government would not devote any resources to an investigation at this stage, except to look into the question of whether the alleged war criminals had broken British immigration rules. While not closing the door to the Wiesenthal Centre, he was not prepared to tackle highly sensitive legal questions on the basis of the evidence with which he had been presented so far. The onus was on them to make a better case.

In a press conference held immediately afterwards, Hurd described the Wiesenthal evidence as 'sketchy' and seemed to douse the allegations with cold water. He repeated what he had told the delegation about the technical obstacles in the way of any action: that British courts had no jurisdiction; that extradition was not an option since Britain had no effective extradition arrangements with the USSR; that, in any case, he was loath to send anyone to face trial under the Soviet legal system. The option of extradition to Israel was also closed because Britain had no relevant treaty with Israel either. All he would concede was a willingness to look into denaturalisation. Although the Wiesenthal delegation told the press that the meeting had been 'very constructive', there was a feeling of disappointment and a sense of resignation that it was going to prove a long haul.[21]

There were signs that it was going to be an uphill struggle
to win the battle for heavyweight opinion, too. The *Guardian*
leaderwriter asked, 'Should we let sleeping dogs lie, or more
precisely alleged agents of the Holocaust lie?' Genocide could
not be forgotten or forgiven, but it was good that no trials could
be held in Britain. At best the paper thought that in cases
where there was *prima facie* evidence of war crimes, denaturalisation, on the grounds of entering the country on false pretences,
followed by extradition to West Germany, was the most appropriate solution. A controversial leading article in *The Times*
concurred with the *Guardian* in distinguishing between the place
of the Holocaust in Israeli consciousness and its place in that of
other countries, but it went much further and drew a distinction
between what it saw as Jewish and Christian attitudes. 'Britain
is a Christian country. Its laws enshrine principles of justice
tempered with mercy, not vengeance.' This exposition was the
first of many which constructed Judaism as a vengeful, unfor-
giving creed opposed to Christian concepts of justice and mercy.
In subsequent debate this line of thinking was to be the subject
of rigorous argument and considerable rancour. Lord Coggan,
a former Archbishop of Canterbury, wrote indignantly to *The
Times* refuting the logic of the editorial, which was 'to say the
least unfortunate and could be offensive to many Jews'.[22]

The *Daily Telegraph* was no less outspoken than *The Times*.
'Nazi-hunting', it declared, 'has become a new and frankly
distasteful bloodsport. It is no reflection of anti-semitism, or
indifference to past atrocities, to feel overwhelming revulsion
against the notion of further war-crimes trials, almost half a
century after the alleged horrors took place. There is a futility,
a sterility, about continuing a search for vengeance beyond
certain limits of time and space.' On a rather less lofty plane
of argument, the leaderwriter then maintained that, 'As far as
we know, none of these men has been guilty of any misbehav-
iour in his postwar life in Britain. They lived out their lives,
bearing whatever burden of guilt, in obscurity.'

This must have been the first time that the *Daily Telegraph*
had ever suggested that years of keeping to the law exonerated
someone from facing trial for a murder they were alleged to

have committed in the past, or that the possibility of a person feeling guilt for a criminal transgression was sufficient cause to abandon investigation or prosecution in their case. But the *Daily Telegraph* was to emerge, through its leading articles, as an unrelenting opponent of the war crimes campaign and its satirical columnist 'Peter Simple', as one of the campaign's most vicious critics. On the same day as the editorial, Simple (Michael Wharton) attacked the 'zealots of the Simon Wiesenthal Centre' for their 'outrageous suggestions' that the law should be changed for what would, in his view, be 'show trials'.[23]

The strength of the backlash was not lost on British Jews, some of whom were unnerved by the venomous press comment. There was already a feeling of resentment in certain quarters that the Wiesenthal Centre was butting in where it was not wanted. Before Hier arrived, Eric Moonman, a senior vice-president of the Board of Deputies of British Jews, the central representative body of Anglo-Jewry, told the *Sunday Telegraph* that he was concerned by the 'lack of quality of the evidence'. Moonman cautioned against accepting Soviet material too readily and warned that 'we must be very careful not to allow ourselves to be manipulated by the Soviets because of the very rapid way in which this information has emerged'. The *Guardian* reported that Moonman was worried that the campaign led by Greville Janner, a former President of the Board of Deputies, might injure British Jews.

Soon it was obvious that for political and, possibly, for personal reasons a split had developed in the leadership of British Jewry. This was both embarrassing and damaging, since it enabled Hurd to claim that his do-nothing policy was not to the distaste of all Jews in Britain, the one group which ought to have been solidly in favour of action. An emergency meeting of the Board of Deputies' executive was held a few days after the Home Office meeting and one member of the Board was reported to have said that Moonman had 'exposed the community to ridicule'. But it would emerge later that other prominent British Jews were unhappy with the campaign: over the next three years, more than one Jewish voice would be raised against the pursuit of war crimes trials. Even at this early stage the well-known *Jewish Chronicle* columnist and writer Chaim Bermant warned against 'being stung by the poison of revenge'.[24]

Notwithstanding what one leading rabbi dubbed the 'crucial differences of opinion' between British Jews, the Board of Deputies eventually presented a united front and addressed itself to the Government. Hurd later wrote to the Board's President, Dr Lionel Kopelowitz, pledging that the Government would carry out its own inquiries to determine how many of the named suspects were alive and whether they had violated immigration laws when they entered Britain. The Home Secretary indicated that at this point he preferred to look at denaturalisation or extradition: 'Beyond that it would be possible to contemplate change in the law, although the case for any such change would depend substantially on the weight of evidence brought forward.'[25]

For the next four months, the researchers from the Wiesenthal Centre devoted themselves to building up the dossiers on the suspects. To his considerable surprise, Efraim Zuroff was given support and assistance via the Russian Embassy in London. Meanwhile, Bob Tomlinson of Scottish Television pressed ahead with parallel investigations of his own for a new programme on war criminals in Britain. Zuroff and Tomlinson both found that *glasnost* had effected a remarkable change in the Soviet system, at least the parts which they encountered. Tomlinson was given access to previously restricted documents, allowed to travel the country and record interviews with witnesses, all with the unstinting help of top Soviet legal officials. As a result, by June he had another hard-hitting programme ready for transmission. Zuroff – thanks largely to Tomlinson's researchers – had new material to submit to the Home Office in the wake of the public interest which the broadcast was bound to create.[26]

An additional, unexpected factor was the clamour for the disclosure of files held by the United Nations which were thought to shed light on the alleged involvement of Austrian President Kurt Waldheim in wartime atrocities. The World

Jewish Congress, which had sparked off the accusations against Waldheim, revealed the existence of the UN War Crimes Commission files and the astounding fact that the former UN General Secretary's name was on them. In March 1987, the Israeli Government demanded access to the files, but was blocked by the members of the Commission – which included Britain. Gradually the other members of the Commission gave way, but Britain remained obdurate. The cause of the Waldheim files was a natural one for the War Crimes Group to take up since it was alleged that, amongst other matters, he was implicated in the execution of British commandos in 1944.

Between May and July, Merlyn Rees and Greville Janner repeatedly asked the Foreign Secretary, Geoffrey Howe, to give Britain's permission for investigation of the files. At the start of July, the War Crimes Group held a press conference at the House of Commons at which Janner said, 'I found it a scandal that these files have been allowed to accumulate hidden, while people who have committed the most vile crimes in human history have, as a result of the hiding of these files, been allowed to escape justice.' An early-day motion tabled by Greville Janner and the Conservative Jewish MP Ivan Lawrence was used to keep up the pressure on Howe. The Waldheim affair added to the widespread suspicion that guilty men had escaped justice after the war and that there had been a cover-up in which Whitehall was persisting. For the MPs in the All-Party Group it was an issue that they could use to keep the subject of war crimes alive while the investigations into suspects in England were going on. In the end, it became a substantial cause in its own right and one that had a successful conclusion when the documents were released at the end of the year.[27]

Luck and careful planning meant that, when the second delegation from the Wiesenthal Centre went to the Home Office on 17 July 1987, it was like dropping a match on to a pile of old newspapers. Rabbi Hier and his companions were greeted by David Faulkner, the Deputy Under Secretary of State, and senior civil servants. Hier explained the significance of the new evidence, particularly the STV interviews with survivors from the unit in which Gecas had served. Faulkner agreed that it was the right kind of material, but could still not promise anything more than stripping of their citizenship those against whom a substantial case could be made.[28]

In the wake of the meeting, the press was gripped by a frenzy of Nazi-hunting that may not have been unconnected with the onset of the 'silly season'. Stories about Nazis and alleged Nazi collaborators proliferated. On 21 July, the War Crimes Group released declassified US documents which showed that Klaus Barbie, the chief of the Gestapo in occupied Lyons, had probably been used by British intelligence after the war. Meanwhile, Gecas was desperately trying to get the STV programme stopped, which only drew more attention to it. On the day that *Crimes of War* was shown on Channel 4, the Home Office announced that seven of the thirty-four individuals named on the Russian list which Tomlinson had forwarded to the DPP were alive. That meant that now thirteen identified suspects were living in Britain.[29]

The MPs now returned to the offensive in the House of Commons, bombarding every possible minister with questions about extradition requests, access to files and calls for a debate on the revelations made by *Crimes of War*.[30] For a while it also appeared as if the USSR and Israel were vying for the right to extradite Gecas. Yet, as Professor Gerald Draper, a former war crimes prosecutor and a distinguished expert in international law, pointed out in *The Times*, the Home Office was in a bind. The alleged murders were not committed by British subjects within the jurisdiction of British courts; the Geneva Conventions Act of 1957 and the Genocide Act of 1969 could not be applied retrospectively; extradition to the USSR was still unacceptable, while Israel did not have an extradition treaty with Britain that was operable in this context. Deportation was an option once a citizen was stripped of his or her citizenship, but this could be done only if it was held to be 'conducive to the public good' and it was not clear that men who had led blameless lives in this country could be held to be a threat to the British public.[31]

When Parliament went into recess at the end of July 1987, Douglas Hurd told MPs that the Home Office was looking carefully at the material provided by the Wiesenthal Centre and the Soviet authorities. As soon as MPs returned to Westminster in October he was under pressure to reveal what conclusions had been reached and what measures, if any, were proposed. Home Office and Foreign Office ministers faced a barrage of questions on the Barbie files withheld by the Public Records Office, the Waldheim files still under lock and key at the UN, and the status of the allegations against individuals living in Britain who were accused of war crimes.[32]

The War Crimes Group did all it could to mobilise public opinion in support of its campaign. It co-operated with *Searchlight* magazine and the Union of Jewish Students in a lobby of the House of Commons and a postcard campaign. On 12 October, Gerry Gable, the anti-fascist activist and editor of *Searchlight*, who had himself undertaken a three-week research trip to the USSR, presented the Home Office with a bulky dossier on Paulis Reinhards. Gable was followed a month later by Natalya Kolesnikova, a state prosecutor from the Moscow Ministry of Justice, who also gave new evidence to Hurd on the named suspects.[33]

Finally, the hint of a breakthrough came when Douglas Hurd met with the All-Party Parliamentary War Crimes Group on 17 November. The Home Secretary told the MPs that a decision would be taken very soon on whether to change the law to enable trials in Britain, or to work on the basis of depriving proven war criminals of citizenship. For the first time, as Greville Janner pronounced excitedly, the advocates of war crimes trials scented 'victory': a spokesman told the *Observer* that they were 'both encouraged and surprised by the extent of the sympathy with their views that some of the worst cases should be brought to justice'. Rupert Allason MP went so far as to predict trials at the Old Bailey within two years.[34]

It was not to be so easy. Despite Hurd's promise to act 'seriously and urgently', weeks passed with no announcement of a Government decision. MPs were uncertain whether the Home Secretary intended to amend the Criminal Justice Bill, which was going through the House at the time, or introduce special legislation. Hopes for enlightenment before the Christmas break were dashed. Opponents of war crimes legislation meanwhile reacted to the signs that movement was taking place by renewing their criticism. Ivor Stanbrook called on the Home Secretary to deny reports that the Government intended to change the law, a step which would in his view be 'contrary to the best instincts of the British people'. Stanbrook complained that the campaign to facilitate trials would 'serve only the motive of revenge and set aside the established rules of evidence that are a hallmark of British justice'. Tony Marlow, a Conservative MP well known for his anti-Israel views, now joined forces with Stanbrook. Because of his opinions on Israel, Marlow had previously crossed swords with several of the Jewish MPs involved with the war crimes campaign. Now he detected a connection between the two. Shortly before the recess, he asked the Home Secretary to be 'extremely wary on this particular issue and take note of the fact that the supporters of this particular proposal are motivated not by justice, but by the demands of propaganda'. Marlow would continue to insist that since the Holocaust was often used to justify Israel's existence, and to deflect criticism from the actions of the Israeli Government, the war crimes campaign was really just a sideline of the pro-Israel lobby.[35]

The opponents of war crimes legislation might have felt less threatened if they had been aware of the trouble Hurd was facing with his own officials. Home Office lawyers made clear their dislike of war crimes trials, while civil servants pointed to the costs which were likely to be incurred. The 'quick fix' of amending the Criminal Justice Bill proved not to be viable since it was feared that such a controversial addition could put the whole bill in jeopardy. Instead, rumours emerged from Whitehall that Hurd was considering an independent inquiry to look into the whole question, from the nature of the crimes to the immigration of alleged war criminals into Britain and all the legal options for dealing with them.[36]

The Government had to be seen to be doing something: continued quiescence in the face of demonstrable public and parliamentary interest could only be politically damaging. The visit by Natalya Kolesnikova at the start of the year also underlined how the changes in Russia removed what was once the chief excuse for remaining passive. Mrs Thatcher had declared that it was possible to 'do business' with Mr Gorbachev; a new legitimacy was conferred on the Soviet judicial system at just the moment when Soviet policy was becoming more outward looking. In the course of her visit, Natalya Kolesnikova offered strong material, particularly with respect to Gecas, and showed that this time the USSR would not allow the matter to die. Hints from the Home Office that an official British investigation was in the offing became more precise.[37]

On 8 February 1988, Hurd announced the establishment of an inquiry. It was to be headed by Sir Thomas Hetherington, a former Director of Public Prosecutions, and William Chalmers, a former Crown Agent for Scotland. The inquiry was charged with obtaining and examining the relevant material held by Government departments or submitted by outside agencies and interviewing persons who seemed to possess information relating to the allegations. Finally it was 'To consider, in the light of the likely probative value in court proceedings in the UK of the relevant documentary material and of the evidence of potential witnesses, whether the law of the United Kingdom should be amended in order to make it possible to prosecute for war crimes persons who are now British citizens or resident in the United Kingdom; And to advise Her Majesty's Government accordingly.'

In the course of his announcement, Hurd told MPs that the passage of time did not lessen the magnitude of the crimes, although it did complicate the investigation of allegations, not to mention the familiar legal problem surrounding the question of how to act if allegations were sustained. The evidence so far submitted by the Wiesenthal Centre and others did not in itself merit a change in the law, but it was clearly of sufficient weight to demand further examination. It was hoped that the inquiry would resolve the inherent difficulties and enable a decision to be made as to how to proceed. The announcement was broadly welcomed by the Opposition front bench, but attracted strenuous criticism from Stanbrook and Marlow. Stanbrook considered that it was 'a bad decision' that would lead to a 'witchhunt'. British courts had never sought to try 'alleged crimes committed long ago by foreigners in foreign countries' because of the inadmissibility of evidence. The Home Office was stepping out on the road to special legislation for a particular class of people – something abhorred by lawmakers. He concluded by asking Hurd, 'Is my right hon. Friend not surrendering to a lobby whose main motivations are hatred and revenge?'

The Home Secretary responded, 'I do not think my hon. Friend's last point is fair,' although Stanbrook was to go on making it inside and outside the House. Tony Marlow's attack was no less passionate. First of all he questioned whether Hurd was moving towards retrospective legislation. But he then speculated whether, if this was so, 'Would we, for example, find ourselves prosecuting the Israeli soldier who savagely beat to death a fifteen-year-old Palestinian boy if that soldier came to stay in this country?' Hurd rejected both points in short order, although Greville Janner, who jumped up next, could not resist referring to Marlow's 'odious question'. Nor did it escape the notice of the press: columnists Edward Pearce and Colin Welch would later deliver a stern verdict on Marlow's jibe.[38]

Opponents of the campaign found a stentorian champion in Peregrine Worsthorne, writing in the *Sunday Telegraph*. Averring sympathy for the Jews, he said that the trials would end up putting them in the wrong by portraying them as 'implacable hunters in search of defenceless victims'. While expressing horror towards the crimes of the 'merciless Germans', he feared that such sentiments would be overwhelmed by the 'mercilessness of the Jewish present'. Sometimes objectionable facts had to be endured. Waldheim was a nasty man who had achieved high office, but no more so than Arik Sharon, the right-wing Israeli Cabinet Minister who had been deeply implicated in the massacre of Palestinians at the refugee camps of Sabra–Shatilla in Beirut in 1982. Ivor Stanbrook likewise added to arguments based on the very real technical difficulties in the way of war crimes trials the accusation that the campaign was essentially the work of a Jewish lobby that was motivated by revenge, a quality he considered inherent in Jewish behaviour and religious thinking. Many Jews resented the attribution of vengeance to their creed and identified this tendency as an anti-semitic canard. So they were hardly appeased when Stanbrook, like Worsthorne, claimed to be acting in their best interests in order to head off anti-Jewish feeling.[39]

Janner and the members of the All-Party Parliamentary War Crimes Group had mixed feelings about the appointment of the Hetherington–Chalmers Inquiry. Was it a delaying tactic? Would the team produce an anodyne report that would enable the Government to drop the whole thing? It certainly set about its work at a leisurely pace. According to a *Jewish Chronicle* reporter, by early April they were still reading basic books on the Holocaust. The 'team' consisted only of Hetherington, Chalmers and one full-time secretary. It was not until the summer that the inquiry roped in archivists, translators and retired policemen to work on strong cases. Then the investigation literally took off, with members travelling to Washington, Jerusalem, Berlin, Vienna and several destinations in the USSR.[40]

While the inquiry was in progress the campaign at home did not go into hibernation. In March, Peter Archer tabled an amendment to the Criminal Justice Bill at committee stage to enable the prosecution of persons who acquired British nationality subsequent to their commission of murder, manslaughter, genocide or torture or to their abetting such acts. The debate on the clause was to be the occasion of an orotund intervention by Ivor Stanbrook, who began by nobly 'exonerating' the proponents of the clause because they were 'misguided, blinkered and not sufficiently imbued with a sense of the real spirit and purpose of British justice'. In his eyes, 'The greatest strength and drive behind such a proposal comes from motives of revenge, hatred and malice.'

Stanbrook repeatedly insinuated that the pro-war crimes lobby was un-British. To ram home this point he remarked, 'Most British people regard justice as being tempered by mercy and even forgiveness. It is not a concept in British eyes to temper justice with revenge. I know that people who propose this sort of idea deny that and say that they do not want revenge, they simply want justice. But that is not so.' Why did 'most British people' differ from the war crimes campaigners? 'Perhaps that is because we are Christians, and part of the Christian philosophy is not to accept revenge as part of its concept of justice. That is the basic human feeling in this country connected with so-called war criminals.' Several members of the All-Party Parliamentary War Crimes Group identified themselves as Jewish, but the cause was not a clearly circumscribed 'Jewish issue' like Israel or the plight of Soviet Jews. To claim otherwise seems to have been a deliberate attempt to marginalise the campaign and stigmatise it, even to tap popular hostility against Jews and to recycle ugly myths about the Jew as 'alien' or 'foreign'.

This dichotomy between British Christians and un-British non-Christians may have irked the members of the committee like Archer (a non-Jew) and Liberal Democrat MP Alex Carlile (a Jew) who supported the clause, but they held their peace. It was only when Stanbrook addressed the question of evidence that he created vociferous outrage. Referring to the 'so-called offences' under discussion, he stated, 'The position is that more than forty years ago something occurred about which there are scraps of information, rumours, stories and so on. Perhaps there is some documentary evidence – pictures, recollections and statements – but all the resources of the famous Simon Wiesenthal Centre have failed to produce evidence more than forty years later.' At this point Alex Carlile, whose parents' family had been wiped out during the Holocaust in Poland, could restrain himself no longer and shouted out, 'Rubbish!'. Whatever Stanbrook intended, the effect of his words was to obfuscate, even to deny, the Holocaust, and it was too much for the Liberal Democrat MP.

Carlile interrupted Stanbrook several times more, asserting that his honourable Friend's oft-demonstrated ability to recall his time in the colonial administration in Nigeria thirty years earlier rendered somewhat suspicious his arguments about the fallible memory of war crimes witnesses. Other members of the committee, such as the Conservative MP Jonathan Sayeed, subsequently took Stanbrook to task for his comments, although much of their rhetoric was wasted since, to the annoyance of his colleagues on the committee, Stanbrook left early to give a radio interview. The most powerful rebuke, powerful because it did not even mention him, came from Llin Golding, the Labour MP whose father had been one of a deputation of parliamentarians to visit Buchenwald after the war. Golding's moving account of what her father told her he had seen in Buchenwald touched all those present. It did not affect the outcome of the debate, which was a foregone conclusion: Archer had merely been flying a kite for war crimes legislation and the clause was withdrawn. But it was a foretaste of bitter oratory still to come.[41]

Members of the War Crimes Group also kept their cause in the limelight by throwing themselves into campaigns on associated issues. The Waldheim affair rumbled on throughout the spring, with a host of parliamentary exchanges over the Government's refusal to allow access to certain files in the Public Records Office. It was believed that these files would shed light on the death of British commandos who were captured in a military area over which Waldheim presided as an intelligence officer. Eventually the Ministry of Defence established its own inquiry by a group of historians and eminent former civil servants under the direction of Professor Harry Hinsley. In August 1989 it delivered its report, clearing Waldheim of direct involvement in the killing of British troops.[42]

Jeff Rooker, the Birmingham Labour MP, harassed the Government over the case of Wilhelm Mohnke, once Hitler's most favoured Waffen-SS general. Mohnke had ended the war in the Führer's personal entourage after a military career littered with massacres and outrages. One of the earliest of his exploits had occurred at Wormhoudt, outside Dunkirk, where his Waffen-SS unit had massacred over eighty surrendered and disarmed British troops of the Warwickshire Regiment. Mohnke had been tried for war crimes in West Germany, but had served little more than a nominal sentence. To the few living survivors of the atrocity, like Bert Evans, Ray West and Alf Tombs, some of whom were Rooker's constituents, it was incredible that the seventy-seven-year-old Mohnke was free at all, not to mention drawing a West German state pension. The files on the massacre were in the Public Records Office, but were closed to the public: Rooker pressed hard for the Government to open the case again and make the files available to historians and war crimes investigators.[43]

In November 1988, the campaign received an enormous boost when the Group published the results of its own investigation based on sources available in the Public Records Office. The ninety-page report, prepared by a team of researchers coordinated by Philip Rubenstein, the secretary to the All-Party Parliamentary War Crimes Group, documented for the first time the way in which East European war criminals had been able to get into Britain after the war. It showed that politicians and civil servants at the time had been aware of this and exposed the dismal record of successive governments in dealing with alleged war criminals. The report did not set out to 'name names' or to prove particular allegations: that would be up to the Hetherington–Chalmers Inquiry, which commanded the necessary resources for proper research. However it represented another milestone in the campaign. Here at last was hard evidence for a story that had been dismissed by many people as sensationalism or deemed by others to be simply unbelievable.[44]

For several days the media were once again saturated by the war crimes issue, and as before there was an immediate backlash. Members of the émigré communities responded angrily to the spotlight turned on them. A Ukrainian community activist Kurs Birzgalis told the *Bradford Telegraph and Argus*, 'These claims are rubbish. It's not true. I came to this country in 1947 and I had every sort of security check.' Gunars Tamsons, chairman of the Captive Nations Committee in Bradford, admitted that 'one or two' might have slipped through – but 'not hundreds'.[45] A *Panorama* programme by Jane Corbyn, 'Shadow of the Swastika', broadcast in December, challenged the aims and methods of war crimes investigators, but the criticisms were angrily rejected. The BBC received complaints from MPs in the War Crimes Group that the programme was both biased and inaccurate, and the programme makers found

themselves on the defensive amidst a mass of claims and coun-
ter-claims about the reliability of their interviewees.[46]

By chance, not long after this, another aspect of Second
World War history which was connected with war crimes flared
up. At the beginning of 1989, a controversy developed over
whether or not Britain should send a member of the royal family
to the funeral of the Japanese Emperor Hirohito. A number of
veterans of the war in South-east Asia and survivors of the
terrible Japanese prisoner-of-war and labour camps were exercised by the paying of royal respect to the deceased head of
state. In their eyes, Hirohito had presided over a country that
had tortured and killed thousands of British soldiers during the
war and done nothing to prevent the atrocities. One former
prisoner of the Japanese even went on hunger strike to publicise
his anger. As in the case of the Holocaust in Eastern Europe,
the past refused to lie down. Seeing that it was a kindred cause
to that espoused by the War Crimes Group, in January 1989
Greville Janner took up the protests of the ex-servicemen and
criticised the Prime Minister for the decision to send the Duke
of Edinburgh to attend the funeral. It was another demonstration that the war crimes campaign was not confined to the
'Jewish lobby', but represented principles of universal concern
and touched on the common history of the British people.[47]

From the autumn of 1988, MPs started to ask for the date
of the inquiry report. All through the spring of the following
year they hounded the Government front bench with requests
for information about the conduct of the investigation, whether
suspects were being watched by the police, and if the report
would be published. To keep the momentum going and to show
that the issue still agitated large numbers of MPs, an early-day
motion was tabled with reference to a *Daily Telegraph* article
'Murderers Amongst Us' which reported that a change in the
law was now being seriously considered by Douglas Hurd. The
motion attracted the names of nearly 130 MPs; a diametrically
opposed amendment in the names of Ivor Stanbrook and Simon
Coombs MP registered but two supporters. John Marshall,
Conservative MP for Hendon South, many of whose constitu-

ents were Jewish, presented to the House of Commons a petition bearing 6,000 signatures in support of war crimes legislation.[48]

Sir Thomas Hetherington and William Chalmers finally presented their report in June. Once it was known that Douglas Hurd had a substantial document in his hands, speculation heightened; once again the thin season for political news meant that almost every newspaper ran Nazi-related stories. As tension mounted in expectation of a Government statement, the opponents of war crimes trials unleashed their strictures. Bernard Levin in *The Times* asked what purpose such trials were meant to serve. Britain had no history of collaboration that was in need of purging; there were serious problems in the way of securing a fair trial – problems of obtaining evidence and questions about the reliability of eyewitness testimony. Above all, trials had no clear point: were they intended as a deterrent? or retribution? or fulfilment of an abstract commitment? Levin saw little value and much harm in them. 'I believe', he wrote, 'that the amount of justice that would emerge from the proposed trials would be far smaller than the harm done by them.' The defendants would probably be let off for lack of evidence and end up garnering public sympathy for their ordeal. He concluded, 'the universe will not be a whit the better or cleaner for purging itself of a dozen or two criminals with one foot in the grave'.[49]

Whereas Greville Janner quickly dispatched a letter to *The Times* to refute Levin's cogent article, Ivor Stanbrook was understandably happy to associate himself with it. He declared, 'What a relief it was to read Bernard Levin's article about the unwisdom of holding war crimes trials in Britain. As a member of the Jewish community he might have been expected to follow the merciless line advocated by Mr Greville Janner.' Having once again characterised Jews as 'merciless', Levin being the exception that proved the rule, Stanbrook then claimed that the War Crimes Group was in danger of damaging Christian–Jewish relations. They wanted 'show trials' made possible by a 'specially made law' which was 'revolting to most British Christians'; the pursuit of alleged war criminals would lead to press harassment that 'would make a fair trial impossible by the traditional standards of British justice'. Stanbrook concluded with what some might have considered a self-fulfilling prophecy: 'Even more dangerously it would revive anti-semitism.'

Jim Richardson, the ex-Director of the Council of Christians and Jews, was mortified by these sentiments. Writing to *The Times*, he noted that if anything might damage Christian–Jewish relations it was giving shelter to war criminals. Later, Merlyn Rees and John Gorst added their protests. Writing as Christians, they said that far from being revolted by the thought of war crimes trials, 'most Christians' were revolted by the thought of the Holocaust, which was an affront to Christian ideals. While Hurd calmly studied the report and discussed its implications the debate raged on, showing the capacity of the war crimes issue to divide and inflame opinion.[50]

On 24 July, the Home Secretary made his statement to the House on the report of the Hetherington–Chalmers Inquiry, in Hurd's words 'a full and impressive document'. It began with a learned examination of the historical background to the events in question and detailed the entry of East Europeans into the UK after the war. Hetherington and Chalmers chronicled the evolution of British war crimes policy during the Second World War and its implementation. They looked at the status of such crimes in international law, the contemporary legal position in the United Kingdom and, by comparison, in other countries such as the USA, Canada and Australia. Finally, after explaining how they had gone about the task of investigating the allegations that had been made, the authors presented their findings, conclusions and recommendations.

Hetherington and Chalmers concluded: 'Some action should be taken in respect of alleged war criminals who are now British citizens or are resident in this country where the evidence is sufficient to justify such action.' Rejecting extradition as an option, they proposed that 'Legislation should be introduced to give British courts jurisdiction over acts of murder and manslaughter committed as war crimes . . . in Germany or German occupied territory during the . . . war by persons who are now British citizens or resident in the United Kingdom.' To make this possible, the report recommended certain changes in the law relating to evidence and committal proceedings. Details of individual cases were confined to a second volume which was not published, but the report stated that there were three cases 'in which there appears to us to be a realistic prospect of conviction on the evidence already available'. In addition, it urged further investigation of three suspects about whom considerable, but not yet sufficient, material had been accumulated. Lastly, it recommended investigation into seventy-five allegations which the inquiry had not been able to deal with in detail.[51]

Douglas Hurd noted that these recommendations raised 'important issues of principle and practicality' that would give everyone cause for thought: would trials serve any useful purpose? would it be possible to assemble a case that would be acceptable before a British court? Set against these caveats, he quoted the words of the authors: 'The crimes committed are so monstrous that they cannot be condoned . . . To take no action would taint the United Kingdom with the slur of being a haven for war criminals.' He was clearly impressed by the views of two cool-headed and sensible men of law, but he recognised that opinion was sharply polarised. The Home Secretary therefore felt that both Houses of Parliament should be allowed to make their views known and he proposed to arrange the necessary debates in the autumn. 'In the light of the views expressed in those debates', he concluded, 'the Government will take a final decision on whether to bring forward a bill on the lines proposed by the inquiry.'

For the Opposition, Roy Hattersley, Shadow Home Affairs spokesperson, concentrated on the 'formidable problems of principle and practice that would be involved in prosecutions'. He was worried about changes to the rules of evidence, the risk of pre-trial by the media and the danger of special legislation. He would have preferred general legislation, such as the Geneva Convention, and warned against the element of retrospectivity. These reservations were tackled at once by Douglas Hurd, who strove to point out that the report did not recommend retrospective legislation, but merely an extension in the scope of

jurisdiction. Retrospective legislation made criminal acts which
were not currently illegal; but the acts in question were clearly
always against the law. The problem lay in a technical hitch
which prevented British courts applying jurisdiction to the men
who had carried out such deeds. Changes in the rules of evidence would pose no difficulty since they were already under
way due to the 1988 Criminal Justice Act, but he accepted that
consideration would have to be given to this matter. It would
also be necessary to extend these changes to Scotland – a
superficially minor adjustment that would, in the event, turn
into a débâcle for the Government.

In the debate which followed the statement, a string of Tory
backbenchers – Ivor Stanbrook, Ian (later Sir Ian) Gow, Sir
John Stokes, Tony Marlow and Nicholas Bennett – rose to
object to the proposal that the law should be altered. To Stanbrook it was 'a tragic mistake' which would 'stir up the
emotions of hatred and revenge': a fair trial would not be
possible. Tony Marlow managed mildly to ruffle Hurd, normally
so impassive, by attributing the campaign to 'a form of moral
blackmail as a means of covering the present behaviour of the
State of Israel'. The Home Secretary thought this description
of the findings by Hetherington and Chalmers was 'grotesquely
astray'.[52]

In the Upper House, Lord Hailsham, a former Lord Chancellor whose word on judicial matters was treated with reverence,
made clear his reluctance to contemplate any changes in the
law such as those proposed in the report. Hailsham was more
outspoken in the press, where he declared that war crimes trials
would be a 'gross perversion of justice' and amount to little
better than 'lynch law'.[53]

Opinion outside Parliament was just as bitterly divided.
Milton Shulman, the Jewish columnist and veteran *Evening
Standard* theatre critic, revealed that as a soldier in 1945 he had
interrogated captured SS men. But he thought it was futile to
go chasing the 'junior scum' in England today. Since on past
performance trials would hardly deter anyone bent on atrocities, the only point was vengeance. 'There is something bizarre
and chilling about the relentless pursuit of these old men when

West Germany and Japan are now numbered amongst our most favoured allies and when the cold war has thawed.' He believed 'The time is out of joint for the scavenging of dreadful reminders of the past. Those who have vested interests in the vengeance business may become victims themselves of the backlash of resentment and revulsion that could undermine all the dedicated work they have already done.'[54]

The leaderwriters had their chance the next day, and on the whole they concurred that the report was so powerful that action had to be taken. The *Guardian* thought that after such a potent conclusion Hurd had no alternative but to seek a change in the law. However, the paper seemed unable to make up its mind and decided a few days later that neither side in the argument had a monopoly of wisdom. The *Daily Telegraph* agreed that the report had 'confounded expectations' and by virtue of the evidence it had collected left the Government in a dilemma. Hurd was right to let Parliament decide and then, perhaps, to consider a limited change in the law. Given the magnitude of the crimes, the *Independent* considered that even retrospective legislation was thinkable in this case.[55]

Columnists and diarists were less in accord. Peter Simple in the *Daily Telegraph* launched a slashing assault on the 'fanaticism and unappeasable thirst for vengeance' which he attributed to the action of Jews campaigning for the removal of a Carmelite monastery from the site of the Auschwitz death camp, a cause he clearly regarded as sharing the same stable as war crimes. Hugo Young in the *Guardian* worried that 'Old men, who have led blameless lives in their adopted country, will be dragged before the court' – a fact which he seemed resigned to accepting in the light of the report. The 'investigative juggernaut', the media circus, the alteration of the law were all 'the price an honest nation pays for its principles'. Richard Ingrams in the *Observer* commented with his customary sarcasm that at a time when the case of the Guildford Four was bringing the entire English legal system into doubt, 'Nothing could be more farcical or macabre' than the attempt to try 'a number of elderly war criminals'.[56]

For Geoffrey Wheatcroft in the *Sunday Telegraph*, as for other journalists, it was hard to talk of international Jewish groups and a Jewish lobby without sounding anti-Jewish, but he felt that he had to be honest and boldly accused British Jews of 'moral arm-twisting'. He asked rhetorically, 'could any other lobby have gone so far in persuading a British Government to fly in the face of English justice by introducing retrospective legislation in order to try men for crimes committed more than 45 years ago far from British soil? How did Mr Greville Janner manage it?' The answer might have been that the campaign had been so successful precisely because it was not just Mr Greville Janner, but embraced many MPs of all parties and persuasions. Nevertheless, Wheatcroft called on the Home Secretary to defy Mr Janner with his 'unusually zealous concern for Jewish interests' and to recall the elements of justice to the 'self-appointed Jewish activists'. Posing as a friend of the very Jews whom he had dealt with so caustically a paragraph before, he warned against a real danger of anti-semitism breaking into flame. By way of complete contrast Woodrow Wyatt, the *News of the World*'s 'Voice of Reason', was more concise, although it is questionable whether he was more convincing with his two-word 'I agree' comment on the content of the report.[57]

Once more, Jews in Britain were alarmed by the vituperation aimed at them over the war crimes issue. Chaim Bermant in the *Jewish Chronicle* again demonstrated his distaste for the whole business: 'There are, one feels, more wholesome outlets for Jewish emotions and more productive calls on Jewish energies.' Later on he warned, 'We are inviting certain hazards for the sake of uncertain benefits.' At a meeting of the Board of Deputies Greville Janner, the target of much of the most unmitigated hostility, personally cautioned Anglo-Jews to expect a 'vicious' opposition to any effort to change the law. Sadly, he was not to be proved wrong.[58]

In October 1989 Nigella Lawson, the *Evening Standard* columnist and daughter of the then Chancellor of the Exchequer, addressed herself to war crimes and affirmed that their prosecution was 'a moral imperative'. Her father Nigel was of Jewish origin, but Nigella was far removed from Jewish life. All the same, as she later told Greville Janner, in the days following

the appearance of her article she endured a torrent of 'disturbing letters from the madder anti-semites who seem to see my
column as just another arm of the world Jewish conspiracy'.[59]

The Struggle for the War Crimes Act

The Hetherington–Chalmers Report transformed the nature of the war crimes debate in Britain. It gave unimpeachable support to the claims which had been made by the war crimes campaigners and confirmed the woeful record of previous administrations. To correct the circumstances which had allowed suspected mass murderers to live securely in Britain for forty years it decisively recommended changes in the law. Now it was up to Parliament, taking account of public feeling, to decide whether legislation was desirable and whether war crimes prosecutions were practicable. For the first time in Britain the debate revolved around concrete proposals, surrounded though they were by thorny constitutional and legal questions. Historical, moral, theological and philosophical considerations fed into, and complicated, the discussion. Almost every MP, peer, columnist and broadcaster in the country felt a right, and took the opportunity, to have his or her say.

The report of the War Crimes Inquiry inspired respect on all sides, not just because it was such a rigorous, lucid and compelling statement – a model of its kind. So much of the force behind the argument and supporting evidence came from the knowledge that neither Sir Thomas Hetherington nor William Chalmers was anything other than a level-headed man with impeccable legal credentials who had no axe to grind in the matter. After the report was published, Sir Thomas freely admitted that at the outset of the work he had been sceptical: 'When I started this inquiry I thought it unlikely that there would be war criminals in this country or that the evidence would be good enough.' He was 'surprised by the size of the crimes, and by the quality of the evidence'. Initially dubious about the reliability of eyewitness testimony over forty years after the event, he was won round by Simon Wiesenthal's argument that 'people who have been through that sort of horror don't forget'. He had met men and women in Eastern Europe who appeared perfectly capable of giving evidence, and it was the sort of testimony that could not be ignored without imperilling the good name of the country. Hetherington saw the problems as clearly as anyone, but he trusted in the British legal system – the DPP, the judges, the juries – to decide on the fitness of proceeding to a trial and then assessing the evidence.[1]

However, there were equally powerful and authoritative advocates of the contrary viewpoint. Lord Shawcross, who had been Attorney General in the Labour Government of 1945–51 and delivered the opening and closing speeches for the British contingent at the Nuremberg Tribunal, emerged as an unwavering opponent of fresh trials. At the end of July 1989, he wrote to *The Times* reiterating and approving the decision by Attlee's Cabinet to end war crimes trials after the Tribunal had concluded its work. Shawcross explained: 'Broadly it was felt that the pacification and reconstruction of the ravaged world would not be assisted by further trials. The remaining criminals were, therefore, so far as Great Britain was concerned, left to the obloquy of mankind and, it may be, the pangs of their own consciences.' As for the current situation he commented:

> I cannot believe that a revival of all these sad and terrible matters by sensational trials of a small handful of aged men, which will take years to conduct and which will start with an assumption of guilt, will help to promote understanding and friendship between the different peoples of the world, will help us to eliminate the evil of anti-semitism – still less – enhance the respect for British justice.[2]

The All-Party Parliamentary War Crimes Group did not underestimate the tenacity of the opposition or belittle the coherence of their arguments. For this reason, it convened in

London a major international conference of experts on war crimes and invited investigators and prosecutors from the United States, Canada and Australia to give a British audience the benefit of their experiences. The conference, held at a Westminster hotel on 23 October, brought together Neal Sher, Director of the OSI, William Hobson, Senior General Counsel for the Crimes Against Humanity and War Crimes Section, Canadian Department of Justice, and Robert Greenwood QC, Director of the Australian Special Investigations Unit of the Attorney General's Department. Their message, informed by years of practice, was simple: war crimes trials were not just a moral and legal imperative, they were wholly feasible if the political will existed to make them a reality.

The conference acquired a sense of drama and urgency for another, unexpected reason. One of the visitors was Rabbi Hugo Gryn, the minister of the West London Synagogue and an Auschwitz survivor. As he exited from his taxi outside the hotel, Rabbi Gryn was confronted by a thinly manned picket from the British National Party, a neo-Nazi group. The men, lined up along the pavement, were distributing a broadsheet which proclaimed on its front page that the Holocaust had not happened: it was a hoax perpetrated on the world by the Jews. Gryn got into a shouting match with the BNP members and had to be restrained by friends who heard the commotion and came out from the hotel. For the rest of the day participants were aware that the decision which Parliament would make could not be isolated from a world in which the Holocaust was demeaned, trivialised and even denied. No sensible advocate of war crimes trials would offer this as the sole reason for making changes in the law or subjecting people to the horrible pressures of a trial, but no one could now overlook the unfortunate resonance of a result which thwarted the principle of bringing to justice alleged war criminals in Britain.[3]

At the conference, John Patten, the Home Office Minister, offered few clues as to the timing of the debate which Douglas Hurd had promised. Moreover, a Cabinet reshuffle in November introduced a certain amount of uncertainty when Douglas Hurd left the Home Office and was replaced by David Waddington. Both sides of the debate girded themselves for combat. Peter Simple poured his wrath on the 'repulsive' idea of retrospective legislation 'in order to satisfy – or at least to slake, for it may be impossible to satisfy – the thirst for revenge of international Nazi-hunters and their assorted sympathisers'. William Deedes, in rather more measured tones, argued that the passage of time demanded silence rather than action. Both writers introduced a note of relativism into the discussion. If Simple wanted to try Communists who had persecuted Balts in 1940 and thereafter, Deedes thought that there was no difference between war crimes in Eastern Europe and the bombing of Dresden. For its part, the War Crimes Group played its hand by calling on constituents to write to their MPs urging support for war crimes legislation.[4]

To the surprise of the MPs in the Group, Geoffrey Howe, now Leader of the House, announced in November that the debate would take place the following month – first in the House of Lords and then in the Commons. Jack Cunningham, on the Labour front bench, was indignant that the unelected House should have the opportunity to make its views heard first; but the members of the War Crimes Group were unhappy for a different reason. Knowing the views and the prestige of Lord Hailsham, along with the negative outlook of other peers, they were apprehensive that the Upper House would give, at best, a lukewarm endorsement to the principle of war crimes legislation.[5]

In the event, the debate in the House of Lords was every bit as grim as the War Crimes Group feared it would be. Lord Elwyn-Jones, a former Nuremberg prosecutor, Attorney General 1964–70 and Lord Chancellor 1974–9, who was a firm advocate of war crimes trials, died that very day after a long illness. Although Lord Mishcon, supporting the principle of prosecutions from the Labour front bench, invoked his name, those in favour tended to be Jewish peers such as Lord Jackobovits, the Chief Rabbi, Lord Beloff and Lord Wolfson. When he rose to speak after nearly three hours of debate, Lord Tonypandy, the former Speaker of the House of Commons, remarked that he was the first non-Jew to advocate trials.

Against the proponents were a stream of previous Law Lords, including Lord Hailsham and Lord Wilberforce, two former prime ministers, Lords Home and Callaghan, and several retired ministers and senior civil servants, including Lords Mayhew and Hankey, who had been involved in policymaking in the late 1940s. They spoke with the authority of those responsible for the suspension of trials and referred to the views of eminent contemporaries including Churchill, Attlee and Bevin. To add to their armoury, they could cite a further missive from Shawcross to that morning's edition of *The Times*, contending that past war crimes trials had not had any deterrent effect. When the debate finished, it was evident that a majority of the House of Lords was against the recommendations of the Hetherington–Chalmers Report.[6]

After this result, the onus was on the House of Commons to demonstrate overwhelming approval for the principle of changing the law to facilitate war crimes prosecutions. The importance of the vote was increased by evidence that the Cabinet was divided: Waddington and Hurd were known to favour action, but the rest of Cabinet was, at best, cool.[7]

The Commons held their debate on 12 December 1989 after Sir Bernard Braine, the Father of the House, moved a motion to endorse the need for legislation. David Waddington summarised the Hetherington–Chalmers Report and made it plain that the Government was in favour of its recommendations. The Opposition front bench concurred with the principle, even if it demurred on several of the practical points of implementing the report. In stark contrast to the Lords, the proponents of trials dominated the proceedings and systematically answered objections to the proposal. True, Roy Hattersley was equivocal and the former Prime Minister Edward Heath unremittingly hostile, but the opposition was confined mainly to crusty Tory backbenchers like Ivor Stanbrook, Quentin Davies, Sir Nicholas Fairbairn, Sir John Stokes and Tony Marlow.

The debate was solemn, but at times acerbic. Conservative backbench MPs repeatedly interrupted Merlyn Rees and later riled Greville Janner. Quentin Davies shouted 'What crimes?' at Merlyn Rees when he was outlining the findings of the

Hetherington–Chalmers Report. Later on, Davies said he wanted crimes such as the Katyn massacre to be included. Similarly, Sir Nicholas Fairbairn interjected noisily, 'What about the Cossacks?', drawing on the recent libel action of Lord Aldington against Nikolai Tolstoy. He wanted to know, mischievously, if British troops who had forcibly repatriated Yugoslavs and Cossacks would be liable to prosecution at some future point.

Robert Maclennan, speaking from the Social and Liberal Democrat benches, took his own colleagues rather by surprise when he adopted the arguments of Lords Mayhew and Wilberforce to the extent of maintaining that, since war criminals had knowingly been allowed to settle in Britain after 1945, the House had no business chasing them now. Ivor Stanbrook repeated his familiar plaint against the 'cruel vendetta' that offended against British law and the British people. He, too, cited other acts that were, arguably, crimes that had escaped punishment – such as the handing over of Chetniks and Cossacks. And he asked, 'What about the leaders of modern Israel, some of whom were responsible for the cold-blooded massacre of British subjects and are now received with warmth and hospitality when they come to Britain?' Would jurisdiction be extended to cover them?

Unlike the Lords, MPs went into the lobbies to register their votes. After three hours of highly charged oratory the result was an overwhelming endorsement of the Hetherington–Chalmers Report, by 348 to 123 votes. This decisive result made the introduction of legislation virtually inevitable and the Home Secretary intimated that he anticipated bringing a bill to the House in the summer of 1990. Greville Janner was jubilant. After the debate he went to Central Lobby, where he was embraced by colleagues and friends, including Ben Helfgott, a survivor of Buchenwald. Later on he told the *Jewish Chronicle*, 'It was remarkable. I could hardly believe the support we got.'[8]

The popular press was jubilant. The *Sun* screamed, 'Hunt and punish the Nazi criminals', and the *Sunday Mirror* gushed, 'At last!' Even the sober and formerly antagonistic *Daily Telegraph* was impressed by the scale of the victory. In its leading article the next day it accepted the verdict of Parliament and resolved that it was now time to ensure that the trials, once they took place, would be fair. The *Economist* pronounced that 'Britain is set to become a less comfortable haven for Hitler's henchmen.' It was right to avoid sending a message to the world that 'Britain has forgotten – or, worse, forgiven.' Yet there were still voices of restraint and anxiety: Geoffrey Wheatcroft in the *Daily Telegraph*, again, Milton Shulman in *The Times*, and Alexander Walker in the *Evening Standard*. Walker made a review of the Costa Gavras film *Music Box*, based loosely on the Demjanjuk trial, into a vehicle for warning that Britain risked entanglement in a juridical and moral nightmare.[9]

War crimes legislation was now placed firmly on the Cabinet's agenda and Mrs Thatcher let it be known that she personally favoured a change in the law. She told the Board of Deputies in February 1990 that she found the arguments 'persuasive', although she also mentioned that she had received 'many letters' from her Jewish constituents. Members of the All-Party Parliamentary War Crimes Group did not allow the Government to forget the issue for a moment and badgered the Leader of the House as well as the Home Secretary to disclose the date for legislation. Despite rumblings of unease from Conservative peers, the Cabinet decided in the last week of February that a bill would soon be introduced to fulfil the recommendations of the war crimes inquiry. The Shadow Cabinet, when it met a fortnight later, resolved to back legislation.[10]

On 8 March, in reply to yet another question from John Marshall, David Waddington announced that the Government had now considered the implications of the two debates the previous December and had prepared a bill which he introduced the same day. It was a short measure and took up only seven pale green pages. The War Crimes Bill was 'to confer jurisdiction on United Kingdom courts in respect of certain grave violations of the laws and customs of war committed in German-held territory during the Second World War; and for connected purposes'. The only other provision enabled the transfer of cases to the Crown Court without committal proceedings, as was already the case for serious fraud cases. In reply to questions a few hours later, Sir Geoffrey Howe told MPs that there would be a free vote on the bill.[11]

The second reading of the War Crimes Bill was held quite quickly, on 19 March 1990. The Home Secretary summed up the arguments in its favour and fended off a series of querulous interventions by his backbench colleagues, including Ivor Stanbrook, Nicholas Bennett and Ian Gow, who all doubted whether a fair trial was possible. Stanbrook caused uproar when he suggested, 'The criminals were not restricted to the so-called Nazis but existed on all sides, including the Allied side.' Anthony Beaumont-Dark, Toby Jessel and Sir Bernard Braine – all fellow Tories – registered their amazement at this historical revisionism, but Stanbrook persisted and refused to give way to MPs who shouted 'Why not?' when he declined to distinguish between the 'calculated and diabolical cruelty' inflicted on one people at one particular time and that perpetrated against another people at a different time. Alex Carlile responded to this apparent denial of the Holocaust as a singular event worthy of a singular response by recounting the story of his mother's experience in the ghettos of Lvov and Warsaw. His moving speech silenced the House. Retorting to those who tried to marginalise the campaign and lay it solely at the door of the Simon Wiesenthal Centre, Jeff Rooker reminded MPs that 'The Bill is not a Jewish issue and it is wholly wrong to put it across that way.' If Britain refused to prosecute war criminals, what hope would there be of persuading the Germans to act against Mohnke?

After Stanbrook, the strongest opposition to the bill came from Edward Heath. He, too, found himself in stormy waters when he argued that the bill was retrospective because those who committed the acts in question might not have been aware that they were breaking any law or the Hague Convention of 1907, let alone committing genocide – which was a recent juridical invention. When he said it was 'debatable' that alleged war criminals knew they were in breach of any law, MPs on all sides raised a chorus of 'Come on!' Even though the Opposition could lay claim to a former prime minister, it was of little avail and after a three-and-a-half-hour debate the bill won its second reading by a handsome majority of 273 to 60 votes.[12]

Now only the House of Lords could stymie the bill and Lord Hailsham left few doubts that he intended to try his best. The resolve of the peers was stiffened by political commentators like Colin Welch, in the *Daily Mail*, who remained jaundiced towards the proceedings: 'We have the ingredients here of a colossal waste of political time, if not of something far, far worse.' *The Times* dubbed the bill 'A kind of wild justice' and disparaged any thought that trials forty years after alleged crimes were committed could be fair. But the *Sun*, like the other 'pops', greeted the second reading with warmth. Meanwhile, Melanie Phillips, in the *Guardian*, took issue with commentators, amongst whom were two of her colleagues, who spurned prosecutions. Fleet Street was as divided as the two Houses of Parliament.[13]

Inevitably the press was excited by the information that a special unit, quickly dubbed the 'Nazi-hunters', was to be set up under the Metropolitan Police to conduct investigations into alleged war criminals. At its head was Detective Superintendent Tony Comben, a forty-seven-year-old police officer who had spent five years with Scotland Yard's SO1 department, which handles international and organised crime. Comben had plenty of experience in international investigations and had only recently been part of the inquiry into the killing of six Jesuit priests in El Salvador.[14] However, the unit would not start operating until the green light came from the Lords and, as Lord Home made clear in newspaper interviews, this was far from certain. Barbara Amiel, Peter Simple, Richard Ingrams and Paul Johnson all fuelled the resistance of the House of Lords from the vantage point of their columns.[15]

The War Crimes Bill had its Commons committee stage on 29 March and 3 April 1990. In the time-honoured fashion of committees, the discussion was intricate and convoluted, focusing on seemingly trivial points such as the definition of German-controlled territory or the date the war ended. Alastair Darling, an Opposition home affairs spokesman, put forward a number of constructive amendments which were eventually incorporated. Otherwise the sittings were animated only by the interventions of Ivor Stanbrook. On two occasions he reprimanded John Patten for not giving his title correctly and upbraided another MP for not addressing the Minister exactly according to parliamentary custom. Patten merely commented, 'I am not prissy about that,' but it was a telling moment. Stanbrook's behaviour was that of a man deeply concerned with propriety: not necessarily for its own sake, but because the defence of the constitution and the authority of the law rested on maintaining a complex system of interlinking outworks. Taken in isolation, the issues which he raised could seem arcane and obtuse: seen as outriders of law and order, they made perfectly good sense. Had Stanbrook been a Jew, his sensibility might have been described most aptly as talmudic.[16]

Having passed through the committee, the bill cleared its report stage and third reading in the House on 25 April, by 135 to 10 votes. It went up to the House of Lords and received its formal first reading the next day. The debate in the Upper House was scheduled to take place on 4 June, but the Lords had the chance to show their mettle a month sooner. On the first day of May 1990, the Law Reform (Miscellaneous Provisions) (Scotland) Bill had its committee stage. Lord Fraser of Carmyllie, for the Government, moved an amendment to extend to Scotland the provisions of the 1988 Criminal Justice Act, which enabled the use of live television links and videotaped evidence in the case of war crimes trials. However, Lord Campbell of Alloway had tabled a further amendment which would have the effect of restricting the innovations to routine criminal proceedings. Lord Campbell, born in 1917, was a distinguished jurist with an interest in European affairs. He argued that since their Lordships had not yet debated the War Crimes Bill, the Government had no business sneaking into a completely alien piece of legislation a clause which was essentially related to the other issue. First the Lords should debate the principle of the bill; once that was done they should consider its implementation, if necessary.

Despite Lord Mishcon's efforts to dissuade the peers from having a mini-debate on the virtues of the War Crimes Bill, this was in effect what happened. One after another they rose to pour scorn, derision or pity on the recommendations of the Hetherington–Chalmers Report. Lords Soper and Longford both appealed to the principles of Christianity. Lord Soper, a prominent Methodist, asserted that Christian tenets of mercy and forgiveness ran counter to the aims of war crimes prosecutions and could not be ignored. He told the peers, 'I do not believe that you can separate the Christian faith from the deliberations of an officially Christian Chamber.' Lord Longford also sought to apply the principle of forgiveness and implied that the War Crimes Bill was the product of an Old Testament, that is Jewish, sensibility which was foreign to Christians. It was his conviction that Jesus had invented forgiveness: 'Rabbis would tell us that it was introduced into the Jewish religion soon afterwards in the Talmud. It is a distinctive Christian virtue.' Side by side with his tributes to the Jews and Jewish ideals, and his fears that the bill might accentuate anti-semitism, Lord Longford was actually reiterating a hotly contested claim about Jewish thought which had been exploited repeatedly by anti-semites in past centuries.

Lords Hailsham, Wilberforce, Grimond and many others also spoke against the Government measure. Lord Callaghan thought it should be rejected so that the Lords could deliberate fully and properly on the War Crimes Bill in its own right. The House divided, unusually, and the result was 137 to 62 against the amendment, although it then accepted without demur the original clause to extend the use of videotaped and live television evidence to Scotland. Once again, a Conservative Government had been ambushed in the House of Lords and mildly humiliated; but for the advocates of the war crimes prosecutions it was a premonition of disaster.[17]

All concerned with the genesis of the War Crimes Bill could see that it was now in deep trouble. There were rumours that the Government would abandon it rather than face a sure defeat at the hands of the Lords. If the Government persisted, there was the danger of a head-on clash that would raise serious constitutional questions regarding the powers of the Upper Chamber. However, some constitutional experts maintained that since the bill was not truly a Government measure (it had not figured in any Conservative Party manifesto), and was passed on a free vote, the Lords were equally at liberty to vote according to their consciences and to reject it without contravening the so-called Salisbury doctrine which held that the House of Lords should never defeat a Government bill on its second reading.[18]

By mid-May the Cabinet made it known that it would press on with the bill, despite the misgivings of Sir Geoffrey Howe and Tim Renton, the Chief Whip. The All-Party Parliamentary War Crimes Group and the Government business managers now set about lobbying the Lords to secure a bare majority for the bill. The War Crimes Group brought Sir Thomas Hetherington to the House of Lords, where he addressed peers in the Moses Room, beneath a huge representation of Moses 'bringing down the tablets of the law to the Israelites'. He rebutted almost every conceivable objection to the proposed legislation, including the claim that in 1948 a prior administration had decided to stop war crimes trials – a decision which actually applied only to the British Zone of Germany. Lord Mayhew, however, contended that the absence of a formal decision to suspend prosecutions in England, too, followed from an unspoken consensus at the time that retribution had run its course. Lord Campbell of Alloway and Lord Walston opened a new front by suggesting that the Hetherington–Chalmers Report was an impressive case for the prosecution – but had done little to investigate the case for the defence or to examine mitigating circumstances. The well-attended meeting did nothing to reassure the bill's proponents.[19]

Outside, the media war heated up. Barbara Amiel wrote powerfully of the problems afflicting the trial of Imre Finta in Canada. Her doubts about his case were vindicated a few days later when he was acquitted – a result which, given the timing, was abysmally bad luck for the war crimes campaign in Britain. On the days running up to the debate, Norman Stone in the *Sunday Times*, Ferdinand Mount in the *Daily Telegraph*, Dominic Lawson in the *Spectator*, and Gitta Sereny – who had once interviewed and written incisively about Franz Stangl, the commander of Treblinka – in the *Independent on Sunday*, all came out against the bill and in favour of the peers.[20]

One line of Finta's defence had been that he was obeying orders, but Melanie Phillips described this as one amongst a number of 'stomach-churning' arguments deployed against the bill. The *Mail on Sunday* belaboured the Lords for 'giving genocide the status of a traffic offence'. Woodrow Wyatt in the *News of the World* referred to the recent wave of anti-Jewish incidents, starting with the outrage at Carpentras, in which a Jewish cemetery was desecrated and a corpse disinterred in a horrible fashion, at the beginning of the month, and warned that a defeat for the bill would give a green light to Jew-haters everywhere. Michael Jones, the political editor of the *Sunday Times*, protested that 'Appeasement will stalk the corridors of the House of Lords tomorrow.' But on the morning of the debate, the leading articles in *The Times* and the *Daily Telegraph* called on the Upper House to defeat the bill.[21]

Their Lordships needed little encouragement. Over sixty peers put their names down to speak for the bill or for the amendment to drop it – and they each exacted their slice of Parliamentary time in an exhaustive debate that stretched from three o'clock in the afternoon until midnight. Every peer who had already spoken against the bill spoke again, with the addition of Lord Shawcross. Summoning up his immense authority, Shawcross justified the wisdom of abandoning trials in 1948 and leaving things that way. In the course of his oration he recalled that the events in Palestine in 1947–8 had impaired the efforts of those, initially including himself, who at the time wanted to press on with war crimes trials. In his summary of Jewish terrorist attacks in Palestine he temporarily groped for the name of the climactic bombing incident, but was quickly assisted by a chorus of peers who sang out 'The King David Hotel!', thus demonstrating that extreme age did not necessarily blunt the memory.

Lord Beloff was swimming against the tide when he put forward arguments for trials, and did his cause no good by two comments that offended his peers. Reviewing the suggestion that a fair trial would not be possible, he jibed that only the

IRA and the House of Lords seemed to believe that British justice was fallible. He also attributed at least some of the opposition to the bill to animus against Jews. Seeing that trials were permitted in Germany, the USA, Canada and Australia, why should Britain stand apart? 'It is difficult to understand the motives of those who wish to place this House in that position. A degree of prejudice has crept into the matter that is very similar to that contained in the official documents of the wartime years . . . . ' Referring to the Carpentras incident, the demonstrations by young neo-Nazis in the newly united Germany and the spate of anti-Jewish attacks in Britain during May, he warned that a defeat for the bill would be an incitement to anti-semitism in Europe and encourage Holocaust denial.

Several peers, such as Lord Callaghan, whose anti-racist credentials could not be questioned, regretted the implication of Beloff's comments that distaste for the bill in any way equated with dislike of the Jews. The point was underlined by two Jewish peers, Lord Goodman and, most dramatically, Lord Bauer. In what was the shortest and pithiest contribution to the debate, Bauer stood up and told the House: 'My Lords, I am of Jewish extraction. My father was killed by the Nazis. I emphatically support the amendment. This bill is another step towards the erosion of the rule of law.' Then he sat down. Other Jewish peers, including Lord Swaythling, who made his maiden speech in the course of the debate, Lord Jakobovits, Lord Morris of Kenwood, Lord Clinton-Davis and Lord Kagan, were joined by non-Jews such as Lord Mason, a founder-member of the All-Party Parliamentary War Crimes Group, and Lord Tonypandy. One of the most potent contributions in favour of the bill was made by Lord Fitt, who observed that in his native Northern Ireland, there were 3,000 unsolved murders. He could not support the amendment which seemed to say to a killer: if you hide successfully for long enough, you will be safe. 'It appears', said Lord Fitt, 'that certain elements within this country are prepared to accept Britain as a haven for yesterday's terrorists.'

Yet the weight of the speeches and the speakers was massively against the bill: Lord Callaghan, once Prime Minister, Lord

Hailsham and Lord Havers, two former Lord Chancellors, Lord Donaldson, the Master of the Rolls, the historians Lords Blake and Dacre, Lord Carver, former Chief of Defence Staff, Lords Carrington and Pym, both of whom had served as Foreign Secretary. Several peers had called on the House not to be bullied by the Commons and when the division was held they were indeed defiant: the amendment was supported by 207 to 74 votes. In an act unprecedented since 1945, the Upper Chamber had defeated a bill passed through the House of Commons by decisive majorities.[22]

Suddenly, an issue that would otherwise have been flogged to death gained a new lease of life. The press was abuzz with the thrill of a constitutional crisis as outraged MPs who had led the campaign for the bill summoned up the cause of democracy against aristocracy. The *Independent* and the *Guardian*, which had sat on the fence, strongly deprecated the Lords' vote. They depicted it as a shameful gesture towards the victims of the Holocaust and an alarming message for contemporary anti-semitism. In its favoured populist style, the *Sun* bawled, 'Put old fools out to grass'; but it was echoed by the more upmarket if equally populist *Today*, which denied the Lords any right to hold up the Commons. It was 'Time to go, my Lords'. The *Mail on Sunday* believed that the 'House of Lords has disgraced itself and the nation' and given 'a vote for the forces of evil'. The *Daily Mail*, however, had second thoughts and now mused that teaching about the Holocaust in schools might be a better use of resources than putting old men on trial. *The Times* simply congratulated the Lords for their decision and said that it exemplified their true function.[23] Public opinion, as revealed by an NOP poll published in the *Daily Mail* on 8 June, showed 60 per cent in favour of the bill and only 31 per cent against. This indicated that the Commons were, indeed, more in tune with popular feeling and reinforced the democratic, constitutional case against the antics of the second chamber.[24]

For all the raging of the war crimes campaigners, the police unit had to be put in mothballs. Sir Bernard Braine was livid and was hardly calmed when Edward Heath, the ex-Prime Minister, who also happened to be running him a very close second for the title Father of the House, congratulated the Lords on their resolution. Thinking that Braine was heckling him, he said, 'May I ask the Father of the House to calm himself. We do not want to lose him.' Braine had actually said nothing and remained silent, but he sent Heath a stiff note and later described him to reporters as a 'slug'. Heath retorted that 'he has gone right over the top. He got so worked up about this war crimes issue that he simply could not control himself. He was apoplectic.'[25]

Sir Bernard was not alone in his fury. Mrs Thatcher was personally affronted by the vote and 'vowed' not to be beaten by the House of Lords. Even though the Cabinet was completely split, with the Leader of the House, the Foreign Secretary and the Attorney General against the bill, the Prime Minister carried the day. As so often before, Mrs Thatcher's personal interest proved decisive: the Cabinet decided to 'let the dust settle' and then to discuss options for ways of proceeding. Putting aside the blandishments of Lord Whitelaw, who pleaded with her to drop the bill, Mrs Thatcher and David Waddington issued marching orders for their troops. On 21 June, Sir Geoffrey Howe intimated that the Government would reintroduce the bill in the next session, although it would consider amendments to secure the support of the Lords.[26]

A month later, the Iraqi invasion of Kuwait gave another twist to the saga. As news of alleged atrocities emerged from occupied Kuwait, Mrs Thatcher threatened Iraqi leaders with war crimes trials. She was soon followed by President Bush and other world leaders. Ironically, Lord Shawcross fulsomely endorsed her approach.[27] Mrs Thatcher was no longer Prime Minister when the Gulf War started, but it injected an unexpected relevance into the war crimes debate as television viewers watched films of captured airmen serving in the coalition forces who had apparently been maltreated; military and political leaders revived the language of the Geneva Convention and rekindled the memory of the Nuremberg Tribunal.

In October 1990, the Home Secretary confirmed his intention to reintroduce the bill. Waddington was by now a convert to the cause: he told David Frost, 'If I were a Jew, I would feel that people should not be protected by a wholly artificial rule of law.' The Queen's Speech on 7 November contained the necessary reference to the bill and the legislative cycle was set to repeat itself. This was, to the *Daily Telegraph*, a 'wholly retrograde step', but the die was cast. Even though the new Prime Minister, John Major, had voted no in the debate on the principle of legislation, he ensured that it would have the explicit backing of the Government. Kenneth Baker, the new Home Secretary in Major's Cabinet, followed the pattern set by his predecessors. Exposure to the full Hetherington–Chalmers Report convinced him that inaction was not an option. Indeed, when the bill was reintroduced, unchanged, on 8 March, it was speedily followed by a procedural motion to allow the Government to operate the 1949 Parliament Act to force it through in spite of the Lords' opposition. The motion was passed by 177 to 17 votes.[28]

The War Crimes Bill had its second reading on 18 March 1991, in the afterglow of the Gulf War. Sir Geoffrey Howe and Sir Ian Gilmour now joined Edward Heath in condemning it, but in spite of the accession of new blood, such as Clare Short, from the Labour benches, the opposition was essentially the same as before – as were most of the arguments. Nevertheless, the bill still managed to inflame passions, and the debate saw several remarkable exchanges between honourable Members. Tony Marlow wondered why the bill excluded war crimes committed in countries under Japanese occupation or in 'Palestine after the war'. He had the feeling that 'we have been mugged in this House by some strong lobby'. But the Home Secretary quickly assured him 'that is not the case' and pointed out that there were no known Japanese immigrants to this country after 1945 who might have committed war crimes. Marlow later repeated his claim that it was all a pro-Israel stunt. 'We are puppets on a string,' he told MPs, the objects of 'the most sophisticated and heavily orchestrated lobby of the post-war world'. David Winnick remarked of this conspiracy theory that, coming from Tony Marlow, the only surprise was the omission of racist comments about black people, too.

Edward Heath enraged MPs when he asked, 'How many of

our troops in the Gulf knew whether the orders that they were
being given were always in accord with international law?' As
he tried to develop the defence of acting in obedience to superior
orders, indignant colleagues on all sides rose to challenge him.
He irritated the Attorney General, Sir Patrick Mayhew, by
implying that trials, if they went ahead, would be 'show trials'.
Mayhew pointed out that it was up to him to decide if a case
went to trial and he implicitly objected to the suggestion that
he would permit such a spectacle. One of Heath's persistent
critics was the formidable Conservative MP, Dame Janet Kel-
lett-Bowman, who could not accept that mass murderers during
the war were not aware that they were committing crimes. After
she had interjected a further comment, Heath turned round
and snapped at her, 'Will my hon. Friend remain quiet, just
for one minute.'

Sir Ian Gilmour caused some astonishment by also arguing
that war criminals were only obeying orders. He was accused
by David Winnick of 'trying to find excuses for those appalling
crimes'. Labour MP Patrick Duffy drew on the Gulf War as
evidence that 'even the most civilised nations' have engaged in
the massive destruction of civilians – as in the bombing campaign during the Second World War. Most MPs, if they did
not find these suggestions offensive, found them completely
unconvincing. In the final vote, the House approved the bill by
254 to 88 votes. After a formal third reading on 25 March 1991,
the bill was passed up to the House of Lords.[29]

For a month the War Crimes Bill went into limbo. The
critical second reading in the House of Lords was set for 30
April, and in the interim rumours flew about that the peers
intended to wreck it or substantially delay its progress. David
Waddington, now leader of the Conservatives in the House of
Lords, certainly faced a rough ride. In rumbustious mood, the
peers defeated the Government by supporting a measure to
abolish the life sentence and savaged a proposal to impose fines
on the parents of juvenile delinquents. Apprehension amidst
the pro-bill lobby was heightened on the eve of the second
reading by hints that Waddington might accept amendments

to the bill in order to mollify the opposition and buy some support.[30]

Lord Mayhew, unrelenting as ever, prepared the ground with a series of questions to Conservative ministers seeking to elicit whether the Government in 1948 knew that there were war criminals in Britain and what action, if any, they took about their presence. His aim was, apparently, to demonstrate that if the Government had decided to drop war crimes trials in 1948 it was not out of ignorance that suspects were known to be in the country even then. His persistence irritated the Government, and at one point Viscount Mountgarret forcefully protested that he was pre-empting the debate.[31]

The war crimes issue had lost none of its potency. When the debate in the House of Lords started at 3.10 p.m., the Chamber was packed and over fifty peers had put their names down to speak. There were two amendments to the bill. The first, put down by Lord Houghton of Sowerby, called for the bill to be delayed for six months. The second, in the name of Lord Campbell of Alloway, sought to extend the bill to cover Japanese war crimes and atrocities committed in the Gulf conflict. Lord Waddington spoke first and left the House in no doubt that the Government would use the Parliament Act of 1949 if either amendment, was carried. Addressing Lord Campbell's amendment he pointed out that the last time the Lords had attempted in such a way to extend the scope of a bill from the House of Commons was in 1906 and before that, 1899; it was an archaic procedure that was no better than seeking the bill's delay.

Lord Houghton, who was actually born in 1899, defended the right of the House of Lords to reject legislation from the Lower Chamber. To embolden his peers he cited their successful opposition to the Government measure to set up an appointed body to govern London in the wake of the abolished Greater London Council. The Government then had meekly accepted the rebuff. Lord Campbell followed, explaining why he wanted to make the bill less selective. His arguments were brushed aside by Lord Mishcon, who pointed out that the core of the debate was purely and simply whether the Lords should

defy the Commons, and what the consequences of their action
would be. However, historians and constitutionalists disputed
Mishcon's argument that the elected chamber must have
supremacy. Lord Jenkins of Hillhead dismissed the much
touted Salisbury – Addison doctrine, since, he maintained, it
was intended only to curb the Lords from blocking legislation
that stemmed from the proclaimed policy of the majority party
in the House of Commons. Not hiding his exasperation, he
declared, 'I simply cannot understand what drives the Government on.'

Jenkins was echoed by Lord Hailsham, who provided an
answer to the former's rhetorical question. It was 'the cloven
foot of populism' that lay behind the Government's insistence
and the Opposition's pusillanimity. This colourful and powerful
oratory was continued by Lord Shawcross in a wily attack on
the Hetherington–Chalmers Report. The two men responsible
for the report, he argued, were fine prosecutors; but they understood little about ensuring a fair defence. To Shawcross the
odds were impossibly stacked against the accused, who could
not hope to get sufficient funds to support a team comparable
to the one which had collected the evidence against them.
Calling on the Lords to defy the Commons, he asserted, 'This
is not a House of Wimps. This is the House of Lords.'

Religious leaders among the peers were less decisive. The
Bishop of Southwark thought that forgiveness was a relevant
consideration only after some judicial action had been taken
against alleged war criminals: something had to be done in
the light of the Hetherington–Chalmers Report. Lord Soper
repeated his advice that it was better to 'love your enemies'
and he was upheld in a curious speech by Lord Longford, who
attributed the war crimes campaign entirely to Jews. He could
understand their desire for trials, but could not figure out how
non-Jews could feel the same way. When he said that this
Jewish-inspired campaign was about 'persecuting' old men,
Lord Glenamara, formerly Ted Short, interjected that Longford
must have meant 'prosecuting'. However, Longford insisted on
using the term 'persecuting' to describe the process which
would be opened up by the bill if it became law.

By contrast, the Bishop of Ripon found 'a moral undergirding' beneath the bill which compelled him to support it. He counselled that it was impossible to consider forgiveness unless a wrong was recognised as such; to deny the bill would be to deny the past, and this would only frustrate the process of healing.

For almost two hours, every peer who had spoken had attacked the bill. When Glenamara rose at nearly 5.30 p.m., he was the first peer to speak in favour of it since Lord Mishcon had sat down soon after the debate had begun. He was followed by Lord Tonypandy and Lord Jakobovits. There was more than a hint of weariness and resignation in the contribution by the Chief Rabbi. He quoted Ecclesiastes, 'This is the end of the matter. Everything has been heard,' as the preface to his point that in all of the long debates people had been talking at or past each other. 'Everything has been said, but has it been heard and answered?' He thought not: the victims cried out for justice, but their silent cries were not heeded. Lord Bridge of Harwich explored the possibility that if the Government front bench would consult with MPs and assure the Lords that it would accept certain amendments to ensure a fair trial, then perhaps the peers would be induced to pass the bill. Despite Lord Callaghan's endorsement of the idea, Waddington sat in his place and gave no indication that he was prepared to consult with the members of 'another place'.

Notwithstanding this, several other peers followed the path of conciliation. Lord Annan, who had served in the Control Commission in Germany after the war, made a cogent argument for passing the bill in order to demonstrate unceasing sympathy for the fate of the Jews and to signal abhorrence of contemporary anti-semitism. The principle and the practice could be dealt with separately. Lord Donaldson announced that he had changed sides and intended to support the second reading in the hope of amending the bill later. This peeved Lord Mayhew when he set out to demonstrate that, despite Waddington's earlier statements, the Government of 1945–51 had known that war criminals were in Britain and had deliberately opted not to act against them. His argument was a hostage to fortune.

Lord Beloff, who began by telling the peers that it was 'the unhappiest day I have spent in your midst, except possibly for 4 June last year', saw little merit in admitting that a previous administration had behaved in a way that might be considered reprehensible.

During the long debate, MPs who were concerned with the future of the War Crimes Bill clustered at the Bar of the House to catch some of the arguments. Sir Nicholas Fairbairn, Tony Marlow, Ivan Lawrence and David Winnick were amongst those who took time from business in the other place to witness the historic exchanges in the Lords. The debate finally concluded at just before 12.30 in the morning of 1 May, and when the division took place Lord Houghton's wrecking amendment was carried by 131 to 109 votes. There was now, in theory, a constitutional crisis.[32]

In fact, it was more a case of the mouse that roared. The very same afternoon, the Speaker of the House of Commons, Bernard Weatherill, responded to the 'numerous inquiries' which he had received about the Parliament Acts and informed MPs that the vote had, indeed, triggered their operation. John MacGregor, the Leader of the House of Commons, then explained that the bill would be submitted for Royal Assent. There was no need for further debate in the Commons, a decision which was supported by John Cunningham for the Labour front bench, even though he considered the bill a 'dubious' measure and had not supported it himself. Several Tory MPs attempted a rearguard action, demanding a debate on the use of a dramatic constitutional device for a purpose such as the War Crimes Bill, but the Speaker ruled them out of order. The mechanism of the Parliament Acts was now irrevocably in motion and nothing that they could say or do could have any effect on the outcome.[33] On 10 May 1991, the War Crimes Bill was signed into law by the Queen. The way was clear to the first war crimes trials in Britain since 1945.

Conclusion

The Arguments and the Issues

The War Crimes Act arrived on the statute book after one of the longest, most emotional and fiercely contested campaigns in British post-war political history. What was it about the proposal to conduct war crimes trials that had the capacity to divide MPs, peers, the media and the public, culminating in a historic constitutional dénouement? This chapter reviews the arguments for and against, and attempts to get beneath them to find out why the subject was so explosive.

Sir Thomas Hetherington and William Chalmers concluded that war criminals had been able to enter Britain after the war and that a certain number were still living in the United Kingdom. They were protected from prosecution in this country by an anomaly of the law, while past governments had regarded extradition to face trial abroad as undesirable for various reasons. There were substantial arguments in favour of doing nothing about these men, even though their presence in the United Kingdom had been finally established, but the authors of the report felt that 'The crimes committed are so monstrous that they cannot be condoned: their prosecution could act as a deterrent to others in future wars. To take no action would taint the United Kingdom with being a haven for war criminals.' Hetherington and Chalmers did not think that the lapse of time since the crimes were perpetrated excused action: 'There is no time limit on the trial of murder and manslaughter by British courts and police prosecutors do investigate and prosecute homicide committed in this country however long ago it was committed.' Discarding certain options for dealing with proven war criminals, such as deprivation of citizenship or extradition, Hetherington and Chalmers favoured legislation to allow prosecutions in this country in the belief that fair trials would be practicable and possible.[1]

This was the case, in essence, as it was presented to Parliament by a string of Government spokesmen such as the Home Secretary, David Waddington, and Earl Ferrers, the Conservative Home Affairs Minister in the Lords. Additional reasons were put forward by partisans of the report and the bill which was based on it, but these mainly anticipated or addressed objections. The extended case for war crimes legislation is best described in response to the case against changing the law. The following paragraphs are a collation of these arguments, and it should be remembered that at different stages in the legislative process some were more prominent than others. For example, the Hetherington–Chalmers Report recommended changes to the rules of evidence that were embodied in the 1988 Criminal Justice Act so that, with respect to England, this question was muted when the War Crimes Bill was eventually debated in March 1990. For Scottish lawyers and in the House of Lords, the changes in the rules of evidence remained hotly disputed.

The antagonists to war crimes prosecutions deployed a range of arguments which can be broken down into three broad categories: constitutional, legal and moral. In the latter category can be included opposition to war crimes legislation on the basis of the motives attributed to proponents of the campaign, often related to stereotypes and preconceptions about Judaism and Jewish behaviour.

The constitutional arguments touched on some of the oldest conventions in the British political tradition. One of these conventions is that administrations should not challenge the decisions of their predecessors. Those who had supported trials in the aftermath of the Second World War and, indeed, those like Lord Shawcross who still supported the principle of war crimes trials for contemporary offences, nevertheless felt that a decision had been taken in 1948 and that it was constitutionally beholden on subsequent administrations to abide by it. The debates in the Houses of Parliament in 1948 and the decision of the Government were frequently alluded to, particularly by those surviving members of the 1945–51 Government, such as Lord Mayhew, or of the civil service which implemented its policy.

The most powerful constitutional objection, however, hinged on the assertion that the bill was retrospective, meaning that it made criminal deeds which were not illegal at the time they were enacted or which the person committing them could not have been expected to know were against the law. Retrospective legislation has been an abomination in England since the seventeenth century when the Crown issued decrees to punish its enemies or to raise monies, usually bypassing Parliament, in ways that constantly caught people by surprise and left them with no defence. Although it is not at all unknown in recent times, the mention of retroactive legislation triggers a furious response. Rigid defenders of the constitution and the British legal system regard retrospective law as one of the most potent threats to individual liberty and respect for the rule of law. This line of thinking was most prominently displayed by MPs Ivor Stanbrook and Edward Heath and Lords Campbell of Alloway and Hailsham.

The retrospectivity argument rested on several doubts about the nature of the acts which were characterised as war crimes and about the spirit in which these acts were carried out. Mr Heath asked more than once whether it could be known for sure that the men now accused of war crimes knew that they were committing crimes at the time. Was it certain that they knew of the Hague Convention of 1907 concerning the treatment of prisoners of war and conduct towards civilians in occupied territories? Was it fair to say that they were carrying out acts of murder or manslaughter when they were obeying orders which derived ultimately from state policy? Finally, could the charge of genocide be held against them when the concept was invented as a juridical category of offence only in 1948? If the answer to these questions was negative, or if there was even a measure of doubt, then the War Crimes Bill was creating a situation in which men could be accused of crimes for carrying out acts that could, at the time, have been construed as innocent or within the law – a classic example of retrospectivity.

Another constitutional theme was that the War Crimes Bill represented an example of selective legislation. Like retrospectivity, selectivity is a concept that was evolved in order to protect the liberty of the subject. To prevent victimisation of groups or individuals by an unscrupulous monarch or Parliament, it is held that laws should be universal and not selective in application. Nicholas Bennett, Julian Amery and Lord Hailsham, amongst others, objected that the War Crimes Bill was based on the recommendations of a report which investigated a small, target group and in its secret annexe actually named certain individuals. This meant that a law would be passed not to address a universal situation or to create a crime which anyone might commit, but to deal with a select body of persons.

To demonstrate the element of selectivity, and to expose other failings in the argument for war crimes trials, opponents asked why the inquiry had examined only crimes committed on German-controlled territory between 1939 and 1945. Ivor Stanbrook and Tony Marlow pointed out that the bill ignored war crimes committed by the Japanese in the Far East or crimes, such as the Katyn massacre, carried out by the Russians on Soviet-controlled territory. They also questioned why the period was so narrowly defined. Several MPs and peers maintained that it would be fairer to pass a statute that made it possible to prosecute in British courts non-British nationals who committed war crimes in any country since 1939, embracing everyone from Jews who killed British soldiers in Palestine in 1946–7 to the Iraqis who murdered Kuwaitis in 1990–1. This would avoid the element of selectivity and, according to Sir Nicholas Fairbairn and Lord Monson respectively, have other merits, such as enabling the trial of Russians who committed atrocities in the service of Stalin or members of the Israeli Government implicated in atrocities in Mandatory Palestine.

A related contention was that war crimes could not be defined precisely and that the bill was establishing a more or less arbitrary category of offence. The use of German-held territory as a geographical limit excluded crimes committed by the Russians in occupied Poland in 1939–41 and in the Baltic states in 1940–1. With the controversy over the post-war repatriation of the Cossacks and the Chetniks fresh in people's minds as a result of the accusations made against Harold Macmillan, Lord Stockton, and Toby Low, Lord Aldington, several MPs like Sir Nicholas Fairbairn wondered whether the actions of British troops in Austria in 1945 might not be deemed by some to be a war crime. Whatever the intention of raising this or that case, the overall import of this line of reasoning was to expose what was seen as the arbitrariness, and hence the unfairness, of the War Crimes Bill.

Nicholas Bennett, Lord Hailsham and many others also asserted that since the legislation was framed to deal with a selected group of men, which by virtue of selection was predefined as suspect, the chances of their having a fair trial would be gravely prejudiced. This suggestion leads on to the legal arguments. These were aimed mainly at the recommendations for procedural changes to enable war crimes prosecutions, but there was also a general legal case which revolved around the need to ensure defendants a fair trial. In the December 1989 debates on the recommendations of the Hetherington–Chalmers Report it was initially thought that there would be three main changes in the law: to permit the use of live television links to relay the testimony of those too old or infirm to travel long distances; to allow the submission of recorded evidence on video and evidence by dead people; and the abandonment of committal proceedings. Due to the passage of the 1988 Criminal Justice Act, by the time the bill came before the House, only the last change required special legislation.

The procedural changes were challenged on various grounds, most powerfully by Ivor Stanbrook, Nicholas Bennett and Lord Hailsham. It was argued that the cross-examination of witnesses over a television link, in a foreign language, would be extremely difficult. The problems of identification would be multiplied by the use of television, with all its weaknesses of reproduction. Evidence presented on video was immune to cross-examination, as was the testimony of people who were deceased. Finally, the abandonment of committal proceedings eliminated a vital element in the defence which formed a traditional safeguard against an unjust trial.

The lapse of time in bringing prosecutions was universally considered by opponents of the bill to make safe identifications all but impossible. How could a person in his or her late sixties or older be expected to remember accurately a face last seen, perhaps fleetingly, fifty years before? Over such a long period, faces change, adding to the difficulties of identification. The trial of John Demjanjuk was often cited as a case in point. Some survivors of Treblinka had identified him as Ivan the Terrible, but many others had not.[2] Moreover, the lapse of time might mean that vital defence witnesses were now dead, although their testimonies might never have been recorded.

Documentary evidence might be used by the prosecution to support verbal testimony, but could this be trusted? Wartime identity cards, post-war eyewitness testimonies by people who had since died and other documents could be fabricated. Many people still distrusted the Soviet Union and its legal system, ascribing to the Russian secret service, the KGB, a capacity and a willingness to wage war on its opponents abroad using the medium of war crimes allegations. How could a defence team, funded by legal aid, command the resources necessary to challenge what might be a massively funded and well-organised plot to discredit anti-Soviet émigrés? The Hetherington–Chalmers team had travelled all over the world to collect evidence. With the help of the Soviet legal establishment they had tracked down and interviewed people in far-flung regions of the USSR. Would defence lawyers be afforded the same facilities and, if so, who would pay? Indeed, the sheer cost of war crimes trials was frequently held to be a potent reason for dropping the crusade. Objectors were also concerned that the defence would be overwhelmed by the press coverage, which would be lurid and one-sided. They feared that, after all the publicity attendant upon the report and the bill, it would be impossible to secure a jury that would be impartial. Moreover, there would be almost irresistible pressure on a judge to secure a conviction.

If there were prosecutions and a jury did convict, what sentence would the judge pronounce? This was a question that brought the central tenets of British justice to bear on the bill. In Roy Hattersley's words, the application of criminal law is intended to achieve specific ends: 'the deterrence of other potential criminals, the reformation of those guilty of crime, the protection of society against the repetition of the offences, retribution and a demonstration of the revulsion which society feels towards the crime and those who committed it'.[3] It was dubious whether war crimes trials had deterred atrocities in general since the late 1940s, and it was hardly credible to suggest that trials were merited so as to deter old men from reoffending, to reform them or to protect society.

Justice might be demonstrated by a successful prosecution for a war crime, but as Lord Campbell of Alloway, Lord Boyd-Carpenter and Sir John Stokes maintained, if an aged defendant was found guilty what sentence could be appropriate retribution? Would a judge sentence a man in his sixties or seventies to a prison sentence – and for how long? If not, then the sentence would be a mockery to the legion of victims. In other words, the War Crimes Bill created crimes for which it was virtually impossible to conceive a just sentence.

It might be contended that the risk of failing to secure a conviction or an appropriate sentence was worth running if, in the course of the judicial process, the truth of the Holocaust was laid before the public. Advocates of trials often referred to their educative value, particularly at a time when the survivors are diminishing in number and young people knew less and less about the terrible events of 1939–45. This reasoning was strongly condemned by Ted Heath, Tony Marlow, Ivor Stanbrook, Lord Campbell and Lord Hailsham, who characterised the establishment of a legal mechanism that would lead to trials with no deterrent value or appropriate retribution as little more than show trials. The business of framing criminal law was not to educate younger generations in the finer points of history: to do so was an illegitimate use of the courts, a distortion of justice and subversive of the rule of law.

If a court could not deal fairly and justly with alleged war criminals, according to the opponents of trials this did not mean that they would go unpunished. It was here that moral,

theological and philosophical arguments came into play. First
of all, it was possible that the guilty men suffered inner torment.
And if they were guilty, would it not be better to let God punish
them in the next world? After such a long period of time, it
was better to forgive, if not to forget, in this world and to
demonstrate to them the virtue of mercy, which they had denied
so ruthlessly to their victims. Many prominent Christians, like
Lord Longford, Lord Soper and the Bishop of St Albans, were
especially assiduous in their efforts to win opinion round to the
exercise of mercy. Others, like Lord Hailsham, appeared to
believe fervently in retribution, but felt it best to leave vengeance to God.

Advocacy of forgiveness was frequently coupled with the
claim that the campaign for war crimes trials was driven by
motives of revenge. This, in turn, was indissolubly linked to
the characterisation of the campaign as Jewish, the product of
a 'Jewish lobby' and the exemplification of an Old Testament
approach to justice. For example, Ivor Stanbrook told *Isis*
magazine:

> The Wiesenthal Centre are fanning the flames of Israeli hatred.
> They're not allowing our young people to grow up with their
> innocence unimpaired. They're determined to maintain this cul-
> ture of revenge that seems to be at the heart of all Jewish, or at
> least Israeli philosophy. The so-called All-Party Parliamentary
> War Crimes Group is a campaign directed by Jewish MPs,
> among others, and, I think, incidentally, by the Israeli govern-
> ment in pursuit of its overall campaign.

Stanbrook also told his interviewer on this occasion that 'There
is a powerful Jewish lobby in the media as you know.'[4]

In the debate in the House of Lords on 4 December 1989,
Lord Hailsham counselled against the need for obnoxious legislation to achieve revenge since, as he reminded the peers, the
Old Testament said, ' "Vengeance is mine; I will repay, saith
the Lord." And you may bet your life that he will.' Lord
Houghton characterised the Chief Rabbi's speech in favour of
the recommendations of the Hetherington–Chalmers Report
as 'dreadful in its literal sense. It was the voice of the Old

Testament as I was taught it, and Jehovah was not a kindly God.' Lady Saltoun of Abernethy, a cross-bencher, asserted that, unlike Wiesenthal, the Christians who had suffered at the hands of the Japanese 'prefer to try to forgive and forget'.[5]

The notion of forgiveness was often connected with a concern for the emergence of the new Europe. To Europeanists like Edward Heath and Lord Pym, the end of the cold war, the unification of Germany and the transformation of politics in Eastern Europe made it the least opportune moment to scratch open old wounds. It was a time to let bygones be bygones, to forgive past crimes and to strive to build for the future, rather than indulge in potentially endless recriminations over the wrongs committed under the *ancien régime*. It would be more profitable to dedicate the time, money and energy which it was proposed should be devoted to hunting down pensioners suspected of war crimes to creating a new world order. Indeed, war crimes trials could send the wrong message to the newly freed peoples of Eastern Europe and encourage them to indulge in an orgy of retribution, causing feuds that would damage the chances of harmony in the future.

Young people, growing up under the new dispensation, would not understand what was at issue in any war crimes trials. Edward Heath and Lord Pym feared that youth would recoil in horror from the sight of relentless judicial action against old men for an outcome of such doubtful value that it would have all the appearance of revenge for its own sake. They would set a bad, instead of a good, example, and one out of keeping with the spirit of the new times. How could it be right to impose months and years of uncertainty on the alleged suspects; what could justify subjecting witnesses to the trauma of reliving their suffering in concentration and death camps? Lord Fraser of Kilmorack spoke for others when he maintained that, for young and old alike, war crimes trials would have a disastrous effect.

In fact, according to many pundits, the application of such a law would be so horrendous that it would cause a backlash against the Jews. Many of those who resisted the legislation did so out of proclaimed concern for the Jewish people in whose

interests it was argued the bill was being passed. Like the
Bishop of St Albans and Lord Longford, they warned that the
bill would have the opposite effect to that which was intended.
It could not deliver justice for the victims or consolation to the
bereaved; on the contrary, it would stir up resentment against
the Jews, wipe out the sympathy which they deserved as a
consequence of their suffering and so perpetuate the forces
which had caused such havoc with Jewish lives in the first
place. Far from acting as a deterrent, it would be an incitement
to hatred.

Indeed, the freeing of public opinion inside the former USSR
gave a new twist to this suggestion. Many dissident nationalists
within the republics of the USSR – particularly the Baltics and
the Ukraine – resent the exhumation of the wartime past. They
see war crimes trials as a Soviet-inspired attempt, or even an
international Jewish plot, to besmirch their aspirations. By way
of counter-attack, they demanded the trial of Lazar Kaganovich, the ninety-seven-year-old survivor of Stalin's Politburo
who was responsible for the terror and famine in the Ukraine in
1930–3. So, alongside public feeling in this country – especially
amongst British Jews, East European immigrants and their
children – has been added the emerging public opinion east of
what used to be the Iron Curtain. The war crimes issue represents one dimension in the evolving relations between East
and West, Jews and East Europeans in Britain, as well as the
large Jewish population of the Ukraine and Ukrainian nationalists. The experiences of Canada and Australia suggest that
trials may well aggravate ethnic tensions.[6]

In the parliamentary debates, in broadcasts, in articles and
in letters to the press, the proponents of war crimes legislation
offered their reply to these arguments. David Waddington and
John Patten dealt repeatedly with the argument that the bill
reversed the decision of a previous administration. In the first
place, they told MPs that no one in the late 1940s seemed
aware of the circumstances being addressed by the current
legislation, so a decision not to prosecute war criminals in
Britain could not have been made. Indeed, no British Government since 1945 had ever abjured the conduct of war crimes

trials on British soil should the need arise. The Labour Government of 1945–51 had only announced that it would suspend further trials in the British Zone of Germany and leave it to the West German authorities to continue actions against war criminals.[7]

The argument that the legislation was retrospective was treated as a red herring since, as the title of the bill indicated, it was intended only to extend the jurisdiction of British courts to cover crimes that were committed by non-British persons in a foreign country. John Patten, Sir Patrick Mayhew and Kenneth Baker patiently repeated to the House that the legislation did not create new offences: it merely corrected an anomaly that prevented British courts from trying men who were guilty of acts that were indubitably criminal at the time they were committed. Was it credible, they and others asked, that those who carried out, or abetted in, the mass murder of thousands of defenceless men, women and children, away from the heat of battle, could have been unaware that they were breaching local and international law? Time and again, proponents of the bill declared that murder was murder, notwithstanding the distance in time and geography from Britain in the 1990s.[8]

The argument of selectivity was met with the stock response that since there were no known perpetrators of Japanese or Soviet war crimes in Britain, it was a pointless exercise to extend the bill to embrace them, too. Like other legislation, the War Crimes Bill was formulated to meet a specific nuisance exposed by a public inquiry. As for British jurisdiction in the case of crimes committed in other countries by non-nationals since 1945, they were covered by numerous international conventions to which Britain had subsequently become a signatory, such as the 1957 Geneva Conventions Act and the 1969 Genocide Act. These acts would cover the eventuality of Iraqis, for example, turning up in Britain while they were wanted for war crimes in Kuwait.[9]

To those who adduced other acts committed during the Second World War – such as the bombing campaign against Germany or the handover of Cossacks and Chetniks – as evidence that the definition of a war crime was arbitrary, the most concise riposte was delivered by Anthony Beaumont-Dark in a memorable exchange with Ivor Stanbrook. 'It is not a matter of saying, "We all did naughty things." I urge my hon. Friend the Member for Orpington [Mr Stanbrook] not to belittle the carnage of the Holocaust by saying that we all did things that we regret. It is not a matter of regret but of record that a great evil took place for which no one responsible should be forgiven – however old, however ancient, or however decrepit they may be.'[10]

Government spokesmen and the legal experts who supported the bill, including Peter Archer and Greville Janner, attended to the legal arguments that a fair trial would not be possible. They submitted that the passage of time was not, in fact, an insuperable barrier. It had been shown in recent war crimes trials in other countries, not to mention the Lord Aldington defamation case in 1988–9, that witnesses could recall faces and details from forty-five years ago. They quoted Kitty Hart and Simon Wiesenthal, who maintained that those who were tormented in the camps had the faces of their persecutors etched on their memories; Alex Carlile cited the case of his own mother, who could remember vividly the days she passed in Warsaw during the ghetto uprising. What was more, courtroom identifications would be buttressed by the use of documents. To those who doubted the reliability of evidence emanating from the USSR, they cited the willingness to use such material in the United States, Australia and Canada. No proven cases of forgeries had yet come to light.

Home Office ministers assured MPs that defendants would be eligible for legal aid and that their representatives would be enabled to collect evidence in foreign countries. Proponents of the legislation dismissed fears of prejudgment as a result of the Hetherington–Chalmers Report or trial by media. Cases were only ever brought to court by the Director of Public Prosecutions on suspicion of guilt; to characterise that as prejudicing a jury would be to make prosecutions impossible. It was also held to be a major slight against judges and juries to argue that they would not be able to see past the circumstances in which a case came to court and the quality of the evidence presented by either side. The same was true for the threatened impact of press hysteria: that tended to accompany every major criminal trial and was a fact of life which the courts had learned to live with.

Advocates of the War Crimes Bill insisted that it did not depart one bit from the principles of British justice. It was common for them to argue, perhaps not as bluntly as Lord Beloff, that they put their faith in the British legal system to ensure that trials were fair. Although committal proceedings would be abandoned – as was already the practice for serious fraud cases – the DPP would still have to decide whether to recommend that a case should go to court. Then the judge would have to assess whether the defendant was fit to take the stand, taking into account age, health and mental faculties: no judge would be so inhumane as to subject an aged, sick and fragile man to the rigours of the judicial process. The judge and the jury would then assess the evidence and hear the arguments as normal: there would be no more pressure to convict than in other 'sensational' cases, and the judge would be sure to bear this in mind in his conduct of the trial. MPs and peers alike argued that it was not up to them to decide the merits of a case in advance and to prevent it coming to court: that was up to the DPP and the judges. Moreover, they noted that three Home Secretaries had seen the secret annexe to the Hetherington–Chalmers Report. It was wrong for Parliament to doubt the wisdom of their decision on the basis of the limited material to which MPs and peers had access.

The champions of the bill insisted that its main and overriding purpose was to provide justice and to prevent murderers circumventing the law which applied to all other residents and citizens of the British Isles. Only occasionally did they suggest that there were other than legal reasons for conducting them. Greville Janner argued that they were necessary in order to teach future generations what had been perpetrated during the Holocaust and to correct the tendency towards Holocaust denial. Llin Golding urged a change in the law because: 'The bill may not lead to the single prosecution of a war criminal who resides in this country, but at least it would give those criminals the bitter taste of fear that, one day, someone may knock at their door and take them away to answer for the suffering and misery they inflicted on so many innocent men, women and children.'[11]

War crimes trials might not deter potential criminals, but at least the pledge to harry the guilty men would not appear to condone such acts. To Lord Fitt, a former Belfast MP, that was a vital factor and by no means an abstract debating point. Not to do so would mark Britain out from other countries and give a poor example to the nations in the new Europe. It would seem to indicate that in the Parliament of the United Kingdom the urge to forget unpleasant periods of history and evade awkward moral and legal obligations was stronger than the desire for justice and the enforcement of the law. It would also signal to other countries that Britain did not regard the persecution of minorities with undue gravity; if tyrants and torturers could escape justice for long enough, then they were secure. This message would be welcomed by the secret police-men, the death squads and the bureaucrats of genocide all around the world. If war crimes trials cost millions of pounds, it was money well spent to avoid this blot on the reputation of British justice and the awful inspiration which it would give to evil and unscrupulous people.

Both Jewish and non-Jewish MPs and peers responded to the admonition that war crimes trials would provoke an anti-Jewish backlash. Non-Jews, like Jeff Rooker, pointed out that the bill was not a 'Jewish' measure and strongly deprecated attempts to characterise the campaign as the work of a Jewish lobby either in California or in Britain. Some Jews, like Lord Beloff, turned the argument around and maintained that rejec-tion of the bill would inspire anti-semites. At a time when racism and anti-semitism seemed on the increase, the denial of justice to the victims of the Holocaust would be interpreted as a sign that little importance was placed on Jewish suffering. Others assured MPs and peers that there would always be a certain amount of anti-semitism, but it was quite wrong to use this as an excuse for not dealing with crimes that resulted from hatred of the Jews in its purest form.

The same line applied to the argument that war crimes trials might sour relations between the contending parties, particularly Jews, on the one hand, and Balts and Ukrainians on the other. In fact, Jews and Ukrainians in Britain have already engaged in argument and dialogue over the war crimes issue. The Ukrainian Civil Liberties Committee in London lodged a protest with the All-Party Parliamentary War Crimes Group after the publication of its report in November 1988, complaining that it had not been consulted and attacking many of the report's findings. Ukrainian activists have written frequently to the *Jewish Chronicle* disputing the allegations against the Galizien Division.[12]

However, the record suggests that these issues will not just disappear and cannot be ignored. It is not inevitable that this encounter with the past should be destructive: Jews and Ukrainians share a history of suffering in the USSR, sometimes at the hands of the Communist Party and the Soviet state and sometimes at the hands of each other. Many Jews were deeply committed to the communist cause and the Soviet regime, which a large proportion of Ukrainians perceived as alien and oppressive; some Jews, like Kaganovich, carried out acts of appalling barbarity. Not all Ukrainians assisted the Nazis and some, like Metropolitan Andrei Sheptyts'kyi, protested against the conduct of both the Germans and their native aides.[13]

To some participants in the debate, the arguments which were used by the opponents of war crimes trials demonstrated that misconceptions about the Jews and Judaism, verging on anti-semitism, needed no further encouragement to burst into the public domain. In particular, the attribution of a spirit of vengeance to proponents of the War Crimes Bill aroused the greatest indignation. This was accentuated by the tendency of the bill's Christian opponents to lay claim to forgiveness and mercy, and the repeated contrast between the virtues of Christianity and the shortcomings of Judaism. The supporters of the bill denied that they wanted revenge and insisted that they were interested only in justice, closing a loophole in the law which allowed men guilty of obscene crimes to evade prosecution. In that sense the contrast between Jewish notions of 'revenge' and Christian ideas of forgiveness was irrelevant. However, once opponents of war crimes trials had labelled them as the product of an alleged Judaic zeal for the cold and unrelenting pursuit of wrongdoers, it was behoven on the other side to rebut the allegation. The most eloquent riposte was delivered by the Chief Rabbi in the House of Lords debate in December 1989. He told the peers, 'My faith abhors vengeance. The Law of Moses denounces as a grave moral offence the bearing of a grudge or the taking of revenge.'[14]

The repetition of this 'vicious canard' which associated Jews with vengeance was intimately related to the identification of the bill with a predominantly Jewish lobby. Consideration of this allegation necessarily leads on to wider discussion of history, memory and the character of British society, all of which were at issue in the debate on the War Crimes Bill. The opponents of the legislation tried to marginalise it by attributing it to one religious–ethnic group and asserting that it was illegitimate to impose the interests of this community on British society and British justice. Supporters of the bill stressed that it was a measure of national importance and universal relevance, and even if it was of special meaning to one community that was no reason to forestall its progress.

At the heart of this debate was a dispute over the character of British society. To the opponents of the bill, like Ivor Stanbrook and Lady Saltoun of Abernethy, it was a question of an 'alien' idea of justice being imposed on British people and British law for the sake of acts committed by foreigners in a faraway place lost in the mists of time. Going further than other speakers in marginalising immigrants in British society, Lady Saltoun asked, 'Is it decent and fitting that we should take such a step in order to enable aliens to be revenged on other aliens for something done in a foreign country nearly half a century ago?' Thus a British-based movement of British-born people concerned with crimes against Jews and, equally, Allied prisoners of war was stigmatised, rather ludicrously, as 'alien'.[15]

To put this selective rejection of history into context, it is important to recall that the war crimes debate occurred during prolonged celebrations of, and meditation on, Britain's recent past. The Hetherington–Chalmers Report was discussed in Parliament soon after the media had been marking the fiftieth anniversary of the outbreak of the Second World War. When the War Crimes Bill arrived in the House of Lords in May 1990, it was narrowly preceded by a vast outpouring of nostalgia about Dunkirk and the 'little ships'. This was followed by an orgy of reminiscences centred on the Blitz. The accusations made against Lord Stockton and Lord Aldington by Nikolai Tolstoy generated an enormous amount of public interest during 1988–90. In 1991, two large volumes of the Cowgill Report, exonerating Lord Stockton of any 'conspiracy' to hand over Cossacks and Chetniks to face certain death at the hands of the Russians and the Yugoslavs in 1945, were published.[16]

There was hardly a murmur of protest that extensive resources should be devoted to these anniversaries or investigations. Clearly, some parts of history were considered more important than others, and whereas it was virtually taken for granted that there would be an insatiable public appetite for the recollections of certain individuals or communities, other people's experiences were simply passed over in silence. What the debate over the War Crimes Bill exposed most painfully was the stubborn refusal in many quarters to acknowledge that Britain is a multi-ethnic society with many strands of history. There is the official history, the history of great public men and women, the history of the nation defined according to the majority community – white, Christian and usually male. But there is also a history of women, of ethnic minorities, of half-forgotten communities far from the centre of metropolitan life. When such groups ask for their history to be recalled, celebrated or mourned, they are dismissed as a 'lobby'. When they seek redress for past injustices, even for something as massive as the Holocaust, involving only the application of the law to known, suspected murderers, they are accused of pursuing a narrow agenda that diverts time, money and energy from the real business of the nation.

In this way, the war crimes debate excavated layers of injustice. The blunder committed in 1946–8 was compounded by the refusal to act against alleged war criminals for forty years.

The guilty men escaped retribution; their victims were denied justice. Not only did the crimes go unpunished, but the story of the crimes was buried, the survivors rendered mute and their history denied. When they pleaded for redress, they were threatened with a repetition of the trauma they had endured.

Opponents of war crimes legislation frequently invoked the changes in Europe – *glasnost*, the reunification of Germany, the collapse of Communist power throughout the old Eastern bloc – to suggest that it was time to forgive and forget, to bury the past. But in so doing they displayed a fundamental ignorance of what was happening in Central and Eastern Europe. Throughout the erstwhile Eastern bloc there are calls for justice against Stalin's henchmen. In 1986, Russian intellectuals including Andrei Sakharov and Roy Medvedev gave their support to a campaign to establish a monument to Stalin's victims. The Memorial Group staged a 'week of conscience' in Moscow and in Leningrad in 1988 and 1989. Progressive journals like *Ogonyok* and *Literaturnaya Gazeta* became platforms for debating the question of how to honour the memory of those who suffered under Stalinism. In January 1989, Memorial held its founding conference and addressed to the Government its demands for an official research centre and a commemorative monument.

Memorial received huge backing from the Baltic republics and the Ukraine who went still further. In May 1989, the nationalist movements in the representative assemblies of the Baltic republics – the Lithuanian Sayudis, the Latvian Duma and the Estonian Council of Deputies – simultaneously passed a resolution on the 'crimes of Stalinism'. The resolution declared that in the 1940s a totalitarian regime had been imposed on them. They demanded legal condemnation of the crimes committed under Stalin and the trial of those responsible who were still alive. In addition, the Supreme Soviet was called upon to declare that the Baltic peoples had suffered 'genocide' and to pay compensation to the victims. Finally, the three bodies wanted a Nuremberg-style tribunal set up to pass judgment on the Soviet secret police, the NKVD.

Since then, debate has raged inside the USSR about how to deal with the past. The Government rejected the most extreme demands of the Baltic republics, but it even baulked at the moderate requests emanating from Memorial. When it was found that several of the NKVD interrogators and court prosecutors who had operated during the purges before and after the Second World War were still alive, the Government deflected calls for immediate trials by appealing to the statute of limitations. The Communist Party Central Committee set up a research body, but it acted sluggishly and has rehabilitated only a few of Stalin's more prominent victims.

Gorbachev delivered a series of reasons for inaction that exactly paralleled those heard in Parliament at almost the same time. It was time to build for the future; it was painful and unhealthy to delve into the past; investigations would bring the party and state institutions into disrepute; the party and the state apparatuses were no longer the same; the suspects were old men, half in the grave, and could not be punished appropriately; inquiries were divisive at a time when unity was required; they would not bring the dead back. Meanwhile, Ivan Shekhovtsov, a state prosecutor who had served under Stalin, has used the courts to challenge the claims made against his one-time master. He argued over the course of eighteen separate submissions that there were no documents to show that Stalin was guilty of any crimes. As in the West, the denial of justice was inevitably accompanied by the repression of history and, in the end, the denial of the crimes themselves.

However, the past will not go away. Until his recent death, Ukrainian nationalists sought the trial of Lazar Kaganovich, once Stalin's right-hand man, whom they blamed for the war on the kulaks, the rich peasants, and the subsequent famine which killed millions of Ukrainians in 1930–3. Memorial continues its struggle to rehabilitate the countless legions of people murdered in the purges and lost in the gulag. To this group, untrammelled historical research and the confrontation with the past is a necessary part of democratisation. In order to build a new Russia, they argue, it is necessary to face the old one.[17]

This phenomenon spreads all across the former Eastern bloc. A decisive moment in the inception of the revolution in Czechoslovakia was the public declaration by its neighbours that the invasion of 1968 had been wrong. When Alexander Dubcek stepped on to the balcony overlooking Wenceslas Square on 24 November 1989, it was the symbolic rectification of a crime committed over twenty years earlier, but never forgiven. The recent graveside ceremony to rehabilitate Imre Nagy, the reforming leader eliminated after the Russians suppressed the Hungarian Revolt in 1956, likewise showed the passion for justice – no matter how late in the day. In the Eastern and Western parts of the 'Common Home', nations, ethnic groups, cultures and religions are asserting their claims and seeking redress against decades of squalor and oppression. History has returned: it stalks the present ruthlessly.[18]

This is true even in Western Europe. France is a country still sundered by the legacy of the war years. The trials of Klaus Barbie, Paul Touvier and René Bousquet were an acknowledgment that for sections of French society the past was not dead and buried: executioners, collaborators, victims were still alive and, while that was the case, then justice could – and, some argued, should – be done. In France, as in Britain, war crimes trials have evoked enormous public debate and proved to be equally divisive. Yet the French authorities finally opted for the judicial process. It is certainly true that the French situation is significantly different: the crimes were committed by Frenchmen against fellow citizens while their country was under occupation. However, the principles remain the same: should crimes be allowed to go unpunished if they occurred over forty years ago or should the legal system be submitted to sundry pressures to accommodate the passion for justice?[19]

If the evolution of the new Europe has any lessons, it is that the past cannot be repressed and the pluralism of nation states is ignored at enormous risk. This is understood nowhere better than in the patchwork countries of Central and Eastern Europe and the Balkans. Emancipation from totalitarianism entails facing up to and accommodating diversity, a process which necessarily extends to history.[20] Conversely, liberal democracy protects itself against the slide into intolerance at the behest of an inflamed majority by insisting on the rights of minorities, respecting their histories and taking notice of their agendas. Justice delayed may not be justice denied, after all; but history denied will never lead to justice.

Notes

Chapter 1: *Collaborators and War Criminals*

1 For a chilling account of Nazi objectives, see Norman Rich, *Hitler's War Aims*, vol. 1: *The Nazi State and the Course of Expansion* (London, 1973), pp. 204–23, and vol. 2: *The Establishment of the New Order* (London, 1974), pp. 326–83.

2 It was only in the course of negotiations between the SS and the Army over co-operation between the two arms that the detection and execution of Jews was formally broached. During the course of July 1941, the operational scope of the Einsatzgruppen was widened to embrace virtually the entire Jewish population. By the autumn, the Einsatzgruppen were killing all Jewish men, women and children and liquidating ghettos that they had set up earlier on in the campaign. See Introduction to Yitzhak Arad, Shmuel Krakowski and Shmuel Spector (eds), *The Einsatzgruppen Reports* (hereafter *ER*), (New York, 1989), pp. i–iii; cf. Andreas Hillgruber, 'War in the East and the Extermination of the Jews', in Michael Marrus (ed.), *The Nazi Holocaust*, vol. 2: Pt 3, *The 'Final Solution' and the Implementation of Mass Murder* (Westport, C.T., 1989), pp. 94–9, and Christian Streit, 'The German Army and the Policies of Genocide', in Gerhard Hirschfeld, (ed.), *The Policies of Genocide: Jews and Soviet Prisoners of War in Nazi Germany* (London, 1986), pp. 2–4.

3 Raul Hilberg, *The Destruction of the European Jews* (New York, 1985), vol. 1, p. 291.

4 *ER*, pp. v–vi. The definitive study is Helmut Krausnick and Hans-Heinrich Wilhelm, *Die Truppen des Weltanschauungskrieges* (Stuttgart, 1981).

5 Anthony Read and David Fisher, *The Deadly Embrace: Hitler, Stalin and the Nazi–Soviet Pact, 1939–1941* (London, 1988), pp. 254–5, 363–70, 465–71.

6 Dov Levin *Fighting Back: Lithuanian Jewry's Armed Resistance to the Nazis, 1941–1945* (New York, 1985), pp. 7–24; Hilberg, *Destruction of the European Jews*, pp. 309–13; J. Lee Ready, *The Forgotten Axis: Germany's Partners and Foreign Volunteers in World War Two* (Jefferson, NC, 1987), pp. 139–45.

7 Levin, *Fighting Back*, pp. 95–7; Avraham Tory [Golub], *Surviving the Holocaust: The Kovno Ghetto Diary* (Cambridge, Mass., 1990), pp. x–xii (for biographical details) and 7.

8 *ER*, No. 8, 30 June 1941, Nos. 14, 19, 21, for 6, 11, 13 July 1941.

9 *Ibid.*, No. 21, 13 July 1941; Yitzhak Arad, *Ghetto in Flames: The Struggle and Destruction of the Jews in Vilna in the Holocaust* (New York, 1982), pp. 48–9.

10 See Yaroslav Bilinsky, 'Methodological Problems and Philosophical Issues in the Study of Jewish – Ukrainian Relations During the Second World War', and Aharon Weiss, 'Jewish – Ukrainian Relations in Western Ukraine During the Second World War', in Peter J. Potichnyj and Howard Aster (eds), *Ukrainian – Jewish Relations in Historical Perspective* (Edmonton, Alberta, 1988); Shimon Redlich, 'Metropolitan Andrei Sheptytsk'yi, Ukrainians and Jews During and After the Holocaust', *Holocaust and Genocide Studies*, 5:1 (1990), pp. 39–52. For the personal recollections of a Jew saved by Metropolitan Sheptytsk'yi and reflections of Ukrainian – Jewish relations, see David Kahane, *Lvov Ghetto Diary* (Amherst, Mass., 1991), pp. 118–50.

11 *ER*, No. 14, 6 July 1941; No. 20, 12 July 1941; No. 24, 16 July 1941; Philip Friedman, 'Ukrainian – Jewish Relations During the Nazi Occupation', *YIVO Annual of Jewish Social Science*, 12 (1958/9), pp. 272–9.

12 Friedman, 'Ukrainian – Jewish Relations', p. 272; Kahane, *Lvov Ghetto Diary*, pp. 5–13; Gerald Reitlinger, *The House Built on Sand* (London, 1960), pp. 166–7; cf. Hilberg, *Destruction of the European Jews*, p. 311.

13 Simon Wiesenthal, *The Murderers Among Us*, ed. Joseph Wechsberg (London, 1967), pp. 29–31.

14 Malvina Graf, *The Krakow Ghetto and the Plaszow Camp Remembered* (Tallahasse, Fla, 1989), p. 30.

15 Hilberg, *Destruction of the European Jews*, p. 311.

16 *ER*, No. 24, 16 July 1941; No. 27, 19 July 1941; No. 43, 5 August 1941; No. 47, 9 August 1941; No. 81, 12 September 1941; No. 112, 13 October 1941; No. 127, 31 October 1941; No. 133, 14 November 1941; Hilberg, *Destruction of the European Jews*, pp. 309, 312.

17 Hilberg, *Destruction of the European Jews*, p. 273. Krausnick and Wilhelm, *Die Truppen des Weltanschauungskrieges*, pp. 596–8.

18 Hilberg, *Destruction of the European Jews*, pp. 369–70; Ready, *The Forgotten Axis*, pp. 158–62; *ER*, No. 48, 10 August 1941.

19 *ER*, No. 19, 11 July 1941.

20 *Ibid.*, No. 21, 13 July 1941.

21 Report on Riga Ghetto Case, Wiener Library Archive (WLA), file 539/22; Frida Michelson, *I Survived Rumbuli* (New York, 1979), pp. 33–4, 61–2.

22 *ER*, No. 111, 12 October 1941.

23 *Ibid.*, No. 17, 7 July 1941; No. 21, 13 July 1941; No. 24, 16 July 1941; No. 26, 18 July 1941; No. 40, 3 August 1941; No. 48, 10 August 1941;. No. 80, 11 September 1941; No. 106, 7 October 1941; No. 111, 12 October 1941; No. 131, 10 November 1941; Hilberg, *Destruction of the European Jews*, pp. 313–14.

24 *ER*, No. 80, 11 September 1941.

25 Hilberg, *Destruction of the European Jews*, pp. 369–72.

26 Tory, *Surviving the Holocaust*, pp. 37–8, 50–1, 159, 195, 289–90, 403–7, 490–1.

27 Michelson, *I Survived Rumbuli*, pp. 72–3, 86.

28 Tadeusz Pankiewicz, *The Cracow Ghetto Pharmacy* (New York, 1987), p. 72.

29 Abraham Lewin, *A Cup of Tears: A Diary of the Warsaw Ghetto*, ed. Antony Polonsky (Oxford, 1989), p. 151.

30 *The Journal of Emmanuel Ringelblum*, ed. and trans. Jacob Sloan (New York, 1958), p. 340.

31 Ready, *The Forgotten Axis*, p. 265; *The Stroop Report* (London, 1980), lists forces used in the clearing of the Warsaw Ghetto.

32 Yitzhak Arad, *Belzec, Sobibor, Treblinka: The Operation Reinhard Death Camps* (Bloomington, Ind., 1987), pp. 7–13.

33 *Ibid.*, pp. 17–22; Hilberg, *Destruction of the European Jews*, pp. 898, 902, 914.

34 Alexander Donat (ed.), *The Death Camp Treblinka: A Documentary* (New York, 1979), p. 122; Samuel Willenberg, *Surviving Treblinka*, ed. Wladyslaw T. Bartoszewski (Oxford, 1989), pp. 56–7, 97.

35 Krolikowski quoted in Arad, *Belzec, Sobibor, Treblinka*, p. 163; Jankiel Wiernik testimony in Donat (ed.), *The Death Camp Treblinka*, pp. 165–6.

36 Miriam Novitch, *Sobibor Martyrdom and Revolt* (New York, 1980), p. 150; Zabecki, quoted in Arad, *Belzec, Sobibor, Treblinka*, p. 67; Willenberg, *Surviving Treblinka*, pp. 59–60, 66–7.

37 Donat, *The Death Camp Treblinka*, p. 122; Julien Hershaut, *Jewish Martyrs of Pawiak* (New York, 1982), pp. 73–4, 104–5, 229–30.

38 Dallin, *German Rule in Russia, 1941–1945: A Study of Occupation Policies* (2nd edn, London, 1981), pp. 111–19; Gerhard L. Weinberg, *The Foreign Policy of Hitler's Germany: Diplomatic Revolution in Europe, 1933–36* (Chicago, 1970), pp. 85–6.

39 B. Baranauskas and K. Rukensas, *Documents Accuse* (Vilna, 1970), pp. 51–4; Hans Werner Neulen, *An deutscher Seite: Internationale Freiwillige von Wehrmacht und Waffen-SS* (Munich, 1985), pp. 275–6.

40 Neulen, *An deutscher Seite*, pp. 281 and 289; T. P. Mulligan, *The Politics of Illusion and Empire: German Occupation Policy in the Societ Union, 1942–1943*, (New York, 1988) p. 85; Ready, *The Forgotten Axis*, pp. 139–41.

41 Baranauskas and Rukensas, *Documents Accuse*, pp. 55–9; Ready, *The Forgotten Axis*, p. 156.

42 John A. Armstrong, *Ukrainian Nationalism, 1939–1945* (2nd edn, New York, 1963), pp. 24–36; Dallin, *German Rule in Russia, 1941–1945*, pp. 114–16; Ready, *The Forgotten Axis*, pp. 11–12; Myroslav Yurkevich, 'Galician Ukrainians in German Military Formations and in the German Administration', in Yury Boshyk (ed.), *Ukraine During World War Two: History and Its Aftermath* (Edmonton, Alberta, 1986), pp. 69–70.

43 Armstrong, *Ukrainian Nationalism*, pp. 48–9; Ready, *The Forgotten Axis*, pp. 18, 23.

44 Armstrong, *Ukrainian Nationalism*, pp. 73–87, 97–107; Dallin, *German Rule in Russia, 1941–1945*, pp. 119–22; Neulen, *An deutscher Seite*, pp. 306–9; Ready, *The Forgotten Axis*, pp. 144–5, 163; Yurkevich, 'Galician Ukrainians in German Military Formations and in the German Administration', pp. 70–2.

45 Ready, *The Forgotten Axis*, pp. 192–5. On the failure of German planning and the weaknesses of the Wehrmacht, see Alan Clark, *Barbarossa* (paperback edn, London, 1966), Book 1; Dallin, *German Rule in Russia, 1941–1945*, pp. 18–19.

46 Ready, *The Forgotten Axis*, pp. 156–7, 162–4.

47 *Ibid.*, pp. 192–5; Joachim Hoffman, *Die Ostlegionen, 1941–1943* (Freiburg, 1986), pp. 11–25.

48 Neulen, *An deutscher Seite*, p. 278; Ready, *The Forgotten Axis*, pp. 216–17.

49 Ready, *The Forgotten Axis*, pp. 257–60.

50 Mulligan, *The Politics of Illusion and Empire*, chs. 4, 11; Ready, *The Forgotten Axis*, pp. 254–60; Joachim Hoffman, *Die Geschichte der Wlassow-Armee* (Freiburg, 1986), pp. 11–31.

51 Mulligan, *The Politics of Illusion and Empire*, pp. 163–76; Dallin, *German Rule in Russia, 1941–1945*, pp. 553–86, 613–36.

52 Gerald Reitlinger, *The SS: Alibi of a Nation, 1922–1945* (2nd edn, London, 1981), pp. 196–201, 205–6; George H. Stein, *The Waffen-SS: Hitler's Elite Guard at War, 1939–1945* (London, 1966), pp. 137–57, 165–89; Ready, *The Forgotten Axis*, pp. 272–6, 301–2,

304–5, 367–71; Mulligan, *The Politics of Illusion and Empire*, pp. 79–86.

53 Neulen, *An deutscher Seite*, pp. 291–2; K.-G. Klietmann, *Die Waffen-SS eine Dokumentation* (Osnabruck, 1965), pp. 373–6.

54 Neulen, *An deutscher Seite*, pp. 291–2; Mulligan, *The Politics of Illusion and Empire*, pp. 79–83, 154–5; Ready, *The Forgotten Axis*, pp. 301–5; Dallin, *German Rule in Russia, 1941–1945*, pp. 596–7.

55 Stein, *The Waffen-SS*, pp. 137–57, 165–89; Ready, *The Forgotten Axis*, pp. 495, 497–8. On the strictly military history of these units, see Neulen, *An deutscher Seite*, pp. 292–5; Klietmann, *Die Waffen-SS eine Dokumentation*, pp. 199–202, 219–22; Hans Stöber, *Die lettischen Divisionen im VI, SS-Armeekorps* (Osnabruck, 1981); Arthur Sigailis, *Latvian Legion* (San Jose, Ca., 1986); H. P. Taylor and R. J. Bender, *Uniforms, Organisation and History of the Waffen-SS*, vol. 5 (San Jose, Calif., 1982).

56 Neulen, *An deutscher Seite*, pp. 283–6; Stein, *The Waffen-SS*, pp. 176–7. For a sympathetic contemporary account of how Estonians were mobilised, see Ants Oras, *Baltic Eclipse* (London, 1948), pp. 237–8.

57 Neulen, *An deutscher Seite*, pp. 286–8; Stein, *The Waffen-SS*, pp. 176–9; Ready, *The Forgotten Axis*, pp. 367–73, 445–6, 491–2, 501.

58 Neulen, *An deutscher Seite*, pp. 310–12; Stein, *The Waffen-SS*, pp. 185–6; Myroslav Yurkevich, 'Galician Ukrainians in German Military Formations and in the German Administration', in Boshyk (ed.), *Ukraine During World War Two*, pp. 76–8.

59 Pavlo Shandruk, *Arms of Valor* (New York, 1959), pp. 279–80; Ready, *The Forgotten Axis*, pp. 272–6, 342–3, 369–70, 467–9, 493–4, 497–9; Yurkevich, 'Galician Ukrainians in German Military Formations', pp. 76–81.

Chapter 2: *Germany, Year Zero*

1 Stephen Spender, *European Witness* (London, 1946), p. 21.

2 The role of the intelligence agencies will be examined in a later chapter. The best overviews are Tom Bower, *Blind Eye to Murder* (paperback edn, London, 1983), and *idem, The Paperclip Conspiracy* (London, 1988), and Christopher Simpson, *Blowback: America's Recruitment of Nazis and Its Effects on the Cold War* (London, 1988).

3 Michael Balfour and John Mair, *Four Power Control in Germany and Austria, 1945–1946* (Oxford, 1956), pp. 7–12.

4 *Ibid.*, p. 12.

5 Mark Wyman, *DP Europe's Displaced Persons, 1945–1951* (Philadelphia, 1989), pp. 17–22; Malcolm J. Proudfoot, *European Refugees: 1939–52. A Study in Forced Population Movement* (London, 1957), pp. 78–93.

6 Wyman, *DP Europe's Displaced Persons*, p. 17; Proudfoot, *European Refugees*, pp. 38–40.

7 Leonard O. Mosley, *Report from Germany* (London, 1945), p. 57; Lord Strang, *At Home and Abroad* (London, 1956), p. 233. Stephen Spender thought that the Germans had no right to complain if people whom they had brutalised behaved in such a way, *European Witness*, pp. 70–4.

8 Proudfoot, *European Refugees*, pp. 110–19, 147–57.

9 See Balfour and Mair, *Four Power Control in Germany and Austria, 1945–1946*, pp. 92–107.

10 Proudfoot, *European Refugees*, pp. 168–75.

11 *Ibid.*, pp. 179–80, 240–1; Jacques Vernant, *The Refugee in the Post-War World* (London, 1953), pp. 30–1.

12 Bower, *Blind Eye to Murder*, pp. 133–6.

13 *Evening Standard*, 3 March 1987.

14 Proudfoot, *European Refugees*, pp. 207–11.

15 Mark R. Eliot, *Pawns of Yalta: Soviet Refugees and America's Role in Their Repatriation* (Urbana, Ill., 1982), pp. 30–49.

16 *Ibid.*, pp. 80–97; Proudfoot, *European Refugees*, pp. 214–18. The grim story is told in Nicholas Bethell, *The Last Secret* (paperback edn, London, 1987).

17 Eliot, *Pawns of Yalta*, pp. 110–11.

18 On the implementation of this change see, for example, Lt-Col. Logan, WO, to I. L. Henderson, FO, 25 June 1946: PRO, FO371/57750; Memorandum by Gen. V. Blomfield, Director of PoWs to GHQ Middle East, 26 June 1946; PRO, WO32/11171. Bethell, *The Last Secret*, pp. 222–45.

19 Yury Boshyk, 'Repatriation and Resistance: Ukrainian Refugees and Displaced Persons in Occupied Germany and Austria, 1945–1948', in Anna C. Bramwell (ed), *Refugees in the Age of Total War* (London, 1988), pp. 206–7; Proudfoot, *European Refugees*, pp. 237–8; Vernant, *The Refugee in the Post-War World*, p. 32.

20 Proudfoot, *European Refugees*, pp. 242, n. 3, 246–8; Vernant, *The Refugee in the Post-War World*, p. 33.

21 The IRO did not actually begin to function until August 1948 and before then the Preparatory Commission of the IRO (PCIRO)

performed its main tasks: Vernant, *The Refugee in the Post-War World*, pp. 33–8.

22 *Ibid.*, pp. 67–8, 75–6, 86–8; Proudfoot, *European Refugees*, pp. 275–92.

Chapter 3: *'Keep the Balts for As Long As Possible, and As Quietly As Possible'*

1 Dov Levin, 'On the Relations Between the Baltic Peoples and Their Jewish Neighbours Before, During and After World War II', *Holocaust and Genocide Studies*, 5:1 (1990), pp. 53–60.

2 A. G. Dickens, *Lübeck Diary* (London, 1947), pp. 44–5, 59–60, 64, 69, 84.

3 Stöber, *Die lettischen Divisionen*, pp. 285–6.

4 Communications between Foreign Office and SHAEF, July 1945: PRO, FO371/47051. Victor Rothwell, *Britain and the Cold War, 1941–1947* (London, 1982), pp. 97–8, 105.

5 Rothwell, *Britain and the Cold War*, pp. 16–19; *idem*, 'Robin Hankey', in John Zametica (ed.), *British Officials and Foreign Policy, 1945–50* (Leicester, 1990), pp. 161, 168 on Brimelow and pp. 156–82 on Hankey.

6 Correspondence, August 1945: PRO, FO371/47051; Correspondence, September 1945: PRO, FO371/47052.

7 Petition, 7 June 1945: PRO, FO371/47051.

8 Valdmanis to Alexander, 30 August 1945: PRO, FO371/47051; Mulligan, *The Politics of Illusion and Empire*, pp. 80–7.

9 Zarine to Foreign Office, 5 September 1945: PRO, FO371/47041; Latvian Legation appeal, 26 September 1945: PRO, FO371/47052.

10 Brimelow comment, 15 September 1945: PRO, FO371/47051.

11 Thomas Brimelow to Lt-Col. Hammer, War Office, 11 October 1945, passing on Warner's concern; and the non-committal information sent by the FO to the Control Commission Legal Department; PRO, FO371/47052.

12 Brimelow to King, 31 October 1945: PRO, FO371/47052; Warner conveyed this position to Zarine, 23 November 1945, and to the Red Cross, 26 November 1945: PRO, FO371/47053.

13 King to Brimelow, 1 December 1945: PRO, FO371/47053.

14 Kenchington to Political Division UNRRA, 27 September 1945: PRO, FO945/711.

15 Brimelow comment, 8 December 1945: PRO, FO371/47053.

16 Inquiry from International Red Cross, 11 December 1945; com-

ments by D. Mackillop, Refugee Department, 18 and 20 December 1945: PRO, FO371/47053.

17 Troutbeck comment, 11 December 1945: PRO, FO371/47053.

18 Brimelow comments, 17, 19 and 21 December 1945: PRO, FO371/47053.

19 ARGUS 225, 20 December 1945; comments by Brimelow, 21 December 1945: PRO, FO371/47053.

20 ARGUS 256, 21 December 1945; Brimelow to Lt-Col. Hammer, War Office, 27 December 1945: PRO, FO371/47053.

21 BAOR instructions, 28 January 1946: PRO, FO1049/612. See also, Minutes of Co-ordinating Committee on Disbandment of Ex-Wehrmacht Prisoners, Central Council of Allied Control Authority, 23 January 1946: PRO, FO371/56711. Ukrainians also resisted fiercely: see Boshyk, 'Repatriation and Resistance: Ukrainian Refugees and Displaced Persons in Occupied Germany and Austria, 1945–1948', pp. 206–9.

22 Lt-Col. Fogarty to PWDP Divn, CCG, 17 July 1946: PRO, FO1049/613.

23 Wyman, *DP Europe's Displaced Persons*, pp. 57–60, 68–85.

24 Record of Zarine's visit, 8 February 1946, and memo, 18 April 1946: PRO, FO371/57750.

25 *Manchester Guardian* report, 18 February 1946; Zilliacus question and reply, 19 February 1946; Orbach question and reply, 20 February 1946: PRO, FO371/55975.

26 Washington Embassy to FO, 23 February 1946: PRO, FO371/55975.

27 Hammer to I. L. Henderson, Refugee Department, FO, 1 March 1946; Brimelow to Hammer, 18 March 1946: PRO, FO371/55975.

28 Mr Pumphry minute, 11 March 1946: PRO, FO371/55975.

29 BERCOMB to TROOPERS, 5 April 1946: PRO, FO945/580.

30 Galsworthy comment, 1 January 1946: PRO, FO371/40753.

31 Rendel to Zarine, 11 May 1946; *Times* letter, 25 May 1946; *Tablet*, 15 June 1946: FO371/57750.

32 Neven-Spence, 17 December 1945: PRO, FO371/47053; Pickthorn question, 4 March 1946: PRO, FO371/55975; Bossom question, 22 May 1946: PRO, FO371/55976; Bossom to Home Secretary, Chuter Ede, 2 December 1946: PRO, FO371/65760; Zarine – Bossom communications and Driberg's intervention: PRO, FO371/47040.

33 Lt-Col. Logan, WO, to I. L. Henderson, Refugee Dept, FO, 25 June 1946; COGA statement on alleged repatriation, 28 June 1946: PRO, FO371/57750; Lt-Col. Lewis, WO, to COGA on

status of Balts, 30 August 1946: PRO, FO945/711; FO to Duchess of Atholl, 20 September 1946: PRO, FO945/368. War Office policy and instructions to DP&PoW officers in the field is contained in the memo by V. Blomfield, Director of PoWs, 26 June 1946: PRO, WO32/11171.

34 Alan Bullock, *Ernest Bevin*, vol. 3: *Foreign Secretary, 1945–1951* (London, 1983), p. 271.

35 Cadogan to Rendel, 17 October 1946; Rendel to FO, 23 October 1946: PRO, FO945/386.

36 C. E. Heathcote-Smith, Vice-Chairman and Honorary Secretary of the Refugee Defence Committee, to FO, 15 January 1947: PRO, FO371/66700.

37 RDC memo, 22 January 1947; COGA Policy on Baltic Personnel, 27 January 1947; COGA figures on ineligibles, CCG to FO, 30 January 1947: PRO, FO371/65754. Further material on the more relaxed British policy is held in PRO, FO371/66700 and FO371/77245.

38 Zarine to Hankey, 21 January and 17 February 1947: PRO, FO371/65754.

39 Zarine to Hankey, 28 October 1946: PRO, FO371/55977; Latvian sailors: PRO, FO371/55975; Brownjohn's comment, 30 November 1946: PRO, FO945/368.

40 File on Baltic PoWs in Britain: PRO, FO371/55797; Hankey to Zarine on policy of transfer, 20 August 1946: PRO, FO371/55980.

41 *Pravda* story, 12 January 1946; response of British military authorities in Copenhagen, 15 January 1946, and Copenhagen to FO, 19 January 1946; Strang to FO, 18 January 1946: PRO, FO371/55974.

42 FO Northern Department to Commander in Chief, Germany, 4 February 1946: PRO, FO371/55974.

43 On Kripens' rank and career, Stöber, *Die lettischen Divisionen*, pp. 308, 311; Zarine to Warner, 29 November 1945; 'Report on attempted suicide of Col Kripens', 16 December 1945: PRO, FO371/47053.

44 Comments by John Galsworthy, 19 and 20 December 1945: PRO, FO371/47053.

45 War Office to FO, 22 January 1946; Brimelow to Isham, 6 February 1946: PRO, FO371/55974.

46 WO to FO, 6 February 1946; Brimelow to Isham, WO, 20 February 1946: PRO, FO371/55794.

47 Stein, *The Waffen-SS*, p. 250.

48 Letter intercept, 28 February 1947; Brimelow to Maj. R. Allen,

JAG, 12 April 1947; War Crimes Group to JAG, 22 April and 15 July 1947; JAG to Brimelow, 18 July 1947: PRO, FO371/65762.

49 Years later, Kripens was named in several publications issued by the Latvian State Publishing House, but this was dismissed as black propaganda, e.g. B. Arklansz and I. Silabriedi, *Political Refugees Unmasked* (Riga, 1965), p. 24.

50 Political Division, BAOR to FO, 20 January 1946: PRO, FO371/55974.

51 Zarine to Hankey, 21 April 1947; Control Commission to FO, 3 June 1947; Hankey to Zarine, 3 June 1947: PRO, FO371/65754; JAG to FO, 24 November 1947; Brimelow to JAG, 2 December 1947: PRO, FO371/65755.

52 A. Wright-Rhodes, HQ Intelligence Division, CCG to FO, 8 September 1947: PRO, FO371/65755.

53 Guidelines on the automatic arrest of certain categories of PoW, including SS volunteers and officers: PRO, FO945/442.

54 Zarine to Hankey, 21 January 1947: PRO, FO371/65754.

55 Hankey to Zarine, 5 February 1947: PRO, FO371/65754.

Chapter 4: *'Good Human Stock': Population Policy, Immigration and Foreign Labour Recruitment*

1 Arthur Marwick, *British Society Since 1945* (paperback edn, London, 1990), p. 19; Alan Sked and Chris Cook, *Post-War Britain: A Political History London* (paperback edn, London, 1986), pp. 26–7.

2 Hugh Dalton, *High Tide and After: Memoirs, 1945–1960* (London, 1962), p. 70; Bullock, *Ernest Bevin*, vol. 3, pp. 126–7.

3 Bullock, *Ernest Bevin*, vol. 3, pp. 233–4, 239–40, 245–6; Kenneth Harris, *Attlee* (London, 1982), pp. 321–3, 339.

4 Bernard Donoughue and G. W. Jones, *Herbert Morrison: Portrait of a Politician* (London, 1973), p. 403; Dalton, *High Tide and After*, p. 195.

5 *Economic Survey for 1947* (London, 1947), Cmd 7046, p. 109; *The Times*, 14 February 1947, quoted in Ben Pimlott, *Hugh Dalton* (paperback edn, London, 1986), pp. 478–9.

6 *The Times*, 18 February 1947, quoted in Pimlott, *Hugh Dalton*, p. 479.

7 Cabinet Papers, PRO, CP 15 (46) 14 February 1946.

8 Keith Sword, 'The Absorption of Poles into Civilian Employment in Britain, 1945–1950', in Bramwell (ed), *Refugees in the Age of Total War*, pp. 233–52.

9 J. Isaac, *British Post-War Migration* (Cambridge, 1954); J. A. Tannahill, *European Voluntary Workers in Britain* (Manchester, 1958).

10 See, for example, G. F. McCleary, *Population: Today's Question* (London, 1938) and *The Menace of Britain's Depopulation* (London, 1939); Fabian Society pamphlets by Louis Ginzbury, *Parenthood and Poverty: The Population Problem of Democracy* (London, 1939) and A. Emil Davies, *Our Ageing Population* (London, 1938); W. B. Reddaway, *Economics in a Declining Population* (London, 1939).

11 *Report of the Royal Commission on Population* (London, 1949), Cmd 7695, p. 134.

12 *Ibid.*, p. 135.

13 *Ibid.*, p. 124.

14 *Ibid.*, pp. 124–5.

15 *Ibid.*, p. 130.

16 *Population Policy in Great Britain* (London, 1948), pp. 109–10.

17 *Ibid.*, p. 112. One chapter deals with eugenics and population policy, putting forward eugenic arguments for voluntary medical examination before marriage, free family-planning advice, and legislation to permit the abortion of foetuses borne by mental defectives as well as limited voluntary sterilisation of those who it was desirable should not become parents.

18 *Ibid.*, pp. 113–14.

19 *Ibid.*, p. 115.

20 *Population and the People: A National Policy* (London, 1945), pp. 42–3.

21 *Ibid.*, pp. 48–50.

22 Greta Jones, *Social Darwinism and English Social Thought: The Interaction Between Biological Theory and Social Theory* (Brighton, Sussex, 1980), pp. 167–71, and *idem*, 'Eugenics and Social Policy Between the Wars', *Historical Journal*, 25:3 (1982), pp. 717–28; Michael Freeden, 'Eugenics and Progressive Thought: A Study in Ideological Affinity', *Historical Journal*, 22:3 (1979), pp. 645–71, and *idem*, 'Eugenics and Ideology', *Historical Journal*, 26:4 (1983), pp. 959–62.

23 E. Stadulis, 'The Resettlement of Displaced Persons in the United Kingdom', *Population Studies*, 5:3 (1951–2), pp. 209–12.

24 Isaac, *British Post-War Migration*, pp. 183–5.

25 Minute by J. M. Troutbeck: PRO, FO371/47053.

26 Isaac, *British Post-War Migration*, pp. 179–80; for the details, see Tannahill, *European Voluntary Workers*, pp. 19–22.

27 Zarine to FO, 18 April 1946: PRO, FO371/57750; Bossom, Parliamentary question, 22 May 1946: PRO, FO371/55076; Society of

Latvians to FO, 9 March 1947: PRO, FO371/65754; Brownjohn to Control Office, 30 November 1946: PRO, FO945/368.

28 Cabinet Papers, PRO, CP, 9 (47), 17 January 1947, CP, 14 (47), 13 January 1947; Tannahill, *European Voluntary Workers*, pp. 23–4.

29 Brownjohn, 30 November 1946: PRO, FO945/368; Wilkinson, 24 January 1947: PRO, FO371/66709; Crawford, 13 December 1946: PRO, FO945/368; Hynd, 21 January 1947: PRO, FO371/66709.

30 Correspondence and comments, November 1946 – July 1947. The quote is from the British Consul in Baden Baden, March 1947: PRO, FO945/470.

31 Boothby to Appleby, 22 April 1947: PRO, FO945/500.

32 Sword, 'The Absorption of Poles into Civilian Employment in Britain', pp. 236–44.

33 On exclusion of *Volksdeutsche*, ACA, Vienna, to CO, London, 9 March 1947: PRO, FO370/66710; on the lifting of the bar on Ukrainians, CO to Lübeck, 24 February 1947: PRO, FO945/497.

34 ACA, British Element, 9 May 1947: PRO, FO945/501.

35 CCG to CO, London, 21 March 1947; Wilkinson minute, 25 March 1947; Hancock minute, 31 March 1947; Wilkinson minute, 2 April 1947: PRO, FO371/66710.

36 CO, London, to CCG, Berlin, 29 March 1947; Wakefield minute, 8 April 1947; Hankey minute, 10 April 1947; Wilkinson to Miss Appleby, Control Office, London, 26 April 1947: PRO, FO371/66710. Keith Sword (ed.), *The Formation of the Polish Community in Great Britain* (London, 1989), pp. 305–8.

37 Discussion concerning the widening of 'Balt Cygnet', February – March 1947: PRO, FO945/497.

38 Extension of 'Balt Cygnet', instructions, 24 February 1947; ACA, Vienna, to CO, London, 25 February 1947; CO, London, to ACA, Vienna, 1 March 1947: PRO, FO371/66709.

39 D. Robinson, Aliens Department, Home Office, to Ivimy, CO, London, 28 March 1947; ACA, Vienna, to CO, London, 31 March 1947: PRO, FO371/66710.

40 Minutes of 1st Meeting of Anglo-French Discussions, re: British Zones of Germany and Austria, 28 April 1947: PRO, FO945/470. Stein, *The Waffen-SS*, pp. 168–79.

41 Minutes of Cabinet meeting, 6 November 1945: PRO, CAB 129/2. See Martin Gilbert, *Exile and Return: The Emergence of Jewish Statehood* (London, 1978), pp. 272–5.

42 Minutes of meeting held to discuss question of Baltic nationals arriving legally or illegally, 17 October 1945: PRO, FO371/47052;

Lt-Col. Hammer, WO, to Mr Pumphry, FO, 10 January 1946; Brimelow to Judge, 15 January 1946: PRO, FO371/55979.

43 CO, London, to ACA, Vienna, 1 March 1947: PRO, FO371/66709; ACA, Vienna, to CO, London, 31 March 1947: PRO, FO371/66710.

44 Winterton to Pakenham, 30 April 1947: PRO, FO371/66711.

45 Iley, ACA, Vienna, to Ivimy, CO, London, 31 March 1947: PRO, FO945/500.

46 The legacy of wartime anti-semitism is detailed in Tony Kushner, *The Persistence of Prejudice* (Manchester, 1989); on the riots, see David Leitch, 'Explosion at the King David Hotel', in Phillip French and Michael Sissons (eds), *The Age of Austerity* (London, 1963), pp. 60–6.

47 Isaac, *British Post-War Migration*, p. 187; Malcolm Proudfoot, *European Refugees*, p. 360, estimated that only 1,000 Jews reached Britain between 1946 and 1950; Vernant, *The Refugee in the Post-War World*, p. 344, states that 2,000 'needy refugees' from camps in Germany and Austria were admitted under a sponsorship scheme, according to a statement by the Home Secretary in the House of Commons, 3 May 1948.

48 Isaac, *British Post-War Migration*, pp. 150–1; Colin Holmes, *John Bull's Island: Immigration and British Society, 1871–1971* (London, 1988), pp. 199–206.

49 Shirley Joshi and Bob Carter, 'The Role of Labour in the Creation of a Racist Britain', *Race and Class*, 25:3 (1984), pp. 53–70; Zig Layton-Henry, *The Politics of Race in Britain* (London, 1984), pp. 19–22.

Chapter 5: The Waffen-SS Comes to Britain I: The Balts

1 Kanty Cooper, *The Uprooted: Agony and Triumph Among the Debris of War* (London, 1979), pp. 121–2.

2 *Ibid.*, p. 132.

3 *Ibid.*

4 House of Lords Debates (Hansard) [HL Debs], vol. 519, cols 1180–1.

5 Wilkinson minute, 30 January 1947: PRO, FO371/66709. For all Cabinet decisions: PRO, HO213/1361.

6 Tannahill, *European Voluntary Workers*, pp. 25–6.

7 Hynd to FO, 21 January 1947: PRO, FO371/66709; Tannahill, *European Voluntary Workers*, p. 26.

8 'Memorandum by Minister of Labour on the Recruitment of

Labour from Displaced Persons', 12 February 1947: PRO, FO371/66709; Minutes of Foreign Labour Committee, 14 February 1947: PRO, FO371/66709; House of Commons Debates, 5th Series (Hansard) [HC Debs], vol. 433, col. 968, 18 February 1947 and cols. 1379–80, 20 February 1947.

9 FO to COGA, 21 February 1947 and FO to COGA, 1 March 1947: PRO, FO371/66709.

10 Tannahill, *European Voluntary Workers*, pp. 36–7.

11 Minutes of Foreign Labour Committee, 14 February 1947, and Corrigendum, 20 February 1947: PRO, FO371/66709.

12 Minutes of 2nd Meeting of Foreign Labour Committee, 26 February 1947: PRO, FO371/66709.

13 Ivimy to ACA, Vienna, 1 March 1947: PRO, FO371/66709.

14 Minutes of Meeting of Allied Commission for Austria, 3 March 1947: PRO, FO371/66710.

15 ACA, Vienna to Control Office, London, 9 March 1947: PRO, FO371/66709.

16 Lübeck to Berlin, 18 March 1947: PRO, FO371/66710.

17 Minute, 24 March 1947: PRO, FO371/66710.

18 COGA to Control Office, London, 24 March 1947: PRO, FO371/66710.

19 Lord Strang, *Home and Abroad* (London, 1956), p. 233.

20 Ivimy to FO, 24 October 1947: PRO, FO945/758.

21 Note of meeting on 24 March 1947 between Mr Pass and G. E. D. Ball, Ministry of Labour, and Mr Pettigrew, Immigration Branch, HO: PRO, FO945/504. Also, Ball to Pettigrew, 28 March 1947, and Ball to Perks, Chief Inspector, Immigration Branch, HO, 28 March 1947: PRO, FO945/504.

22 COGA, Lübeck, to CO, London, 18 February 1947: PRO, FO945/470.

23 Washington Embassy to FO, 17 May 1947; FO to Washington, 20 May 1947; Inverchapel to FO, 24 May 1947; FO to Inverchapel, 4 June 1947: PRO, FO371/66711.

24 Zarine to Brimelow, 22 October 1947: PRO, FO371/66714.

25 Wilkinson minute, 28 October 1947: PRO, FO371/66714.

26 Boothby minute, 28 October 1947; Brimelow minute, 29 October 1947; Boothby to Zarine, 31 October 1947: PRO, FO371/66714.

27 Zarine to Boothby, 10 November 1947: PRO, FO371/66714.

28 Zarine to Hankey, 12 November 1947: PRO, FO371/66714.

29 Dr Franz Burger to Miss Wyatt, 17 November 1947: PRO, FO371/66714. On the work of CIO, Tannahill, *European Voluntary Workers*, pp. 68–9.

30 Rouse to Boothby, 2 December 1947: PRO, FO371/66714.

31 Wilkinson minute, n.d.; Walmsley minute, 10 December 1947: PRO, FO371/66714.

32 Refugee Dept, FO, to POWDP Div., Lemgo, 17 December 1947: PRO, FO371/66714.

33 Boothby to Rouse, 2 January 1948: PRO, FO371/66714.

34 Note of meeting and Wilkinson's comment, 12 March 1948: PRO, FO371/72039.

35 S. T. Kobryner to Ministry of Labour, 10 April 1948: PRO, FO371/72039.

Chapter 6: *The Waffen-SS Comes to Britain II: The Ukrainians*

1 Bethell, *The Last Secret*, pp. 253–63.

2 Shandruk, *Arms of Valor*, pp. 290–3; Brigadier Anthony Cowgill, Lord Brimelow and Christopher Booker, *The Repatriations from Austria in 1945: The Report of an Inquiry*, 2 vols (London, 1991), pp. 8, 93–4, 98. According to this account, the surrendered division appears to have walked over 300 miles, across the southern Carnic Alps, to Riccione with no logistical support or transport in approximately eighteen days. That an unsupplied, war-weary and hungry division of 10,000 men managed this without being molested on the way or creating something of a fuss as they passed through the densely populated and partisan-controlled north-east of Italy may be considered to be stretching credulity.

3 Ukrainian Socialist Party to Attlee, 26 December 1945; Bishop John Buchko to D'Arcy Osborne, 9 January 1946; Brazilian Ukrainians to FO, 2 February 1946; Ukrainian Canadian Committee, 28 February 1946: PRO, FO371/56791. The members of the unit themselves addressed a collective petition to Bevin via the Camp Commandant, 14 February 1946: PRO, FO371/57750. Pavlo Shandruk assigned Bishop Buchko a major part in the salvation of the division: Shandruk, *Arms of Valor*, pp. 290–2; Mark Aarons and John Loftus, *Ratlines* (London, 1991), pp. 173–81, 189–94.

4 Stokes to FO, 6 March 1946; Stephen Thorne of the Quakers, to Attlee, 8 March 1946: PRO, FO371/56791. Christopher Mayhew, junior Minister at the FO, also received a petition from the men in October 1946, forwarded by Alderman Hynd, MP for Hackney Central, 29 October 1946: PRO, FO371/56793.

5 Panchuk to Bevin, 27 March 1946: PRO, FO371/56791.

6 Briefing paper, 29 March 1946; note of meeting, 29 March 1946:

PRO, FO371/56791; CP 30 May 1947, 53 (4): PRO, FO3871/56792. On Morgan, see Wyman, *DP* Europe's Displaced Persons, pp. 73, 58, 144–5.

7 A. B. Bartlett to Warner, 19 September 1946; Hankey to Bartlett, 28 September 1946: PRO, FO371/56793.

8 Hlynka to COGA, London, 24 September 1946; COGA to FO, 27 September 1946: PRO, FO371/56793.

9 Memorandum from the Supreme Ukrainian Liberation Council, 16 October 1946: PRO, FO371/56793.

10 Hynd to Mayhew, 29 October 1946; Brimelow minute, 6 November 1946, Wilkinson minute, 8 November 1946: PRO, FO371/56793.

11 Mayhew to Hynd, 12 December 1946: PRO, FO371/56793.

12 CCG to Brimelow, 30 November 1946: PRO, FO371/56793; Wilkinson memorandum, 20 February 1947: PRO, FO371/66709.

13 Wilkinson minute, 20 February 1947: PRO, FO371/66709.

14 Ambassador to Rendel, 25 February 1947: PRO, FO371/66710.

15 Mayhew memorandum, 24 February 1947: PRO, FO371/66710.

16 Isaacs to Bellenger, 3 March 1947: PRO, FO371/66709.

17 Boothby, FO, to Bevan, Ministry of Labour, 1 March 1947; Boothby and Rendel comments, 3 March 1947: PRO, FO371/66709.

18 Bevin to Attlee, 3 March 1947: PRO, FO371/66709.

19 Rendel also asked Mayhew to lean on John Hynd to admit DPs from Italy into Germany: Rendel to Mayhew, 3 March 1947, and Mayhew minute, 3 March 1947; Mayhew to Hynd, 3 March 1947: PRO, FO371/66657.

20 The screening commission arrived in Italy in the first week of February. It is curious that no reference is made by FO officials to its establishment and dispatch before it is first mentioned in mid-February. But someone had already thought of the problem of screening and must have ordered Maclean into action at the turn of 1946/7.

21 Maclean to FO, 22 February 1947: PRO, FO371/66605.

22 *Newsnight*, BBC 2, 11 December 1989.

23 Maclean to FO, 26 February 1947: PRO, FO371/66605.

24 Report of Refugee Screening Mission in Charge of SEP Camp 374, 21 February 1947: PRO, FO371/66605.

25 Bethell, *The Last Secret*, pp. 253–5; Denis Hills, 'You Are the Grey Mass', *Spectator*, 23–30 December 1989, pp. 13–14.

26 *Newsnight*, BBC 2, 11 December 1989.

27 Mark R. Elliott, *Pawns of Yalta*, p. 172.

28 Burgess to Wilkinson, 31 March 1947; Edmonds minute, 31 March 1947; Tuck, WO, to Edmonds, FO, 31 March 1947; Edmonds to Tuck, 2 April 1947: PRO, FO371/66710.

29 Chancellor, WO, to FO, 14 April 1947; Edmonds, FO, to Chancellor, WO: PRO, FO371/66711.

30 Minute of meeting, 1 October 1947: PRO, FO371/66712.

31 Interview with Beryl Hughes, Oxford, 17 November 1988.

32 Carew Robinson, HO, to Boothby, FO, 11 April 1947: PRO, FO371/66711.

33 Boothby, FO, to Robinson, HD, 23 April 1947: PRO, FO371/66711.

34 Robinson, HO, to Boothby, FO, 2 May 1947: PRO, FO371/66711.

35 Wilkinson, FO, to Robinson, HO, 13 May 1947: PRO, FO371/66711.

36 Robinson, HO, to Wilkinson, FO, 19 May 1947: PRO, FO371/66711.

37 C. Parkinson, HO, to Capt. Kerr, WO, 31 May 1947: PRO, FO371/66712.

38 Wilkinson and Boothby minutes, 18 July 1947: PRO, FO371/66712.

39 Minutes of meeting at Home Office to review position and prospects of the Ukrainians, 10 July 1947; Boothby minute, 27 July 1947: PRO, FO371/66712.

40 Brimelow, FO, to J. H. Mallard, WO, 13 June 1947: PRO, FO371/66344.

41 Sargent to Zaroubin, 20 August 1947: PRO, FO371/66344.

42 *Soviet Monitor*, 26 June 1947; McNeil comment, 11 July 1947; Zaroubin to FO, 26 July 1947; Sargent to Zaroubin, 24 August 1947: PRO, FO371/66712.

43 Wirth to Driberg, 7 June 1947; Driberg to FO, 13 June 1947: PRO, FO371/66712.

44 Hyman to Crossman, 18 June 1947; Crossman to McNeil, 23 June 1947: PRO, FO371/66712.

45 L. W. Carruthers to McNeil, 19 June 1947: PRO, FO371/66712.

46 HC Debs, vol. 438, cols 1980–1, 18 June 1947.

47 McNeil to Driberg, 30 June 1947; McNeil to Crossman, 11 July 1947: PRO, FO371/66712.

48 Wilkinson minute, 30 June 1947; Boothby minute, 11 July 1947; P. Gore-Booth to Carruthers, 9 July 1947: PRO, FO371/66712.

49 Panchuk to McNeil, 18 July 1947: PRO, FO371/66712.

50 Lt-Col. Chandler, WO, to Brimelow, FO, 27 November 1947; Boothby to Chandler, 12 December 1947: PRO, FO371/66714.
51 Zaroubin to FO, 10 November 1947: PRO, FO371/66347.
52 FO to Zaroubin, 18 November 1947: PRO, FO371/66347; Hughes, HO, to FO, 27 November 1947; Director of PoWs to FO, 22 December 1947; FO to US Embassy, 2 January 1948: PRO, FO371/66348.
53 Zaroubin to FO, 27 February 1948; Wilkinson minute, 3 March 1948: PRO, FO371/71662.
54 A. E. Lambert, FO, to Under Secretary of State, HO, 9 March 1948; Lambert, FO, to War Office, 9 March 1948; War Office to FO, 18 March 1948; Roy, HO, to Under Secretary of State, FO, 25 March 1948: PRO, FO371/71662.
55 Wilkinson minute, 6 April 1948; C. R. A. Rae minute, 7 April 1948; Lambert minute, 9 April 1948; Wilkinson minute, 12 April 1948; Boothby, 12 April 1948; Hankey minute, 19 April 1948: PRO, FO371/71662.
56 Hankey to Zaroubin, 21 April 1948: PRO, FO371/71662.
57 Zaroubin to FO, 29 June 1948; C. R. A. Rae, Lambert, Wilkinson minutes, 1 July 1948; Hankey to Zaroubin, 28 August 1948: PRO, FO371/71663.
58 Hughes, HO, to C. R. A. Rae, FO, 3 July 1948: PRO, FO371/71663.
59 Lambert, FO, to Hughes, HO, 28 August 1948: PRO, FO371/71663.
60 Hankey minute, 6 July 1948; A. A. Stark minute, 31 July 1948: PRO, FO371/71663.
61 Panchuk to FO, 8 April 1948; Panchuk to WO, 6 July 1948; C. R. A. Rae minute, 23 July 1948: PRO, FO371/71636.
62 Tannahill, *European Voluntary Workers*, pp. 31–3.
63 Interview with Beryl Hughes, Oxford, 17 November 1988.
64 Tannahill, *European Voluntary Workers*, p. 33.
65 Wilkinson to Bevan, 20 July 1947: PRO, FO371/66712.
66 Danish Embassy to FO, 13 March 1948; FO to Danish Embassy, 31 March 1948; Danish Embassy to FO, 21 April 1948; C. R. A. Rae to Panchuk, 10 May 1948; Panchuk to C. R. A. Rae, 18 May 1948: PRO, FO371/71636.
67 Savery to Hancock, 24 April 1948; Wilkinson to Panchuk, 8 April 1948; Panchuk to Wilkinson, 24 April 1948: PRO, FO371/71636.
68 Panchuk to FO, 13 August 1948; Wilkinson minute, 23 August 1948: PRO, FO371/71636.
69 Albert Hunt, 'Bitter in Yorkshire', *New Society*, 21 November 1986,

pp. 14–16; Colin Holmes, *John Bull's Island: Immigration and British Society, 1871–1971* (London, 1988), p. 238; Tannahill, *European Voluntary Workers*, pp. 103–4. See also D. White, 'The Ukes of Halifax', *New Society*, 21 June 1980, pp. 201–2. On the ABN, Simpson, *Blowback*, pp. 269–72.

70 T. W. E. Roche, *The Key in the Lock: A History of Immigration Control in England from 1066 to the Present Day* (London, 1969), pp. 176–8; Sir Thomas Hetherington and William Chalmers, *War Crimes: Report of the War Crimes Inquiry* (London, 1989), pp. 40, 42; *Observer*, 5 May 1991.

Chapter 7: *EVWs, the Cold War and the Intelligence Connection*

1 Anthony Glees, *The Secrets of the Service: British Intelligence and Communist Subversion, 1939–51* (London, 1987), pp. 1–35.

2 Rothwell, *Britain and the Cold War*, pp. 114–23; Glees, *The Secrets of the Service*, pp. 35–58; Elisabeth Barker, *The British Between the Superpowers, 1945–1950* (London, 1986), pp. 6–8; Julian Lewis, *Changing Direction: British Military Planning for Post-War Strategic Defence, 1942–1947* (London, 1987), pp. 90–7, 101–7.

3 Clement Attlee, *As It Happened* (London, 1954), p. 147.

4 Warner memorandum, 2 April 1946: PRO, FO371/56832. See Lewis, *Changing Direction*, pp. 167–77, 262 for discussion and pp. 359–63 for full text.

5 'The Strategic Aspect of British Foreign Policy', Foreign Office Strategy Paper, 5 October 1946: COS(46)239(0). Quoted in Lewis, *Changing Direction*, p. 288; for full discussion see pp. 285–9, and partial text, pp. 363–9.

6 'Future Defence Policy', 22 May 1947: DO(47)44. For the full text of this document, see Lewis, *Changing Direction*, pp. 370–87, and discussion, pp. 315–31. See also Barker, *The British Between the Superpowers*, p. 100.

7 Trevor Barnes, 'The Secret Cold War: The CIA and American Foreign Policy in Europe, 1946–1956. Part 1', *Historical Journal*, 24:2 (1981), pp. 399–415.

8 Minutes of meeting of Chiefs of Staff, 10 December 1947: DEFE 4/9 COS(47)153; minutes of Cabinet Defence Committee, 5 January 1948: CAB 131/6 DO(48); minutes of Chiefs of Staff meeting, 30 April 1948: DEFE 4/13 JP(48) 50, all cited in Barker, *The British Between the Superpowers*, pp. 103–8.

9 Barker, *The British Between the Superpowers*, pp. 106–7.

10 Minutes of meeting of Chiefs of Staff, 11 September 1948: DEFE

4/16 JP(48)28(Final), cited in Barker, *The British Between the Super-powers*, pp. 108–9; J. L. Gaddis, *Strategies of Containment: A Critical Appraisal of Postwar American National Security Policy* (paperback edn, Oxford, 1982), pp. 55–88; Kim Philby, *My Silent War* (paperback edn, London, 1989), pp. 221–2.

11 Joint Planning Staff, 11 June 1948: DEFE 4/13 JP(48)63(Final), cited in Barker, *The British Between the Superpowers*, pp. 111–2.

12 Paul W. Blackstock, *The Secret Road to World War Two: Soviet Versus Western Intelligence, 1921–1939* (Chicago, 1969), pp. 65–99; Nigel West, *MI6: British Secret Intelligence Operations, 1909–1945* (London, 1983), pp. 17–19, 23–4, 26–7, 39; Tom Bower, *The Red Web* (London, 1989), pp. 1–4, 13–14, 23. Bower, who gained rare access to several SIS officers and their agents, quotes from interviews to give an insight into their operations, although there is, naturally, a dearth of documentary evidence to support the oral testimony.

13 West, *MI6*, pp. 169, 173; Bower, *Red Web*, pp. 14, 16, 22, 30, 40–3; Ants Oras, *Baltic Eclipse* (London, 1948), pp. 84–8.

14 Anthony Cave Brown, *The Secret Servant* (London, 1988), pp. 143–4; Bower, *Red Web*, p. 23.

15 Oras, *Baltic Eclipse*, pp. 84–8, 269–73. Only one SOE agent was sent into the Baltic during the war. Ronald Seth had taught English at Tallinn University and fled to Helsinki in 1939. On reaching England he joined RAF intelligence, but was seconded to SOE. His 1942 mission to Estonia was a disaster. Although he made contact with some friendly Estonians he was soon captured by the German Security Police and survived only by deserting to the Nazi cause which, as he later explained in his memoir, *A Spy Has No Friends* (London, 1948), was a pretence to escape.

16 Bower, *Red Web*, pp. 41–5.

17 Glees, *The Secrets of the Service*, pp. 278–80; Bower, *Red Web*, pp. 58–9.

18 Bower, *Red Web*, pp. 41, 58–9.

19 Neulen, *An deutscher Seite*, pp. 279–80; Mulligan, *Politics of Illusion and Empire*, pp. 85–7.

20 Intelligence Bureau to Political Division, Lübeck, 28 February 1946: PRO, FO1049/414.

21 C. E. King, Political Division, Lübeck, to Intelligence Bureau, 12 April 1946: PRO, FO1049/414. A good deal of material concerning Plechavicius is, however, withheld from another Foreign Office file in the PRO, FO371/55076.

22 Bower, *Red Web*, p. 94.

23 *Ibid.*, pp. 59–60.

24 *Guardian*, 28 June 1988. Rumnieks was imprisoned for many years; on his release he continued to live in Latvia as an old-age pensioner.

25 Bower, *Red Web*, pp. 110–12.

26 *Ibid.*, pp. 145, 149.

27 *Observer*, 9 July 1989; Bower, *Red Web*, p. 149; *Newsnight*, BBC 2, 11 December 1989.

28 Klietmann, *Die Waffen-SS*, pp. 223–4; E. G. Krätschmer, *Die Ritterkreuzträger der Waffen-SS*, (Olendorf, 1988), pp. 660–4.

29 There were 2,000 Estonian soldiers in British captivity in December 1945: PRO, FO371/57750. During 1946, Estonian DPs submitted petitions to the FO, with the backing of the Estonian diplomat, for an enlargement of their political and educational activities: PRO, FO371/57750. Bower, *Red Web*, pp. 129, 181–2.

30 Bower, *Red Web*, pp. 110, 129, 145.

31 Stöber, *Die lettischen Divisionen*, p. 308; E. Avotins, J. Dzirkalis and V. Petersons, *Dauvagis Vanagi: Who Are They?* (Riga, 1963), pp. 53–5. The latter is a Soviet publication of cold-war vintage which sets out to discredit émigré Latvian nationalists, but much of the material it presents has since been verified independently.

32 On Valdmanis' 'outstanding work': PRO, FO1049/613; on Dauvagis Vanagi, Simpson, *Blowback*, pp. 204–8.

33 Simpson, *Blowback*, pp. 204–8.

34 Janums to Mackenzie, FO, 9 March 1949: PRO, FO371/77245.

35 Mackenzie, FO, to Stoney, WO, 25 March 1949; Stoney, WO, to Mackenzie, FO, 29 March 1949: PRO, FO371/77245. Other material pertaining to Janums is withheld in file N2600/1822/59. MI3 was the section which dealt with Germany.

36 Zilliacus question, 19 February 1946; Orbach question, 20 February 1946: PRO, FO371/55975; *New York Times*, 4 February 1946, 1, cited in John Loftus, *The Belarus Secret* (New York, 1982), p. 175, n. 4; Avotins, Dzirkalis and Petersons, *Dauvagis Vanagi*, pp. 58–9. The story also made the front page of the London *Jewish Chronicle*, 8 February 1946.

37 *Labour Service and Industrial Police in the European Command, 1945–1950* (Karlsruhe, 1952), cited by Simpson, *Blowback*, pp. 204–8.

38 C. R. A. Rae, memorandum of meeting with Mr Panchuk and M. Andrievsky, 15 April 1948: PRO, FO371/71636. It is also impossible to determine the repercussions of this encounter in the absence of relevant files, e.g. N4982/13/38, which are withheld from the public. Andrievsky and Panchuk returned to the FO in

March 1949 and met with Hankey, by then head of the Northern Department and a prominent member of the FO's Russia Committee. See minutes of meeting between Hankey, Panchuk and Andrievsky: PRO, FO371/77586.

39 Bower, *Red Web*, p. 169.
40 The utilisation of alleged war criminals was not confined to useful East Europeans. Klaus Barbie was only the most notorious war criminal who passed through the hands of the British and then the US intelligence services before being helped to 'disappear'. See Tom Bower, *Klaus Barbie* (London, 1984).
41 Simpson, *Blowback*, p. 73 and *passim*; Bower, *The Paperclip Conspiracy*.
42 BAOR Interrogation Report on Nikolai Poppe, 11 November 1946: PRO, FO371/56838; Simpson, *Blowback*, pp. 118–20.
43 Walter Schellenberg, *The Schellenberg Memoirs* (London, 1956), pp. 318–19.
44 Kurochkin to Robertson, 29 July 1946: PRO, FO371/56871.
45 Maj.-Gen. M. Shoosmith, Chief of the Intelligence Division, COGA, to Office of Deputy Military Governor, COGA, 3 October 1946: PRO, FO371/56871.
46 Poppe to Haloun, 12 September 1946; Pratt to FO, 11 October 1946: PRO, FO371/56871.
47 G. P. West, Control Office, Berlin, to Mr Pumphry, FO, 15 October 1946; Berlin to Control Office, London, 20 October 1946; Lambert, FO, to West, COGA, 1 November 1946; Brimelow, FO, to F. Pickering, Intelligence Division, 1 November 1946: PRO, FO371/56871.
48 CO, London, to CO, Berlin, 1 November 1946: PRO, FO371/56871.
49 Lambert to Beckett, 27 November 1946; Brimelow minute, 24 November 1946; Beckett, Legal Adviser, minute, 25 November 1946; Lambert minute, 4 December 1946: PRO, FO371/56838.
50 Hankey and Warner minutes, 6 December 1946: PRO, FO371/56838.
51 Shoosmith to Control Office, London, 18 December 1946: PRO, FO371/56838.
52 Brimelow note of meeting, n.d.: PRO, FO371/56838.
53 Col. Peter P. Rhodes, Director of Intelligence, to Deputy Director of Intelligence, HQ EUCOM, 22 May 1947: NR3/775119. See Simpson, *Blowback*, pp. 118–20 and nn. 24–5, pp. 315–16.
54 Simpson, *Blowback*, pp. 120–2.
55 NSC 10/2 was the main instrument authorising subversion under

which émigré groups were protected and taken to the USA: Barnes, 'The Secret Cold War. Part 1', pp. 414–15; Loftus, *The Belarus Secret*, pp. 8–9, 70–85, 105–19; Simpson, *Blowback*, pp. 96–106.

56 Richard Harris Smith, *OSS: The Secret History of America's First Central Intelligence Agency* (Berkeley, Calif., 1972), pp. 239–41.

57 Charles Thayer, *Hands Across the Caviar* (London, 1973), pp. 160–1; Charles E. Bohlen, *Witness to History* (New York, 1973), pp. 69–87.

58 Thayer, *Hands Across the Caviar*, pp. 162–4, 165–71; Johnny von Herwarth, *Against Two Evils: Memoirs of a Diplomat-Soldier During the Third Reich* (London, 1981), pp. 305–6.

59 Simpson, *Blowback*, pp. 80–9, 112–18.

60 Trevor Barnes, 'The Secret Cold War: The CIA and American Foreign Policy in Europe, 1946–1956. Part 2', *Historical Journal*, 25:3 (1982), pp. 656–7; Simpson, *Blowback*, pp. 170–5; Loftus, *The Belarus Secret*, pp. 70–5, 109–10; Philby, *My Silent War*, pp. 214–25.

61 Bower, *Red Web*, p. 54; Philby, *My Silent War*, pp. 215–16.

62 Yury Boshyk, 'Repatriation and Resistance: Ukrainian Refugees and Displaced Persons in Occupied Germany and Austria, 1945–1948', pp. 204–5.

63 Resolution of Ukrainian EVWs at Knightthorpe Hostel, 1949; Stetsko request to FO, 15 June 1949: PRO, FO371/77584. Several sub-files in this file are withheld: N1599 and N2467, which deal with the Ukrainian underground in the USSR. Readers may draw their own conclusions. No less than five files – N7597, N9709, N9092, N102151, N10558 – on the activity of Stetsko and Ukrainians in Britain and Germany during 1949 are retained from PRO, FO371/77585. For R. M. A. Hankey's disapproval of Ukrainian political activity in Britain, see report of meeting between Hankey, Panchuk and Andrievsky: PRO, FO371/77586.

64 The SIS-sponsored airborne insertions into Poland and the USSR were no more successful than the missions to the Baltic, probably for the same reason. The teams disappeared and it is almost certain that they were captured immediately by the KGB operating on a tip-off from Kim Philby. Philby, *My Silent War*, pp. 223–5.

65 Loftus, *The Belarus Secret*, pp. 77–81.

66 Major L. H. Manderstam, *From the Red Army to SOE* (London, 1985), pp. 118–22, 133, 136–52.

67 Interview with Beryl Hughes, Oxford, 17 November 1988. A good

deal of material on the Vlasov movement is withheld from PRO, FO371/77585.
68 HC Debs, vol. 169, cols 950–1, 19 March 1990.

Chapter 8: *Justice Delayed*

1 Rebecca West, *A Trail of Powder* (London, 1984), p. 3. The article reprinted in this collection originally appeared in the *Daily Telegraph* in 1946.
2 The word 'Holocaust' did not gain currency until the later 1950s: Gerd Korman, 'The Holocaust in American Historical Writing', in Marrus (ed.), *The Holocaust in History*, vol. 1: *Perspectives on the Holocaust*, pp. 292–3.
3 On the end of the 'Operation Reinhard' camps, see Arad, *Belzec, Sobibor, Treblinka*, pp. 370–6. For the liberation of Majdanek, see Jon Bridgman, *The End of the Holocaust: The Liberation of the Camps* (London, 1990), pp. 20–1.
4 Bridgman, *The End of the Holocaust*, pp. 33–4, 82–3.
5 N. Pronay, 'Defeated Germany in British Newsreels: 1944–45', in K. R. M. Short and Stephen Dolezel (eds), *Hitler's Fall: The Newsreel Witness* (London, 1990), pp. 30–2, 40–5; Bridgman, *The End of the Holocaust*, pp. 110–12.
6 Bridgman, *The End of the Holocaust*, pp. 103–7.
7 *Ibid.*, pp. 20–1, 33; on *The Times*, see *Jewish Chronicle*, 22 September 1944, p. 10. There is no analysis of the response in England comparable to the study on the USA by Robert H. Abzug, *Inside the Vicious Heart* (New York, 1985), esp. pp. 169–73, although Tony Kushner, 'The British and the Shoah', *Patterns of Prejudice*, 23:3 (1989), pp. 11–13 compresses into a few pages evidence and comment that maps the ground most impressively.
8 Gilbert, *Exile and Return*, pp. 275–83.
9 Leonard Dinnerstein, 'The US Army and the Jews: Policies Toward the Displaced Persons After World War II', in Marrus (ed.), *The Nazi Holocaust*, vol. 9: *The End of the Holocaust*, pp. 514–15; *America and the Survivors of the Holocaust* (New York, 1982), pp. 28–34, 46–7; Wyman, *DP*, pp. 134–7; Ursula Buttner, 'Not nach der Befreiung. Die Situation der deutschen Juden in der britischen Besatzungszone 1945 bis 1948', *Das Unrechtsregime*, vol. 2: *Verfolgung-Exil-Belasteter Neubeginn* (Hamburg, 1986), pp. 375–82.
10 Nicholas Bethell, *The Palestine Triangle* (London, 1979), pp. 202–19.

11 Gilbert, *Exile and Return*, pp. 283–6; Bethell, *Palestine Triangle*, pp. 219–39.

12 Bethell, *Palestine Triangle*, pp. 226–7, 232–4, 253–77, 279–80.

13 These incidents were fully reported in the *Jewish Chronicle* (*JC*): *JC*, 3 January 1947, p. 12; 15 November 1946, p. 1; 22 November 1946, p. 1; 17 January 1947, p. 12.

14 Bethell, *Palestine Triangle*, pp. 316–36, 340–2.

15 *Ibid.*, pp. 336–40; Leitch, 'Explosion at the King David Hotel', in M. Sissons and P. French (eds), *The Age of Austerity* (London, 1963), pp. 70–2.

16 See *JC*, 25 May 1945, pp. 5 and 8; 2 November 1945, p. 10 on the Hampstead petition.

17 Wyman, *DP* Europe's Displaced Persons, pp. 144–5.

18 *JC*, 10 October 1947, p. 10; on press anti-semitism: 3 October 1947, p. 10, and 30 January 1948, p. 10; on anti-schechita bills: 8 October 1948, p. 10. John Gross, 'The Lynskey Tribunal', in Sissons and French (eds), *The Age of Austerity*, pp. 255–75.

19 Colin Cross, *The Fascists in Britain* (London, 1964), pp. 199–202; David Leitch, 'Explosion at the King David Hotel', pp. 60–6; Tony Kushner, *The Persistence of Prejudice* (Manchester, 1989), pp. 199–200; Neil Nugent, 'Post War Fascism?' in K. Lunn and R. C. Thurlow (eds), *British Fascism* (London, 1980), pp. 210–14; R. C. Thurlow, *Fascism in Britain: A History 1918–45* (London, 1987), pp. 233–59.

20 West, *Trail of Powder*, p. 11; Peter Calvocoressi, *Nuremberg: The Facts, the Law and the Consequences* (London, 1947), pp. 24–5; *Reynolds Daily News*, 16 December 1945, cited in Ann Tusa and John Tusa, *The Nuremberg Trial* (London, 1983), p. 222; Birkett quoted in Tusa and Tusa, *The Nuremberg Trial*, p. 370.

21 Calvocoressi, *Nuremberg*, pp. 89–90, 108–9.

22 *Ibid.*, p. 123; West, *Trail of Powder*, pp. 253–5.

23 Calvocoressi, *Nuremberg*, pp. 120–1; West, *Trail of Powder*, pp. 255–6.

24 Sir John Wheeler-Bennett, *Friends, Enemies and Foreigners* (London, 1976), pp. 114–15.

25 The Rt Hon. Lord Hankey, *Politics, Trials and Errors* (Oxford, 1950), pp. 125–30.

26 Montgomery Belgion, *Epitaph on Nuremberg* (London, 1946), pp. 25–35, 58–65, 89–90. Hankey also contributed a postscript to Viscount Maugham's tract, *U.N.O. and War Crimes* (London, 1951), which argued that there was no such thing as a 'crime against humanity'.

27 Kushner, *The Persistence of Prejudice*, p. 85; on the Right Club, Richard Griffiths, *Fellow Travellers of the Right* (paperback edn, Oxford, 1983), pp. 353–5.

28 HC Debs, vol. 445, cols 673–90, 4 December 1947.

29 HL Debs, vol. 155, cols 669–70, 5 May 1948.

30 HC Debs, vol. 442, cols 404–5, 16 June 1948; vol. 454, cols 927–8, 26 July 1948.

31 *Ibid.*, vol. 454, cols 1469–90, 28 July 1948; vol. 457, cols 57–84, 26 October 1948.

32 HC Debs, vol. 457, col. 66, 26 October 1948.

33 Christian Streit, 'The German Army and the Policies of Genocide', in Hirschfeld (ed.), *The Policies of Genocide*, pp. 7–9 and Jurgen Forster, 'The German Army and the Ideological War Against the Soviet Union', in *ibid.*, pp. 25–6.

34 HC Debs, vol. 457, cols 256, 272, 26 October 1948. There was also a major debate in the Lords, led by the Marquess of Reading, who tabled a motion 'That in view of the length of time that has elapsed since their capture and the circumstances of their detention since that date, the proposed trial of certain senior German general officers as war criminals is not in accordance with the principles of British justice and that the proceedings should therefore be discontinued': HL Debs, vol. 159, cols 157–86, 2 November 1948. For the implementation of this policy: PRO, FO1063/56–9.

35 HL Debs, vol. 162, cols 389–91, 5 May 1949. During his contributions to the public debate on the war crimes bill in 1989–90, Christopher, now Lord, Mayhew clarified the stages by which the revised policy emerged: for example, *Guardian*, letters, 29 March 1990.

36 HC Debs, vol. 465, col. 247, 17 May 1949. On the Manstein affair, see Wheeler-Bennett, *Friends, Enemies and Foreigners*, pp. 114–15.

37 On Manstein's trial: *JC*, 10 September 1948, p. 11; on twenty-five year sentence against Gen. Gottlob Berger, Einsatzgruppen controller, and seven-year sentence on Ernst von Weizsäcker, Nazi diplomat: 22 April 1949, pp. 1, 10; on trial of Falkenhausen, Governor of Belgium: 13 October 1950, p. 1; release of diplomat, Weizsäcker: 20 October 1950, pp. 10, 11; on release of convicted war criminals in Germany: 9 February 1951, p. 12. Public awareness or concern faded with amazing rapidity. According to Mass Observation, by September 1947 'people are no longer moved by

the thought of Jewish suffering in the concentration camps': cited by Kushner, 'The British and the Shoah', p. 13.

38 *JC*, 1 May 1953, p. 14.

39 *Observer*, 22 August 1954.

40 Lord Russell of Liverpool, *The Scourge of the Swastika: A Short History of Nazi War Crimes* (London, 1954), p. 250.

41 *JC*, 23 March 1951, p. 12.

42 For example, Derrick Sington, *Belsen Uncovered* (London, 1947); G. M. Gilbert, *Nuremberg Diary* (London, 1948); Dr Eustace Chesser, *Doctors of Infamy* (London, 1951); Alan Bullock, *A Study in Tyranny* (London, 1952); H. R. Trevor-Roper, *Hitler's Table Talk* (London, 1953). In *The Holocaust and the Historians* (Cambridge, Mass., 1981), pp. 31–4, Lucy Dawidowicz is scathing towards Bullock and Trevor-Roper, especially.

43 One of these concerned two Belgians who in July 1948 were accused of collaboration and murder. The case was dropped due to insufficient evidence.

44 Information on Dering is taken from Mavis M. Hill and L. Norman Williams, *Auschwitz in England: A Record of a Libel Action* (London, 1965).

45 CROWCASS Final Consolidated Wanted List, June 1948; H. O'Grady, FO, to T. Randall, Paris, 5 November 1948: PRO, FO371/70811.

46 Hancock, FO, to Roy, 5 March 1948; Roy to Hancock, 6 March 1948; Northern Department memorandum, 11 March 1948: PRO, FO371/71585.

47 Bevin minute to memorandum, 11 March 1948: PRO, FO371/71585.

48 Home Secretary Chuter Ede to Bevin, 18 April 1948: PRO, FO371/71585.

49 *JC*, 3 September 1948, p. 5; HC Debs, vol. 445, cols 684–7, 4 December 1947.

50 The case is recorded in Hill and Williams, *Auschwitz in England*.

51 Polish arrest warrant, 28 September 1948; correspondence, September–October 1948: PRO, FO372/6451.

52 *Leicester Mercury*, 11 November 1960; All-Party Parliamentary War Crimes Group, *Report on the Entry of Nazi War Criminals and Collaborators into the UK, 1945–1950* (London, 1988), pp. 78–9.

53 The details of the British response came to light when Patrick Ground MP took up the case with the Foreign Office in 1983: see Baroness Young, FO, to Ground, 21 December 1983, cited in *Report on the Entry of Nazi War Criminals*.

54 *JC*, 24 March 1961, p. 21. On 1948–9 activities of Baltic Jews: PRO, FO1060/4 and FO1060/200.

55 *JC*, 12 April 1957, p. 40; 24 October 1958, p. 20; 24 September 1962.

56 For an account of the trial, see Lord Russell of Liverpool, *The Trial of Adolf Eichmann* (London, 1962).

57 Hannah Arendt, *Eichmann in Jerusalem: A Report on the Banality of Evil* (New York, 1963). For a riposte, see Gideon Hausner, *Justice in Jerusalem* (London, 1967).

58 For a highly partisan but concise account of the Hilberg and Arendt controversies and their impact, see Dawidowicz, *The Holocaust and the Historians*, pp. 130–9.

Chapter 9: *The War Crimes Campaign in Britain, 1986–1989*

1 On the role of the Simon Wiesenthal Centre, see Efraim Zuroff, *Occupation: Nazi-Hunter* (Southampton, 1988), pp. 175–221.

2 For a description of the origins and operations of the OSI, Allan A. Ryan Jr, *Quiet Neighbours: Prosecuting Nazi War Criminals in America* (New York, 1984); Rochelle G. Saidel, *The Outraged Conscience: Seekers of Justice for Nazi War Criminals in America* (Albany, NY, 1984); Henry Friedlander and Earlean M. McCarrick, 'Nazi Criminals in the United States: The Fedorenko Case', *Simon Wiesenthal Center Annual*, 2 (1985), pp. 63–93.

3 Eli Rosenbaum, 'The Investigation and Prosecution of Suspected Nazi War Criminals: A Comparative Overview', *Patterns of Prejudice*, 21:2 (1987), pp. 17–24. This article also compares the USA, Canada, Australia and Britain, but concludes in early 1987. For an update, see the comments of OSI Director Neal Sher at the 'Time for Justice' Conference, reported in the *Guardian*, 24 October 1988.

4 The above account is based on Harold Troper and Morton Weinfeld, *Old Wounds: Jews, Ukrainians and the Hunt for Nazi War Criminals in Canada* (Chapel Hill, NC, 1989), chs 3–7.

5 For the record of events in Australia, see Mark Aarons, *Sanctuary: Nazi Fugitives in Australia* (Melbourne, Victoria, 1989), pp. 269–96.

6 Scottish Television, *Crimes of War*, Channel 4, 22 July 1987.

7 Renton to Janner, 20 October 1986, *Chronology of Events*, All-Party Parliamentary War Crimes Group, March 1987, p. 1.

8 *Chronology of Events*, p. 1; *The Times*, 24 October 1986.

9 *Sunday Times*, 26 October 1986; *Scottish Daily Record*, 29 October 1986 and 17 November 1986.

10 Janner to John Biffen, Leader of the House of Commons, HC Debs, vol. 105, col. 703, 20 November 1986; *Chronology of Events*, pp. 1–2.

11 *Daily Telegraph*, 13 January 1987; *Chronology of Events*, p. 2.

12 Scottish Television, *Britain – The Nazi Safe House*, 28 January 1987, and Channel 4, 4 February 1987.

13 Janner to Biffen, HC Debs, 6th Series, vol. 109, col. 1152, 5 February 1987. Bower, *The Paperclip Conspiracy*.

14 Editorials in *Daily Mirror*, 6 February 1987, and *Sunday Mirror*, 8 February 1987.

15 *The Times, Guardian, Independent*, 25 February 1987.

16 *Independent*, 26 February 1987.

17 Kinnock to Biffen etc., HC Debs, vol. 111, col. 419, 26 February 1987.

18 *Daily Mirror, London Daily News, Guardian, Independent*, 27 February 1987.

19 *Sunday Express*, 1 March 1987. See also *Guardian*, 3 March 1987, and *Sunday Today*, 11 March 1987.

20 *Observer*, 1 March 1987.

21 Zuroff, *Occupation: Nazi-Hunter*, pp. 190–2; *Guardian, Daily Telegraph*, 3 March 1987.

22 *Guardian, The Times*, editorials, 4 March 1987. *The Times*, letters, 6 March 1987. Simon Wiesenthal also wrote a retort, *The Times*, letters, 11 March 1987.

23 *Daily Telegraph*, editorial and diary, 4 March 1987.

24 *Sunday Telegraph*, 1 March 1987; *Guardian*, 2 March 1987; *JC*, 6 March 1987.

25 *JC*, 13 March 1987, 27 March 1987.

26 Zuroff, *Occupation: Nazi-Hunter*, pp. 192–7.

27 Janner to Wakeham, HC Debs, vol. 118, col. 636, 2 July 1987; *Daily Telegraph*, 2 July 1987. The files were eventually released in January 1988; they proved to be a great disappointment: see *Time*, 7 December 1987.

28 Zuroff, *Occupation: Nazi-Hunter*, pp. 198–9.

29 All-Party Parliamentary War Crimes Group, Press Release, 21 July 1987; *Observer*, 19 July 1987, and *Guardian*, 20 and 22 July 1987.

30 Janner to Secretary of State for Scotland, HC Debs, vol. 120, col. 76, 20 July 1987; David Winnick to Chris Patten, Minister of State for Overseas Development, and Janner to John Wakeham, Leader of the House, HC Debs, vol. 120, cols 341–4, 23 July

1987; Janner to Hurd, Home Secretary, HC Debs, vol. 120, col. 526, 24 July 1987.

31 *JC*, 31 July and 28 August 1987; *The Times*, 26 August 1987.

32 Rupert Allason and Greville Janner to Linda Chalker, Minister of State at the Foreign Office, HC Debs, vol. 120, cols. 770, 21 October 1987; Winnick to Hurd and Timothy Renton, Minister of State at the Home Office, HC Debs, vol. 121, col. 14–15; Janner to Wakeham, HC Debs, vol. 121, col. 458, 29 October 1987; Janner to David Mellor, Minister of State at the Foreign Office, HC Debs, vol. 121, cols 718–9, 21 October 1987.

33 *JC*, 30 October 1987; *Mail on Sunday*, 15 November 1987.

34 *Guardian, Independent, Daily Telegraph*, 18 November 1987; *Observer*, 22 November 1987.

35 Winnick to Wakeham, HC Debs, vol. 122, col. 1224, 19 November 1987; Stanbrook to Wakeham, HC Debs, vol. 123, col. 391, 26 November 1987; Winnick to Hurd, Stanbrook and Marlow to Hurd, HC Debs, vol. 123, cols 1093–5, 3 December 1987.

36 *Guardian*, 4 December 1987; *Daily Telegraph*, 7 December 1987; *Independent*, 16 and 19 January 1988.

37 *Guardian*, 1 February 1988.

38 HC Debs, vol. 127, cols 28–36, 8 February 1988. Edward Pearce, *New Statesman*, 12 February 1988; Colin Welch, *Daily Mail*, 9 February 1988.

39 *Sunday Telegraph*, 14 February 1988; *JC*, 19 February 1988.

40 *JC*, 12 February 1988; 8 April 1988; 29 July 1988.

41 House of Commons Official Report, Standing Committee H, Criminal Justice Bill [Lords] 23rd Sitting, 24 March 1988.

42 HC Debs, 16, 18, 22, 29 February, 30 and 31 March, 21 April 1989. *The Times*, 30 August 1989.

43 *JC*, 29 March 1988; *Daily Telegraph*, 21 April 1988; HC Debs, Janner, Winnick, Rooker to Wakeham, 21 April 1988; Attorney General to Dayell, 5 May 1988; Rooker to Freeman, MoD, 28 June 1988; Roger King to Ian Steward, MoD, 1 July 1988; 6, 13, 19 July, Rooker. Also, 13, 23 February 1989. On the Mohnke case, see Leslie Aitken, *Massacre on the Road to Dunkirk* (London, 1977).

44 All-Party Parliamentary War Crimes Group, *Report on the Entry of Nazi War Criminals and Collaborators into the UK, 1945–1950* (London, November 1988). The report was followed in February 1989 by one dealing with the legal aspects, *Nazi War Criminals in the UK: The Law*, which anticipated many of the legal proposals in the Government's own subsequent inquiry.

45 *Bradford Telegraph and Argus*, 18 November 1988.

46 'Shadow of the Swastika', BBC 1, 12 December 1988. The War Crimes Group and Wiesenthal Centre accused the programme of bias and inaccuracy. For the subsequent controversy see *JC*, 18 December 1988; *Private Eye*, 23 December 1988 and 3 February 1989.

47 HC Debs, vol. 145, col. 1176, 26 January 1989.

48 Winnick to Hurd, HC Debs, vol. 139, col. 11, 24 October 1988. *Daily Telegraph*, 23 May 1989; Gorst to Hurd, HC Debs, vol. 151, col. 92, 18 April 1989; Winnick to Hurd, HC Debs, vol. 154, col. 215, 11 May 1989; Carlile to Hurd, HC Debs, vol. 152, col. 568, 12 May 1989; Lawrence to Hurd, HC Debs, vol. 154, col. 108, 17 May 1989; petition, 16 June 1989; HC Debs, vol. 154, col. 1213, 16 June 1989.

49 *The Times*, 8 June 1989.

50 *The Times*, letters, 15, 27, 29 June and 2 July 1989.

51 Cmnd 744, Sir Thomas Hetherington and William Chalmers, *War Crimes: Report of the War Crimes Inquiry* (London, July 1989), summary of recommendations, pp. 106–7.

52 HC Debs, vol. 157, cols 731–45, 24 July 1989.

53 HL Debs, vol. 510, cols 1146–7, 24 July 1989; *The Times*, 24 July 1989.

54 *Evening Standard*, 24 July 1989.

55 *Guardian, Daily Telegraph, Independent*, 25 July 1989; *Guardian*, 29 July 1989.

56 *Daily Telegraph*, 28 July 1989; *Guardian*, 29 July 1989; *Observer*, 30 July 1989.

57 *Sunday Telegraph*, 30 July 1989. For rejoinders, see *Sunday Telegraph*, letters, 6 August 1989. *News of the World*, 30 July 1989.

58 Bermant comments: *JC*, 21 July and 4 August 1989; Janner's comments and reports on Anglo-Jewish responses, 21 and 28 July 1989.

59 *Evening Standard*, 24 October, 13 December 1989; Nigella Lawson to Janner, 9 December 1989, files of the All-Party Parliamentary War Crimes Group.

Chapter 10: *The Struggle for the War Crimes Act*

1 Interview, *Independent*, 12 August 1989; profile, *Guardian*, 24 October 1989; and author's notes of meeting addressed by Sir Thomas Hetherington in the Moses Room, House of Lords, 22 May 1990. Sir Thomas served in the Royal Artillery in 1945–8, including a

spell in Palestine. As DPP he dealt with the prosecution of Jeremy Thorpe and handled the case of the Yorkshire Ripper.

2 *The Times*, 29 July 1989.

3 All-Party Parliamentary War Crimes Group, 'Time for Justice' programme (London, October 1989); *The Times, Daily Telegraph*, 24 July 1989.

4 *Daily Telegraph*, 26, 30 October 1989.

5 HC Debs, vol. 162, cols 227–8, 237–8, 23 November 1989.

6 Letters, *The Times*, 4 December 1989; HL Debs, vol. 513, cols 604–79, 4 December 1989.

7 *JC*, 8 December 1989.

8 HC Debs, vol. 163, cols 880–912, 12 December 1989; *Independent*, 14 December 1989; *JC*, 15 December 1989.

9 *The Sun, Daily Telegraph*, 14 December 1989; *Economist*, 16 December 1989; *Sunday Mirror*, 17 December 1989. Wheatcroft in *Daily Telegraph*, 12 December 1989; Shulman in *The Times*, 16 December 1989; Walker in *Evening Standard*, 18 December 1989.

10 *JC*, 19 January 1990; *Sunday Express*, 21 January 1990; *JC*, 16 February 1990; *Sunday Times*, 25 February 1990. Marshall to Howe, HC Debs, vol. 164, col. 1097, 11 January 1990; Marshall to Patten, HC Debs, vol. 165, col. 170, 16 January 1990; Marshall to Howe, HC Debs, vol. 166, col. 1014, 8 February 1990; Marshall to Howe, HC Debs, vol. 168, col. 392, 1 March 1990. Shadow Cabinet decision, *Guardian*, 16 March 1990.

11 War Crimes Bill, 8 March 1990; HC Debs, vol. 168, cols 820–1, 8 March 1990, and Howe replies to questions, HC Debs, vol. 168, cols 1006–14. The use in war crimes trials of live television links and the admissibility of evidence recorded on video was now catered for by the 1988 Criminal Justice Act.

12 HC Debs, vol. 169, cols 887–970, 19 March 1990.

13 *Sun*, 19 March 1990; *Daily Mail, The Times*, 20 March 1990; *Guardian*, 23 March 1990.

14 *Sunday Telegraph*, 25 March 1990.

15 *Daily Telegraph*, 21 March 1990; *The Times*, 23 March 1990; *Observer*, 25 March 1990; *Spectator*, 31 March 1990.

16 HC Debs Official Report, Standing Committee A, War Crimes Bill, 1st Sitting, 29 March 1990, 2nd and 3rd Sittings, 3 April 1990.

17 HL Debs, vol. 518, cols 926–59, 1 May 1990.

18 *The Times, Guardian*, 2 May 1990; *Guardian, JC*, 4 May 1990; *House Magazine*, 4 May 1990; *JC*, 11 May 1990.

19 Author's notes, 22 May 1990.

20 *The Times*, 18 May 1990; *Daily Telegraph*, 26 May 1990; *Sunday Times*, 27 May 1990; *Daily Telegraph*, 1 June 1990; *Spectator*, 2 June 1990; *Independent on Sunday*, 3 June 1990.

21 *Guardian*, 25 May 1990; *Mail on Sunday*, *News of the World*, *Sunday Times*, 3 June 1990; *The Times*, *Daily Telegraph*, 4 June 1990.

22 HL Debs, vol. 519, cols 1080–1206, 4 June 1990.

23 *Independent*, *Guardian*, *Sun*, *Daily Mail*, *The Times*, *Today*, 6 June 1990; *Mail on Sunday*, 10 June 1990.

24 *Daily Mail*, 8 June 1990; *News of the World*, 10 June 1990; *Independent*, 14 June 1990. Opinion poll, *Daily Mail*, 8 June 1990.

25 *Sunday Times*, 10 June 1990.

26 *The Times*, *Daily Express*, 6 June 1990; *Evening Standard*, 12 June 1990; *The Times*, 13 June 1990; *Sunday Telegraph*, 17 June 1990; *Independent*, 18 June 1990; *The Times*, *Daily Telegraph*, *Daily Mail*, 22 June 1990.

27 *Sunday Telegraph*, 9 September 1990; *The Times*, 17 October 1990.

28 *Independent*, *Guardian*, 14 October 1990; HC Debs, vol. 180, col. 6, 7 November 1990; *Daily Telegraph*, 8 November 1990; HC Debs, vol. 188, cols 901–13, 12 March 1991.

29 HC Debs, vol. 188, cols 23–112, 18 March 1991; HC Debs, vol. 188, cols 738–9, 25 March 1991.

30 *Sunday Telegraph*, 7 April 1991; *Independent*, 19 April 1991; *The Times*, 30 April 1991.

31 HL Debs, vol. 528, cols 225–70, 24 April 1991; *Independent*, 25 April 1991.

32 HL Debs, vol. 528, cols 619–744, 30 April 1991.

33 HC Debs, vol. 190, cols 315–17, 1 May 1991.

Conclusion: *The Arguments and the Issues*

1 *Hetherington–Chalmers Report*, 9.18, p. 94.

2 For the case of John Demjanjuk, one against and one for the prosecution, see Willem A. Wagenaar, *Identifying Ivan* (London, 1988), and Tom Teicholz, *The Trials of Ivan the Terrible* (London, 1990).

3 HC Debs, vol. 169, col. 896, 19 March 1990.

4 *Isis*, April 1989.

5 HL Debs, vol. 513, cols 604–79, 4 December 1989.

6 Troper and Weinfeld, *Old Wounds*, pp. 340–7; Aarons, *Sanctuary: Nazi Fugitives in Australia*, pp. 293–6.

7 HC Debs, vol. 163, col. 889, 12 December 1989; HC Debs, vol.

169, cols 968–9, 19 March 1990; HC Debs, vol. 188, col. 110, 18 March 1991.

8 *Ibid.*, vol. 169, cols 925–6, 19 March 1990; HC Debs, vol. 188, cols 23–5, 969, 18 March 1991.

9 *Ibid.*, vol. 188, col. 111, 18 March 1991.

10 *Ibid.*, vol. 169, col. 907, 19 March 1990.

11 *Ibid.*, vol. 188, col. 85, 18 March 1991.

12 *JC*, letters, 17 April 1987; 22, 29 May 1987; 15 November 1989; report of debate between Jews and Ukrainians in London: *JC*, 22 September 1989; F. Kurlak, Chairman, Ukrainian Civil Liberties Committee, to Merlyn Rees, 24 January 1989, files of the All-Party Parliamentary War Crimes Group.

13 Robert Conquest, *The Harvest of Sorrow* (paperback edn, London, 1988) p. 328; Redlich, 'Metropolitan Andrei Sheptyts'kyi' op. cit.

14 HL Debs, vol. 513, col. 615, 4 December 1989.

15 *Ibid.*, vol. 513, cols 604–79, 3 December 1989.

16 Cowgill, Brimelow and Booker, *The Repatriations from Austria in 1945*.

17 The account of developments in the USSR is based on Walter Laqueur, *Stalin: The Glasnost Revelations* (London, 1990), pp. 259–76. Kaganovich died in September 1991.

18 Misha Glenny, *The Rebirth of History: Eastern Europe in the Age of Democracy* (London, 1990).

19 These issues are discussed by Patrick Marnham, *Independent*, 9 April 1991.

20 Timothy Garton Ash, *The Uses of Adversity* (London, 1989), pp. 241–2. This is a persistent theme, explored with brilliance by Glenny, *The Rebirth of History*.

Appendices

1. *East European Waffen-SS Units*

2nd SS-Infanterie-Brigade (mot)
Formed in September 1941, during 1941–2 the Brigade absorbed three Latvian Schutzmannschaft-Bataillonen (police battalions) which were combined into the 1st Latvian Infantry Regiment. After transfer of further Latvian Schutzmannschaft units, in May 1943 the Brigade became the Lettische SS-Freiwilligen-Brigade (Latvian Volunteer Brigade).

Lettische SS-Freiwilligen-Brigade
In the winter of 1941–2, the 2nd SS-Infanterie-Brigade (mot) was reinforced by two Latvian Schutzmannschaft-Bataillonen and gained a third in early 1943. The Latvian regiment formed from these police units was joined by another regiment also created out of Schutzmannschaft battalions. In May 1943, the restructured 2nd SS-Infanterie-Brigade (mot) was redesignated the Lettische SS-Freiwilligen-Brigade (Latvian Volunteer Brigade). In January 1944, it was expanded into the 19th Lettische SS-Freiwilligen-Division (19th Latvian SS Volunteer Division).

Lettische SS-Freiwilligen-Legion
The Latvian Volunteer Legion, established in January 1943, nominally encompassed all Latvians in the existing Latvian Waffen-SS and police units. From March 1943, it served as an umbrella body for Latvian front line and police formations.

15th Waffen-Grenadier-Division der SS (lettische Nr. 1)
Created from scratch in February 1943, the unit was initially known as the 15th Lettische SS-Freiwilligen-Division (15th Latvian SS Volunteer Division).

19th Waffen-Grenadier-Division der SS (lettische Nr. 2)
Formed in January 1944 as the 19th Lettische SS-Freiwilligen-Division (19th Latvian SS Volunteer Division) this unit was built out of the two original Latvian regiments of the 2nd SS-Infanterie-Brigade (mot), later the Lettische SS-Freiwilligen-Brigade (Latvian Volunteer Brigade), with an additional regiment and ancillary units.

Estnische Legion
The Estonian Legion was inaugurated in October 1942 two months after Estonian volunteers were first invited to serve in the Waffen-

SS. The unit was trained at the SS training centre at Heidelager. In March 1943, the Legion numbered 37 officers, 175 NCOs and 757 other ranks.

3rd Estnische SS-Freiwilligen-Brigade
The 3rd Estonian SS Volunteer Brigade was an expansion of the Estonian Legion, beginning its existence in May 1943.

20th Waffen-Grenadier-Division der SS (estnische Nr. 1)
Launched in January 1944, the 20th Waffen-SS Estonian Division grew out of the Estnische Legion (Estonian Legion) and the 3rd Estnische SS-Freiwilligen-Brigade (3rd Estonian SS Volunteer Brigade).

14th Waffen-Grenadier-Division der SS (galizische Nr. 1)
Formed in July 1943, in addition to volunteers the unit absorbed the Ukrainian 204th Schutzmannschaft-Bataillon (police or guard battalion) and also 2000 men of the Wachbataillon Heidelager (another guard unit). Initially designated the SS-Freiwilligen-Division 'Galizien' (SS Volunteer Division 'Galizien'), the unit was redesignated the 14th SS-Freiwilligen-Grenadier-Division (galizische Nr. 1). After refitting in Neuhammer, Silesia, following the disastrous battle of Brody, the division was known as the 14th Waffen-Grenadier-Division der SS (galizische Nr. 1). In the last months of the war, the unit's Ukrainian commanders rechristened it the 1st Ukrainian Division of the Ukrainian National Army.

(Source: Klietmann, *Die Waffen-SS*)

2. Main Refugee and Relief Organisations Operating in Germany, 1945–51

Intergovernmental Committee on Refugees (IGCR)
Formed as a result of the Evian Conference on Refugees in July 1938, the IGCR provided limited assistance to refugees. From July 1946 it took some responsibility for DPs, lobbying governments to accept DPs and fund DP-related projects, supplying internationally recognised travel documents and developing settlement programmes for non-repatriables.

United Nations Relief and Rehabilitation Administration (UNRRA)
Created by the Allies in 1943, UNRRA was intended to aid only those persons displaced by the war. It was responsible for determining who was a DP, arranging their repatriation to their homes and maintaining them in camps in the interim. UNRRA was subject to controversy over its initial reluctance to aid Jews who had been sent to camps in their own countries and refugees who voluntarily left

areas under Soviet occupation after the war had ended. While Jews were accepted as charges of UNRRA in December 1945, the Soviet Union protested against the maintenance of DPs who refused to return to homes now under Russian domination or those who fled to the Western Zones of Germany. In July 1946, UNRRA extended its aegis to Poles and Balts who had served in the German forces, provided that the military authorities could certify that they were conscripts and had not been willing collaborators or war criminals. UNRRA passed the 640,000 DPs still in its charge to the PCIRO when it was wound up in June 1947.

Preparatory Commission of the International Refugee Organisation (PCIRO)

The International Refugee Organisation (IRO) was inaugurated by the UN in February 1946, but the Eastern bloc countries objected to it having any role other than repatriation. Debate over its constitution and the lengthy process by which each member state individually adopted it meant that IRO's full operations were delayed until August 1948. In the meantime, from July 1947 a Preparatory Commission took over the work of IGCR and UNRRA. PCIRO determined the eligibility for DP status and assisted the resettlement of successful applicants.

International Refugee Organisation (IRO)

IRO operated from July 1947 as PCIRO and as the IRO proper from August 1948 until it was dissolved at the close of December 1951.

(Source: Vernant, *The Refugee in the Post-War World*)

3. Summary of recommendations of the Hetherington–Chalmers Report, July 1989

10.1. Some action should be taken in respect of alleged war criminals who are now British citizens or are resident in this country where the evidence is sufficient to justify such action (*Paragraph 9.18*).

10.2. Legislation to allow prosecution in this country is preferable to extradition. Other courses, such as deprivation of citizenship and deportation, and prosecution under the terms of the Royal Warrant of 1945, would not be satisfactory (*Paragraphs 9.20 and 9.54*).

10.3. Legislation should be introduced to give British courts jurisdiction over acts of murder and manslaughter committed as war crimes (violations of the laws and customs of war) in Germany or German occupied territory during the period of the Second World War by persons who are now British citizens or resident in the United Kingdom (*Paragraphs 9.22–9.30*). Such legislation should be brought into force as quickly as possible (*Paragraph 9.56*).

10.4. Certain procedural changes will also be desirable. There are considerable differences between English and Scots law in this respect. In England and Wales we recommend that the procedure of transfer to the Crown Court without any committal proceedings, which was introduced for serious fraud cases by sections 4–6 of the Criminal Justice Act 1987, also be applicable to war crimes trials (*Paragraph 9.43*).

In Scotland we recommend that provision be made to allow a witness outside the United Kingdom to give evidence through a live television link, with the leave of the court, *as section 32(1)(a) of the Criminal Justice Act 1988 provides for English courts* (*Paragraph 9.34*) and that recorded statements of persons now dead should be admissible as evidence (*Paragraph 9.41*).

In both jurisdictions we recommend that such provision as seems necessary be made to make admissible (i) video recordings of evidence taken abroad by letters of request (*Paragraph 9.37*), (ii) documents held in archives, if authenticated by the archivist, without his having to testify orally (*Paragraph 9.42*).

We also recommend such provision as seems necessary be made to allow the taking of evidence on commission in Scotland and the consideration of making similar provision in England and Wales (*Paragraph 9.38*).

10.5. Consideration should be given by the prosecuting authorities to prosecuting in three cases in which there appears to us to be a realistic prospect of conviction on the evidence already available (*Paragraph 9.14*). This action should be taken at the earliest opportunity as some preparations for prosecution could precede the enactment of any legislation (*Paragraph 9.55*).

10.6. Further investigations should be undertaken in three cases in which we have carried out detailed investigations, but are not yet satisfied with the available evidence (*Paragraph 9.10*). Investigation should also be carried out into 75 cases of allegations which were not being investigated in detail (*Paragraphs 9.11 and 9.14*). Investigations should continue to attempt to trace the 46 suspects remaining untraced in this country (*Paragraph 9.12*). All these investigations should commence as soon as possible (*Paragraph 9.55*).

10.7. No further action should be taken in 94 cases where the suspect is dead, has left the United Kingdom, or has not been traced and there is no evidence that he ever came to this country. No further action should be taken in 72 cases where the allegation falls outside our terms of reference, where there is insufficient material to allow further investigation, or where we have found the allegations to be unsubstantiated, grounded solely on malice, or contradicted by facts we have ascertained (*Paragraph 9.13*).

10.8. Appropriate arrangements should be made with the authorities of countries where potential witnesses are available, particularly the Soviet Union, so that they can be interviewed and, where appropriate, permitted to travel to give evidence in British courts (*Paragraph 9.33*). Arrangements should also be made for evidence to be taken in pursuance of a letter of request and videotaped; or by the use of a live television link (*Paragraphs 9.34–9.37*).

10.9. Adequate resources should be made available in England and Scotland to the respective investigating and prosecuting authorities and to the courts to allow war crimes to be fully investigated and, where appropriate, prosecutions to take place. The accused in such cases should be entitled to legal aid in order to ensure that they are adequately defended (*Paragraph 9.55*).

(Source: Hetherington and Chalmers, *Report of the War Crimes Inquiry*)

Select bibliography and sources

The vast bulk of documents on which this study is based are held in the PRO, as indicated in the notes for each chapter. Printed primary sources – collections of documents, diaries, memoirs – and important secondary works are listed below. To avoid an unwieldy bibliography references to other sources and newspaper articles appear only in the notes.

Aarons, Mark and Loftus, John, *Ratlines*. London, 1991.

Aarons, Mark. *Sanctuary. Nazi Fugitives in Australia*. Victoria, 1989.

Abzug, Robert H. *Inside The Vicious Heart*. New York, 1985.

All-Party Parliamentary War Crimes Group, *Report on the Entry of Nazi War Criminals and Collaborators into the UK, 1945–1950*. London, 1988.

Arad, Yitzhak. *Belzec, Sobibor, Treblinka. The Operation Reinhard Death Camps*. Bloomington, Ind., 1987.

Arad, Yitzhak. *Ghetto in Flames. The Struggle and Destruction of the Jews in Vilna in the Holocaust*. New York, 1982.

Arad, Yitzhak; Krakowski, Shmuel; and Spector, Shmuel (eds). *The Einsatzgruppen Reports*. New York, 1989.

Arendt, Hannah, *Eichmann in Jerusalem. A Report on the Banality of Evil*. New York, 1963.

Arklansz, B. and Silabriedi, I. *Political Refugees Unmasked*. Riga, 1965.

Armstrong, John A. *Ukrainian Nationalism 1939–1945*. New York, 1963.

Attlee, Clement. *As It Happened*. London, 1954.

Avotins, E; Dzirkalis, J; and Petersons, V. *Dauvagis Vanagi. Who Are They?* Riga, 1963.

Balfour, Michael and Mair, John. *Four Power Control in Germany and Austria 1945–1946*. Oxford, 1956.

Baranauskas, B. and Rukensas, K. *Documents Accuse*. Vilna, 1970.

Barker, Elisabeth. *The British Between the Superpowers 1945–1950*. London, 1986.

Barnes, Trevor. 'The Secret Cold War: The CIA and American Foreign Policy in Europe, 1946–1956. Part 1', *The Historical Journal*, 24:2 (1981).

Barnes, Trevor. 'The Secret Cold War: The CIA and American Foreign Policy in Europe, 1946–1956. Part 2', *Historical Journal*, 25:3 (1982).

Belgion, Montgomery. *Epitaph on Nuremberg*. London, 1946.

Bethell, Nicholas. *The Last Secret*. London, 1987.

Bethell, Nicholas. *The Palestine Triangle*. London, 1979.

Bilinsky, Yaroslav. 'Methodological Problems and Philosophical Issues in the Study of Jewish–Ukrainian Relations During the Second World War' in Peter J. Potichnyj and Howard Aster (eds). *Ukrainian–Jewish Relations in Historical Perspective*. Edmonton, Alberta, 1988.

Blackstock, Paul W. *The Secret Road To World War Two. Soviet Versus Western Intelligence 1921–1939*. Chicago, 1969.

Bohlen, Charles E. *Witness to History*. New York, 1973.

Boshyk, Yury. 'Repatriation and resistance: Ukrainian refugees and displaced persons in Occupied Germany and Austria, 1945–1948', in Anna C. Bramwell (ed), *Refugees in the Age of Total War*. London, 1988.

Bower, Tom. *Blind Eye to Murder*. London, 1983.

Bower, Tom. *Klaus Barbie*. London, 1984.

Bower, Tom. *The Paperclip Conspiracy*. London, 1988.

Bower, Tom. *The Red Web*. London, 1989.

Bridgman, Jon. *The End of the Holocaust: The Liberation of the Camps*. London, 1990.

Bullock, Alan. *A Study in Tyranny*. London, 1952.

Bullock, Alan. *Ernest Bevin*, vol. 3, *Foreign Secretary 1945–1951*. London, 1983.

Buttner, Ursula. 'Not nach der Befreiung. Die Situation der deutschen Juden in der britischen Besatzungszone 1945 bis 1948', *Das Unrechtsregime*, vol 2, *Verfolgung-Exil-Belasteter Neubeginn*. Hamburg, 1986.

Calvocoressi, Peter. *Nuremberg. The Facts, the Law and the Consquences*. London, 1947.

Cave Brown, Anthony. *The Secret Servant*. London, 1988.

Chesser, Dr Eustace. *Doctors of Infamy*. London, 1951.

Clark, Alan. *Barbarossa*. London, 1966.

Cooper, Kanty. *The Uprooted. Agony and Triumph Among the Debris of War*. London, 1979.

Conquest, Robert. *The Harvest of Sorrow*. London 1988.

Cowgill, Brigadier Anthony; Brimelow, Lord; and Booker, Christopher. *The Repatriations From Austria in 1945. The Report Of An Inquiry.* London, 1991

Cross, Colin. *The Fascists in Britain.* London, 1964.

Dallin, Alexander. *German Rule in Russia 1941–1945. A Study of Occupation Policies.* London, 1981.

Dalton, Hugh. *High Tide and After. Memoirs 1945–1960.* London, 1962.

Davies, A. Emil. *Our Ageing Population.* London, 1938.

Dawidowicz, Lucy. *The Holocaust and the Historians.* Cambridge, Mass., 1981.

Dickens, A. G. *Lübeck Diary.* London, 1947.

Dinnerstein, Leonard. 'The US Army and the Jews: Policies Toward The Displaced Persons After World War II', in Michael Marrus (ed) *The Nazi Holocaust*, vol. 9, *The End of the Holocaust.* Westport C.T. 1989.

Dinnerstein, Leonard. *America and the Survivors of the Holocaust.* New York, 1982.

Donat, Alexander (ed). *The Death Camp Treblinka. A Documentary.* New York, 1979.

Donoughue, Bernard and Jones G. W. *Herbert Morrison. Portrait of a Politician.* London, 1973.

Eliot, Mark R. *Pawns of Yalta. Soviet Refugees and America's Role in Their Repatriation.* Urbana, Ill., 1982.

Fabian Society. *Population and the People. A National Policy.* London, 1945.

Freeden, Michael. 'Eugenics and Ideology', *Historical Journal*, 26:4 (1983).

Freeden, Michael. 'Eugenics and Progressive Thought: A Study in Ideological Affinity', *Historical Journal*, 22.3 (1979).

Friedlander, Henry and McCarrick, Earlean, M. 'Nazi Criminals in the United States: The Fedorenko Case', *Simon Wiesenthal Center Annual*, 2 (1985).

Friedman, Philip. 'Ukrainian–Jewish Relations During the Nazi Occupation', *YIVO Annual of Jewish Social Sciences*, 12 (1958/59).

Gaddis, J. L. *Strategies of Containment. A Critical Appraisal of Postwar American National Security Policy.* Oxford, 1982.

Garton Ash, Timothy. *The Uses of Adversity.* London, 1989.

Gilbert, G. M. *Nuremberg Diary.* London, 1948.

Gilbert, Martin. *Exile and Return. The Emergence of Jewish Statehood.* London, 1978.

Ginzbury, Louis. *Parenthood and Poverty: the Population Problem of Democracy.* London, 1939.

Glees, Anthony. *The Secrets of the Service. British Intelligence and Communist Subversion, 1939–51.* London, 1987.

Glenny, Misha. *The Rebirth of History. Eastern Europe in the Age of Democracy.* London, 1990.

Graf, Malvina. *The Krakow Ghetto and the Plaszow Camp Remembered.* Tallahasse, Fla., 1989.

Griffiths, Richard. *Fellow Travellers of the Right.* Oxford, 1983.

Gross, John. 'The Lynskey Tribunal', in Phillip French and Michael Sissons (eds) *The Age of Austerity.* London, 1963.

Hankey, The Rt Hon Lord. *Politics Trials and Errors.* Oxford, 1950.

Harris, Kenneth. *Attlee.* London, 1982.

Hausner, Gideon. *Justice in Jerusalem.* London, 1967.

Hershaut, Julien. *Jewish Martyrs of Pawiak.* New York, 1982.

Herwarth, Hans von. *Against Two Evils. Memoirs of a Diplomat-Soldier During the Third Reich.* London, 1981.

Hetherington, Sir Thomas and Chalmers, William. *War Crimes. Report of the War Crimes Inquiry.* London, 1989.

Hilberg, Raul. *The Destruction of the European Jews.* 3 vols. New York, 1985.

Hilgruber, Andreas. 'War in the East and the Extermination of the Jews' in Michael Marrus (ed) *The Nazi Holocaust,* Vol. 2, Pt 3, *The 'Final Solution' and The Implementation of Mass Murder.* Westport, C.T., 1989.

Hill, Mavis M. and Williams, L. Norman. *Auschwitz in England. A Record of a Libel Action.* London, 1965.

Hoffmann, Joachim. *Die Ostlegionen 1941–1943.* Freiburg, 1986.

Hoffmann, Joachim. *Die Geschichte der Wlassow-Armee.* Freiburg, 1986.

Holmes, Colin. *John Bull's Island. Immigration and British Society, 1871–1971.* London, 1988.

Isaac, Julius. *British Post War Migration.* Cambridge, 1954.

Jones, Greta. 'Eugenics and Social Policy Between the Wars', *Historical Journal,* 25:3 (1982).

Jones, Greta. *Social Darwinism and English Social Thought. The Interaction Between Biological Theory and Social Theory.* Sussex, 1980.

Joshi, Shirley and Carter, Bob. 'The Role of Labour in the creation of a racist Britain', *Race and Class,* 25:3 (1984).

Kahane, David. *Lvov Ghetto Diary*. Amherst, Mass., 1991

Klietmann, K-G. *Die Waffen-SS eine Dokumentation*. Osnabrük, 1965.

Korman, Gerd. 'The Holocaust in American Historical Writing', in Michael Marrus (ed) *The Holocaust in History*, vol 1, *Perspectives on the Holocaust*. Westport C.T., 1989.

Krätschmer, R. G. *Die Ritterkreutzträger der Waffen-SS*. Oldendorf, 1982.

Kushner, Tony. 'The British and the Shoah', *Patterns of Prejudice*, 23.3 (1989).

Kushner, Tony. *The Persistence of Prejudice*. Manchester, 1989.

Laqueur, Walter. *Stalin. The Glasnost Revelations*. London, 1990.

Layton-Henry, Zig. *The Politics of Race in Britain*. London, 1984.

Leitch, David. 'Explosion at the King David Hotel', in Phillip French and Michael Sissons (eds) *The Age of Austerity*. London, 1963.

Levin, Dov. 'On the Relations Between the Baltic Peoples and their Jewish Neighbours Before, During and After World War II', *Holocaust and Genocide Studies*, 5:1 (1990).

Levin, Dov. *Fighting Back. Lithuanian Jewry's Armed Resistance to the Nazis, 1941–1945*. New York, 1985.

Lewin, Abraham. *A Cup of Tears. A Diary of the Warsaw Ghetto*. Ed. Antony Polonsky. Oxford, 1989.

Lewis, Julian. *Changing Direction. British Military Planning for Post-War Strategic Defence, 1942–1947*. London, 1987.

Loftus, John. *The Belarus Secret*. New York, 1982.

Manderstam, Major L. H. *From the Red Army to SOE*. London, 1985.

Marwick, Arthur. *British Society Since 1945*. London, 1990.

Maugham, Viscount. *U.N.O. and War Crimes*. London, 1951.

McCleary, G. F. *Population: Today's Question*. London, 1938.

McCleary, G. F. *The Menace of Britain's Depopulation*. London, 1939.

Michelson, Frida. *I Survived Rumbuli*. New York, 1979.

Mosley, Leonard O. *Report from Germany*. London, 1945.

Mulligan, T. P. *German Occupation Policy in the Soviet Union, 1942–1943*. New York, 1988.

Neulen, Hans Werner. *An deutscher Seite. Internationale Freiwillige von Wehrmacht und Waffen-SS*. Munich, 1985.

Novitch, Miriam. *Sobibor Martrydom and Revolt*. New York, 1980.

Nugent, Neil, 'Post War Fascism?' in K. Lunn and R. Thurlow (eds) *British Fascism*. London, 1980.

Pankiewicz, Tadeusz. *The Cracow Ghetto Pharmacy*. New York, 1987.

PEP. *Population Policy in Great Britain*. London, 1948.
Philby, Kim. *My Silent War*. London, 1989.
Pimlott, Ben. *Hugh Dalton*. London, 1986.
Pronay, Nicholas. 'Defeated Germany in British Newsreels: 1944–45', in K. R. M. Short and Stephen Dolezel (eds) *Hitler's Fall: The Newsreel Witness*. London, 1990.
Proudfoot, Malcolm J. *European Refugees: 1939–52. A Study in Forced Population Movement*. London, 1957.

Read, Anthony and Fisher, David. *The Deadly Embrace. Hitler, Stalin and the Nazi-Soviet Pact 1939–1941*. London, 1988.
Ready, J. Lee. *The Forgotten Axis. Germany's Partners and Foreign Volunteers in World War Two*. Jefferson, NC., 1987.
Reddaway, W. B. *Economics in a Declining Population*. London, 1939.
Redlich, Shimon, 'Metropolitan Andrei Sheptyts'kyi, Ukrainians and Jews During and After the Holocaust', *Holocaust and Genocide Studies*, 5:1 (1990).
Reitlinger, Gerald. *The House Built On Sand*. London, 1960.
Reitlinger, Gerald. *The SS. Alibi of a Nation 1922–1945*. London, 1981.
Rich, Norman. *Hitler's War Aims*, vol 1, *The Nazi State and the Course of Expansion*. London, 1973.
Rich, Norman. *Hitler's War Aims*, vol 2, *The Establishment of the New Order*. London, 1974.
Roche, T. W. E. *The Key in The Lock. A History of Immigration Control in England from 1066 to the Present Day*. London, 1969.
Rosenbaum, Eli. 'The Investigation and Prosecution of Suspected Nazi War Criminals: a Comparative Overview', *Patterns of Prejudice*, 21:2 (1987).
Rothwell, Victor. 'Robin Hankey', in John Zametica (ed) *British Officials and Foreign Policy 1945–50*. Leicester, 1990.
Rothwell, Victor. *Britain and the Cold War 1941–1947*. London, 1982.
Russell of Liverpool, Lord. *The Scourge of the Swastika. A Short History of Nazi War Crimes*. London, 1954.
Russell of Liverpool, Lord. *The Trial of Adolf Eichmann*. London, 1962.
Ryan, Jr., Allan A. *Quiet Neighbours. Prosecuting Nazi War Criminals in America*. New York, 1984.

Saidel, Rochelle G. *The Outraged Conscience. Seekers of Justice for Nazi War Criminals in America*. Albany, NY, 1984.
Schellenberg, Walter. *The Schellenberg Memoirs*. London, 1956.
Seth, Ronald. *A Spy Has No Friends*. London, 1948.
Shandruk, Pavlo. *Arms of Valor*. New York, 1959.
Sigailis, Arthur. *Latvian Legion*. San Jose, Ca., 1986.

Simpson, Christopher. *Blowback. America's Recruitment of Nazis and Its Effects on the Cold War.* London, 1988.

Sington, Derrick. *Belsen Uncovered.* London, 1947.

Sked, Alan and Cook, Chris. *Post-War Britain. A Political History.* London, 1986.

Sloan, Jacob (ed). *The Journal of Emmanuel Ringelblum.* New York, 1958.

Smith, Richard Harris. *OSS. The Secret History of America's First Central Intelligence Agency.* Berkley, Ca., 1972.

Spender, Stephen. *European Witness.* London, 1946.

Stadulis, E. 'The Resettlement of Displaced Persons in the United Kingdom', *Population Studies*, 5:3 (1952).

Stein, George. H. *The Waffen SS Hitler's Elite Guard at War 1939–45.* London, 1966.

Stöber, Hans. *Die lettischen Divisionen im VI. SS-Armeekorps.* Osnabrük, 1981.

Strang, Lord. *At Home and Abroad.* London, 1956.

Streit, Christian. 'The German Army and the Policies of Genocide', in Gerhard Hirschfeld (ed), *The Policies of Genocide. Jews and Soviet Prisoners of War in Nazi Germany.* London, 1986.

Stroop Report, The. London, 1980.

Sword, Keith. 'The absorption of Poles into civilian employment in Britain, 1945–1950', in Anna C. Bramwell (ed) *Refugees in the Age of Total War.* London, 1988.

Sword, Keith (ed). *The Formation of the Polish Community in Great Britain.* London, 1989.

Tannahill, J. A. *European Voluntary Workers in Britain.* Manchester, 1958.

Taylor, H. P. and Bender, R. J. *Uniforms, Organisation and History of the Waffen-SS.* Vol. 5. San Jose, Ca., 1982.

Teicholz, Tom. *The Trials of Ivan the Terrible.* London 1990.

Thayer, Charles. *Hands Across the Caviar.* London, 1973.

Thurlow, Richard. *Fascism in Britain. A History, 1918–45.* Oxford, 1987.

Tory [Golub], Avraham. *Surviving the Holocaust. The Kovno Ghetto Diary.* Cambridge, Mass., 1990.

Trevor-Roper, H. R. *Hitler's Table Talk.* London, 1953.

Troper, Harold and Weinfeld, Morton. *Old Wounds. Jews. Ukrainians and the Hunt for Nazi War Criminals in Canada.* Chapel Hill, NC., 1989.

Tusa, Ann and Tusa, John. *The Nuremberg Trial.* London, 1983.

Vernant, Jacques. *The Refugee in the Post-War World.* London, 1953.

Wagenaar, Willem A. *Identifying Ivan*. London, 1988.

Weinberg, Gerhard L. *The Foreign Policy of Hitler's Germany. Diplomatic Revolution in Europe 1933–36*. Chicago, 1970.

Weiss, Aharon. 'Jewish-Ukrainian relations in Western Ukraine During the Second World War', in Peter J. Potichnyj and Howard Aster (eds), *Ukrainian-Jewish Relations in Historical Perspective*. Edmonton, Alberta, 1988.

West, Nigel. *MI6 British Secret Intelligence Operations 1909–1945*. London, 1983.

West, Rebecca. *A Trail of Powder*. London, 1984.

Wheeler-Bennett, Sir John. *Friends, Enemies and Foreigners*. London, 1976.

Wiesenthal, Simon. *The Murderers Among Us*. Ed. Joseph Wechsberg. London, 1967.

Wilhelm, Heinrich. *Die Truppen des Weltanschauungskrieges*. Stuttgart, 1981.

Willenberg, Samuel. *Surviving Treblinka*. Ed. Wladyslaw T. Bartoszewski. Oxford, 1989.

Wyman, Mark. *DP. Europe's Displaced Persons, 1945–1951*. Philadelphia, 1989.

Yurkevich, Myroslav. 'Galician Ukrainians in German Military Formations and in the German Administration', in Yury Boshyk (ed) *Ukraine During World War Two. History and its Aftermath*. Edmonton, 1986.

Zuroff, Efraim. *Occupation Nazi-Hunter*. Southampton, 1988.

Index